Perspectives on Play

PEARSON
Education

We work with leading authors to develop the strongest
educational materials in education, bringing cutting-edge
thinking and best learning practice to a global market.

Under a range of well-known imprints, including
Longman, we craft high quality print and electronic
publications which help readers to understand and apply
their content, whether studying or at work.

To find out more about the complete range of our
publishing, please visit us on the World Wide Web at:
www.pearsoned.co.uk

Perspectives on Play
Learning for Life

Avril Brock
Sylvia Dodds
Pam Jarvis
Yinka Olusoga

Harlow, England • London • New York • Boston • San Francisco • Toronto • Sydney • Singapore • Hong Kong
Tokyo • Seoul • Taipei • New Delhi • Cape Town • Madrid • Mexico City • Amsterdam • Munich • Paris • Milan

Pearson Education Limited
Edinburgh Gate
Harlow
Essex CM20 2JE
England

and Associated Companies throughout the world

Visit us on the World Wide Web at:
www.pearsoned.co.uk

First published 2009

© Pearson Education Limited 2009

ISBN: 978-1-4058-4673-8

British Library Cataloguing-in-Publication Data
A catalogue record for this book is available from the British Library

Library of Congress Cataloging-in-Publication Data

Perspectives on play : learning for life / Avril Brock . . . [et al.].
    p. cm.
  Includes bibliographical references and index.
  ISBN 978-1-4058-4673-8 (pbk.)
1. Play. 2. Early childhood education. 3. Child development. I. Brock, Avril.
  LB1139.35.P55P47 2008
  372.21—dc22

                               2008024444

10 9 8 7 6 5 4 3
11 10

Typeset in 9.75/13 Minion by 73
Printed by Ashford Colour Press Ltd., Gosport

Remember,
You don't stop playing when you get old,
You get old when you stop playing!

Anon

This book is dedicated to:

- Jackie Brock, for her perseverance and support; to Kirsty, David, Melissa, Simon, Joe and Tom for their playfulness and, of course to JJ, for keeping the sustenance ongoing during the long hours of writing.

Avril Brock

- My two boys, Alex and Mark, who still encourage me to play with them, learn new skills and with whom I have many cherished moments that I have drawn upon as I contributed to this book. Also to Jos, my husband, and other family members, who have always believed in me and been by my side as I chase my dreams.

Sylvia Dodds

- My parents and grandparents who were the bows and my children who are the arrows: 'the archer sees his mark on the path of the infinite'.

Pam Jarvis

- My mother Marion Olusoga and to my partner Dan Austin, both of whom provided support and encouragement during the writing of this book and who remind me to make time for playfulness in my own life. It is also dedicated to my other major accomplishment of the last 12 months, my daughter Mia. I like to think that Mia and I produced my chapter together as I was seven months pregnant at the time. As I wrote, her kicking and playing inside the womb was a constant source of wonder to me as I looked forward to being able to watch her play and learn as she grows up.

Yinka Olusoga

Contents

Contents

Section 3   Supporting Children's Play   173

Contents

List of Figures and Tables

List of Abbreviations

ADD	Attention Deficit Disorder
ADHD	Attention Deficit Hyperactivity Disorder
ASBOs	Anti-social Behaviour Orders
CACHE	Council for Awards in Children's Care and Education
CAH	Congenital Adrenal Hyperplasia
CGFS	Curriculum Guidance for the Foundation Stage
CPD	Continuing Professional Development
DAP	Developmentally Appropriate Practice
DCD	Dyslexia and Dyspraxia
DCSF	Department for Children, Schools and Families
DfEE	Department of Education and Employment
DIL	Developing Independent Learning
EAL	English as an Additional Language
ECEC	Early Childhood Education and Care
ECERS-E	Early Childhood Environment Rating Scale English
ECERS-R	Early Childhood Environment Rating Scale Revised
ECM	*Every Child Matters* (DfES 2003b)
EPPE	Effective Provision for Preschool Education
ERA	Education Reform Act (1988)
EYFS	Early Years Foundation Stage
EYP	Early Years Professional

IATC	Internet Addiction Treatment Centre
IVF	In Vitro Fertilisation
JNCTP	Joint National Committee on Training for Playwork
NAECCE	National Advisory Committee on Creative and Cultural Education
NAEYC	National Association for the Education of Young Children
NC	National Curriculum
NGO	Non-Government Organisation
NLS	National Literary Strategy
NNS	National Numeracy Strategy
OECD	Organisation for Economic Co-operation and Development
Ofsted	Office for Standards in Education
PICL	Parents Involved in Children's Learning
PBA	Play-based Assessment
Post	The [UK] Parliamentary Office for Science and Technology
PPSG	Playwork Principles Scrutiny Group
PTSD	Post-Traumatic Stress Disorder
QCA	Qualifications and Curriculum Authority
R&T	Rough and Tumble [play]
REPEY	Researching Effective Pedagogy in the Early Years
SATs	Standard Assessment Tests
SEN	Special Educational Needs
SENCO	Special Needs Coordinator
SPEEL	Study of Pedagogical Effectiveness in Early Learning
SPRITO	Sport and Recreation Industry Lead Body
TDA	Training and Development Agency
TTA	Teacher Training Agency
UN	United Nations
UNESCO	United Nations Educational, Scientific and Cultural Organization
UNICEF	United Nations (International) Children's (Emergency) Fund
WRI	White Rose Initiative
VAK	Visual, Auditory and Kinaesthetic
ZPD	Zone of Proximal Development

Author Acknowledgements

Avril Brock

This book would not have been written without the help of family members, friends, neighbours, colleagues, students, teachers, nursery nurses, managers and lots of children. Particular thanks go to:

The families: David, Kirsty and Melissa; Jackie, Joe and Tom; Annabelle, William and Claudia; Fiona and Emily; Ken, Helen, Jed and Holly; Jo and Theo; Stuart, Pauline, Alex and Jack.

The practitioners: Cynthia; Dawn; Francesca; Helen; Joan; Julie; Maggie; Marianne; Margaret; Naseem; Paul; Sarah; Scott; Tiffany.

The students: BA/MA Early Childhood Education/Early Years students studying at Leeds Metropolitan University and Bradford College.

Sylvia Dodds

My contribution to this book would not have been possible without the many individuals who have influenced my practice over the years. From the very first child I taught who showed me that teachers make a difference, the classes of children who have enjoyed playing as much as I have, the student teachers and teaching assistants who have shared my passion for teaching and learning, the colleagues who facilitated my reflection and encouraged me to be the best practitioner I can be and the learning environments that have shaped my own lifelong learning.

Thank you to the students, parents and administrators at River Oaks Public School, Oakville, Ontario, Canada who gave their permission to use photos of primary children at play. These include Caitlin Bevington, Ocean Bryan, Tevin Doyley, Julianna Macmillan, Nicole Porter, Gillian Sandison, Amber Syme, Lex Jeffrey, Olivia Olberholster, Jasmine Stiff and Maddie and Katelyn Hill.

I would like to give special thanks to my extended family (My mum and dad Jeff; My inherited mum and dad Sheila and Neil; The Parrys and the Woodies) who have never stopped learning and still love to play.

Finally, to my co-editors and friends Avril, Pam and Yinka, for their inspiration and encouragement in making this dream a reality.

Pam Jarvis

My acknowledgements are for my husband Chris Jarvis for his help with putting the glossary together for this book and my children Claire, Sian and Andrew Jarvis for giving their permission for some observations of their childhood play and various photographs of them to be used in this book. I would additionally like to thank both my husband and children for putting up with a working Christmas 2007 due to endless editing! Many thanks are also offered to all the children, colleagues and students who have participated in my research over the past six years who, due to research ethics, must remain anonymous.

Yinka Olusoga

I would also like to give thanks for the help I received whilst researching and writing this book. Particular thanks go to:

My co-editors, Avril, Pam and Sylvia for their generous and invaluable professional and personal support during and after my pregnancy.

The practitioners: Verna Kilburn who inspired me to become a teacher and on whom my practice is modelled. Maureen Small, nursery nurse, for her guidance, wisdom and professionalism and Denise Johnston, teacher, for her insight and humour on teaching and on motherhood.

The students: Early Childhood Education and Primary students at Leeds Metropolitan University, Bradford College and the University of Leeds.

My siblings: David, Kemi, Peter, Moremi, Daniel and Vin: who would have thought that playing with you as we grew up was (and still is) actually research?

Please note: the names of all the research participants have been anonymised.

Publisher Acknowledgements

We are grateful to the following for permission to reproduce copyright material:

Figure 2.2 Reproduced by permission of SAGE Publications, London, Los Angeles, New Delhi and Singapore, from Scaffolding learning and co-constructing understandings by Jordan, B. in Anning, A., Cullen, J. and Fleer, M. (Eds) (2004) *Early Childhood Education: Society and Culture*, (© Jordan, B. 2004); Figure 2.3 from Curricular quality and day to day learning activities in pre-school, Sylva, K., Taggart, B., Siraj-Blatchford, I., Totsika, V., Ereky-Stevens, K., Gilden, R. and Bell, D. in *International Journal of Early Years Education* Vol 15 No 1 March 2007, Taylor and Francis, reprinted by permission of the publisher (Taylor & Francis Ltd http://www.tandf.co.uk/journals); Figure 2.7 adapted Fig Whiting and Whiting's Psycho-cultural Model from *The Cultural Nature of Human Development* (2003), Rogoff, B. by permission of Oxford University Press, Inc.; Figure 6.6 adapted from Kolb's experiential learning model from Wallace, M (1999) When is experiential learning not experiential learning? in Claxton, G., Atkinson, T., Osborn, M. and Wallace, M. (Eds), *Liberating the Learner* (1996) Routledge, with permission from Taylor and Francis Books Ltd.

We are grateful to the following for permission to reproduce photographs:

Figure 1.1 Reproduced by permission of UK21 / Alamy, Figure 1.4 Reproduced by permission of Homer Sykes Archive / Alamy; Figure 1.5 Reproduced by permission of Sarah Winterflood / Alamy; Figure 3.1 Reproduced by permission of Janine Wiedel Photolibrary / Alamy; Figure 4.4 Reproduced by permission of Bubbles Photolibrary / Alamy; Figure 7.3 *Bonobo playface* Photograph by

Frans de Waal; Figure 8.1 Reproduced by permission of John Callan/reportdigital.co.uk; Figure 8.3 Reproduced by permission of Jim West / Alamy; Figure 8.4 Reproduced by permission of Paul Box/ reportdigital.co.uk.

We are grateful to the following for permission to reproduce the following texts:

Page 269 From When We Were Very Young by A. A. Milne © The Trustees of the Pooh Properties Published by Egmont UK Ltd London and used with permission; "Spring Morning" by A A Milne from 'WHEN WE WERE VERY YOUNG' by A.A. Milne, illustrations by E.H. Shepard, copyright 1924 by E.P. Dutton, renewed 1952 by A.A. Milne. Used by permission of Dutton Children's Books, A division of Penguin Young Readers Group, A Member of Penguin Group (USA) Inc., 345 Hudson Street, New York, NY 10014. All rights reserved; Page 274 The 'Telegraph letter 2006' reprinted with permission of the authors, Sue Palmer and Dr Richard House; Page 277 'On the Trail of Santa Claus' by Cole Moreton from *The Independent on Sunday*, 23 December 2007, copyright The Independent; Page 277 Game Over for China's Net Addicts from www.redherring.com with permission of FosterReprints (Reuters) Copyright 2007 Reuters. Reprinted with permission from Reuters. Reuters content is the intellectual property of Reuters or its third party content providers. Any copying, re-publication or redistribution of Reuters content is expressly prohibited without the prior written consent of Reuters. Reuters shall not be liable for any errors or delays in content, or for any actions taken in reliance thereon. Reuters and the Reuters Sphere Logo are registered trademarks of the Reuters group of companies around the world. For additional information about Reuters content and services, please visit Reuters website at www.reuters.com. License # REU-4025-JJM.; Page 278 'Speak to us of children' from *The Prophet* by Gibran, K. (1923), Random House.

In some instances we have been unable to trace the owners of copyright material, and we would appreciate any information that would enable us to do so.

List of Contributors

Avril Brock is a senior lecturer in childhood and early years in Carnegie Faculty of Sport and Education at Leeds Metropolitan University. She is the course leader for the MA Childhood Studies and the MA early Years in the Faculty. She has worked in higher education since 1989, lecturing in the Department of Teacher Education at Bradford College for sixteen years until moving the LeedsMet. Prior to this she was a deputy head teacher and primary/early years teacher in West Yorkshire, often working with linguistically diverse children. Both Avril's books 'Into the enchanted forest: language, drama and science in primary schools' [Trentham, 1999], her most recent publication 'Communication, language and literacy from birth to five' written with Carolynn Rankin [Sage, 2008], as well as her contributions to Jean Conteh's 'Promting learning for bilingual pupils 3-11 [Sage, 2007] reflect this interest in diversity and language development. Avril's PhD research is entitled 'Eliciting early years educators' thinking: how do they define and sustain their professionalism' and this has turned into longitudinal research, as she has recently revisited the participants in the study. Throughout her work in Higher Education, Avril has participated in several Socrates, Comenius and Erasmus European funded international projects and is involved in international, interdisciplinary partnerships with colleagues in West Yorkshire and the USA.

Sylvia Dodds has extensive experience of early years and primary education as a classroom practitioner, subject manager, mentor and deputy head-teacher in the North of England. Whilst at Bradford College, West Yorkshire, England she pioneered continuing professional development opportunities for teaching assistants managing the Diploma of Higher Education and later the Foundation Degree (Supporting and Managing Learning) and delivering taught programmes of study. In response to workforce reform she also spent several years working as a Higher Level Teaching Assistant (HLTA) trainer and lead-assessor as well as providing training and consultancy to schools and LA's. As an initial teacher trainer she has lectured in the areas of mathematics, science and technology and currently supports as initial teacher training programme at Charles Sturt University, Burlington, Ontario campus in Canada. Her research interests include assessment, questioning and developing the engaging and creative classroom. She was awarded a Master in Education: Lifelong Learning from the Open University in which she researched in the areas of Learning, Curriculum and Assessment; Mentoring and Lifelong Learning.

Dr Pam Jarvis has taught in school, further and higher education. She is a qualified teacher, graduate psychologist and social scientist, with many years of experience in developing and teaching developmental, social science and social policy modules for Education/Child Development programmes in further and higher education; most recently within the area of Early Years Professional training. She is currently working on the Early Years and Children's Agenda team at Bradford College and as an Open University tutor, where she has supported child development and psychology students on a wide range of programmes at undergraduate and Masters level. She is an active researcher in child development and education, who has most recently focused on the areas of play-based learning and 'student voice'. Dr Jarvis was awarded a PhD by Leeds Metropolitan University in 2005 for her thesis 'The role of rough and tumble play in children's social and gender role development in the early years of primary school'.

Yinka Olusoga is a senior lecturer in early childhood education at Leeds Metropolitan University. She has worked in higher education since 2000, initially running a Teacher Training Agency-funded project based at the University of Leeds, before moving into teacher training. She is an experienced primary and early years teacher and has taught in the Foundation Stage, Key Stage One and Key Stage Two in Birmingham, Liverpool and London, in a range of inner city and multi-cultural settings.

Her research focuses on educational sociology, policy and history. She has particular interests in personal and social education and development and in the role of friendship in children's lives. She is currently engaged in PhD research and is examining the symbolic and practical purposes of personal and social education within the primary curriculum.

Jackie Brock, after gaining her BSc degree in German with Japanese, followed by a BA in Theology, spent seven years working in Japan teaching English and religion in Japanese to university students. During that time she worked on her Masters degree and is currently writing her doctoral thesis. On returning to the United Kingdom, Jackie has been working as a research assistant in the fields of religion and early years education, contributing to research on early language development and play.

Dr Fraser Brown is Reader in playwork and course leader of the BA (Hons) Playwork course at Leeds Metropolitan University. For ten years he was Director of the playwork training agency Children First, and previously held an advisory post with the National Playing Fields Association (NPFA). He began his playwork career on an adventure playground in Runcorn, and for two years was District Leisure Officer in Middlesbrough. His publications include *Foundations of Playwork* (Open University Press, 2008); *The Venture* (Play Wales, 2007); *Playwork: Theory and Practice* (Open University Press, 2003) and *School Playgrounds* (NPFA, 1990). He has a worldwide reputation for his research into the effects of therapeutic playwork on a group of abandoned children in Romania. He is Chairperson of the charity, Aid for Romanian Children.

Dr Jonathan Doherty is principal lecturer and head of Early Childhood Education at Leeds Metropolitan University where he has responsibility for training intending teachers at undergraduate and postgraduate levels in the 3–7 age range. His teaching and research interests include developmental psychology, special needs and children's motor development. Jonathan has sat on a number of national working parties and consultancies and has presented his work to national and international audiences. Books include *Supporting Physical Development and Physical Education in the Early Years* (Open University Press, 2003); *Physical Education and Development 3–11* (David Fulton, 2007) and *Right from the Start: A Textbook on Child Development* (Pearson, in press). His doctoral research considered higher order thinking in relation to children's movement.

Jane George has extensive experience in the voluntary sector, in toddler groups and playgroups and managing and teaching for the Pre-School Learning Alliance. She has worked in community education developing and delivering parent and toddler at play classes in areas of social deprivation and to various cultural groups. Working in colleges across West Yorkshire, she has developed and delivered a variety of Early Years programmes across the range of further and higher education. She was awarded an MEd in 2003. In her current role of programme manager for Early Years and Children's Agenda at Bradford College she teaches and manages the curriculum across the full range of Early Childhood Studies programmes, which includes Council for Awards in Children's Care and Education (CACHE) levels Entry, 1, 2 and 3 in Child Care and Education, the Foundation degree in Early Years, the BA Hons early childhood studies, the postgraduate certificate in Early Years Practice and the early years professional Pathway. She is also an Early Years Professional Status assessor.

Dr Phil Jones, School of Childhood and Community, Leeds Metropolitan University is author of *Drama as Therapy* (Routledge) and *The Arts Therapies* (Routledge). His books have been translated into a number of languages and published in China, Korea and Greece. He has held the posts of course leader in advanced training in art therapy and dramatherapy, postgraduate diploma in Dramatherapy and Foundation in Art, Drama and Dance Movement Therapy. He has lectured on the arts therapies in a number of countries including the United States, Canada, Germany, Greece, Portugal, France and the Netherlands.

Foreword

Towards the end of this book, the authors use a phrase which for me resonates very strongly. The phrase refers to '*two play-arid decades over the closing years of the twentieth century*'. It is a reference to the relentless diminishing of playful encounters and engagement for children and young people across our western society. In particular, this book draws attention to the huge reductions in play opportunities that we have witnessed in England since the introduction of the Education Reform Act (ERA) in 1988, the attendant and relentless quest to test children and the pressure on schools and teachers to teach children to pass these tests, all of which subsequently ensued, post-ERA. As a result, huge efforts, firm intentions and educator commitment are now needed to reinstate play as high status and as valued in our schools in particular, but also in some cases in our early years settings, some of which have also succumbed, perhaps understandably, to the pressures for increasing adult-directed activities and for diminishing child-initiated activities – or play as it is better known. A new balance now needs to be struck and this book will be an asset to those choosing to strike it on behalf of children everywhere, in or out of schools.

The authors believe the time is right for a turnaround on play and are hugely optimistic that play is returning to its rightful place in the legacy of human experiences, most especially for young children. They state this firmly from the outset and set out in the ensuing chapters to do all they can to speed the movement towards maximum exposure to playful learning for all as an entitlement rather than as a 'gift' from adults.

One key focus is the birth to 5 age range where the authors anticipate that the impact of the Early Years Foundation Stage will go some way towards re-engaging educators from a wide range of settings with a playful learning philosophy and pedagogy and with associated debates; but the book is also rightly concerned that play does not stop at age 5 years. Examples are given of older children playfully investigating the given curriculum and show how problem solving might make a natural transition across the age ranges. In support of this, the book takes a very useful approach to professional development, which is to blend the theoretical with the illustrative and with practical tasks and questions for readers working with children of all ages and in a wide range of contexts. This publication could support a setting/school-based approach to engaging with the complexities of play with the tasks and illustrative material offering a way forward for joint reflection. The materials would also suit those wanting to work at a more intensive level of professional development as, for example, collaborative action researchers following the tasks and reflections together.

However, this book is not only about play in early years settings or in schools; it usefully takes a much broader perspective and signals this clearly in Chapter 1 with a triple focus, on socio-pyschological perspectives on play, play as learning and, from a playwork perspective, a focus on the innate and naturalistic aspects of play, each of which draws on potentially complementary but very different ways of seeing and understanding play. The three perspectives however bring useful illumination rather than conflict and serve to open the reader's mind to new routes to understanding play and its complexities. A 'journey' metaphor does feature in the book and the use of practical examples, many of which have arisen from research by the authors, helps to illustrate their own journeys of understanding as well as also contributing to that of the readers.

Each of the chapters has a complementary focus and key areas are addressed across the book including culture, gender and identity, special educational needs, rough and tumble play and unusually but very helpfully, play as dramatherapy. This eclecticism is very welcome and helps to reiterate the authors' claims to a unique approach to a book on play. The recent UNICEF report on the poor quality of life in the United Kingdom for its children has had considerable impact; the book draws on this work and reiterates the need to now look towards improving the quality of life for children in the United Kingdom; play is at the heart of this, and a better understanding of play now needs to be at the heart of practitioners' perspectives – this book is in no doubt of that. We need new ways of thinking and new kinds of pedagogy.

This is a detailed and rich text and represents a drawing together of some familiar theoretical perspectives in accessible and interesting ways for its readers alongside some theoretical complementarities that will bring new insights. The book recognises its readers as likely to be people with a passion for play and speaks to them all, novice and expert, from an informed and equally passionate perspective. Those who do not have a passion for play may well find themselves acquiring one the more they read.

Professor Pat Broadhead
Professor of Playful Learning
Leeds Metropolitan University

Introduction

This book seeks to explore and further develop the theory and practice of play. It celebrates the central place of play within the learning of children from birth to the end of their primary education and affirms its rightful status as a vehicle for learner development. The book portrays and analyses the varied theories, issues, ideologies, perceptions and practice of play. Its aim is not only to stimulate the reader, but also to provide the wherewithal for practitioners to articulate, justify, proclaim and provide evidence for the necessity of play. It also supports current developments that seek to place active, play-oriented learning experiences as the foundation for lifelong learning.

Early years is at the forefront of pedagogic change and since the introduction of the Curriculum Guidance for the Foundation Stage, with its play-based pedagogy, there is at last some recognition for the importance of play within educational settings. This book addresses the recent paradigm shift towards the resurgence of the recognition that children's thinking and learning processes are qualitatively different to those of adults. As such, the authors write from many varied perspectives that nevertheless agree on one key issue: the impetus to give children a 'voice' within their own developmental

activities. The book examines key international policies such as the focus by the United Nations upon the Rights of the Child, and national English policy statements – the Children's Acts, Every Child Matters, Excellence and Enjoyment, the Ten Year Plan, the Early Years Foundation Stage and The Children's Plan (2007) amongst others.

The reader will explore play-based activities in an impressive arena of settings, including the classroom, the playground, the home and local community, and settings abroad. The book introduces, explores and demonstrates how play can be used as a vehicle for learning in a range of curriculum areas within the primary setting, including supporting the Primary National Strategy, National Curriculum and the National Strategies for Literacy and Numeracy. Play is explored from a wide variety of perspectives, and given its rightful place within children's development: as a holistic 'learning for life' activity that can be widely utilised, but not imprisoned within the formal teaching and learning process. To this end it examines play provision from different perspectives, including those of educators, social workers, therapists, carers, parents, service providers and members of multidisciplinary professional teams.

Issues of diversity and inclusion, including English as an additional language (EAL), special educational needs (SEN) ethnicity and gender, form an important part of the text. Several writers have been engaged in developing theory and practice within their own specific areas of expertise; as such they have provided chapters that present completely new perspectives upon the topics in question. These include the use of a biocultural perspective in the analysis of outdoor free play, sociopsychological analysis of the impact of play, research on eliciting early years educators' thinking and the success of playwork and playtherapy across the globe.

The book aims to encourage its readers to examine research perspectives and consider implications for practice. It facilitates the development of reflective practitioners who will use it as a starting point for improving practice but also as a tool in identifying key points for their continuing personal and professional development, particularly with regard to accessing a huge breadth of cutting-edge theory and empirical evidence and information from an exhaustive range of perspectives, contained within one lively, wide-ranging volume.

The book will not only be a valuable resource for students studying within childhood studies, qualified teacher status (early years/primary), early years professional status and playwork programmes within higher education, but also for early years, primary and play practitioners. Wider perspectives from the fields of playtherapy and playwork demonstrate how play can contribute to the emotional, social, academic, physical and cultural development of learners of all ages.

Chapter details

Chapter 1 introduces the reader to three perspectives on play that in turn examine the usefulness of play (including evolutionary, arousal modulation, meta-communicative and cognitive development theories as well as identifying play texts and therapy alongside psychological development), the need to harness play for learning and the importance of a play-based curriculum, and finally the place of playwork in the holistic development of the child. It also considers the problem of defining 'play' and 'not play', and the sometimes problematic/strained linkage of 'play' to 'education' and 'development'. The authors provide starting points for theoretical perspectives that are explored in context in later chapters.

In Chapter 2 Yinka Olusoga concentrates on a socio-cultural, social and cultural-historical perspective proposing that children need time and space to play and highlighting the vital role of the practitioner as guide, scaffold and facilitator of learning. The zone of proximal development (Vygotsky), scaffolding (Bruner) intersubjectivity, sustained shared thinking and co-construction are some of the notions explored in depth in this chapter alongside the work by Barbara Rogoff. Concepts of childhood, gender, the role of play, the role of adults, safety versus risk and the needs of society are shown to impact on children's experiences of, and opportunities for, play both within and outside the home.

In Chapter 3 Avril Brock focuses not only on perspectives of the early childhood curriculum in England but also draws on influences and perspectives from Europe, the United States and New Zealand. The Early Years Curriculum Group asserted in 1989 that early years education in the United Kingdom was well established, acknowledged and emulated for many years throughout the world and that it was a catalyst for high-quality work with young children and their parents, based on important educational principles and founded on good practice. However, throughout the 1990s in England there were immense pressures on early years education to conform to a more formal approach that was being demanded by policy makers. Many early years educators looked to Europe and the wider world to gain inspiration and support for their ideologies that would support a strong play-based pedagogy. The author examines educators' perspectives of these issues within the debates around developmentally appropriate curricula and current national frameworks such as the Early Years Foundation Stage (EYFS).

In Chapter 4 Avril Brock is joined by Jonathan Doherty, Jackie Brock and Pam Jarvis to offer national and international evidence from eminent neuroscientists, developmental psychologists and early years researchers demonstrating the complexity of play in children under 3. The authors explore how babies and toddlers learn about themselves and the world that surrounds them and the importance of the role of the early years practitioner. The reader is provided with examinations of practice, particularly in the area of early physical play along with practitioner perspectives and observations of babies in action. From this chapter the reader will not only explore why play is vital for cognitive, linguistic, social, emotional and physical development but it highlights how it is possible to capitalise on the capabilities of this group of learners.

Avril Brock, in Chapter 5, focuses on children between the ages of 3 and rising 6, promoting play opportunities for learning in the Early Years Foundation Stage whilst meeting the demands of early curricula through a play-based pedagogy. She explores how early years professionalism has come to involve specific expertise, including practical and professional knowledge of the pedagogy and the processes of learning through play steered by statutory frameworks. Contributions from professionals in playgroups, nurseries, parents and trainee practitioners provide numerous opportunities for the reader to reflect on their own philosophy of early education and pursue lines of enquiry to develop thinking and practice. This chapter further develops ideas from the previous chapter offering practical ideas from early years educators for promoting play in educational and care settings into Key Stage One.

Chapter 6 sees Sylvia Dodds broaden the notion of play as a vehicle for learning beyond the commonly acknowledged remit of the early years curriculum into the primary phase of education (6–11 year olds). She explores and analyses different aspects of play currently used within different curriculum areas, for example investigation in science, problem solving in mathematics, communication and role play in language, imaginative and thematic work, asserting the existence of a link between primary teaching and learning to 'play-based roots'. It examines classroom starting points that can be utilised to enhance learning in the primary curriculum, based on case study, educator perspectives and the author's own classroom experiences. It provides the reader with reflection points on play-oriented learning promoting cross-curricular and integrated approaches

to practice that develop, extend and excite the imagination of the lifelong learner. After having explored this chapter the reader will realise that play-based pedagogy has a place in the primary curriculum and that they, the practitioner, are only limited by their own imagination!

Chapter 7 provides a summary of groundbreaking research that has been undertaken with both human and non-human animals in the area of rough and tumble (R&T) play and children's play language. Pam Jarvis also introduces us to her investigations of children's rough and tumble play through a longitudinal, ethnographic study of the R&T play of a small group of children during the 18 months covering the last term of their nursery year, their reception year and the first term of their time in Year 1. Key findings highlight the narratives that these children attached to their R&T play, and the single and mixed gender relationships that they built within their R&T activities. The reader is also provided with the chance to reflect upon the place of outdoor free play within the current early years curriculum and is exposed to suggestions for improving their own free play support practice balancing day-to-day provision more equally between support for the development of cognitive *and* social skills, based upon a biocultural model of the juvenile human being as a complex, linguistic primate.

In Chapter 8 Jonathan Doherty explores the notion of inclusive education, the place of play in the education of children with special educational needs and the approaches practitioners can utilise to ensure creative environments for inclusive play. Throughout the chapter the reader is encouraged to reflect upon their own knowledge and practice, take up key points for consideration whilst remembering that we all need to play and have a right to play.

Chapter 9 sees Fraser Brown examine the playworker's view of play offering a working definition of playwork and an analysis of key debates currently taking place in the profession. The reader is introduced to powerful research in the field but more interestingly to the work of the White Rose Initiative with a paediatric hospital in Romania. Throughout the chapter the author successfully illustrates the range of ways in which the principles of playwork can be applied in practice.

Chapter 10 provides the reader with a review of arts therapies practice with children. Phil Jones examines the different contexts of work with children (from general education to more specialist provision) along with summaries of findings relating to the variety of different aims, ways of working and outcomes in art, music, drama and dance therapy. All these are considered in relation to play-based or play-related processes within the therapy. A series of research vignettes and examples from practice provide the backdrop for key reflections in dramatherapy as well as an illustration of how therapists see dramatherapy space as a way of enabling children to play out elements of their life, creating a playful relationship to reality.

In Chapter 11 Pam Jarvis and Jane George take a closer look at current debates that surround the play in the lives of children in the twenty-first century. They examine play in sibling interaction and explore why play with a wide range of peers is essential for healthy human development. The chapter identifies some of the reasons for decreasing opportunities for play in school as well as how practitioners need to work towards extending the opportunities for provision of out-of-school free play. The reader will hear what the 'student voice' has to say about school in the twenty-first century and will learn of initiatives to open up spaces for children's independent play.

Chapter 12 draws the book to a close, further arguing that a play-based approach can be used by creative practitioners to enhance learner development in any discipline. It draws the reader's attention to the fact that in some ways play, for the child in the twenty-first century, shows little resemblance to the play of previous generations. With the advent of technology, the development of the internet and the potential for online game playing with strangers located across the globe, the nature of play not only for children but human beings as a species is relentlessly changing. Despite the dangers of such developments the editors conclude the development of transferable skills and independent thinking via play-based activity is at the heart of meeting the core needs of children. Learners of today not only need to have such lifelong learning attributes in their repertoire of skills, but also need to be ready to take on the challenges of the world of the future. By the close of the book the reader will see that play, whatever one's age or stage of development, has a fundamental role in learning for life.

Chapter structure

Throughout the book the authors encourage the reader to engage with theory and curriculum development, explore links to practitioner perspectives and reflect on personal practice. Within the chapters themselves readers will encounter many of the following items:

- An **Introduction**, identifies the *key points, aspects* or *issues* that the chapter aims to explore.

- **Key theory and research** provides an examination of key theoretical perspectives, issues, ideologies, perceptions and practice of play.

- **Ideas in action** moves from the research to an examination of actual practice. This includes a wide range of evidence, from observations and case studies to vignettes, scenarios and episodes. Extracts from lecturers', teachers' and students' work, photographs, interviews, and so on, will also demonstrate the relevance and currency of the focal points of the chapter, providing a mixture of text and pictoral stimuli for the reader.

- **Stop and reflect** provides the reader with questions or commentaries that prompt connection to Ideas in action and starting points for research or examination of personal philosophy and practice.

- **Improving practice** offers the practitioner key points for reflection, opportunities to identify areas for personal and professional development or additional observations from settings.

- **Summary and review** aims to provide concluding remarks and a synopsis of the chapter material that offers the reader the opportunity to reinforce and consolidate their understanding.

- The final section, **Transforming Thinking and Practice: Over to You!** gives the reader the opportunity to further research the main and further ideas with additional **Questions for consideration** and/or **Ideas for research**.

- **Further reading** directs the reader to supplementary professional and academic reading, websites, new reports and a list of resources and their practical applications pertinent to the chapter and provides the opportunity for further study. These sources are complemented by a full reference section at the end of the book.

Features of the text

Throughout, each chapter utilises a range of presentational tools (icons, highlighting, and sidebars) that will be used to facilitate the orientation of the reader and the communication/examination of key ideas and points.

Key terms are presented within shaded boxes in the margin where they first appear and provide a brief definition to assist the reader in seeking clarity and understanding. These are then presented in a composite Glossary at the end of the book with further explanations as deemed necessary.

Where authors discuss issues/theories/ideas that are explored in other chapters in the book, these are highlighted within a shaded LINK box in the margin adjacent to the line where the former appears.

The Value of Play?
Psycho-social, Educational
and Playwork Perspectives

Chapter 1

Three Perspectives on Play

PAM JARVIS, AVRIL BROCK AND FRASER BROWN

Introduction

This book enters the world at an exciting time for the children's agenda in Britain, being launched in 2008, the same year as the **Early Years Foundation Stage** (EYFS) in England, which is endorsed with government intentions for a child-led, play-based statutory framework for children from birth to 5+. Wales also completes its launch of its play-based Foundation Phase for 3–7 year olds in 2008, while Northern Ireland introduced its new holistic, child-focused Foundation Stage for 5–7 year olds in September 2007. As might have been expected, the EYFS is already causing controversy in the English press, with *The Times* proposing that the EYFS is, in fact a 'stealth curriculum' which is 'a threat to all toddlers' (Frean, 2007). However, government funding has been provided to ensure that care and education for children under 6 will be led

> **Early Years Foundation Stage**
> Statutory guidelines for the education and care of children aged 5+ in England, to be introduced September 2008.

by adults in the new role of 'Early Years Professional' (EYP), who will be trained to fulfil a similar function to that of the Scandinavian 'pedagogue'. Such pedagogues are charged with developing the whole child – body, mind and emotions – within a specific historical and cultural background, whilst facilitating each child's potential for creativity and socialisation with others (Moss and Petrie, 2002). From September 2008 Scotland will also offer a new qualification for leaders of early years practice, who will attain an equivalent level to the English EYP.

The Children's Plan, published in December 2007, sets out the aspirations of the Brown New Labour Government for the development of children's services in England from 2008 to 2020. This includes provision of play areas and a comprehensive review of the primary curriculum, including the consideration of a more gradual transition from play-based learning to a more formal curriculum for 6–7 year olds.

As such, it is a fortuitous time to deliver a new book that presents so many different facets of play, and whilst it cannot claim to cover every single aspect, it contains a wealth of practice-based research and reflection from many very different perspectives. These range from a synthesis of culture, biology and evolution in a new 'biocultural' theory of play, to the innovative use of dramatherapy play, the pivotal role of playwork, and the importance of play in the early years/primary school classroom and playground. Authors will also explore recent discoveries about the developing brain that indicate a crucial role for play during the first months of life, the essential place of play in the lives of children with special needs, and the impact of social, cultural and gender issues upon children's play activities.

The concept of play and play-based learning is currently emerging from some very bleak times in Britain, culminating in the publication of the UNICEF report 'An overview of child well-being in rich countries' (2007), which rated the United Kingdom in bottom place. British children were least likely to find their peers 'kind and helpful' and most likely to engage in underage drinking and sexual behaviour. Fewer than 20 per cent of British children reported 'liking school a lot'. British children also reported the lowest sense of subjective well-being amongst children in the **OECD (Organization for Economic Cooperation and Development)** nations (UNICEF, 2007). Such a finding highlights the problems that have necessitated a comprehensive national initiative to 'transform practice', moving England in particular out of a dark era when children were firmly caught in the vice of the National Curriculum from the age of 4½. Reception classes were thereby led to engage in practices where children barely past their fourth birthdays spent their first school year in an oppressive regime which prescribed that large parts of the school day must be spent in desk-based, outcome-driven learning. Sociological changes in many post-industrial societies, particularly in the Anglo-American nations, including a huge increase in vehicle numbers, the geographic dispersal of the extended family and a decrease in average nuclear family sizes, have resulted in the curtailment of children's

> **OECD (Organisation for Economic Cooperation and Development)**
> An international organisation helping governments tackle the economic, social and governance challenges of a globalised economy (OECD website).

opportunities to independently engage in social free play. An increasingly sophisticated mass media has also heightened parent perception of traffic and 'stranger' danger, simultaneously negatively impacting upon opportunities for outdoor free play for children in such societies.

The period spanning the end of the twentieth century and the beginning of the twenty-first has brought a wealth of new opportunities for the world's children, but each set of new opportunities has been accompanied by a new set of risks. New technologies that have revolutionised teaching methods have also created new e-forums for children to engage in unpleasant behaviour, sometimes leading to serious, sustained bullying. Mass opportunities for long-distance travel and mass access to the internet have opened worldwide travel and a wealth of multi-cultural learning opportunities for children and adults. However, such technological advance has also spawned international industries in drug trafficking and pornography, resulting in an increased risk of the exploitation of children, both as workers within such dark industries and as users. The balance between risk and opportunity is also inequitably allocated between children from the rich western and poor eastern nations, with many of the poorest forgoing play and education to work long hours to produce luxury goods for the richest. This is currently a focal point for ongoing international concern, which will hopefully lead to more multi-nation derived solutions with the potential to underpin increasing cooperation towards positive intervention strategies as we move into the 2010s.

As England steps forward into a new programme for early years services that has been clearly endorsed by the new **Department for Children, Schools and Families (DCSF)** as supportive of play-based learning, we must remember that there is still a lot more to do for our children in England, including the pressing need to develop a smoother 'ramp' into mainstream education, with more room for child-led, play-based learning in the later stages of primary school and, as part of the same

> **Department for Children, Schools and Families**
> A new government department, replacing the Department for Education and Skills.

initiative, across Britain as a whole, to explore and facilitate the play and recreation needs of older children and teenagers, and the play needs of children of all ages in out-of-school environments.

The authors of this book offer a wide-ranging set of practical and theoretical ideas to help facilitate training for those with an ambition to go forward to contribute to future local, national and international play and education initiatives. In order to offer a suitably broad introduction to such a text, this chapter will present three alternative perspectives of the role of play in children's lives: psycho-social, educational and playwork, which provide different, but not incompatible standpoints and constructs for examining the complex concept of play. This book arose from our realisation that when we talked together as colleagues we were communicating similar values and aiming for equivalent results. We are all in agreement that play is crucially important for children's development, learning and well-being, reflecting the fact that the concept of play itself is infinitely flexible, offering choices and allowing for freedom of interpretation.

The challenge offered to the reader by this chapter is to accommodate and reflect upon what the similarities and differences may be between each perspective and, additionally, to engage with the following over-arching debates:

- Should play serve the needs of the child, rather than the needs and expectations of adults?

- What real choices are offered to contemporary children in their everyday play experiences?

- Is play about experiencing and doing, or about achieving a specific end result?

- How flexible should children's play be, with regard to offering freedom of movement and expression?

Perspective 1: The usefulness of play

PAM JARVIS

This part of the chapter will focus on the developmental usefulness of play for the child, particularly with regard to providing the psychological foundation for the social and intellectual skills that human adults need

to function in the increasingly complex social environment that sociologists call 'the global village'. In this way, play is about a flexible, self-directed experience, which both serves the needs of the individual child, and the future society in which s/he will live in adulthood.

Introducing evolution

If we use **evolutionary theory** as our starting point, we must presume that the urge to play that is present within young human beings and many species of non-human animals advantages the survival of the creature in some way. If there was no inherent advantage in playful behaviours, animals that play during their developmental years would not have survived to pass their **genes** down to their descendants. It is therefore generally theorised among **developmental psychologists** and **ethologists** that play provides essential practice experience for young animals; that they can use their playful behaviour to develop skills which they will use in adulthood to advantage the survival potential of themselves and their own offspring. Bruner (1976, p. 67) emphasises the huge importance of play in his comment 'animals do not play because they are young, but they have their youth because they must play'.

> **Evolutionary theory**
> A theory proposing that features which give a particular creature an advantage in the environment it inhabits are more likely to survive in that species, due to the fact that more successful animals are more likely to survive to mate and pass on their genes to the next generation.
>
> **Genes**
> The functional unit of inheritance controlling the transmission and expression of one or more traits (Merriam Webster).
>
> **Developmental psychologist**
> A psychologist who specialises in the psychology of infants and children, particularly how this changes as the child matures.
>
> **Ethologist**
> A person who studies animals in their natural environment.

Ideas in action

The value of play experience (Author's observation notes)

Five-year-old Nathan, one of the Reception class boys, was one of the most active children within my observation sample, and was frequently to be found engaged in highly active play. However, when it came to his turn to be the focus of one of my **focal child observations**, he was involved in an incident at the beginning of the relevant play session where he mistakenly hurt another boy in play fighting. His actions were mistaken for real aggression by the supervising adult, which resulted in a 'time out' punishment. When this was over, Nathan sought out the boy he had accidentally injured, apologised and explained that the incident had been an accident; the boy accepted the apology. Nathan then asked the boy to come with him to speak to the supervising adult and tell her what had happened. She listened to what they had to say, and asked the boys to shake hands, which they did. Nathan then walked away alone, still looking upset and sucking hard on his thumb (which had been in and out of his mouth since the situation arose). He continued to look rather morose, while Chris, one of his closest friends, jumped around him, clearly trying to entertain. Nathan turned around and smiled at Chris, but continued to stand quite still in the middle of the playground, with his thumb in his mouth.

> **Focal child observation**
> An observation carried out by focusing on one child, recording everything that the child does and says for a stated amount of time.

Playtime is useful even when it is not 'fun'!

I recorded a reflection in my observation notes, that the socially sophisticated measures that Nathan took to try to rectify his accident over a period of half an hour (albeit with the typical 5-year-old stress-diffusing mechanism of a thumb firmly in his mouth) would have been beyond the social repertoires of some adults. Whilst Nathan's experiences certainly did not make for a pleasant play period for him, it can be strongly argued that many such playground-based social events, even those which have quite negative results, are highly developmental experiences for the child concerned. These form a set of ongoing learning experiences relating to the human social world, which are both relevant to the child's independent management of his/her day-to-day life and underpin his/her eventual adult potential to deal competently with the vast range of complex social situations, including misunderstandings, that one meets in the adult world.

Stop and reflect

How would human beings learn to deal independently with difficult social situations if they did not experience sufficient independent free play opportunities in their daily lives during early development?

The more complex the adult society, the longer animals spend in their developmental period, and the more complex the play activities in which they engage. The most complex societies on earth, requiring an extensive range of cognitive, physical and, above all, social skills are those found amongst the great apes – gorillas, orang-utans, bonobos, chimpanzees, and the most complex of all – our own species, *Homo sapiens*, or, more commonly, human beings.

> ***Homo sapiens***
> Latin name for the version of the human species currently living on Earth.

This section therefore starts from the position that play is, pre-eminently, a useful activity through which much learning is accomplished.

The problem of defining 'play' and 'not play'

It is easy (particularly for early years practitioners) to casually discuss the concept of 'play' without fully specifying what we mean. Which activities undertaken within a pedagogical environment are 'play' and which are not? How do we define the difference between children's 'work' and children's play? Reed and Brown (2000) suggested that play may be hard to define because it is something 'felt' rather than 'done', commenting that there is no agreed universal definition for play in the literature. Ramsay (1998, p. 23) defined play as a social vehicle for 'exploring differences and developing common themes'. But how can this encompass all types of play; for example, how would solitary play fit this definition?

The following criteria for defining play were proposed by Garvey (1977, p. 10):

- It is enjoyable to the player.
- It has no extrinsic goals, the goal being intrinsic, the pursuit of enjoyment.
- It is spontaneous and voluntary.
- It involves active engagement by the player.

But are these definitions over-exclusive? It could be argued that this list excludes sport, as sporting activity involves certain extrinsic goals and inhibition of spontaneous behaviour, yet sport is still undertaken as an enjoyable leisure pursuit by many human beings, both children and adults. If we see the term 'play' as equivalent to 'having fun' (Anderson, 1998, p. 107), it becomes clear how different individuals and different demographic groups may perceive what is and is not 'play' very differently, and how many diverse behaviours might qualify as 'play'. Play thus appears to be a **relative** behaviour category. It may be that where an individual reports that they were playing, they probably were: 'it is fruitless to devote time and effort to defining what play is and what it is not . . . by de-emphasising the label "play" it might be easier to get on with the problem of studying the development of behaviour' (Meaney and Stewart, 1985, pp. 11–12).

> **Relative**
> A thing having a relationship to or necessary dependence upon another thing (Merriam Webster).

Play and psychological development

The linkage of 'play' with 'the development of behaviour' is a common focus for developmental researchers.

Ideas in action

'Work' or 'play'? (Author's observation notes)

One afternoon, whilst I was carrying out an observation of the Reception home corner, the teacher told the children to tidy up, as she wanted to read them a story before they went home. Four and a half year old Rory tidied briefly around the home corner, then, with the area behind him still in a state of some disarray, started to carefully organise the play knives and forks in the home corner drawer. He was taking a long time over this, moving them from slot to slot, muttering to himself as he did so. He then stopped and looked over towards some other children who were passing pencils to one another at a nearby table, commenting to me 'they are just playing'. 'What are you doing, then, Rory?' I asked. 'I'm working', he said proudly. 'Putting the knives and forks away?' I asked. 'Yes', he replied, returning to moving them from slot to slot.

Stop and reflect

Are adults really more competent at defining differences between 'work' and 'play' than children, or might they, like Rory, also be inclined to define what they are doing themselves as 'work', and what others are doing as 'play'?

Consequently, although it is generally accepted that human beings of all ages play, play research has mainly been carried out within the human developmental **paradigm**, investigating the play of children, and the role of play within their learning and developmental processes. Many theories of play have therefore focused upon the function that different *types* of play may have for specific aspects of children's development, rather than seeking exclusive categorisations of 'play and not-play'. As such, many researchers have attempted to categorise the

> **Paradigm**
> A philosophical or theoretical framework of any kind (Merriam Webster)

most common types of play observed in children's behaviour. Hutt (1979, p. 115) divided play types into three main categories, which she referred to as:

- epistemic: play associated with development of cognitive/intellectual skills;
- ludic: play associated with development of social and creative skills;
- games with rules: for example team sports or chess.

Whether and how adults study children's play is 'based on a set of values about the nature and function of childhood . . . held by the society in which a child lives' (Sylva and Czerniewska, 1985, p. 40); however, there are very many differences between human cultures in both time and geography; as such, we have to accept at the outset of our play studies that it is impossible to narrowly and simplistically define a complex activity such as play. It is therefore unlikely that we will ever come to any firm, universally agreed definitions of 'play' and 'not play', but nevertheless, many insightful theories of play have been created over the past 200 years. The following sections list a small selection of these.

Classical theories (nineteenth and early twentieth centuries)

For a long time, play was considered to be just something that children did which did not merit the effort of adult attention. As is typical of many aspects of western culture, there is a brief reference to children's play in Ancient Greek writings that was not followed up until the time of the 'Enlightenment', from the late eighteenth century onwards.

Energy regulation theories

These propose that play is just a way of 'letting off steam' and using up energy that has not been used elsewhere, or conversely, restoring energy through relaxation activities. The idea of 'letting off steam' originated in Ancient Greek texts with Aristotle's concept of 'catharsis'. In the eighteenth century

> **Catharsis**
> Elimination of a complex by bringing it to consciousness and affording it expression (Merriam Webster).

> **Philosopher**
> A person who seeks wisdom or enlightenment (Merriam Webster).

> **Mammal**
> A group of warm-blooded, hairy animals that secrete milk to feed their young.

> **Primate**
> A member of a group of mammals that developed particularly large brains and an ability to grasp objects. It encompasses both apes and monkeys.

> **Physiology**
> The organic processes and phenomena of an organism (Merriam Webster).

German **philosopher** Friedrich Schiller defined play as 'the aimless expenditure of exuberant energy' (Mellou, 1994, p. 91). However, the German poet Moritz Lazarus (1883, in Mellou, 1994) proposed that play is a way to *restore* energy lost in work, directly opposing surplus energy theories. British philosopher Herbert Spencer (1820–1895) used Darwinian evolutionary theory to propose that the more highly evolved the animal, the more 'surplus energy' it had, and the more complex its play would be (Mellou, 1994). It is true that the only creatures which appear to play are birds (in a very simple way) and **mammals**, with **primates** showing the most extended and complex forms of play. However, we know nowadays that there are many differences between the species, particularly in terms of brain **physiology**, which means that the picture is not quite as simple as differing levels of 'surplus energy' between species.

> **Darwin's theory of evolution**
> A theory which proposes that features that give a particular creature an advantage in the environment it inhabits are more likely to survive in that species, due to the fact that more successful animals are more likely to survive to mate and pass on their genes to the next generation.

Recapitulation theory
G. Stanley Hall (1920) viewed childhood as a link between the animal and human way of thinking and behaving. This is a theory that draws upon **Darwin's theory of evolution** in a rather strange way. Hall proposed that play helped children work out primitive instincts

which exist in human beings via the evolutionary process, but which would not be helpful in a more civilised human lifestyle. Hall's stages follow what he proposes is the evolutionary path: animal, savage, tribal society, modern society. However, we now know that western people are no more 'evolved' than people who still live in a tribal environment, and that it is technology that makes the superficial difference, not basic human instincts and behaviours, which can be seen in all human environments.

Western people
People from Europe, Australia or North America.

Human instincts
A natural or inherent aptitude, impulse, or capacity, specific to the human species (Merriam Webster).

So this theory has been discredited as it is based upon an outdated understanding of 'instincts' and 'evolution'.

Practice or Pre-exercise theory

This theory was proposed by Karl Groos (1896, 1901). Groos based his theory on practical observations rather than the philosophical speculations used by his play theory predecessors. Groos proposed that young animals and human children learn in play, practising skills that they need to develop for adulthood. Groos was also one of the first researchers to consider the idea that adults may use play in a similar way. He developed (1901) an early, very basic 'taxonomy' of play, listing the following types: experimental play (rule-based games), socio-economic play (chasing and play fighting) and imitative, social and family games (make believe play).

Taxonomy
An orderly classification of a group of related concepts.

Ideas in action

Case study: Recapitulation theory in popular fiction?

In 1954, William Golding published his world-famous book, *Lord of the Flies*, which tells the story of some pre-adolescent British boys marooned without adults on a tropical island. As the story unfolds, the boys make a good start in trying to organise their society along the lines of western social codes, but it rapidly deteriorates until they are behaving in a dangerous, wild, savage fashion, which includes painting their faces and carrying out tribal dances. This behaviour eventually results in the violent deaths of two of the group. Golding's rationale for this novel appears to be directly drawn from Hall's theory, in that he seems to propose that the unchecked play activities of western children are likely to lead to undeveloped, primitive and 'savage' behaviours, which will be ultimately harmful to their safety. The book's characters are drawn as in desperate need of firm guidance from more 'highly evolved' western adults.

Stop and reflect

What might this tell us about the author's attitude towards children's independent free play activities?

Play therapy

Psychoanalytic theory was originated by Sigmund Freud (1854–1938), who believed that play had an important role in children's emotional development. Freud reintroduced the term catharsis, in terms of a 'cathartic effect', believing that, through play, children could remove negative feelings associated with traumatic events. Freud's daughter Anna subsequently originated and developed Freudian play therapy over the mid-twentieth century. Play therapy can be used to help children who have had traumatic experiences, breaking the memory down into small segments and encouraging the children to 'play out' the troubled feelings, offering a variety of play experiences for this purpose, for example dolls, sand, water, art materials (Gitlin Weiner, 1998). Much use was made of play therapy in the years directly after World War II to help children who had been traumatised by violent events in Nazi-occupied Europe.

Arousal modulation theory

Arousal modulation theory was developed by Berlyne (1960), who proposed that play was the result of a

Ideas in action

Case study: Play as therapy

Van Dyk (2006) described a play therapy schedule that she carried out with a 4-year-old boy called Jason who had witnessed his father attacking his mother. Jason was encouraged to use 'small world' figures in the sand tray, during which he picked a Darth Vader figure to represent 'dangerous dad', with whom he does not want to be left alone during home visits. He was also encouraged to draw pictures representing his feelings, describing one picture as 'somebody . . . fighting with the kids and they gonna take him to jail'. As Jason continued his play therapy sessions, his behaviour at school and at home improved, particularly his ability to concentrate.

Improving practice

Play 'therapy' in everyday life

Children who are not 'in therapy' can also benefit from activities drawn from play therapy concepts. One example that works well with girls aged from 8 upwards is to seat a small group (four to eight) around a table upon which there are several bottles of different coloured nail varnish. Each girl in turn has to talk about a feeling that she had, and pick a colour to represent it. The group are then invited to use the varnish to paint their fingernails, choosing a different colour for each finger to represent different feelings that they have, chatting about this as they do so.

Stop and reflect

Can you think of a more gender-balanced, similar activity that children could carry out during an art activity, which involves using different colours to represent different feelings? Consider how this could be converted for children in different developmental stages.

Figure 1.1 A modern childhood?
Source: UK21/Alamy

drive in the central nervous system to keep arousal at an optimum level. Ellis (1973) proposed that children use play to increase stimulation and level of arousal. In Berlyne's model children respond to a given environ- ment to increase arousal; in Ellis's children actually create that arousal in their actions upon the environ- ment. Arousal modulation theory can be related to the current debate about the role of boredom versus

Ideas in action

Case study: A twenty-first-century childhood

Today, 8-year-old Aimee will get up at 6am, dress and eat breakfast quickly so her mother can get her to the childminder by 7.30am, on the way to work. Aimee will then be in school from 8.45am to 3pm. Her childminder will pick her up and take her to her 30-minute piano lesson; she will then go back to the childminder's house, where her mother will pick her up at 4.30pm. Aimee will then be taken back to her own home, where she will eat dinner and get ready for Brownies, where she will be between 6.30 and 7.30pm. Her father will collect her from Brownies, take her home, bath her and put her to bed at 8.30pm. On other days of the week Aimee goes horse riding and to a gymnastics class. She attends dancing classes on Saturday mornings. She is an only child, and lives on a busy road, where she cannot engage in outdoor play unaccompanied by adults. The only regular chance she gets to play undirected by adults is in her school playground. However, her school has recently reduced the lunch break, so this equates to one 15-minute break in the morning and approximately 20 minutes at lunchtime, depending on how quickly she finishes her lunch. Aimee's mother complains that Aimee can be 'difficult' during the school holiday periods; she seems unable to settle down to anything (other than watching television) for longer than a few minutes and, despite being surrounded by expensive educational toys, she constantly complains to adults that she is 'bored'. This indicates that Aimee lacks strategies to balance her own levels of arousal.

Stop and reflect

How do you think this might effect Aimee's future teenage and adult life? Discuss this with colleagues.

---

potential over-stimulation in childhood. The question is whether by removing boredom by a constant round of stimulating experiences, twenty-first-century child-rearing practice is removing children's development and practice of independent self-directed activities that regulate their own arousal levels. The sociologist Corsaro (1997) suggested that, in modern western societies, children's time is increasingly taken up by adult-directed activities, and that consequently modern western childhood is being 'colonised' by adults in this way.

Metacommunicative theory

Metacommunicative play theory was developed by Gregory Bateson (1955). Bateson proposed that in pretend play children learn to operate on two different levels, that is, in the scenes that they are acting out, while still maintaining their existence in the real world. Garvey (1977) proposed the term 'break frame' for what children do when problems or disagreements arise and they come out of their make-believe to solve

> **Metacommunicative play**
> Metacommunication is communicating about communicating, used to describe conversations where people are talking about aspects relating to communication; children frequently do this in their play interactions.

> **Play text**
> An imaginary story a child or group of children create to underpin and explain their play actions (can also be called a 'play narrative').

the issue, then re-enter into the pretend scenario. This indicates that children do not just learn about the role itself, but about the concept of *playing* a role and how this relates to reality.

Play texts

It has been shown that '**play texts**' that is, what children pretend about, are highly related to their actual environments and experiences (for example western children playing at 'families', 'schools' or fantasy roles drawn from media sources).

Bateson (1955) proposed that pretend play within this specific context produces an adult with a particular cultural and social self-image; a necessary part of being a fully functional adult human being. Jarvis (2006, 2007) studied children's playground-based play texts, finding them to be complex and highly gendered (see Chapter 7).

Cognitive development theories

Cognitive development theories propose that play is a vital part of building up a set of mental representations (Piaget called these 'schemas') of the world around the child. This is achieved in very small 'bites', each piece of learning in a particular area building upon the previous piece over the entire period of development, with the young adult finally achieving a 'cognitive map' of how the world s/he lives in actually works. For example, all human beings learn about the basic operation of gravity (why we would not purposely drop a basket of eggs), but only those who live in an area with motor vehicles know that you have to look and listen carefully before you cross a road that initially appears to be clear. The two most prominent theorists in this area are Jean Piaget (1896–1980) and Lev Vygotsky (1896–1934).

Piaget proposed a developmental system of 'assimilation and accommodation', the child either assimilating a new experience (taking it into thought without creating a new concept, for example you lick an ice cream and you also lick an ice lolly) or accommodating it (creating a new concept in thought, for example you can't pick up spaghetti with just a spoon, or a knife and fork, you have to learn a new action with a spoon and a fork). The child moves into accommodation by a process of 'equilibration', which means needing to balance all related schemas against one's current picture of reality (Piaget, 1955).

Vygotsky proposed the concept of a 'zone of proximal development' (Vygotsky, 1978). The 'ZPD' is an area of competence that a

> **Schema**
> A term from Piagetian theory, referring to a collection of concepts or ideas that are highly organised within the brain.

> **Assimilation**
> From Piagetian theory, to use an existing schema to deal with a new experience; in teaching the term can be used to mean to absorb, take in, fully understand a particular element of learning.
>
> **Accommodation**
> From Piagetian theory, to build a new schema in response to a new experience.
>
> **Equilibration**
> To bring into balance. In Piagetian theory, this specifically refers to bringing one's ideas into balance with reality.
>
> **Zone of Proximal Development (ZPD)**
> From Vygotskian theory, the gap between the learner's current level of development as compared to his/her immediate potential level of development when s/he is aided by an adult or more competent peer.

Ideas in action

Case study: A 'breaking frame' example

Five-year-olds Sophie and Elizabeth are playing in the home corner. They have previously agreed that Sophie is the mummy and Elizabeth is the baby. Sophie puts Elizabeth to bed and goes into the kitchen area. Elizabeth gets up and wanders in after her, picks up a toy saucepan and puts it on the cooker. Sophie turns around and, 'breaking frame', says, 'You're the baby, you can't use the cooker.' Elizabeth says, 'But what if baby *tried* to use the cooker?' Sophie moves back into the mummy role (the 'pretend frame'), adopting a scolding tone: 'Naughty baby, get away from that cooker, you'll burn yourself.' Elizabeth starts pretending to cry, Sophie says, 'Oh, no, baby, what have you done?' She takes Elizabeth's hand and says, 'Shall we get a bandage?' Elizabeth nods her head, still 'pretend crying'.

Stop and reflect

What do Sophie and Elizabeth learn about caring for younger children and babies from this interaction?

Ideas in action

Playground play texts (Author's observation notes)

On a bitterly cold winter's day, the children were briefly in the playground during a light fall of snow. I observed Rory, Elliot and Adam absorbed in an energetic chasing game, which they had to leave when they were called back into school. Directly we arrived back in the classroom I sat down with them to ask them about their game. The resulting conversation is reported below:

Pam Jarvis:	What were you playing?
Rory (to Elliot):	What were we doing?
E:	We were helping Adam.
R:	We were helping Adam not to freeze.
PJ:	Helping Adam not to do what?
R:	Not to freeze. It was snowing and blowing in my eyes.
PJ:	Yes, I know, it was very cold.
R:	If you freeze you never get out.

Narrative

Literally something that is spoken (narrated), the term is often used by social scientists to refer to the way people explain things by explaining a background 'story'.

This play text would appear to reflect some of the 'super-hero' **narratives** frequently played out in western action cartoons and fantasy films.

Improving practice
Play texts research: Suggested activity

You could carry out a focal child observation in an outdoor play area, focusing upon the play texts that the child creates in his/her collaborative play with others during that session. Once you feel comfortable with the focal child technique, you could subsequently do several such observations, focusing on children from cultures the same as and different from yourself, considering how differing cultural backgrounds may (or may not) have implications for the play texts that children create. If you are in a setting where you know the children well, you might also be able to discuss their play activities with them, in an attempt to find out what the texts they are creating mean to them. Make sure to time your conversation carefully, making sure that you do not interfere with or curtail their play, or conversely, wait for too long afterwards, as young children very quickly forget. For the average 4–7 year old, 'too long afterwards' means when they have moved on to a different activity. A good time to talk to children about their playground-based play texts is at the end of playtime, as they walk back across the playground after the bell has gone.

Stop and reflect

What might these boys be learning about adult male roles, responsibilities and relationships from collectively designing and playing out this play text?

Peers

Those belonging to the same societal group, especially based on age, grade, or status (Merriam Webster).

child can access with help from an adult or in collaboration with **peers**, but cannot achieve alone. For example a child building a Lego model may not be able to work out how s/he uses the different shaped bricks to make a wheel arch on a model of a car, but an adult may help by demonstrating and breaking down the task (Jerome Bruner later referred to this as 'scaffolding'). Two or more children may also 'put their heads together' and work out by discussion, trial and error how it is done.

Conclusion

This part of the chapter has introduced the usefulness of play and in doing so has explored a range of

Ideas in action

Improving practice

Vignette: Schema focus

Three-year-old children may easily accept the existence of Santa Claus, given their very limited knowledge of everyday practical physics, but by the time they are 6 or 7 they will be asking questions such as, 'How can he come down the chimney if we haven't got one?' and 'How can he get round all the children in the world in one night?' This indicates that the process of equilibration is occurring, and sooner or later the child will realise that the concept of Santa is a myth rather than a reality, as his existence is not commensurate with the other knowledge that they now have about the world.

Stop and reflect

By focusing upon the specific questions that children ask, we can discover what ideas they may be currently engaged in bringing to a new state of equilibration.

Improving practice

Studying the ZPD: Suggested activity

Some learning may involve working on the ZPD with both teachers and peers. You can consider this through designing/engaging in/observing any activity that involves an adult demonstration followed by group work. For example, show children aged 6 or over how to make a simple Lego model or a simple craft item such as a decorative paper garland (which could be linked to learning about various religious festivals). Demonstrate how to carry out the task, and then compare how children complete it either working alone, working with a peer of similar ability and working with a peer of slightly higher ability. You should particularly focus on how children discuss the task, and what they appear to gain (or occasionally lose) from such discussion.

---

theoretical perspectives rooted in developmental psychology, many of which will be revisited and further explored by various authors in the later chapters of this book. It has outlined the vital link between play and psychological development, and suggested that play does not always have to result in an obvious or even a positive outcome to usefully contribute to the child's current and future social competence, which is both to his/her own benefit, and the benefit of the society in which s/he lives.

Ideas in action

Improving practice

Observation focus idea: Suggested activity

Why not carry out a 10–15-minute **focal area observation**, and then see how many of the above theories you could apply to the behaviour that you recorded?

> **Focal area observation**
> An observation carried out by focusing on one area, recording everything that occurs within this area for a stated amount of time.

Perspective 2: Capitalising on play – harnessing it for learning

AVRIL BROCK

Introduction

This section on educational play promotes play for learning. Children are both pre-programmed and motivated to play – it is quite simply, as Susan Isaacs declared in the 1920s, 'their life's work'. From an educational perspective children's disposition to play, their inherent motivation and driving purpose to play, should be harnessed to promote learning and fulfil educational potential. Play is important for learning – educators 'milk' it; hijack it from children; use it as a vehicle to develop

Ideas in action

Valuing play (Author's interview data)

What is so wrong with playing at this age? That's where the root of all learning comes from as far as I'm concerned, exploration, experimentation, that's the way I feel that children learn best and it's our job to direct that and channel it. Our planning will provide support to develop what the children are interested in, whilst meeting the demands of the early learning goals. It's about being practical but also being creative in what you're doing with the children and trying to stimulate them in as many sensory ways as you can.

People don't always see the value and really don't realise what goes into it. They think we turn up on the day, we open up nursery and that's it, children come in and you just play with them, not that there's hours of preparation, planning, finding and making resources. Yes, even my own girlfriend doesn't realise.

Mike, nursery nurse

Education Action Zone
Schools that receive special assistance from the Department for Education and Employment to run projects designed to raise pupils' achievement levels.

English as an additional language (EAL)
Where English is not the child's first language.

partner in an early years team in a nursery that had been recently integrated into the school. The team was developing the links and curriculum across the then newly introduced Foundation Stage.

This nursery nurse believed strongly in the power and importance of play, promoting the curriculum through quality play experiences. He was also very aware of the status of play and that public perception from parents, other educators and policy makers was not always understanding or in favour of play being promoted in educational settings.

It is therefore important to be both knowledgeable and articulate about the importance of play in educational contexts. Educators must be articulate and prepared to justify their provision for a play-based curriculum and pedagogy to a range of audiences.

Improving practice

Many early years educators find it hard to understand why some people, including educators of older children, belittle play, when it is such a powerful motivating force that yields such rich results. The nursery nurse in the above quote was interviewed for a PhD research thesis. He worked in a nursery within an inner city school in an **Education Action Zone**, which had a very mixed catchment of children, including a percentage learning **English as an additional language**. He worked as an equal

Stop and reflect

Do we need to justify play and do *you* feel able to articulate this to an external audience? Reading this book should help you in the process of being accountable for play!

Cognition
The processing of information; how one understands the world.

Curriculum
A body of knowledge/skills to be transmitted to the learner; the coursework and content taught at a school; a programme of learning.

cognition and all aspects of the **curriculum**. – why not? Particularly if it is both effective and enjoyable. Children play naturally; through a developmental process; to discover their environment; to learn

about what and why things happen and, primarily, to have fun.

The importance of play

Educators of young children, therefore, believe that play is the most valuable tool for learning. **Intrinsic motivation** is valuable because it results in **child-initiated** learning. Educators need to provide stimulating playful environments that promote practical activities

Intrinsic motivation
The stimulus for learning inherent in children that is not dependent on external factors such as money or grades.

Child initiated
Allowing children the opportunity to develop their knowledge and skills through play without adult direction.

and the use of interesting resources and so enable children to initiate their own learning experiences (the chapters throughout this book will provide many rich examples).

By the beginning of the nineteenth century the idea of childhood not just being a preparation for adult life, but existing in its own right as a special period of life, was gaining acceptance. Philosophers, psychologists and early educationalists were the pioneers of theories regarding the importance of play for learning and education. Here is a brief introduction to some of these:

- Pestalozzi's (1746–1827) ideas influenced Robert Owen when he set up the first infant school in Scotland in 1816, promoting suitable learning environments for young children that included free outdoor play.

- Wilderspin (1792–1866) promoted literacy, language and numeracy, through both rote learning and the availability of materials and active practical experiences.

- Froebel (1782–1852) suggested the significance of educative play in young children's development for children to absorb knowledge, and to develop imagination and language. He developed a **child-centred approach** and stressed active learning.

Child-centred approach
Education that tailors the teaching and learning style to the particular interests of the child, e.g. allowing a child who has an interest in trains to read about trains, write a story about trains, etc.

- Steiner (1861–1925) was concerned with children's individuality, their whole development through experiencing a creative and balanced curriculum. He proposed that the role of the adult, the environment and the provision of natural resources as play materials were important.

- Montessori (1870–1952) advocated the value of play in children's learning and provided real-life learning experiences in a structured, planned environment, which developed the inner lives of children through sensory and scientific experiences.

- Isaacs (1885–1948) promoted play and exploration through active involvement, encouraging children's clear thinking and independent behaviour. She studied child psychology scientifically, through undertaking systematic child observations, examining the influence of language on thought and emotions.

- McMillan (1860–1931) firstly provided environments to support children's health, but she also believed in the importance of first-hand experiences and active learning, particularly that play was important for their development of imagination, feelings and emotions.

- Vygotsky (1896–1934) believed that the quality of children's social and cultural relationships was crucial; that adults and peers support children's learning and that play created a zone of proximal (potential) development, which enabled them to function at a high level.

- Bruner (1915–present) sees children as active learners, who need first-hand experiences to help them develop their thinking and learning. Like Vygotsky, he believes that the adult is important for **scaffolding** children's learning.

Scaffolding
Assistance provided by an adult or more experienced peer in context to aid a child's learning.

- Piaget (1896–1980) was concerned with the thoughts and ideas children have, examining how they learn through stages, including how play and **discovery learning** is important for development and that imaginary play led to games with rules.

Discovery learning
Inquiry-based learning/instruction.

Adapted from Beardsley and Harnett (1998); Curtis and O'Hagan (2003); Broadhead (2004); Bruce (2004).

Ideas in action

Making sense of the world through play (Author's observation notes)

I visited Mina, aged 14 months, and her mother to interview them about Mina's early language development. Mina was extremely shy of me for the first 30 minutes and kept her distance. However she had seen me place my small digital recorder on the coffee table and as soon as she had plucked up her courage, she came to sit with me, immediately grasping the recorder. It fitted neatly in her hand and within seconds she had worked out how to turn it on and off and listen to the recordings. Her next task was to 'take photos' with my digital camera. This was a larger instrument, but again she had no trouble manipulating it, holding it correctly to take photos, whilst modelling appropriate poses and smiles. She then manoeuvred herself to my handbag and systematically selected items one by one. Firstly she took out the purse, followed by appointment cards, lipsticks, perfume, pens, memory sticks, mobile phone and glasses. She used each item appropriately – except for the memory sticks! The purse went in her plastic

handled box, which she used as a handbag, as she copied what her mum does with hers. She scribbled on my notepad with each pen. She experimented wearing my glasses on the front, top and back of her head. She made her 'smelling face' as she pretended to apply the lipstick and perfume. How did she know that the small round bottle had a top that could be removed? 'Ah, beautiful' declared her mum, whenever Mina showed her each new acquisition.

Stop and reflect

In your observations of children, upon which contexts do they most readily base their play? How often is this from previously 'modelled' adult behaviours?

Comment

My handbag was more appealing at this time than the array of toys on the floor, so was Mina playing,

Figure 1.2 Exploring through play

▶

experimenting or working? I think she was doing all three. She had already, at 14 months, learned the purposes of the handbag items, through watching, imitating and exploring. She was learning as she handled the objects, using all her senses to use and examine them. She didn't talk much during these activities, but you could see there was much evidence to indicate her thinking processes. Her mother commented that she and Mina's father felt that they could often observe their daughter thinking things through as she played. As Hutchin (1996) observed, children draw on a range of experiences, which they have in every aspect of their daily lives. Mina has learned through watching, listening and reflecting, and has already had many opportunities to imitate, imagine and repeat actions through her playful activities.

This is quite a long list of renowned figures, who have provided evidence for their beliefs, demonstrating a breadth of knowledge regarding the importance of play for learning and education. Educators need not only to consider these aforementioned theories, they also need to be able to explain their provision of play experiences to a wider audience. They need to be able to articulate this knowledge in a way that parents, policy makers and the public at large understand and accept that a play-based curriculum and pedagogy is an essential part of children's education. Both early years and primary educators need not only to understand the value of play and so put it into practice with children, but also be able to *explain* and *celebrate* play-based learning with others. Educators need to provide rich learning environments that promote all types of play – spontaneous, structured, imaginative and creative, and so enable children to fulfil their learning potential.

Mina is learning through her play and early years educators have become skilled at capitalising on young children's inclination to learn, their appetite for new experiences and their inclination to 'play' first and foremost. What then defines a 'play' experience as being different from a 'work' experience in school and other educational settings? Are 'play' experiences only those that are freely chosen by the children themselves? Are having fun or enjoyment key elements in defining what play is? When an adult in a **Foundation Stage**

> **Foundation Stage**
> Prior to September 2008, this was the first part of the National Curriculum, aimed at children between the ages of 3 and 5+.

setting directs children to paint a picture, create a construction with the large blocks or complete a jigsaw – is this play or work? When a child chooses to plant bulbs in the garden, bake a cake or listen to a story – is this work or play? All children have a right to relax, play and join in with a wide range of activities (Article 31, **UN Rights of the Child**), to free play as well as structured learning, and this is of value in itself

> **UN Rights of the Child**
> An international agreement providing a comprehensive set of rights for all children.

as part of the child's cognitive and creative development. Play is fun, rewarding, enjoyable and complete in itself.

A play-based curriculum

In this way it can be seen that play for learning occurs naturally. The educator's role is to provide a multitude of opportunities in which children are motivated to become involved, individually and collaboratively. These activities need to be planned for potential and optimal learning. The educator needs to be able to analyse these learning opportunities, make decisions about when and how to be involved and move the play forward; all the time observing and analysing the achievements and benefits for learning. This does not preclude having fun and enjoyment, as these should be essential components of learning through play. Children's individual needs must be met for successful learning and development. The activities and experiences provided by educators need to be structured through a cycle of planning, organisation, implementation, assessment and evaluation. As Riley (2003)

Ideas in action

Outdoor social free play (Author's observation notes)

Zack and his older brother Kurt were playing in their garden. They threw, caught, kicked and hit balls playing golf, football and basketball; they climbed ladders and trees in their role as firefighters; they used gardening tools in the soil and sandpit; drove a tractor, car and tricycle round and round the garden and were mechanics in overalls using a range of tools and implements; they played team games and races with the adults. In a span of three hours, there was no whingeing, lots of collaborative play, imaginative thinking, exploratory language and socialising with the adults.

Zack (aged 4) was playing in my garden. Amongst lots of self-initiated activities, he carefully watered the flowers and worms with a water pistol, watched the sparrows eating seed from a feeder and saw the water boatmen swimming in the pond. He observed, asked questions and discussed what was happening. (see Figure 1.3 on p. 26)

educators!). I took advantage to create a PowerPoint on physical development and outdoor play for my lecture that week. I analysed the boys' activities for learning and development for the students' enlightenment. Zack and Kurt experienced a majority of the **early learning goals** in the Foundation Stage Curriculum for Physical Development. In the second scenario Zack was not only experiencing the early learning goals for 'knowledge and understanding of the world' in the Early Years Foundation Stage, but also meeting aspects of personal, social and emotional development and communication, language and literacy.

> **Early learning goals**
> The six areas of development and learning, which define what children are expected to achieve during the Early Years Foundation Stage.

Improving practice

These two scenarios offer insights into children's experiences in the outdoor environment. The adults initiated none of these activities, but they capitalised on them, or at least I did (there's no 'off duty' for early years

Stop and reflect

Access the Early Years Foundation Stage document – if you don't have a copy – view or print it from the DCSF website. Read and reflect on the early learning goals for physical development.

---

proclaims, a rigorous and comprehensive grasp of a holistic curriculum is required, not only in the Foundation Stage, but also in Key Stage One, with **developmentally appropriate** learning experiences offered across all curriculum subjects.

> **Developmentally appropriate**
> Practice based on what is known about how children develop taking account of age, social situation and emotional well-being.

Moyles *et al.* (2002) in their *Study of Pedagogical Effectiveness in Early Learning* (*SPEEL*) determine that quality teaching and learning is characterised by practitioners' ability to apply knowledge of young children's learning to promoting their progression and

achievement, and in identifying and measuring the effectiveness of the provision. A nursery nurse in a Foundation Stage unit explained to me about the system she and the early years coordinator had organised for the children. (see 'Ideas in Action' on p. 27)

Instrumental theories of play

That play is essential for learning has been validated by many contemporary researchers in the field of early years education, including Hutt *et al.*, (1989); Moyles (1989); Anning (1991); Bruce (1991); Hall and Abbott (1991); Wood and Attfield (1996); Bennett, *et al.* (1997); Sayeed and Guerin (2000); Drake (2001);

Figure 1.3 At play in the garden

problem solving through play (Wood and Attfield, 1996, 2005; Anning *et al.,* 2004). Play-based learning is highly motivating and enables young children to self-direct their learning, encouraging engagement and concentration (Riley, 2003). Moyles (1989) develops Norman's (1978) model of accretion to show that play builds on personal experiences and knowledge to create new concepts and experiences:

- accretion – acquiring new knowledge, facts, information and skills;

- restructuring – reorganising existing knowledge to accommodate the new and seeing patterns, structures and principles;

- tuning – restructuring guides the acquisition of further new knowledge.

Play emphasises the restructuring, enrichment and discovery – building on personal experiences and knowledge to create new concepts and experiences. This affirms Froebel's (1782–1852) belief that play is the way that children integrate their learning, gain understanding, apply this understanding and begin to work in more abstract ways. All these theories offer insights into the way play enables children to develop their ideas, thoughts, feelings, relationships, knowledge and understanding of the world around them.

In 1967 the Plowden Report gave play a strong endorsement. It stated that play was important for children's development and that wide-ranging and satisfying play is a means of learning.

MacIntyre (2001); Riley (2003) and Broadhead (2005). The first problem to be encountered is its definition, as 'play' can cover a range of behaviours related to varied activities (Wood and Attfield, 1996, 2005). Play is an 'umbrella word' (Bruce, 1991) and a 'jumbo category' (Hutt *et al.,* 1989) that encompasses a multiplicity of activities, many of which are conducive to learning. Throughout the last two centuries there have been a wide variety of theories that all proclaim the importance of play from different perspectives; as Bruce (2004, p. 129) observes, 'different theories offer support in different ways'. The complexity of this 'simple' activity called play can be seen in Table 1.1 (see p. 28).

However there are critics of providing play experiences as a means for learning and of the quality of the actual provision that may be provided in educational settings, as shown in Table 1.2 (see p. 29).

There is substantial evidence from many researchers that children can demonstrate higher levels of verbal communication, creative thinking, imagination and

Adults who criticise teachers for allowing children to play are unaware that play is the principal means of learning in early childhood; it is the way through which children reconcile their inner lives with external reality. In play, children gradually develop concepts of causal relationships, the power to discriminate, to make judgments, to analyse and synthesise, to imagine and to formulate. Children become absorbed in their play and the satisfaction of bringing it to a satisfactory conclusion fixes habits of concentration that can be transferred to other learning.

(CACE, 1967; in Pollard, 2002, p. 143)

Ideas in action

Organising and resourcing 'play for learning' (Author's interview data)

A few years ago our children were entering school with no pre-school experience and they'd been thrown into a Reception class and expected to do work at a National Curriculum stage, when all they wanted to do was play. They were not ready to sit down and work or ready to sit down for 20 minutes and listen to a story in English. All they wanted to do was explore and play with play-dough for the first time, splash in water, play with the sand.

So now when they come in there are a lot of activities set up for them – the sand and water and the home corner is ongoing and we alternate the painting table, flat painting, finger painting. They choose for the 20 minutes and then we find that they do come and sit on the carpet, that they are so much more ready to listen.

When they're playing I think their language develops a lot better than sitting and listening, when they're talking to one another. You maybe have a Gujerati girl speaking to a Punjabi girl and they have to speak in English because neither of them speak the same home language.   Peta, nursery nurse

Improving practice

This nursery nurse articulated her appreciation and increased understanding of the children learning through play. Of the children in the unit 98 per cent spoke English as an additional language and the nursery nurse and her teacher were making changes that suited the children's particular needs. Building on their knowledge of the children's previous experiences and their individual needs, they had decided to allow the children free play when they entered the classroom in the morning. Her team evaluated their practice through ongoing observations and monitoring of the children's learning and they determined that their free play provision was effective in meeting the children's needs. They found that the children's play was focused, that they did move and select from a range of experiences, they were able to concentrate for prolonged periods, engaging in cooperative play, using both home language and English. The team supported the children and provided experiences that allowed them to meet the objectives of the early learning goals. Educators need to be concerned with demonstrating that their provision promotes effective learning. They should engage in ongoing analysis of children's learning; they need to be **reflective practitioners**, examining both the curriculum and the **pedagogy** that occurs in their practice.

Reflective practitioners
Practitioners who actively evaluate their professional competence and look for ways in which to improve their knowledge and expertise.

Pedagogy
The art, science, or profession of teaching.

Stop and reflect

How often do you stand back and objectively analyse the quality of provision and the impact it has on learning? What constraints do you feel inhibit the existence of 'free play'?

However, there have been ongoing criticisms of the Plowden ideology in that it allowed too much freedom with too little direction, which actually resulted in less and less play occurring in many Reception classes in the late 1980s and 1990s. Since this time the debate has moved backwards and forwards between the two polarities of free-flow play and formal instruction. The core of the debate seems to be: should the primary aim for young children be that they become confident, capable members of society, or that they become knowledgeable regarding subject content? These two polarisations are not at all mutually exclusive and educators, including teachers, nursery nurses and others working in care and education settings need to make informed decisions about provision for the early years child. Many teachers have found that it is difficult to justify learning through

Table 1.1 Instrumental Theories of Play

View of play	Source	Date
Suitable learning environments – outdoor play	Pestalozzi	1805
Educative play; child-centred approach	Froebel	1837
Play to develop inner life; multi-sensory learning	Montessori	1900
Play as rehearsal for future adulthood	Groos	1920
Play as an expression of inner conflict	Freud	1920
Play is children's work	Isaacs	1958
Play as a means for learning	Piaget Bruner Vygotsky	1962 1974 1978
Practice play; symbolic play; play with rules	Piaget	1962
Play on a spiral curriculum; learning through first-hand experiences	Bruner	1966
Play dispositions	Katz	1967
Play reconciles children's inner lives with external reality	Plowden	1967
Play is emotional and a means to control fears	Paley	1978
Play as a cultural tool; socio-cultural learning in ZPD; supported by adults	Vygotsky	1978
Ludic (explorative) and epistemic (creative) play	Hutt *et al.*	1989
Play as a spiral of learning	Moyles	1989
Play and schema	Athey; Nutbrown	1989
Socio-dramatic play important for cognitive, creative and socio-emotional abilities	Smilansky	1989
Play as a process with no product – free-flow play	Bruce	1989
Levels of involvement	Laevers	1996
Teaching through play	Bennett *et al.* Wood and Attfield	1997 1996, 2005
Playfulness	Parker-Rees	2001
Play on a social continuum	Broadhead	2004
Play to promote self-regulation and meta-cognition	Wood and Attfield Whitebread	2005 2005

play because they have felt pressurised to conform to a more formal delivery. This pressure occurs through inspection, head teachers, other teaching colleagues and parents. Educators require underpinning knowledge and understanding of psychological, socio-cultural and eco-logical theories and the relevance of these to meet young children's needs, as well as knowledge of how educators teach and how children learn. In the 1990s, the move towards a traditional subject-based curriculum resulted in most Initial Teacher Training courses focusing mostly

Table 1.2 Critical Theories of Play

View of play	Source	Date
Play is just a means to let off steam and to exercise	Spencer	1878
Children think work is sitting still or producing something	Tizard *et al.*	1984
Play is heavily idealised	Meadows and Cashdan	1988
Play does not have to be worked at, it is deemed less valuable than activities that have measurable outcomes	Cleave and Brown	1989
Play activities can be low in intellectual challenge	Hall and Abbott	1991
Play tends to be seen as trivial by a male-dominated society that emphasises the power of rational thought	Anning	1994
Play is seen as the enemy of education	Hirst	1994
Difference between rhetoric and reality in teachers providing play	Bennett *et al.*	1997

on how to deliver subject knowledge. Issues about these different perspectives on knowledge base, curriculum and pedagogy will be explored in later chapters.

Despite a constant validation of play and a widespread agreement that early years education should be play based from contemporary early years theorists – Rumbold (DfES, 1990); Bennett *et al.* (1997); House of Commons (2000); Qualifications and Curriculum Authority (QCA) (2000); Moyles *et al.* (2002) – its place in the curriculum was not secure and embedded until recently. Its status and value continued to be questioned at the level of policy by Government until its validation in the *Curriculum Guidance for the Foundation Stage* (QCA, 2000). Unfortunately there is still a lack of affirmation from parents, and even from primary teachers and head teachers, regarding the place of play in school.

The *Researching Effective Pedagogy in the Early Years* (Siraj-Blatchford *et al.*, 2002) research demonstrates that some practitioners have a narrow conceptualisation of play – that it was only relevant to some areas of the curriculum. Siraj-Blatchford *et al.* propose that these practitioners seemed to believe that the involvement of imagination was a necessary component before play could be considered to be play. Similarly, when Siraj-Blatchford and Sylva (2005) evaluated the implementation of the foundation phase for the Welsh Assembly Government, they found that some practi-

tioners were not confident about what a play-based pedagogy entailed, and failed to grasp what is meant by children being actively involved in their own learning. There was a general perception that play is accepted as part of what children do outdoors but not indoors!

The debates about the educational value of play derive from this lack of clarity about what is and what is not play (Riley, 2003). This therefore reiterates the importance of educators gaining a through understanding of broadly what constitutes play in an education environment and how to provide rich learning environments. This is important for both early years settings and primary schools.

Conclusion

Do educators provide enough 'quality' time for children to learn through play? Is there a real understanding by educators to provide and to justify why time for play experiences needs to occur in a rich learning environment in both early years settings and schools? Siraj-Blatchford *et al.* (2002) proposed that the richest play experiences occur in nursery, indicating that perhaps schools need to examine their practice, visiting these areas of excellence to help their provision become richer,

Ideas in action

Play for 'rich' learning

Brock's (1999) research demonstrates how children from 5 to 8 years gained curriculum knowledge through practical experiences in an 'Enchanted Forest'. This was a holistic dramatic environment that enabled the children to play, explore and problem solve collaboratively in an imaginative setting, through story, role-play and drama. The main curriculum area promoted in the Forest was science, but the children also gained a wealth of literacy, technological, geographical and artistic knowledge and skills. The children not only had meaningful experiences, through which they gained understanding of difficult concepts, they had an exciting and enjoyable time! The children were given time to reflect and articulate their knowledge and understanding back to adults, and even when interviewed several years later, they could remember the concepts.

Improving practice

Broadhead (2006a) advocates that when children play they need time:

- to allow reciprocity and momentum to build;

- for shared goals to be constructed and for play themes to be developed;

- to become friends;

- for problems to be set and solved both socially and cognitively.

Our current society is generally so extremely time poor and we are always rushing children to get on to activity – both in educational settings and in the home environment. In this way, do we teach children that completion is more important than quality, that accomplishment is more important than thinking, that achievement is more important than in-depth understanding? It is therefore crucial that we take on board Broadhead's (2006) advice and provide time for children to develop in holistic and valuable ways.

Stop and reflect

Do you find yourself agreeing with this point of view? Can you think of evidence in practice that supports your standpoint?

and so meet children's developmental needs. The new Early Years Foundation Stage promotes a curriculum and pedagogy that is play based from birth to 5 years. The Primary Review, a large-scale research project is ongoing at the time of writing (late 2007), and although this initiative does not include the word 'play' in any of its ten themes, it does at least include the collection of a body of **pupil voice** data, which will no doubt refer to play-based learning at some points. Many local education authorities are not only encouraging that this play-based pedagogy continues throughout Key Stage One, they are actively ensuring that it is taking place. These are exciting times

> **Pupil voice**
> Research undertaken to collect interview data from pupils who have been asked to give honest opinions about their experiences in education, and possibly make suggestions for positive change.

for advocates for play for learning; perhaps the pioneers of play will soon be able to take a sigh of relief and gasp 'AT LAST!'

Perspective 3: Playwork

FRASER BROWN

Introduction

> One thing that observation of children makes clear ... is that children *will* play everywhere and with anything. (Ward, 1978, p. 86)

A child might be sitting in a classroom, or making their way home from school, or waiting at a supermarket checkout. The setting matters little. If something stimulates the urge to play, nothing will get in the way. Most adults fail to recognise that fact. Nor do they understand the immense developmental benefits that come from informal play. Playworkers on the other hand see play as intrinsically important. For that reason, they are often heard to say that play is important for its own sake. However, to suggest that is the sum total of the playworker's view would be to trivialise the subject as well as the profession. The most commonly expressed view in the playwork literature is that play has value not just in terms of individual child development, but also that it contributes to the evolution of the species (Hughes, 2001). How does this work?

Playwork Principles

The recently redrafted *Playwork Principles* define play in the following terms:

1   All children and young people need to play. The impulse to play is innate. Play is a biological, psychological and social necessity, and is fundamental to the healthy development and well-being of individuals and communities.

2   Play is a process that is freely chosen, personally directed and intrinsically motivated. That is, children and young people determine and control the content and intent of their play, by following their own instincts, ideas and interests, in their own way for their own reasons.   (PPSG, 2005)

This is an ethos that reflects many previous statements by respected playwork organisations. For example, the National Occupational Standards for Playwork state:

Children's play is freely chosen, personally directed behaviour, motivated from within; through play, the child explores the world and her or his relationship with it, elaborating all the while a flexible range of responses to the challenges she or he encounters; by playing, the child learns and develops as an individual.   (SPRITO, 1992)

And finally, the Joint National Committee on Training for Playwork says:

Play is an innate drive and is essential for human development. It is manifested as behaviour that is freely chosen, personally directed and intrinsically motivated. The value of play derives from the play process itself, not from any extrinsic goal, reward or end product. Play is often spontaneous and unpredictable. Through play children experience their world and their relationship with it.

(JNCTP, 2002)

Obviously, as Sutton-Smith (1997) has pointed out, definitions such as this cannot be said to be accurate, since they clearly do not apply to all possible instances of play. In fact he represents them as an idealisation of play. Nevertheless, the 'freely chosen, personally directed . . . intrinsically motivated' mantra is now quite widespread amongst playworkers, probably in response to the type of work they recognise as being their most effective. On a daily basis playworkers see the positive benefits that accrue to children from widening their freedom of choice; enabling them to take control of their environment; and enhancing their self-esteem. As has already been mentioned, this not only benefits the individual, but also enables the human species to survive. Ironically it is Sutton-Smith who is most often quoted in support of that view, because it is he who offers such a cogent argument concerning the links between play and species survival.

Sutton-Smith (2008) identifies a close link between Damasio's (1994) primary emotions (shock, fear, anger, sadness, happiness and disgust) and various forms of play (teasing, risk, contest, festivals, flow experiences and profanity). He takes this one stage further to suggest that through a dialectical process of action and rebuttal, we learn the survival skills that enable the individual to cope with the daily trials of life. For example teasing involves harassment, which when met with resilience may be seen to prepare us for social initiation procedures in later life; risks involve dangers being confronted with courage, which prepares us for the chances we take with our physical and economic fate; and so on. He also suggests that play might be seen as an evolutionary mechanism; the means by which human beings adapt to an ever-changing world. We are born with the potential to be adaptable. Through play we develop and refine that ability. We now know that play activity stimulates the brain in such a way that brain cells retain their 'plasticity'. If we don't play, our brain cells rigidify, and our flexibility of thought is reduced. Ultimately we become unable to cope with change, which could have dire consequences both for the individual and for the future of our species. Thus, Sutton-Smith is making the not inconsiderable claim that play is at the very heart of the evolutionary process.

One strand of playwork theory that follows this line of thinking is based upon Haeckel's (1901) theory of recapitulation, and its subsequent development by first Hall (1904) and then Reaney. This is the idea that each stage in a child's development corresponds to successive adult forms of evolutionary history, and that this is represented in current and future play behaviour. Reaney (1916) suggested that this life summary reveals itself as play periods that correspond to the various evolutionary stages of human history (animal, savage, nomad, pastoral and tribal). Her analysis of this actually makes something of a mockery of her own ideas. For example, she equates the pastoral and tribal stages with doll play, gardening and team games played by children of between 12 and 17 years (Schwartzman, 1978, p. 47). Most children are engaged in those activities at a much earlier age. Nevertheless, the idea has been taken up strongly by the leading playwork theorist Bob Hughes (2001), who suggests that children have a fundamental biological drive to play, and that there are clear links between certain play forms and the behaviour patterns of our human ancestors. Hughes's interpretation, which is rooted in his own experience of working with children, makes more sense than Reaney's earlier analysis. He translates the stages in a contemporary context as follows:

- animal – children interacting with the elements
- savage – cruel interaction with other species
- nomad – ranging for mental mapping
- pastoral – mastery play, for example gardening
- tribal – membership of gangs and clubs

In an earlier part of this chapter, Pam Jarvis stated that Hall's original idea of recapitulation has largely been discredited. In terms of his interpretation of evolutionary theory, that is obviously true. However, the general idea of recapitulative play should not be dismissed merely because its early interpretation was incorrect. There can be little doubt that modern-day children are born with a genetic make-up that suits a bygone age. Biological evolution has certainly not kept pace with social evolution. In the great sweep of human history it is only during the last millennium that we have begun to live an indoor existence. However, throughout history it seems certain that human babies have come into the world genetically equipped for an outdoor life. That is still the case. We can only guess at the effects of the mismatch between biological expectations and social reality. Both Sebba (1991) and Wilson (2002) suggest that children who are submerged in indoor surroundings are likely to grow up psychologically and physically detached from their environment. They are then likely to develop a negative and critical approach to the world, rather than a positive and accommodating one.

Hall (1904) suggested it would be counterproductive to push a child ahead of its natural stage of development, and Hughes (2003) has taken this idea as a cautionary warning of the dangers of a certain form of play deprivation. He says children are born with a genetic expectation of the type of play they should experience. If that does not happen, they may become very ill as a result. If children are deprived of the opportunity to light fires, stamp on insects, play games of chase, and so on, we run the risk that they will grow into adults who still feel the need to enact those forms of behaviour (but in a distorted adult mode). Thus, for Hughes, one of the most important roles of the playworker is to recreate environments that allow children to experience fundamentally recapitulative play.

A second strand of thought that derives from evolutionary psychology is my own theory of compound flexibility (Brown, 2003a). This is the idea that the most productive developmental relationship is that between the child and a flexible play environment, and that adults have a responsibility to create and maintain opportunities for that relationship to work effectively. In an ideal world the child would be able to experiment with, and exercise control over the environment. This would produce positive feelings, which would in turn encourage the development of self-acceptance and self-confidence. With the development of self-confidence the child inevitably becomes a better problem solver, and thus is able to make better use of the environment. It is that interrelationship between flexibility in the

Figure 1.4 Playing in the street

Source: Homer Sykes Archive/Alamy

environment and the development of flexibility in the child that I termed 'compound flexibility'.

The relevance of this theory to playwork lies in the idea that the world in which the UK's children are growing up is an inflexible place. The role of playwork is to create environments which provide the sort of flexibility that is fast diminishing. As a society the United Kingdom is increasingly suspicious of children (perhaps because we see them in our communities less and less); the growth of traffic means children are no longer able to play on the streets; parental fears mean children are driven to and from school, which means they don't get to play with their friends immediately before and after school; we have a National Curriculum that tells children exactly what they should learn during the whole of their school life; we use ASBOs to control their boisterous excesses; and so on. As mentioned before, early in 2007 the UNICEF report, *An Overview of Child Well-being in Rich Countries*, placed the United Kingdom bottom of all the western nations in terms of the quality of life of its children. During the same week a second child was shot in London. The Government's immediate response was not to question the way in which UK society treats its children, but to suggest a new law enabling us to lock up more 15 year olds.

It is a reasonable assumption that play has significant benefits, otherwise why would human beings expend so much time and energy on the activity. If there

Figure 1.5 No ball games allowed

Source: Sarah Winter Flood/Alamy

was nothing to be gained, the activity would have been selected out in the course of evolution. So, why does such a risky activity persist? The most likely explanation lies in the creative process which Bruner (1976) calls combinatorial flexibility. Combinatorial flexibility is a process that not only enables the acquisition of information about the world, but also encourages the development of flexibility and creativity in problem solving. It is based on the idea that most artefacts in a child's play environment have a flexible potential. For example, a child who is playing with a doll, a ball and a box, has the potential to play many different games, and become involved in a wide range of creative activities. Each artefact has its own inherent flexibility, while in combination they have even more potential flexibility. Thus, the investigative and experimental nature of play inevitably leads to the development of problem-solving skills. The role of the playworker is to develop environments that offer the child the opportunity, in the words of Brian Sutton-Smith (1992), 'to control their own little microcosm of the world'.

Playwork is rooted in an understanding that children learn and develop through their play. There are many instances in modern society where that process is interrupted or impaired. Playwork involves identifying and removing barriers to the play process, and enriching the child's play environment. Playwork is a generic term for a profession that encompasses those occupations where the medium of play is used as the major mechanism for redressing aspects of developmental imbalance (Brown and Webb, 2002). This may be something as straightforward as providing an after-school club for children who would otherwise have nowhere to play. On the other hand it might be something as complex as creating an environment to assist the recovery of children who have suffered severe play deprivation. Thus, playwork takes place in many different settings. The following examples show the breadth of that work, and also provide the opportunity to explore exactly what play means to a playworker.

Play: a theory of loose parts

The children in the adventure playground described in 'Ideas in Action' on p. 35 were free to recycle the materials in whatever way they saw fit. Therefore, not only were they in control of their environment (an unusual experience for children), but they were also able to explore its potential. This situation reflects one of the most basic ideas underpinning the work of an adventure playground, namely Nicholson's 'theory of loose parts'. He explains it thus: 'In any environment both the degree of inventiveness and creativity, and the possibility of discovery, are directly proportional to the number and kind of variables in it' (Nicholson, 1971, p. 30).

Not surprisingly, over a lengthy period of time, these children became more and more inventive and creative. Nevertheless they continued to walk away from their work once it was complete. Sylva *et al.* (1976) suggest an explanation for this. When playing, children tend not to worry about achieving set goals. In play, they suggest *means* are generally more important than *ends* – process is often more important than product. In the adventure playground example the process of construction was clearly far more important to the children than the end product, the den.

Essential play needs

It is a basic playwork tenet that all children have similar play needs (Hughes, 2001). The content of play may vary according to a child's culture, but the fundamental nature of play holds firm across all cultures. Children everywhere need to socialise, run about, investigate their environment, create new worlds, and so on. This holds true for *all* children, including those with disabilities, so we should not allow ourselves to be unduly distracted by a particular child's disability. Thus, in the example provided in 'Ideas in Action' on p. 36 it was important to view Liliana as a little girl with the potential to learn and develop through her play, rather than as a child with a visual impairment. Having overcome that initial prejudice it then became possible to start from scratch. That non-prejudicial, non-judgemental frame of mind, which Fisher (2008) calls 'negative capability', is an essential part of the playworker's make-up. In this frame of mind it becomes second nature for the playworker to interpret the children's play cues accurately. Else and Sturrock (1998) highlight the importance of appropriate interpretation of play cues. In fact they

Ideas in action

Lessons from the adventure playground (Author's observation notes)

Many years ago I was employed on an adventure playground. It was the sort of facility where children used scrap materials to create their own play environment. To begin with, although their efforts were enthusiastic, they usually contained fundamental flaws. Six-inch nails were used where one inch would do, with the result that the wood split; uprights were not buried deep enough in the ground, so their structures fell down; the roofs of dens were not protected, so everyone got soaked when it rained; and so on. The children did not appear to be bothered by any of these things. In fact, once construction was finished they generally moved on to something else.

Comment

As I saw it (wrongly) I had a responsibility to help the children improve their building abilities. I was not especially skilled in construction techniques, so could only offer rudimentary advice. Students from the engineering course at the local college spent a day on the site, but wanted to do everything to a plan, which meant the children got bored. A couple of local dads who worked on building sites were quite knowledgeable, but really didn't have the patience to engage fully with the children.

Eventually, I realised the children were not unduly bothered by their failures. So long as the materials were available to try again, that is just what they did. Often they knocked down their own creations so the materials could be reused in a new project. Over the years they became highly skilled in their work. They constructed dens, built climbing frames, rope swings, seesaws and the like. However, I noticed that the pattern of involvement remained the same as in those early days. In other words, the children were enthusiastic about the activity of construction, but relatively disinterested in the end result. More often than not the den would be handed over to a group of toddlers, while the children who had constructed the den moved on to build again elsewhere.

---

suggest that continuous misinterpretation of play cues may lead to childhood neuroses. In this particular case it was important to understand Liliana's little noises, and her clasping of my hands, and interpret those cues accurately as an invitation to repeat the song (see 'Ideas in Action' on p. 36).

What was it about the singing that led to such an immediate connection between myself and Liliana? Trevarthen (1996) suggests that rhythm is one of the most fundamental developmental building blocks. Having spent a comfortable nine months in the womb, building an awareness of the mother's rhythms, babies come into the world with a strong sense of rhythm, which they then use to interpret social relationships. For example, they are able to recognise the mother's voice pattern as the same rhythm they heard while safe inside the womb. It is therefore not surprising that there is such a strong bond between mother and child.

However, this connection is not limited to the mother alone. Babies are able to identify sounds outside the womb. Rhythmical sounds heard regularly are likely to be firmly embedded in the baby's memory at birth. Thus they are ready to relate to the father, siblings, grandparents, and others, so long as those people's rhythms are heard fairly soon after birth. This is a theme taken up recently by Davy (2008) who suggests 'babies are "pre-designed" for perceiving rhythmic patterns that provide a structure for organising experiences in human interactive events'. In the case of Liliana, by using the simple device of a rhythmical song to help her feel secure I was able to form a relationship very quickly.

The fact that I was able to go back later that afternoon, and pick up the playful activity where we had left it, demonstrates the strength of the playful connection. Elsewhere I have talked about the peculiar strength of

Ideas in action

Liliana, a challenging situation (Author's observation notes)

In the summer of 2005 I was training a group of Romanian playworkers who were working in a paediatric hospital with a group of abandoned children. On my final day I came upon a very agitated 4-year-old girl who had been left in a ward totally alone. She stood at the bars of her cot rocking back and forth, making strange hooting noises. Every so often she walked rapidly round the cot, before settling back into her rocking.

Her doctors said she was 'blind and mentally retarded'. This diagnosis made me uncomfortable, as she was clearly aware of my presence, and appeared to be reacting to my movements (albeit not in a very positive fashion). There was obviously something wrong with her eyesight, but a quick experiment with moving lights showed she had some level of residual vision – seeing shadows, at the very least. An added complication was her fear of men's voices. This was confirmed when I called her name, 'Liliana'. Straight away she retreated to the back of the cot.

The playworkers were wondering how they could work with her. How could they get beyond the obstacle of her poor sight?

Stop and reflect

I started singing to Liliana quietly: 'Twinkle, Twinkle, Little Star'. She calmed down immediately, moving her head to locate the sound. At the end of the song she made a noise in the back of her throat, which I interpreted as a request to sing again – a kind of play cue. I did this three times, and each time she moved closer to the sound.

Then I started to clap gently in time to the rhythm of the song. When I stopped, she reached for my hands and put them together – another cue for me to sing. I repeated the song three more times, and each time she gave the same cue. On the last occasion she not only took my hands, but also started clapping them together in time to the song. Finally she picked up the rhythm of the song in her own hand movements, and clapped in time to my singing.

This whole sequence took no more than five minutes. In that short space of time I was able to show the Romanian playworkers how to start making a relationship with Liliana by using rhythm and music.

Later that afternoon I went back into her ward, to find her rocking and hooting again. I called her name, 'Liliana'. She came across the cot, and felt for my hands. Clasping them together in hers, she started to clap our hands together in a rhythm that I recognised – 'Twinkle, Twinkle, Little Star'. This was truly a magic moment.

relationships forged during play (Brown, 2008). For most children, playing is the only experience they ever have of being in control of their own world. On all other occasions an adult is in charge. Therefore, when working with children in a playwork setting it is crucial for the adult to resist the temptation to take control. Otherwise it ceases to be a high-quality play experience for the child. For children to find themselves in a largely equal relationship with an adult is rare and powerful. The fact that I was able to interpret and respond to Liliana's play cues carried a strong message for the child: this is someone who respects me; this is someone to be trusted.

Play: the pursuit of independent ideas

This is how a playworker would interpret the events in Cardboard City: the idea that children should be free to choose what they want to do in a play setting is a fundamental principle of playwork, rooted in a definition that sees play as 'freely chosen, personally directed and intrinsically motivated' (PPSG, 2005). By providing an environment rich in all kinds of loose materials, the playworkers are offering the children not only a 'loose parts environment' (Nicholson, 1971), but also reflecting Portchmouth's observation, 'it helps if someone, no

Ideas in action

Cardboard City (Based on an original observation by Janice Smith, playworker)

The children arrive in the playwork setting, and as normal are invited to choose what they would like to play with. In the store room there is a variety of different sized cardboard boxes and all kinds of loose materials, such as wood, blankets, dressing-up clothes. Most of the children ignore these materials and choose equipment they have played with previously. Two younger children spot the materials and ask the playworker whether they can have those. Once they have the materials they start a discussion on what they might do with the boxes. They go through the usual suggestions like making a boat, or creating a theatre for a puppet show. The younger of the two children says, 'I know, let's play at being tramps in the streets.' He explains to the other child that he has been shopping in the town centre with his mum and saw two tramps living in a cardboard box.

The two children set about arranging the cardboard boxes in different ways. One of them says, 'Let's make a window so the tramps can see outside.' They set about making a window, but find it really hard to cut through the card with the scissors they have available.

They ask a playworker if they can have a sharp knife to cut their window. The playworker asks whether the children have used a penknife before, and if so in what way. The eldest child explains that he often helps his grandad in his shed, and is allowed to use a knife. The playworker suggests they draw their window and then come back and get the knife. As they do this, the playworker watches from a discreet distance while the older child uses the penknife to cut out the window.

At this point a couple more children, who have been standing by watching, ask to play. The two children have a discussion and agree that the newcomers can join in, but cannot share their boxes, as they are going to be tramps who are about to go to sleep. As a group, the children set about making more dens and introduce some material they have found to put over the dens to keep them warm. Once the dens have been made the children put on some of the dressing-up clothes, as they think this makes them look poor. Then they lay in their dens with blankets on. As the other children come near, they start begging for money, which the other children find very funny.

matter how lightly, puts in our way the means of making use of what we find' (1969, p. 7). The children's discussion about how to use the materials shows Pepler's (1982) idea that children's play is similar in nature to the problem solving of adults. The children start by exploring the most obvious solutions to their 'problem' of what to play, but find those unsatisfactory, so they move on to a novel or more imaginative choice. The fact that it is the younger of the two children who comes up with the idea ('let's play at being tramps on the streets'), demonstrates the way in which play can cause children to engage with their 'zone of proximal development'. Vygotsky (1976) suggests children may be helped to explore their ZPD with the input of an adult or more capable peer. In play, even a younger child may be *more capable* as a result of his or her life experience. Vygotsky (1978, p. 102) says, 'play contains all developmental tendencies in a condensed form and is itself a major source of development'. The way in which the child's previous experience of shopping with his mother affects the subsequent choice of activity shows the impact of context on the content of play (Sutton-Smith, 1977).

Tinbergen (1975) describes certain independent forms of play as apparently being clumsily executed, chaotically arranged and performed with abandon. To the casual observer the behaviour of these two children might well appear to fit that description. However, that is the paradox of play (Bateson, 1955) – play is rarely what it seems – in play, actions often have different meaning. When the children decide to make a window, the playworker's reaction is crucial. The fact that they feel able to ask the playworker for a sharp knife is a good indicator of a trusting relationship between the children and their playworker. The positive response of the playworker indicates an awareness of the special abilities and experience of particular children. An informal risk assessment was carried out, taking account of a range of factors, including the experience and ability of the child. The playworker's handling of the process of the children cutting out their windows is a good example of Bruner's (1976) concept of 'scaffolding', whereby the adult provides organisational structure in order to assist the child's learning process. It also illustrates the need for playworkers to develop good peripheral vision, as recommended by Hughes (1996).

The children who are standing to one side watching the activity are clearly engaged in looking-on play. Once they are accepted, they become engaged in joining-in play. The game then broadens its scope and it is possible to identify elements of cooperative play. These are all forms of social play as identified by Parten (1933). The children dress up to look like poor homeless persons, which shows the quality of their observation, and the complexity of their aspirational role-play (Freud, 1974). It also shows the importance of make-believe play (Singer and Singer, 1990). The whole observation illustrates the playwork approach, which seeks to encourage the development of self-esteem, through children being able to pursue their own ideas (Roberts, 1996).

Conclusion

We stated in our introduction to this chapter that: 'this book arose from our realisation that when we talked together as colleagues we were communicating similar values and aiming for equivalent results'. We are all in agreement that play is crucially important for children's development, learning and well-being'. Such similarity and agreement is demonstrated in our answers to the chapter questions:

- Should play serve the needs of the child, rather than the needs and expectations of adults?

We have all articulated our beliefs that play should serve the needs of the child rather than the expectations of adults. Jarvis and Brock give rather more emphasis to the need for the child to use play as preparatory learning for the adult society, Jarvis in terms of sociability, and Brock in terms of intellectual skills; while

Brown's view of play is rather more organic. However all the authors clearly agree that children should be free to choose their play activities rather than be continually chided and directed by adults towards narrow 'curriculumised' activities.

- What real choices are offered to children in their everyday play experiences?

Continuing from the point above, all three authors agree that whether play is undertaken as an individual or social activity, it should always hold real choices for the children who are engaging in it. Jarvis asks 'How would human beings learn to deal independently with difficult social situations if they did not experience sufficient independent free play opportunities in their daily lives during early development?' Brock proposes: 'Educators need to provide stimulating playful environments that promote practical activities and the use of interesting resources and so enable children to initiate their own learning experiences'; while Brown sums up the overall position of all three authors: 'If we don't play, our brain cells rigidify, and our flexibility of thought is reduced. Ultimately we become unable to cope with change, which could have dire consequences both for the individual and for the future of our species'.

- Is play about experiencing and doing, or about achieving a specific end result?

All three authors emphatically see play as very much about experiencing and doing. Jarvis gives the example of 'Nathan', learning quite a hard lesson through free play by taking responsibility for the consequences of a careless accident; Brown gives the example of an adult helping a child with reduced sensory capacity to access 'experiencing and doing' through his description of his work with 'Liliana'; while Brock sums up more everyday experiences of British children 'experiencing and doing' at different developmental stages in 'Mina's' fascination with the contents of an adult's handbag, and 'Zack and Kurt's' busy afternoon in her garden. These are three very different uses of example, but all have a clear emphasis for children's need to 'experience and do' rather than to be herded by adults down narrow conceptual tramlines towards a predetermined end result.

- How flexible should children's play be, with regard to offering freedom of movement and expression?

All three authors would emphatically answer 'very flexible, with as much freedom of movement as possible' to this question. Brown questions a national regime that imposes a monolithic National Curriculum to dictate exactly what children must learn, and ASBOs to deal with those it sees as dangerously out of control; Brock questions the wisdom of forcing children into such a curriculum at the age of 4½; while Jarvis gives the example of 'Aimee', a child whose every waking hour is relentlessly timetabled and directed by adults, asking the reader to consider what impact this enforced schedule will have upon the adult she will eventually become.

Whilst there are clearly some differences in emphasis and use of underpinning theory by the three authors of this chapter (for example the different 'takes' of Jarvis and Brown on Hall's recapitulation theory), there is clearly a large area of agreement in the emphasis on the vital need for children to experience adequate time for free play in order for healthy developmental processes to unfold, and a concern that the culture of child care and education practice that has evolved over the last 25 years in the post-industrial culture of western Europe and the United States has not allowed children sufficient time, independence and freedom to explore and develop their full human potential through independent free play.

The subsequent chapters in this book will focus on specific aspects of this debate in turn, and engage you in undertaking reflection and practice-based research to come to your own set of conclusions. As you move through the chapters, it is hoped you will begin to construct your own considered position on the importance of play for healthy development, which, it is hoped, will underpin your transformation and continuing development of practice as the first generation of child care and education professionals in the twenty-first century.

Chapter 2

'We Don't Play Like That Here': Social, Cultural and Gender Perspectives on Play

YINKA OLUSOGA

A lot of our children come to school unable to play. We have kids from really deprived backgrounds and children who come with no English who have only just arrived in the country. They either don't play at all or their play tends to be disruptive and inappropriate. We have to spend a lot of time teaching them how to play properly. You have to tell them, 'We don't play like that here' and you have to show them how to use the play equipment and space safely. Some children get it straight away, but others take a lot of telling.

(Karen, Reception teacher)

Introduction

In the previous chapter we saw all three authors argue that the need to play is universal: all young children have a biological urge to play and through that play they develop cognitively, physically and socially. They also established that this view is supported by a range of research from the fields of developmental psychology, education and playwork and has gained widespread international recognition via endorsement from organisations such as the United Nations.

This chapter will argue that although the urge to play may be universal, the forms that the play takes and the status it is bestowed are not. How children play, with what and with whom they play varies according to their social, cultural and historical contexts. What is recognised as play in one society or community may not be recognised in another. Indeed how play is perceived in any community is a function of that community's model of childhood and of how it has developed socially to meet the challenges and opportunities of its physical and economic environment. As we shall see, the implications of this argument are significant both in terms of how children's access to play is safeguarded and in terms of how the role of adults in facilitating that play is managed.

The starting point for this chapter will be socio-cultural theory. In particular we will examine the work of Lev Vygotsky and of Barbara Rogoff, both of whom argue that child development and play are fundamentally social processes. We will then consider the role of play in developing and maintaining social and cultural identity in young children. The focus will then shift to the institutional contexts within which young children play – particularly educational and care contexts where children experience play outside of the family. We will establish that educational and care settings are not socially and culturally neutral places and we will consider the implications of this for practitioners in addressing the needs of all children in increasingly socially and culturally diverse societies.

The chapter aims to address four key questions:

1   What role do social and cultural contexts play in shaping children's play?

2   How can play support or hinder the development of social, cultural and gender identity in children?

3   How are adult and child play agendas pursued within educational and care settings?

4   How, and to what extent, should educational and care practitioners accommodate diverse models of play?

Socio-cultural perspectives on learning and play

Since the 1970s, socio-cultural theories and perspectives have become increasingly important in the study of child development and education. Earlier developmental psychology and cognitive psychology approaches, such as those used by Jean Piaget, sought to establish regularities, stages and universal biological 'laws' to explain, analyse and categorise how all children develop and learn. The approach mirrored that of traditional science, in that research subjects were studied out of their usual contexts under experimental conditions in laboratories, engaged in specifically designed cognitive tasks. Instead, the socio-cultural approach acknowledges the profound influence of differing cultural contexts and social processes on development and learning. Consequently, in the case of child development and learning, the study of research subjects moves from the laboratory to children's familiar environments (that is the home, the playground, the classroom) and from the administration of contrived and decontextualised cognitive tasks to close observation and analysis of children's actual experiences and activities. In doing so the socio-cultural approach opens up new avenues for understanding the significance of differences as well as similarities between the experiences and patterns of development of children from different cultures and different times. This also offers opportunities for researchers and practitioners to see their own contemporary, local cultural practices regarding child rearing and education in a new and revealing light. As Fleer *et al.* (2004, p. 175, drawing on Vygotsky) explain: 'Research framed from a socio-cultural perspective is less about revealing "the eternal child" and more about uncovering 'the historical child'.

The 'socio-cultural' paradigm encompasses a range of perspectives and theories that are referred to via various terms such as **socio-culturalism** and **cultural–historical theory**. Historically, its most important theorist is Lev Vygotsky, a Russian psychologist whose pioneering work in the Soviet Union in the 1920s and 1930s only came to international attention in the 1970s when his works were translated from the original Russian. Charged by the Soviet authorities with developing public education to meet the needs of hitherto marginalised children, he developed a set of theories that focused on human development and the process, and promotion, of learning. Central to all of his work is an understanding of human development as a journey accomplished via social and cultural processes (Daniels, 2001; Wood and Attfield, 2005). He argues that it is via interaction and

> **Socio-culturalism**
> Describes the role of the community and culture in underpinning the psychological development of the human being. The theory suggests that psychological development is rooted in the collective ideas and conventions of a specific culture.
>
> **Cultural–historical theory**
> Describes the role of the 'collective mind' (or 'distributed cognition') that exists in a community's culture in underpinning the future of that society.

activity with the people, materials, tools and symbols of his/her social and cultural environment that the child learns and develops; biological processes alone cannot accomplish this.

This view of the critical role of social and cultural interaction is supported when one considers cases where children have been denied access to human social and cultural networks during their early development – so-called 'feral children'. This includes severely neglected children and, in extreme examples, children who have grown up totally isolated from human contact. For children who become isolated from human contact after their first five to six years, physical development seems to progress much as would be expected, though dietary stress may stunt their growth. Their linguistic and cognitive development appears to stall and sometimes regress, but once they are returned to human society, they seem to be able to recover and develop their language and social skills to varying degrees of success. However, in the case of feral children who have been isolated from human contact from their earliest years, all development appears affected. In particular their linguistic and cognitive development has been severely restricted. The lack of social and linguistic interaction during the key phases of brain development during childhood has left permanent scars. Despite interventions from carers and psychologists these children have been unable to make up this lost ground and never develop the linguistic and social competence of children brought up within ordinary human social and cultural communities (Candland, 1993; Newton, 2002).

Social theories of learning, development and play

The zone of proximal development

Vygotsky's (1978) influential concept of the zone of proximal development was introduced in Chapter 1. He defined the ZPD as: 'the distance between the actual development level as determined by independent problem solving and the level of potential development as determined through problem solving under adult guidance or in collaboration with more capable peers'

(Vygotsky, 1978, p. 86). The ZPD can be represented diagrammatically as shown in Figure 2.1.

Vygotsky saw the ZPD as the fundamentally important space within which learning and development actually occurred. Within the ZPD, via a process of interaction with other, more experienced members of the community, there is the potential for the child's existing understanding and use of key concepts, skills and knowledge to be transformed to a higher level (Daniels, 2001; Rogoff, 2003; Wood and Attfield, 2005). Key features of the ZPD are:

- active engagement in joint activity, leading to:
- social interaction between participants of varied states of experience, knowledge and understanding, requiring:
- the use, interpretation and manipulation (leading ultimately to internalisation) of language (verbal and non-verbal, involving the use of signs and symbols).

In addition, the ZPD also offers the practitioner the opportunity to:

- tap into the intrinsic interests and motivation of the learner; and
- establish a two-way process, where the learner and the practitioner each contribute to the process of problem creating and problem solving (Wood and Attfield, 2005, p. 102).

Lev Vygotsky

Figure 2.1 Vygotsky's zone of proximal development

Level of potential development
(What the child can do under adult guidance or in collaboration with more capable peers)
That is, psychological tools and mental processes which are currently beyond the child's independent use

Zone of proximal development
'those functions that have not yet matured but are in the process of maturation, functions that will mature tomorrow but are currently in an embryonic state'
(Vygotsky, 1978, p. 86)

Level of actual development
(What the child can do independently)
That is, psychological tools and mental processes that have matured

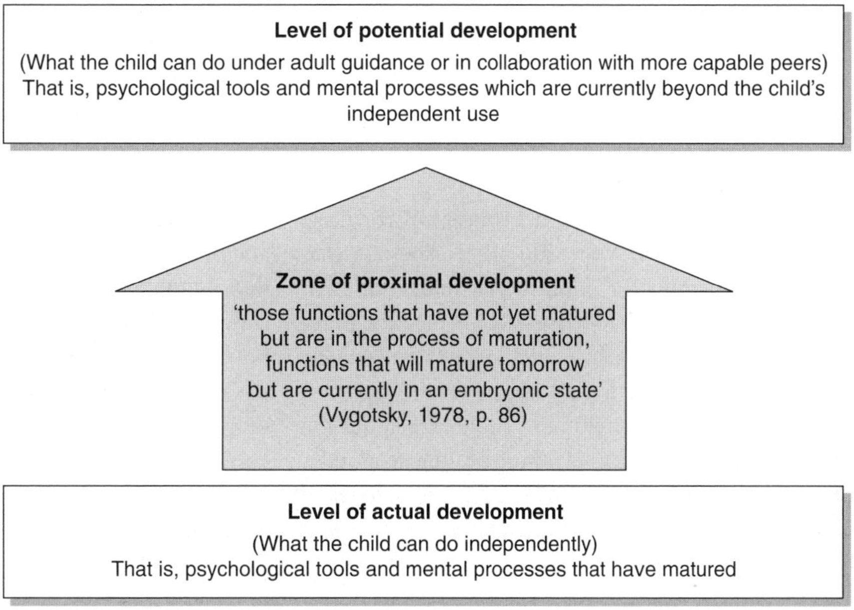

The ZPD and play

Vygotsky saw play as a crucial activity for development and learning. Play combines opportunities for joint activity, for social interaction, for use of language and other symbols, for harnessing the power of the child's own interests and for engaging in problem creating and problem solving: all ingredients of the ZPD. In play the child is self-motivated, resilient and able to take risks. Vygotsky argued that whilst involved in play, children were able to operate effectively at the very limit of their ZPD, where learning takes place. He wrote: 'In play a child is always above his average age, above his daily behaviour; in play it is as though he were a head taller than himself' (Vygotsky, 1967, p. 552; cited in Rogoff, 2003, p. 298).

The use of signs and symbols is a particularly critical feature of play. In play children learn that one object can stand in for another. A piece of swirling blue fabric can be a river, a box can become a boat and a stick can be a crocodile. In order to use these signs those involved in the play have to communicate and interpret ideas and develop shared meaning via the use of language. Vygotsky identified language, and other symbol systems such as drawing, writing, mapping and so on, as **psychological tools** which enable the learner to develop and master mental processes – that is, new ways of thinking (Daniels, 2001, p. 15). The exact form and use

Psychological tools
Describes the ways in which human beings support the building of knowledge, e.g. story telling, writing, possibly even the internet!

Mediation
To bring about a negotiation process in which the interacting individuals liaise in order to develop understanding.

Internalisation
To make something that is initially external to the self part of one's mind – e.g. in learning a language.

of psychological tools varies according to the child's social and cultural context. In the ZPD the learner's engagement with these psychological tools and higher-level mental processes is mediated by the adult or more experienced peer. An important part of **mediation** involves the adult or experienced peer making their use of these psychological tools and mental processes external and explicit to the learner. This mediation enables the learner to develop, practise and refine their use of these psychological tools and their mastery of new ways of thinking via a process of **internalisation**. Mediation is a significant concept in that it acknowledges the active role of the child and the more experienced other within the ZPD. In mediation, learning is not something that just happens to the

43

child, but is a process that the child actively negotiates, with the support of someone who already has greater mastery of the psychological tools and mental processes in question.

The ZPD and the practitioner

The ZPD has been an influential concept, particularly in primary and early years education. The fact that Vygotsky recognised the status of play in development and learning within the ZPD has confirmed the practice of many practitioners involved in the education and care of young children. Within the ZPD there is a specific and skilled role for the adult in helping the child to move from one level of functioning to another. Vygotsky spoke of the adult 'instructing' the child within the ZPD. He argued that instruction is 'only useful when it moves ahead of development' and 'awakens a whole series of functions that are in a stage of maturation lying in the zone of proximal development' (Vygotsky, 1978, p. 212). This is significant as here Vygotsky is arguing that learning precedes development. For practitioners this means that part of the skill in working within the ZPD is to pitch adult support and intervention at the correct level – that is, connected to but building on from the mental processes that the child has already mastered. Too little movement will not stimulate learning and therefore development, too much will overwhelm and confuse. The use of the term 'instruction' has provoked some debate and some have argued that it is a mis-translation of the Russian word *obuchenie*. They argue that other terms such as 'teaching' and 'teaching-learning' are more appropriate

Ideas in action

The role of the adult or more experienced peer in internalisation (Author's observation notes)

Three-and-a-half-year-old Sadie and her mother are visiting an adult friend, Anya. In the afternoon Anya and Sadie decide to make a cake for dessert. As they begin Anya starts to narrate all of her actions to Sadie. She names equipment that needs to be collected, stating what each item will be used for. She produces the recipe and talks through it, listing ingredients and emphasising the concept and language of ordination (that is, doing things in the correct order). As they begin to measure ingredients and begin the process of mixing, rubbing and chopping she models the physical skills alongside the correct use of the terminology. Sadie's role however is an active one. Where she already has knowledge and/or skills, she identifies and uses them – for example, she can identify and collect some of the equipment and ingredients herself and is already proficient at pouring liquids with care. She also tries out the new words that Anya introduces and discusses the new concepts and skills she is engaging with, using them to narrate her own actions to herself and others. When her mother joins them, for example, Sadie is keen to point out to her that she is being careful to use her fingertips when rubbing the butter into the flour so that it doesn't melt.

Later that evening, whilst engaged on her own in small world play, Sadie reviews the baking activity by having her toy horses act out making a cake as she revisits the language and skills of the baking task.

Comment

During this joint activity involving the baking of a cake, the running commentary that Anya and Sadie provide describes and directs what they are both doing. This serves to externalise the psychological tools and mental processes they are drawing on in their approach to the task. By having them made explicit, Sadie is able to experiment with them. This is the first step on the way to internalising them for future deployment as tools for her own use. The fact that Sadie can call on the vocabulary and describe the skills involved in the baking activity later that day during her independent play shows that the process of internalisation has begun.

as Vygotsky was referring to 'all of the actions of the teacher in engendering cognitive development and growth' (Daniels, 2001, p. 10).

What happens in the ZPD? Models for defining and refining 'instruction'

Having established the concept of the ZPD, Vygotsky was less clear in his definitions and descriptions of the specific sorts of actions that an adult (or more experienced peer) should take in order to promote learning and therefore development. As we saw above, his term 'instruction' does not manage to convey the complexity and variety of potential strategies for working with a child within the ZPD. For some, in a western context, 'instruction' would appear to imply a formal, didactic role for the adult that would turn an informal play-based activity into a 'lesson' with the adult firmly in charge. Consequently, many other researchers have turned their attention to theorising and modelling the processes that occur within the ZPD.

The concept perhaps most closely linked to the ZPD is 'scaffolding'. Indeed, many practitioners and students assume that the term was coined by Vygotsky himself, whereas, in fact the term comes from the work of Jerome Bruner (Bruner et al., 1976). Bruner was particularly interested in Vygotsky's claim that learning leads development. This would seem to indicate that in the ZPD the learner is making use of psychological tools and engaging in higher mental processes before he/she has gained mastery (that is, conscious control) over them. Bruner described the analogy of scaffolding as follows:

the adult or the aiding peer serves as a vicarious form of consciousness until such time as the learner is able to master his own action through his own consciousness and control. When the child achieves that conscious control over a new function or conceptual system, it is then that he is able to use it as a tool. Up to that point the tutor in effect performs the critical function of 'scaffolding' the learning task to make it possible for the child, in Vygotsky's words, to internalise external knowledge and convert it into a tool for conscious control.

(Bruner et al., 1976, p. 24; cited in Wood and Attfield, 2005, p. 94)

Scaffolding defined in this way requires the adult (or experienced peer) to shape but not dominate the learning process. The aim is not to haul the learner up the scaffolding but to support the learner as they negotiate a pathway through the activity. However, how different practitioners practise scaffolding depends on their own interpretation of it as a concept.

Recent research in the early years context has refocused attention on the concepts and practices involved when adults mediate and scaffold children's learning and development. Two key ideas in this field (which are also extremely relevant to thinking about how adults facilitate and utilise play for learning and development) are:

- co-construction; and
- sustained shared thinking.

Co-construction

At the heart of the concept of co-construction is a Vygotskian view that the human mind is created and shaped via joint activity with other people. In this model, the mental processes that underpin the individual's knowledge, skills and understandings are co-constructed through the mediating interactions the child has with the knowledge, skills and understandings that are distributed amongst the adults and more experienced peers with whom they engage in joint activities.

Jordan, discussing the findings of case study research based on adult–child interactions in play-based early years settings, makes a key distinction between scaffolding learning *for* children and co-constructing learning *with* children (Jordan, 2004, p. 40). See Figure 2.2.

A useful concept for analysing these two lists of attributes is '**intersubjectivity**'. In the earlier practitioner vignette about scaffolding, we saw one interpretation of the concept that kept the adult firmly in charge of the focus and conduct of the activity and of the types of adult–child interaction.

> **Intersubjectivity**
> Shared meanings between people; they 'read' symbols in the same way.

Ideas in action

Case study: Practitioner interpretations of the practice of scaffolding

I'd say that good teaching can be seen in the balance between hearing the voice of the adult and that of the child or children. One week I had a supply nursery nurse who never seemed to stop talking during a session and when you listened to her, it was just a stream of constant, almost random questions. I watched her as she joined a group of five children at the play-dough table at the start of a session. They'd all been busily exploring the feeling of the play-dough, not making anything in particular, just chatting about what they had been doing before school. Within seconds of joining them, she told them that they should all make a picture of a house using the play-dough and began to make one herself to show them how. She then began firing questions: 'What colour is that?', 'What shape are those?', 'How many more to make three?' One after another, with virtually no gap in between, she asked closed questions that she (and most of the children) already knew the answer to. The children abandoned their own conversation and tried to deal with what increasingly resembled an interrogation! Within minutes some of the group began to drift off, eventually leaving two girls, sat there looking startled as the questions kept coming at the same pace, with only two of them left to answer them. She tried to attract other children to join the activity but they began to give the play-dough table a wide berth. One of the children who'd left the activity came up to me and said, 'My head hurts, Miss'. So does mine, I thought!

Improving practice

At the start of the next week I reflected on what had happened and I contrasted the noise and feel of the classroom during the previous week to the usual sound of the classroom when my usual nursery nurse Kathleen is with me. I realised that with Kathleen, I never hear this type of interaction. I watched her taking the same activity – playing at the play-dough table – and saw that she was always engaged in genuine conversation with the children. She listened before joining in. The conversation ebbed and flowed as ideas and links occurred to the children and to her. Her voice didn't dominate the classroom, she didn't just ask questions but also answered them, sharing her own ideas and experience, and the questions are linked to what they were actually talking about, instead of being just dropped in from nowhere. Children remained talking to her, actively engaged in an activity for ages – some returned to the conversation hours and even days later.

Some people (and I'd say that the supply nursery nurse is one of them) think that teaching and even playing means taking total charge of an activity and forcing the children along a predetermined path of your choosing – the adult is the person who creates the activity and the child is led almost passively through it. Instead I think teaching should involve listening, pausing and sharing – both parties need to be active and creative.

Yasmin, nursery teacher

Stop and reflect

This practitioner is describing two different approaches to scaffolding by giving two different examples from practice. In the first the adult takes over organisation of the play activity, changing its focus and its pattern of interaction – without being asked to! The children rapidly lose interest and motivation. In the second approach the practitioner begins by listening and then matching her input to the focus and pattern of interaction of the activity in which the children are already engaged. Here the children maintain interest and motivation.

- Where does control lie in each of these approaches?
- How might the position of control affect children's engagement in the ZPD?

Figure 2.2   Scaffolding learning *for* children versus co-constructing learning *with* children

Scaffolding	Co-construction
Interactions that include:	Interactions that include:
• Questioning techniques, with particular knowledge outcome in the teacher's head	• Co-constructing meanings, including hearing children and getting to know what they think
• Providing feedback on cognitive skills noticing children's small achievements and voicing this	• Questioning techniques with no particular knowledge outcome in the teacher's head, aware of their interests, not interrupting them, allowing silences, following the child's leads
• Demonstrating and modelling skills	
• Supporting children's problem solving and experimentation, with a predetermined outcome or task in the teacher's mind	• Making links in thinking across time and activities through revisiting children's ideas and interests, making links between many sources of ideas, knowing children really well
• Telling children specific knowledge facts, in the context of their interests, developing limited intersubjectivity with children.	• Developing full, two-way intersubjectivity with children, through sharing their own ideas with children to extend their current interests, often as in-depth projects, entering the child's fantasy play, valuing and giving voice to children's activities, respectfully checking that a child would like the offered assistance.

(Taken from Jordan, 2004, pp. 40–1)

As Wood and Attfield argue (2005, p. 94): 'scaffolding has been interpreted to imply a one-to-one relationship in which the teacher, expert, or more knowledgeable other remains in control of what is to be learned, and how the teaching will be carried out – essentially a *transmission* model.'

In an activity based on the model of co-construction, the focus moves away from transmission of knowledge and skills from the adult or more experienced peer to achieve an outcome or goal that they have identified. Instead the focus shifts to the interests and motivations of the learner. The role of the adult or more experienced other is to establish joint problem solving and intersubjectivity – a state where both parties work to identify and establish shared meaning and from that work towards an outcome or goal. Berk and Winsler (1995, pp. 27–8; cited in Jordan, 2004, p. 33) argue that: 'Intersubjectivity creates a common ground for communication as each partner adjusts to the perspective of the other . . . constantly striving for a shared view of the situation.'

Intersubjectivity therefore raises the status and role of the learner, allowing them to become a motivated co-constructor of their own learning and development. In co-construction, the learner can be proactive in identifying and seeking sources of support (Wood and Attfield, 2005, p. 104). Intersubjectivity also affects the adult/more experienced peer role, requiring a collaborative, listening and open approach to the learner and to the activity. With this shift in control, co-construction offers the learner an opportunity to be, in the words of Jordan (2004, p. 33), 'a powerful player in his/her own learning'. She goes on to state:

Co-construction thus places emphasis on teachers and children together studying meanings in favour of acquiring facts. Studying meaning requires teachers and children to make sense of the world, interpreting and understanding activities and observations as they interact with each other.

Play offers an ideal space for the study of meaning. In play the roles and rules of the world can be experienced and explored by the child in a safe environment, free from the consequences possible in the real world. Language and other psychological tools can be practised and manipulated. Co-construction offers education and care practitioners a valuable model of how to operate within this play space. Striving to achieve intersubjectivity and to arrive at shared understandings of meaning requires a more subtle, and less intrusive approach than is sometimes achieved via scaffolding alone.

Sustained shared thinking

The concept of sustained shared thinking arises from the twin research studies *Effective Provision for Pre-school Education* [EPPE] (Sylva *et al.*, 1997–2002) and *Researching Effective Pedagogy in the Early Years* [REPEY] (Siraj-Blatchford *et al.*, 2002). These projects have examined broad educational outcomes and specifics of practice in a large-scale, Government-funded longitudinal study in England. A key finding of the REPEY study relates to the types of interactions and play interventions that occur between adults and children in successful, quality early years settings. The research has found that learning and development are most effectively promoted when children and adults engage in **sustained shared thinking** (Siraj-Blatchford *et al.*, 2002). This is defined in the REPEY study as:

> **Sustained shared thinking**
>
> Introduced by Iram Siraj-Blatchford, this phrase describes the ability of an adult to intuit a child's interest and level of understanding and to subsequently successfully interact with him/her to develop a concept or skill.

An episode in which two or more individuals 'work together' in an intellectual way to solve a problem, clarify a concept, evaluate activities, extend a narrative, etc. Both parties must contribute to the thinking and it must develop and extend.

(Siraj-Blatchford *et al.*, 2002, p. 8)

In sustained shared thinking, the nature, quality and frequency of 'adult–child verbal interactions' is crucial to children's learning and is quite different from that involved in 'direct teaching', as described in Figure 2.3.

What is striking about the two descriptions is the location of control within the two types of adult–child interaction. In direct teaching, the adult role is a controlling, organising and dominating one. The adult selects the task, organises the resources and participants, controls the flow of information and decides when the task begins and finishes. Though the child may actively engage in the task, s/he does not have ownership or control of it and his/her participation is channelled along a restricted pathway. In contrast, during sustained shared thinking control is shared and is passed between the participants at various stages during the course of engaging

Figure 2.3 The nature, quality and frequency of adult–child interactions in sustained shared thinking and direct teaching

Sustained shared thinking	Direct teaching
Interactions that include:	Interactions that include:
• scaffolding	• questioning
• extending	• modelling
• discussing	• instruction
• modelling	• task management
• playing.	• reading to the target child
	• organising
	• allocation of tasks.

(Taken from Sylva *et al.*, 2007, p. 57)

in the task. The task itself may change and develop in response to ideas from either party. Looking again at these two descriptions it is clear that sustained shared thinking is a more helpful model for adults to use when engaging and intervening in children's play and closely resembles the description of co-construction we discussed earlier.

Cultural–historical theories of learning, development and play

Human development as a cultural–historical process

As stated in the introduction to this chapter, one branch of socio-culturalism is called the cultural–historical perspective. This perspective emphasises the cultural nature of human development (Wenger, 1998; Rogoff, 2003). Researchers working from this perspective have again been critical of traditional, developmental psychology approaches that seek to discover set 'stages' of child development which can be applied universally to all children, living in all cultures. Especially (as writers such as Rogoff have pointed out) as theorists taking this approach have tended to base their theories on data gathered using research subjects from exclusively western, and often middle-class, backgrounds (Rogoff, 2003, p. 84). From a cultural–historical outlook, this model, taken from the physical sciences, is inappropriate and inadequate to explain the complexities of human experiences and functioning across the range of communities in which children grow and develop. Rogoff has also argued that it also fuels the ongoing and essentially redundant nature/nurture debate regarding how human development takes place.

From the cultural–historical perspective, the nature/nurture debate presents a misleading either/or **dichotomy**. It pitches biology against culture as competing forces and potential explanations of aspects of human behaviour. Similarities in behaviour across cultures are often ascribed to biology and differences to culture. Rogoff argues that this separation of biology and culture is artificial and that instead we should view humans as 'biologically cultural', with nature and nurture operating as inseparable influences on human development (2003, pp. 63–5). She writes:

> We are prepared by both our cultural and biological heritage to use language and other cultural tools to learn from each other . . . Being human involves constraints and possibilities stemming from long histories of human practices. At the same time, each generation continues to revise and adapt its human cultural and biological heritage in the face of current circumstances. (p. 63)

Cultural–historical theory argues that children develop in **communities of practice** (Lave and Wenger, 1991) in which they are active participants. They learn to recognise, use and manipulate the signs and symbols of their communities to reproduce and sometimes to transform them (Wenger, 1998). Via participation and interaction they grapple with the 'socially negotiated character of meaning' (Lave and Wenger, 1991, p. 50). Achieving mastery of a new skill, symbol or process – that is, learning –

> **Dichotomy**
> Division into two mutually exclusive, opposed, or contradictory parts.

> **Communities of practice**
> Describes how differences may exist between different groups in that they may have different ways of accomplishing everyday tasks, e.g. educating children or preparing food.

> **Transformation of practice**
> Describes how things may change in a society when new discoveries are made; e.g., the invention of the microwave over created a difference in the way food is prepared in western households; such changes may permeate into the culture and create wider effects, such as a curtailment of 'home cooking'.

results in a **transformation of practice**, as they can now draw on these as tools in their future cultural participation (Rogoff, 1998; cited in Jordan, 2004, p. 37). Their ways of behaving and thinking are changed by the very act of learning.

In her influential research Barbara Rogoff examines play as a key element in the transformation of practice. She identifies play as an important medium within which the exploration and mastery of cultural signs and symbols can take place as children participate in their communities of practice. She agrees with Vygotsky about the significance of social processes, but has researched further into the impact of cultural diversity on the specific processes and outcomes of children's development. Furthermore, she maintains that a cultural–historical approach to understanding children's learning and development will prove to be more illuminating than traditional cognitive psychology approaches as it allows an understanding of differences as well as similarities to be developed (Rogoff, 2003). Understanding the unfamiliar aspects of other cultural communities and their practices (including play practices) also has the added benefit of what has been described as 'making the familiar strange', that is, the assumptions, beliefs and traditions which underpin one's own culture and its processes can be noticed for the first time, countering the usual state of affairs where familiarity leads to invisibility. As the French sociologist Bourdieu has written regarding the study of other cultures: 'this detour through an exotic tradition is indispensable in order to break the relationship of deceptive familiarity that binds us to our own tradition' (2001, p. 3; cited in Webb *et al.*, 2002, p. 72).

Rogoff's work involves consideration of, firstly, the relationship between the individual and the culture/community that individual experiences via activities such as play and, secondly, of how we understand, define and problematise the concept of 'culture'. Two models

Ideas in action

Case study: Membership of communities of practice

We each belong to many communities of practice, and during any one day we may move between several of them as we go about our usual activities. For example, I may have breakfast with my family, drive to work by car, do my job as a university lecturer all day and then spend the evening with friends at a music venue. In doing so I will have engaged in several different communities of practice.

In addition, as we go through life we enter new communities of practice and leave behind others. Figure 2.4 presents a brief map of my own involvement in communities of practice. My membership of each of them has introduced me to specific vocabulary, skills, knowledge, attitudes and perspectives and consequently this has shaped how I view the world. My most recent new community of practice is that of (western) motherhood and

my involvement in it has resulted in ongoing transformation of practice. In the 14 weeks since my daughter was born I have learned new skills, my use of language has changed as new words have been introduced (and some old, rather rude words discarded) and my understanding of babies and motherhood has changed from one based solely on theory to one rooted in exhausting but rewarding experience!

Stop and reflect

Try mapping your own involvement in communities of practice. During the course of one day, identify those in which you engage. Can you think of any communities of practice of which you are not yet a member but that you think you may be in the future?

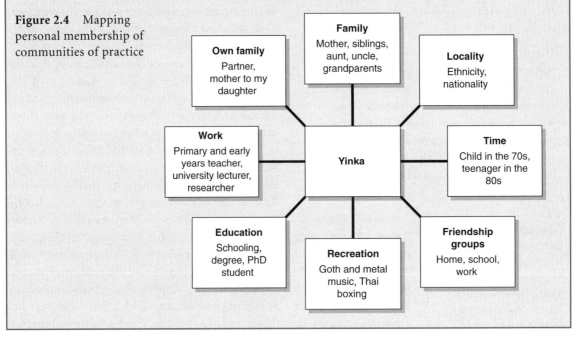

Figure 2.4 Mapping personal membership of communities of practice

that explore the first of these issues (namely the relationship between the individual child and its community) have been key to developing Rogoff's thinking. They are:

1 Whiting and Whiting's psycho-cultural model (1975); and

2 Bronfenbrenner's ecological model (1979).

Whiting and Whiting's psycho-cultural model places the child within a chain of social and cultural factors. This chain includes both the immediate social and cultural surroundings in which the child interacts and the more removed cultural processes in which the child, and those people around the child, participate (Rogoff, 2003, p. 43).

Ideas in action

Case study: Experiencing an unfamiliar community of practice

This chapter focuses on different cultures in different parts of the world, but we can also consider how culture changes in time. A good example of this can be seen in the Channel 4 'reality' television programme called *The 1900 House*, filmed in 1999. A modern family agreed to live for three months as a family would have done in 1900, and to be regularly filmed over this period. The family soon found that the 'community of practice' they had entered was very different to the one they had left. Simply getting dressed in the morning was a difficult task, especially for the women, with intricate layers of underwear including a corset with lacings. The family had made a pact with the producers not to purchase goods that would not be available in 1900, but after a few weeks the mother and eldest daughter broke this promise by buying modern shampoo/conditioner because they found their hair became completely unmanageable when it was washed in the soft soap that women of the time had used (McCrum and Sturgis, 1999).

After the programme had aired, the producers received many letters from the public, some from people in their 80s and 90s pointing out that the family had had so much trouble with various aspects of 1900s life because they were simply doing things 'wrong'. For example, Victorian women washed their hair less frequently than modern women, and brushed it vigorously night and morning, which spread the natural oils through the hair. Also, Victorian women's hair was usually long, plaited at night and pinned up in various styles during the day; it was very seldom worn loose around the face, so it did not have much chance to matt and tangle. Just as a genuine 1900 family would be baffled by a microwave oven, a central heating thermostat or a laptop PC, the 1999 family placed in a '1900 house' were unable to rely on culturally transmitted learning to manage their lives in the situation in which they were placed; they were outside their 'community of practice'. This even extended to something as deceptively simple as personal grooming, which progressed into a situation that caused a surprising amount of anguish.

Improving practice

Victorian children

Children love to role-play, and they love to hear stories. See if you can draw on the resource of your own local community (parents are often the best first contact) to see if you can get adults to come in and tell the children stories about their lives in other cultures, or in earlier times, and if possible to bring in some resources to 'show and tell'. When Pam Jarvis (one of the other editors of this book) took in the photographs (Figures 2.5 and 2.6) of her grandparents as visual aids to show her twins' classmates to supplement some stories about late Victorian childhood that she had been told by her grandmother, the children listened avidly. They were absolutely fascinated with the photographs, particularly

Figure 2.5 Victorian boys

the one of her grandfather, who had a clear facial like-ness to her own son. She remembers one of the class saying, 'He's real, he's a real Victorian, he's all dressed in Victorian clothes in an old photo, but he must be real because he looks just like Andrew.'

If you can create some experiences like this for the children you work with, it would add to the experience if you could produce some related resources that the children can use in their role-play afterwards (for this example, it could be some Victorian-style clothes for the dressing-up box). Whilst they will not be able to fully enter another 'community of practice' in this way, they will at least become more able to reflect on and become more open to the idea that their own societal practices are not the only way to do things, and that there are very different societies, both in time and in geography.

Figure 2.6 Victorian girls

The chain begins with the physical and natural environment and then moves to historical factors such as migrations, inventions and borrowings from other groups. This is followed by the group's maintenance systems, which include its subsistence patterns, means of production, settlement patterns and social systems for organising such aspects as defence, law and control and the division of labour. The chain then reaches the individual child and factors such as innate needs, drives and capacities as well as learned behaviours, including skills, abilities, values and conflicts. These learned be-haviours then admit the adult into participation in what are termed the 'projective–expressive systems' of the group, that is, aspects such as religion, beliefs, ritu-als, arts and recreational pastimes.

Rogoff argues that a major difficulty with the model is that it assumes that factors earlier in the chain affect those further down it, that is, that earlier factors have a determining effect on the development of later factors. In this model, the child's (and ulti-mately the adult's) behaviours are heavily determined by social factors that are in turn determined by

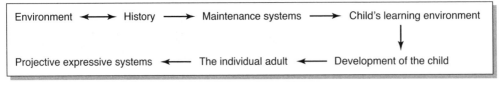

Figure 2.7 Whiting and Whiting's psycho-cultural model
Source: Adapted from Rogoff, 2003, p. 43.

> **Agency**
>
> The capacity, condition, or state of acting or of exerting power (Merriam Webster).

historical and geographical factors. Cultural processes and individual processes are portrayed as different entities with the former causing the latter. As a result, in this model, the individual child or adult has little power or '**agency**' and is dominated by the cultural context.

Bronfenbrenner's ecological system presents similar difficulties for Rogoff. The child is located within a concentric model that has been likened to a set of Russian dolls. At the centre lies the child, immediately surrounded by the microsystems of home, school, neighbourhood and religious setting with which the child personally interacts. Surrounding this are the mesosystems where the different aspects of the microsystems interact (that is, home interacts with school as parents interact with teachers). Next come the exosystems, which include settings in which the child is not directly involved but that influence the child's experiences (for example parental workplaces, local government and the mass media). Here decisions are taken, on factors such as maternity leave arrangements, on the provision of child care facilities or public health services, which will ultimately have an impact on the experiences of the child. The macrosystems make up the final, outer level of the model. They are the dominant beliefs and ideologies that provide an underpinning set of assumptions which shape the various social institutions of the culture. (For example, in the past two decades beliefs and a political ideology focused on economic activity and social inclusion in the United Kingdom have shaped the institutions of schools and child care settings to provide 'wraparound' care to enable parents to work.)

Bronfenbrenner argues that within his model there is mutual accommodation between the individual growing child and the changing properties of the settings in which the child is located – each exerts a modifying effect on the other. However, Rogoff argues that the model is still a hierarchical one, with the larger, outer contexts constraining the smaller, inner ones. It is, however, useful for establishing a view that in order to understand the experiences and development of children it is necessary to consider settings and contexts with which the child has indirect contact as well as those that provide direct interaction (Rogoff, 2003, pp. 44–8).

So, if we are to reject the idea of cultural contexts determining the development and experiences of individuals, what is the alternative? Rogoff (2003) proposes that in cultural–historical theory we should not see culture as a separate, external set of processes which influence the individual. Instead she argues that: 'people contribute to the creation of cultural processes and cultural processes contribute to the creation of people' (p. 51).

The consequences of this view are, firstly, that culture can be understood as dynamic as it is reproduced but also changed by the actions of individuals, and secondly, that individuals (including children) have agency; they can choose how to behave, whether to conform or to rebel against the dominant cultural processes. Rogoff (2003, p. 11) states: 'Humans develop through their changing participation in the socio-cultural activities of their communities, which also change.'

Thirdly, conducting research into development and learning from this cultural–historical perspective requires recognition of the cultural nature of everyday activities, of the tools, traditions, structures and institutions and of the ways in which people use and transform them. This also means that practices and processes from the west cannot be viewed as culturally neutral 'norms' against which to judge other communities.

Rogoff (2003, pp. 11–12) lists the following key principles to guide understanding of her take on the cultural–historical approach. These principles, as we shall see later, have particular relevance for anyone working with children from socially and culturally diverse backgrounds:

- Culture isn't just what other people do.
- Understanding one's own cultural heritage, as well as other cultural communities, requires taking the perspective of people of contrasting backgrounds.
- Cultural practices fit together and are connected.
- Cultural communities change, as do individuals.
- There is not likely to be 'one best way' of doing things.

Ideas in action

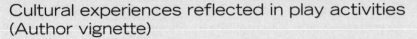

Cultural experiences reflected in play activities (Author vignette)

Once when I was 4, my best friend Harley and I were caught climbing trees in the compound of Harley's house in Nigeria by one of the maids. We were dragged in to see our parents and told off as climbing trees was dangerous because of the snakes that might be in them. Soon after that we were at my house when there was a big commotion when someone spotted a snake in the grass. Harley and I were made to sit inside the house and watch through the window while my father and some men from the neighbourhood, armed with long knives, sticks and nets, caught the snake and killed it by chopping it up and burning it. We then became fascinated by the idea of becoming snake hunters. We would gather pan lids, sticks and blankets and sneak around the room pretending to catch and kill snakes like my father had, whispering instructions to each other and using hand signals as we zeroed in on our pretend prey.

Comment

When I share this memory with friends in England they often express shock that two 4 year olds could have been allowed to, indeed encouraged to, watch a group of people kill an animal in such a graphic way. However, from the Nigerian perspective, teaching children the dangers of snakes was an important part of good parenting. Learning how to protect your family from poisonous snakes was a key life skill that boys such as Harley in particular were expected to learn.

The story also demonstrates other cultural aspects such as the gendered division of labour, community cohesiveness and social class divides, but no one has ever commented on them; their focus is always on whether I as a young child should have been exposed to violence and death.

So how is development facilitated within the cultural–historical approach? Lave and Wenger (1991, p. 95) have proposed that children learn and develop via participation in their communities; in learning they are 'both absorbing and being absorbed in the "culture of practice"'. Rogoff (2003) has developed this into a concept of **guided participation** in a community of practice. In guided participation, children learn by taking part in the practices of their community and being guided by its values. This guidance can be experienced in ways that may be seen as positive or negative (depending on the observer's personal and cultural point of view). For example, it can include being praised or being shamed, or learning how to cooperate and compromise with others

> **Guided participation**
> Describes how children are led to participate in the community into which they were born by being supported by adults to engage in mundane/everyday activities, many of which will vary from culture to culture.

or to use violence to dominate an interaction (Rogoff, 2003, pp. 283–4). The guidance may be intentional, for example an adult setting out to teach a child a new skill or concept, or unintentional, for example where a child observes someone else undertaking an activity and is later able to mimic it. Guided participation can also involve trying to exclude children from some practices and forms of learning that are considered unsuitable for children by their community (for example excluding children from certain religious practices or imposing a sex and violence watershed on television schedules).

Guided participation involves interactions between the child and adults or other children. These interactions involve both parties attempting to:

- bridge their different perspectives to arrive at shared meaning;

- structure each other's participation in shared activities.

Bridging different perspectives involves the participants using verbal and non-verbal communication to arrive at shared meaning (achieving the state of inter-subjectivity that we discussed earlier). Mutually structuring each other's participation is achieved via adults (or older children) granting or denying access to certain activities, organising resources or drawing on narrative traditions in their interactions with children, and via children seeking involvement with, or proximity to activities that they find attractive, and by them practising and toying with routines and rules in play and other activities.

Rogoff identifies these processes of guided participation as being universal, though the precise forms they take will vary from community to community. For example, she writes:

> children's play builds on what they observe, but what they have the opportunity to observe differs greatly depending on whether they are included in the full range of their community's activities or are segregated from many settings that are restricted to adults.　　　　　　　　　　　　　(2003, p. 299)

The previous vignette demonstrates this point. In some communities death and killing of animals are not experienced or observed by children. In others they are an important part of a child's 'education' from the earliest age, and for adults to deny children access to the experience would be seen as negligent.

The concept of children engaging in cultural processes within 'communities of practice' inevitably leads to questions regarding what is meant by 'culture' and by 'community'. The politics of recognising and labelling people by their membership of perceived cultural groupings has been criticised for being inadequate and divisive by theorists from different disciplines (Appiah, 1994; Taylor, 1994). Rogoff agrees and argues that culture is not a 'static social address carried by individuals' (2003, p. 63). Rather than ascribing people to separate cultural categories that focus on one aspect of a person's identity, she argues that we should instead focus on the individual person's involvement and participation in cultural communities. This approach better fits the actual lived experiences of people in that it acknowledges that communities can be built around cultural aspects of life other than ethnicity and that many people in fact participate in more than one community.

Play as a site for guided participation

What constitutes play, who is involved in play, where it occurs and what artefacts, materials and processes children can access during play – the details of none of these features is universal to all communities. Rogoff's research is particularly useful in highlighting that the western view of play, its model of childhood and its image of the child, is culturally constructed and reflects specific social, historical and ideological contexts. Let us take three different aspects of play to illustrate the point:

1　Where do children play?

2　With what do they play?

3　With whom do they play?

In the west most children, like Holly (see 'Ideas in Action on p. 56), tend to spend large parts of the day away from the home in child-focused care and educational settings and institutions. They therefore do not get to see their parents during the day or to witness their parents' work activities either inside the home or in the workplace. In the child-focused institutions the children play with resources designed for use by children, manufactured to meet legally enforced safety requirements. They play with fixed groups of other children of their own age and with adults employed to engage in activities with them, often on a one-to-one or small group basis. They are introduced to songs and stories designed for children. Once home, many children will play with their parents as well as with siblings, again using play resources designed for children and often on a one-to-one basis.

Rogoff contrasts this with examples from other cultures. For example, in many cultures in places such as Africa, Central and South America and Oceania, working-class and rural children do not attend child-focused settings but spend their days with their families and communities in and around the home. They get to witness their families as they conduct work activities within a largely agricultural economy and are often expected to participate in these activities. They do not have access to large amounts of play resources specifically designed for children. Instead they often have access to the everyday objects that adults in their families and communities use in their work.

Ideas in action

The role of adults in the play of her 3-year-old child (Parent reflection)

Holly's been going to nursery since she was 1 and she's used to being with her friends all day, surrounded by toys and to having a lot of adult attention – one of the reasons we chose that nursery is because it has a really good staff to child ratio. After nursery, at home, once she's had her dinner she wants to play with me or Daddy all the time and that makes getting on with jobs very difficult. I can't make our dinner until her Daddy comes home, because she wants me to play dolls or something with her. She's very good and always knows what she wants to play but it can be very tiring. Then once her Daddy's home she plays rough and tumble with him and I clear up. Then I make our dinner whilst he baths her. At weekends I take her to the urban farm. They've got a supervised petting zoo and adventure playground so she can play safely and it gives me a break.

We do sometimes find the long holidays hard. Holly really misses nursery and all of her friends so I often put her into nursery for a day or two over the holiday. She enjoys it and I can get on with getting all my jobs done.

Helen, parent of Holly

Stop and reflect

- What do you notice about Holly's play? Specifically, who is involved in playing with her?

- Which aspects of family life are excluded from Holly's experiences?

Moreover, some of these objects are potentially dangerous, such as the machetes used by Efe children under a year old in the Congo and knives and the fire handled by children of a similar age in New Guinea (Sorenson, 1979 and Wilkie, 1989; cited in Rogoff, 2003, p. 5). As adults in these communities are engaged in work activities for much of the day, the primary care givers and playmates for babies and small children are other children, who often take on this responsibility at ages 5–7. They often combine child care, play and contribution to the domestic chores of the family and provide role models for their charges as they do so. Infants and small children therefore spend the day with children and adults of varying ages, often joining in their work activities and being introduced to the work songs, stories and conversations of their elders. Parents will not take on the role of playmate directly, but often will instruct older children to fulfil the role, with some supervision (Rogoff, 2003, p. 122).

Comparing the two descriptions does serve to highlight certain assumptions in the western models of childhood and of the child, and of the role of play in the life of the child. In contemporary Britain, for example, childhood is seen as a distinctly different and increasingly ghettoised phase of being. However, this is not universal – geographically or historically. For example, prior to the Industrial Revolution children in Britain spent their lives in the company of adults and other children of various ages in and around the home. It was only with the advent of statutory education in the late nineteenth century that children increasingly spent much of their day in the company of children and during the early twentieth century that they were organised into increasingly narrow, age-specific class groupings.

This type of experience reflects a particular image of the child. Rogoff writes:

> An alternative to children's observing and participating in the activities of their communities is for adults to introduce them to mature skills in specialized, child-focused settings that are created to instruct children, outside of mature community activities. A prime site for this is school, which is usually organized to keep children away from adult settings and to 'prepare' them to enter mature roles by giving them non-productive, specialized exercises . . . These specialized child-focused activities include play with adults as playmates or as organizers of children's play, lessons given at home in preparation for later engagement in school or work activities, and adults serving as peers in child-focused conversations. (2003, pp. 140–1)

Research carried out by Halldén (1991) (examining parents' views of their young children and the role of parents and other adults in their development and learning), proposes two ways of viewing the child that are relevant to this discussion:

1   the child as project
2   the child as being.

In the 'child as project' image, the child is viewed in terms of its future potential and as someone to be moulded and shaped by parents, family and educational institutions. Goals and activities are set for the child by adults, outcomes are predetermined and developed from a top-down perspective that is constantly preparing the child for future ages and roles. The 'child as being' image implies that the young child develops autonomously as an individual and has his/her own driving force to learn and grow. The 'child as being' needs adults as supporters, not instructors, and can identify his/her own goals and activities, relevant to his/her own current needs and interests. The 'child as being' image gives significantly more power and agency to the child than the 'child as project' image. It is also more consistent with the concepts of co-construction and intersubjectivity discussed earlier in the chapter.

Implications of cultural perspectives on play for those working with children

In this section we will consider some potential issues for care and education practitioners that arise from taking a socio-cultural/cultural–historical perspective. These are:

- culture, identity and play
- gender, identity and play
- the role of the practitioner in managing play.

Culture, identity and play

Rogoff (2003) argues that appreciation of cultural perspectives of children's development and play experiences is increasingly important as societies become more culturally diverse. Care and educational institutions are not culturally neutral spaces. They are themselves communities of practice, with values, behaviours and attitudes that are embedded and taken for granted by those who work in them. Furthermore, both Bourdieu (1977) and Apple (2004) have argued that these institutions reflect and actively promote the specific values, behaviours and attitudes of the dominant political and cultural classes within any society; indeed, that is one of their prime functions. For example, in the case of English care and educational institutions which we will consider for the remainder of this chapter, the curricula and everyday practices draw on the values, dispositions and attitudes that are more familiar to the children of the social, cultural and ethnic majority, namely, the dominant, white, middle classes. They reflect what Bourdieu called a certain 'habitus', that is, the social inheritance expressed in habit, disposition and 'unthinkingness in actions' that confer on the individual: 'dispositions to act in a certain way, to grasp experience in a certain way, to think in a certain way' (Grenfell and James, 1998, p. 15).

> **Habitus**
> A set of thoughts, values, tastes and behaviours that have been culturally acquired in childhood which the individual nevertheless frequently presumes are universally 'normal' and/or 'what everyone does'.

As such the assumptions, language, idioms and artefacts used in these settings are more familiar to children of the white middle classes than to children from other social, cultural or minority ethnic groups. Children of the dominant classes will find that their habitus fits in easily with school. Children of the dominated classes, by contrast, are more likely to find that their habitus is either absent from, or ridiculed and/or 'demonised' by, that of the school. Returning to the opening vignette of this chapter, we can see in the teacher's description a graphic portrayal of this process at work. Some children are seen to know how to 'play properly' whilst the play of others is rejected as unsuitable. Children's identity as 'good' players/learners and 'bad' players/learners is made explicit very early in their engagement with the setting.

Ideas in action

Acknowledging cultural identity in the classroom (Practitioner observation)

Asha had been in nursery for about 12 weeks. Her family was from North Africa and didn't speak English. Asha came to nursery everyday but wouldn't really join in with the other children. She always either sat in the listening corner, playing music tapes, or went to the sand, repeatedly filling and emptying buckets. She didn't speak to other children and apart from passing objects to them sometimes, she made no attempt to communicate with them. At this time I was given £200 to spend on equipment and for the first time it came with no conditions – usually I'm told to spend any money on something specific, such as books or maths equipment. After discussion with my nursery nurse, we decided to spend it on dressing-up clothes, in particular on clothes that reflected different ethnicities. We looked in the catalogue and got four outfits – 'Asian Girl', 'Asian Boy', 'African Girl' and 'African Boy'. The Asian Girl outfit was a red embroidered full-length tunic and a long, matching veil. I didn't tell the children we were getting new stuff, I just put it all in the home corner and waited to see what would happen.

Asha came through the door at the start of the session and instantly noticed the 'Asian Girl' outfit. As soon as registration was over she went straight to the outfit, put it on and, the only way I can describe it is that she 'became' her mother. The way she walked,

the way she held herself, everything was transformed. She then went into the home corner where two other children were already playing. She instantly took on the role of mother and the other two became children. In her play she talked and talked, and even though she was not speaking English, everyone seemed to know what role she was playing and they played along too. It was like watching her blossom. At last she was able to interact with the other children. As the week went on she played like this every day, making contact with more of the children. By the end of a month, still wearing the outfit, Asha was playing with children in the other areas of the classroom and her English was really starting to develop.

Practitioner reflection

At first I felt really pleased that the outfit seemed to have made such a difference to Asha, but eventually I felt guilty that she'd had to wait for so long for me to provide the play equipment that had helped her to play and interact with other children. It made me think about the huge responsibility I have as a teacher to help all children access opportunities to play and to feel represented and wanted in the classroom.

Musrat, nursery teacher

Brooker (2005), discussing her research into cultural diversity and early years ideology, argues that part of the process of schooling is to transform the 'child' into a 'pupil'. However, she found that the process was more difficult for ethnic minority children within her research sample. They began school with a different cultural understanding of the role of the child and the teacher in school. They also had different experiences of play and of the involvement of children in the work and everyday lives of their families. For them transformation from child to pupil involved learning a complex set of behaviours, discourses and expectations and, to a varying extent, leaving their own cultural ways of being, and therefore part of their identity, at the school door. Furthermore, Brooker argues that the way in which this process occurs can have lasting effects on the child's actual development and self-image as a learner (2005, p. 116). Levinson's (2005) research with children from traveller backgrounds in England establishes that for some children this rejection of their play culture in school can serve to undermine their cultural identity and isolate them from their peers. This reflects Bourdieu as it acknowledges that school is a specific cultural context (or in Rogoff's terms, 'community of practice') and that different children's home experiences will vary in how similar or different they are to the school context: school itself is a community of practice. The experience of the child who finds his/her home experiences and culture are present and valued in school is reflected in Wenger's statement that: 'When we are with a community of practice of which we are a full member, we are in familiar territory. We can handle ourselves competently. We experience competence and we are recognised as competent' (Wenger, 1993, p. 152; cited in Cowie and Carr, 2004, p. 99).

Gender, identity and play

Rogoff (2003) argues that young children are actively developing their understandings of gender and gender roles. In doing so they explore the concepts of 'boy' and 'girl' – often examining the extremes of each role within their community – and this is reflected in their play. Holland's (2003) work on war, weapon and superhero play in the early years brings into focus some key issues about gender and play within care and educational settings. These settings are gendered spaces, reflecting the fact that early years and primary workforces are predominantly female. This inherent female bias is potentially (and unconsciously) reflected in the values, attitudes and behaviours that are encouraged and those that are rejected when children engage in play. Whereas historically approaches to education in England presented different curricula and expectations based on gender (for example the Elementary Code of 1900 had boys studying drawing whilst girls did needlework), in recent decades the practice has been to discourage gendered approaches to the curriculum and provision in practitioners, parents and children. Children's, and in particular, boys' engagement in violent or pseudo-violent play has generally come to be regarded as unhealthy and inappropriate in these settings. Policies of zero tolerance – of stopping such play as soon as it starts – have become widespread as a way of containing and attempting to eradicate such play within

Ideas in action

Refocusing children's war, weapon and superhero play (Student observation)

A PGCE student, recalling her recent school experience, stated:

> We had a pirate ship for our role-play area and the children (a few) kept trying to make swords to use in the area. I discouraged them from doing this because they were fighting with them each time. I tried to get them to make treasure maps and telescopes instead – this way they still got to use their creative skills, but in a positive way.

When asked what she thought was prompting these children to want to take part in play fighting in the first place she replied, 'TV, movies and computer games. Children want to imitate super heroes and make weapons. If children weren't exposed to these ideas in the media, they wouldn't be imitating them in their play.' She also described how, once she had altered the play theme some of the boys lost interest in the role-play area, but more girls started joining in.

Stop and reflect

- How true is this assertion about the influence of the media?
- If play-fighting were the direct consequence of television, films and computer games, then it would be a fairly modern phenomenon. Is it?
- Why might the actions of the student teacher in changing the play theme have had different effects on the boys and the girls in the group?

institutional settings (Holland, 2003). Holland argues that these policies are problematic for a number of reasons.

Firstly, they are based on the idea that war, weapon and superhero play leads to the development of violent attitudes and behaviours outside of the play arena. Such a causal (as opposed to an associative) link is however not proven by the research (Holland,

2003). These policies also do not distinguish between real violence and pretend violence, treating both as equal (as witnessed by the 9 year old I once saw pleadingly exclaiming to a lunchtime supervisor, 'But Miss, our phasers are only on stun!'). Furthermore, the practice of such policies generally involves practitioners intervening and closing down such play as soon as they spot it. The play is not observed for any length of time to ascertain the spirit of the play or the motives of the players. It is merely shut down. However, although the play may be stopped the underlying motivations of children engaging in war, weapon and superhero play continue to exist. In fact they are so powerful that children tend to continue to subvert play and play resources in order to continue exploring these themes (for example creating their own guns from construction materials, moving away from adults to less overlooked play spaces within the setting, and so on). Again, the lack of observation of this play by adults means that the motives driving children and the complex concepts (such as death, loyalty, responsibility and resilience) they may be trying to gain mastery over by engaging in this play are lost.

Moreover, the types of play that practitioners often try to substitute for war, weapon and superhero play often reflect this lack of understanding as to why children are engaging in it in the first place. Physical play (running around and 'letting off steam') or noisy play are seen by some practitioners as suitable replacements for war, weapon and superhero play, reflecting a view that children engage in them due to excess energy levels rather than as a means of engaging in cognitive and social development. In other cases the war, weapon and superhero play is refocused by practitioners towards what they consider to be more suitable topics and interactions (as in the earlier student teacher observation). The success of this is often quite limited as it ignores the play themes or narratives that are underlying the pre-existing play. Some children are able and willing to make the switch from co-constructing their play with peers to having it tightly controlled and scaffolded by an adult, whilst others will lose interest in the new play and wander off. In practice, zero-tolerance policies disproportionately affect boys as they are more likely to engage in war, weapon and superhero play (or to be perceived to be engaged in it) than girls are. In shutting down such play, unquestioningly, practitioners are denying them a key form of expression.

> The concept of play narratives will be explored in Chapter 7, which examines 'rough and tumble' play.

The role of the practitioner in managing play

One of the key duties of care and education practitioners is to manage play in their settings and to reconcile children's learning and developmental needs with wider societal concerns. Their duty is not just to the children in their care, but to the expectations of parents, colleagues, employers and to society as a whole. Responding to this duty often requires them to balance conflicting pressures and to make professional judgements when faced with complex situations involving health and safety and child protection dilemmas. 'Ideas in Action' on p. 61 provides two observations that illustrate these issues.

Health and safety and play

One of the practical reasons often given for stopping war, weapon and superhero play is health and safety. Such play is seen as potentially (or even inevitably) dangerous and likely to escalate and 'get out of hand' unless stopped almost before it has started. This attitude has grown in recent years to encompass other types of physical, noisy and boisterous play, reflecting an increasingly litigious, blame-oriented culture.

Child Protection and play

Some children who engage in apparently inappropriate play may be doing so as a direct result of traumatic experiences in their home lives that they are attempting to revisit and come to terms with during play. A zero-tolerance policy creates a danger that practitioners will become habituated to closing down play without considering and addressing the motives behind it. For traumatised children, there is a risk that merely stopping this play without seeing and hearing the themes it explores will leave them further isolated, and without a 'voice' to express their concerns.

Ideas in action

Gender and practitioner perceptions of play (Student observation)

I think that teachers tend to notice what they think of as 'aggressive' play in boys more than in girls. On one placement the teacher was constantly telling boys off for play-fighting. They'd use some of the wooden blocks as guns and pretend to shoot each other. They were giggling all the time and never actually touched each other but she had a 'no guns' policy and always noticed and stopped this kind of play. On the other hand, some of the girls developed a game whilst playing Sleeping Beauty where they would all be fairies with wands. One girl, Natalie, always liked to be in charge, and she'd use her wand almost as a weapon, threatening to turn other girls into horrible creatures unless they did as she wanted. Sometimes another girl would respond by using her wand to do something nasty back. This would then go back and forth with wands waving everywhere. Like the gun play, it was all pretend and no contact was made, but I felt that sometimes there was real aggression behind it as each one tried to dominate the play. However, the teacher never stopped this play and said that the girls were being creative and developing language skills when engaged in this sort of fantasy play. To me it seemed like a double standard.

Lynn, student teacher

Improving practice

This observation reinforces the argument that detailed and focused observation is a key tool in understanding and developing children's play. Between what the eyes 'see' and what the brain 'perceives' is the filter of personal experiences, attitudes, values and expectations, which can disadvantage or privilege certain groups of children unintentionally. Observation and a reflective practice approach are key professional tools that can open up practitioners, helping them to notice what children are actually doing and how they themselves filter and colour what they notice and fail to notice in children's play.

Ideas in action

The growth of the health and safety culture in settings for children (Author's observation notes)

One nursery I visited had taken extreme care to promote health and safety. In the classroom several large tubular metal columns held up the ceiling. These had been carefully wrapped in thick padding from floor to around 1 metre in height. In addition, padding had also been placed around corners of walls and of large pieces of furniture. Talking to the practitioners in the setting I found that no directive to do this had come from the local authority or the Health and Safety Executive and no injuries had been reported involving the columns, walls or indoor furniture; nevertheless the decision had been made by managers to effectively 'bubble-wrap' the setting. However, the practitioners had noticed that several of the boys were now deliberately hurling themselves against the padded columns, corners and furniture and were enjoying the sensation of bouncing off these obstacles; indeed, sometimes they were jumping off chairs to achieve maximum velocity and impact! This new game seemed far more likely to result in an injury than would have been likely had the columns remained uncovered.

Stop and reflect

- What models of childhood and of the duty of care of practitioners does this incident reflect?
- Should children be comprehensively protected from any possible chance of hurting themselves? Is this in fact possible (especially given the way that this set of precautions back-fired)?
- Does the *in loco parentis* duty of responsibility of practitioners (which should match the level of reasonable care and attention given by a parent) extend to bubble-wrapping entire rooms?
- What are the potential downsides of isolating children from genuine contact with the real environment?

Ideas in action

Case study: Child protection and managing difficult or 'unsuitable' play

Julia was still very new to nursery and was in the home corner exploring the equipment but generally not interacting with the other children around her. After some time she picked up a doll, wrapped it in a blanket and held it to her chest. Then, with her other hand Julia picked up one of the telephones and began frantically dialling. At this point I moved away from the area to support some other children using construction. After some moments I became aware that Julia was shouting and as I looked up she was still 'on the phone' but was shouting for the police to come to arrest her husband before he hurt someone; her language at this point included a number of pretty hard-core swear words. Other children around her had stopped what they were doing and were staring at her. I went to Julia and interrupted her play, asking her to come and do some painting with me. I was concerned not only at the other children hearing the language she was using and repeating it but at the heightened emotional state Julia appeared to be in. Julia came and painted with me and then went on to paint by herself at the easel. At break, as I was discussing the incident with my nursery nurse, a teaching assistant who lived near Julia came in and told us that the previous night the police had been called to Julia's house and her dad had been arrested. Afterwards Julia's mum had told neighbours that she had called the police because he had become violent towards her and had hit her whilst she was holding her baby son.

Julia's play for the sake of the other children and their parents as she was using language that was totally unacceptable and which other parents would not want their children exposed to. However, in stopping her play, I was removing the symptom without addressing the cause. I know that children who have suffered trauma and abuse are often given play therapy to work through difficult memories and experiences, and yet I was denying that opportunity to Julia so as not to upset other children or offend their parents. In telling her not to use certain language in the setting, I was preventing her from authentically processing her experience in a safe environment, away from the pressures of home. I felt that nothing in my training or experience could support me in knowing how to proceed.

Elizabeth, nursery teacher

- How could a practitioner provide meaningful opportunities for Julia to explore her experiences without making things more uncomfortable for her?
- Is it something the practitioner should even try?
- Should Julia be referred to specialist help such as play therapy (see Chapter 10)?
- What are the dilemmas arising in meeting Julia's needs whilst protecting those of the other children in the setting?

Stop and reflect

The dilemma posed by this incident was that my responsibility as a teacher meant I had to interrupt

Summary and review

This chapter has explored social and cultural aspects of play and of the practice of adults in managing children's play experiences and now returns to the original four questions set out in the Introduction.

- What role do social and cultural contexts play in shaping children's play?

The argument for the universal importance of social interaction to children's learning and development has been established by a number of socio-cultural theorists and research studies. However, it has also been established that this interaction takes place within the child's specific cultural community(ies) as they learn via guided participation in the cultural practices that surround them. The role of adults within these social interactions/guided participation is open to cultural and individual interpretation. The actions (and inactions) of practitioners will reflect their own interpretations of cultural practices (and professions are also communities of practice) and understanding of theory.

- How can play support or hinder the development of social, cultural and gender identity in children?

Play is a key site for guided participation. In some cultures children experience play as a central feature of a child-focused set of interactions with parents and other adults in home and care/educational settings. In other cultures play is more peripheral and takes place alongside children's involvement in the work and everyday tasks of their families and communities. Whilst it is still a significant feature of these children's experiences, their play interactions are different, more often involving other children rather than adults, with the child joining in the activities of others rather than taking part in decontextualised child-focused activities within separate settings for children.

Play within the community of practice is fundamental to establishing and exploring aspects of personal identity including cultural and gender identities. However, care and educational settings also constitute communities of practice and promote (intentionally and unintentionally, explicitly and implicitly) a specific set of cultural practices. Play experiences within such settings have the potential either to support and value the identities that children bring with them or to marginalise and reject those identities. Either has lasting consequences for the child and his/her developing self-image as a person and as a learner.

- How are adult and child play agendas pursued within educational and care settings?

The adult–child relationship within care and educational settings is not an even one. Adults inherently hold more of the power however they choose to exercise it. Adults can control the use of time and space, the resources provided and the language and discourses available for expression of thoughts, ideas and feelings. Adult agendas however are also strongly influenced by external pressures from parents, other practitioners, official bodies and society at large. Training, experience and individual interpretation of theory and **practice wisdom** are also powerful influences. As a result different practitioners develop and pursue their own play agendas in different ways. Practices such as scaffolding and co-construction offer models that explore how power and control can be shared between adults and children in play.

However, consideration of controversial aspects of children's play, such as war, weapon and superhero play, illustrates how, despite the uneven distribution of power, children can still pursue their own play agendas. Furthermore, the fact that children consistently pursue such play, even when adults often go to great lengths to prevent it, also presents challenging questions for practitioners. This is especially significant when adults' power and control over play agendas can disproportionately affect specific, and often already disadvantaged, groups of children.

- How, and to what extent, should educational and care practitioners accommodate diverse models of play?

This is a key question, the answer to which ultimately depends on the personal philosophy and approach of the practitioner and the setting and on the attitude to and experience of diversity in the society in question. The socio-cultural perspective would

> **Practice wisdom**
> A feature of a professional culture, similarly to habitus, 'practice wisdom' is a set of thoughts, values and behaviours, but in this instance it is shared between members of a profession (e.g., teachers, doctors) and is acquired through training and subsequent frequent association between professional colleagues.

▶

endorse a view that participation as a full member of a community supports the development of a full social, cultural and gender identity. This can be challenging for practitioners when dealing with potentially 'difficult' play that involves issues such as violence or gendered behaviours which go against society's aspirations for children and childhood.

However, in the modern culturally diverse society that exists in Britain, accommodating diversity is established as part of the key duty of practitioners to promote equality of opportunity. This means that each practitioner needs to be attentive to the social, cultural and gender differences and similarities that each child brings to a setting and to the fact that both are aspects of the child's essential and developing identity. An inclusive approach requires practitioners to strive to become aware of their own cultural biases and assumptions in order to assess and address their influence on their individual practice.

Transforming thinking and practice: over to you!

Cultural–historical theorists argue that a helpful way forward for the practitioner might be to consider a reflective and cross-cultural approach that will open up new ways of looking at familiar and 'alien' ways of being. This practice can help us to realise that we are *all* steeped in cultural practices, as we learn from reviewing our own practices from points of view gleaned from alternative cultures. Researching how another culture approaches specific professional practices such as assessing and documenting learning, or what they consider to be appropriate markers for development is illuminating and will generate questions about your own personal and societal assumptions.

Questions for consideration

The potential for questions is a key aspect of the cross-cultural approach but it is easy to become overwhelmed by them. It might be useful to decide on a specific issue to focus on such as gender and play, cultural identity and play or difficult/dangerous play. You can then seek to establish and articulate:

- your own current approach to the issue;
- the theories, experiences and assumptions that underpin that approach;
- alternative ways of approaching the issue that other cultures have taken;

- the theories, experiences and assumptions that underpin these alternative approaches;
- how these new perspectives can raise new questions about your own current approach and the theories, experiences and assumptions that underpin it.

Ideas for research

Video is an effective tool for developing reflective practice. Video can allow practitioners to capture small but significant moments that are overlooked in the dynamic and complex practice of the setting. You could ask permission to video your own practice and/or the play that children are engaged in during a session in a familiar setting. Afterwards review the video, preferably with a critical friend. What do you notice about your own practice, including your attitudes and preferences? What do you notice about the children's play and interests? What happens when instead of intervening in play, you stand back and let it continue under the children's control?

Further reading

Anning, A., Cullen, J. and Fleer, M. (eds) (2004) *Early Childhood Education: Society and Culture.* London: Sage.

Daniels, H. (2001) *Vygotsky and Pedagogy.* London: Routledge Falmer.

Rogoff, B. (2003) *The Cultural Nature of Human Development.* New York: Oxford University Press.

Children at Play: A Journey through the Years (0–11)

Chapter 3

Curriculum and Pedagogy of Play: A Multitude of Perspectives?

AVRIL BROCK

I'm happy with the early learning goals and I'm glad that the curriculum recognises the importance of play and that you can learn through play. I have more confidence in my teaching and that what I am providing is right for the children. I am more comfortable structuring their learning through play. I just wish they would take this play-based pedagogy through into Key Stage One as well.

(Lianne, Reception teacher)

Introduction

Education today is characterised by ongoing debates about how best to teach children and discussions about what sort of practice is most likely to contribute to their development and learning. These are such complex phenomena that no one theory is sufficient to explain them. Historically many prominent educators have espoused their own theories and practices. This chapter will explore conceptualisations of **pedagogy** and then present discussions about definitions of curriculum, as

> **Pedagogy**
> Encompasses principles, theories and practice relating to teaching and learning.

learning, from varied perceptions. Although there is a strong focus on the English education system, and its new curriculum for children aged 0–6, the Early Years Foundation Stage, a number of international models of curriculum and pedagogy will also be presented, such as Montessori, High/Scope, Reggio Emilia, Steiner/Waldorf and the Danish Forest Schools approaches. The centrality of play within education is key to these discussions and is a primary vehicle for delivering the curriculum to children. By the end of this chapter you should be able to answer these questions:

- What is meant by pedagogy and what do I need to know for practice?

- How can international models influence my practice?
- What is meant by curriculum and what is the role of play within it?

What is pedagogy?

Pedagogy is a complex concept and there are varied contemporary definitions. Pedagogy encompasses practice and the principles, theories, perceptions and challenges that inform and shape teaching and learning. According to Jackson and Tasker (2004) pedagogy is the distinctive knowledge base of education. It is considered to be the total provision of teaching that includes the methods, activities, materials and all other practical matters intended to achieve learning, whilst simultaneously taking the learner's development into account (Pollard, 2002). These educational interactive processes between teacher, learner and the learning environment need to be intertwined with care and with personal, cultural and community values (Siraj-Blatchford, 2004).

As previously alluded to, there is no single 'effective' pedagogy. Educators need to employ a whole gamut of pedagogical skills and knowledge, what Turner-Bisset (2001) terms a 'pedagogical repertoire'. Shulman (1987) highlighted several categories of teaching for secondary teachers to provide an appropriate pedagogical framework for educators. Siraj-Blatchford et al. (2002) developed these to encompass the following four points:

1 pedagogical content knowledge – 'subject' knowledge and awareness of the child's level of learning;

2 pedagogical interactions – face-to-face social or cognitive interactions;

3 pedagogical framing – provision and organisation of materials, space, routines;

4 pedagogical strategies – practices that support learning – social interactions, assessments, organisation of resources or management.

Perhaps Siraj-Blatchford et al.'s (2002) framework needs an additional category of pedagogical *relationships* that takes into account knowledge and experience of both articulating and communicating with the varied **stakeholders**. These include children, their families

> **Stakeholders**
> Those who have an interest in children's education such as parents, teachers, and governors, policy-makers and the children themselves.

> Examine the Ideas ⇨
> for research in Chapter 2 that may enable you to explore some of the key issues.

> REPEY is explored ⇨
> further by Olusoga in Chapter 2.

> Chapter 5 explores ⇨
> these issues and furthers your understanding of the range of Continuing Professional Development Opportunities with which you might engage.

and the local community; other educators; the general public and policy makers. This not only implies being able to *inform* but also to *listen*. Communicating with this breadth of stakeholders means being able to communicate in varied ways, to be able to co-construct interpretations of curriculum and pedagogy and to develop socio-cultural knowledge of the different communities and partnerships. This requires both ongoing commitment and effort – it is again another complex process in this field of education.

In 2000 and 2001 the Labour Government funded two projects designed to explore effective pedagogy in the early years. These DfEE commissions were the *Researching Effective Pedagogy in the Early Years* (Siraj-Blatchford *et al.*, 2002) and the *Study of Pedagogical Effectiveness in Early Learning* (Moyles *et al.*, 2002). The SPEEL study brief was to investigate practitioners' perceptions and understanding of effective pedagogy and to produce a framework that could be used alongside the Curriculum Guidance Foundation Stage. Stakeholders' descriptions of key terms were identified, as were the components of effective pedagogy comprising 129 statements under the three areas of focus: practice, principles and professional dimensions (Moyles *et al.*, 2002). The findings from this research emphasise that early years pedagogy is an extremely complex phenomenon, and that teachers' skills are acquired through a complex combination of training, experience and personal understanding. The research appears to have raised practitioners' awareness of the complexity of pedagogy and the researchers assert that the respondents' articulation of and reflection on practice is key to improving practice. Issues about head teachers/managers' understanding, the practitioners' own roles, the importance of play, children's attendance at settings and the involvement of parents is also deemed to contribute to effective pedagogy.

REPEY project findings demonstrated that the most effective pre-school practice 'achieve[s] a balance between the opportunities provided for children to benefit from teacher-initiated group work, and in the provision of freely chosen yet potentially instructive play activities' (Siraj-Blatchford and Sylva, 2004, p. 716). The research analysis shows the importance of adult–child interaction and the findings indicate that the more effective settings have well-qualified staff, who are able to match curriculum and pedagogy to children to promote cognitive challenges and 'sustained shared thinking'. This requires supporting children talking, thinking things through, rationalising their ideas and engaging in problem solving in intellectual ways. Siraj-Blatchford and Sylva (2004, p. 724) suggest 'that the higher the amount of good pedagogic practice, the greater was the effect on children's cognitive progress'.

Scaffolding is one such pedagogy that encourages 'sustained shared thinking' through appropriate adult/teacher interventions. The adult needs to consider each child's 'zone of proximal development' (Vygotsky, 1978), supporting and promoting understandings within a social context. Both adults and the children involved contribute to the learning process, with the adult monitoring interactions and thinking through the discursive processes. An adult identifies a child's current understanding, supports and gradually withdraws to allow confident and independent performance.

Look back to Chapter 2 where you were introduced to the notion of the ZPD.

Effective educators need more than just subject-based knowledge; they need to have a good working understanding of how concepts, knowledge, skills, processes and attitudes fit into teaching and learning. They need also to be good 'scaffolders', in the sense of being mentally flexible and being able to consider how their practice may be viewed from the learner's side of the relationship. Knowledge from whichever curriculum is selected needs to be embedded into children's frames of reference through meaningful experiences. As Sylva and Siraj-Blatchford (2004) suggest, in the 2000–2007 Foundation Stage (children aged 4–6) a balanced pedagogy is needed, comprising one-third each of experiences that are: child initiated; child initiated/teacher involved and teacher directed. Teaching children continues to become more complex and demanding, requiring particular skills in educators that go beyond the direct transmission of knowledge. The most effective educational institutions plan a curriculum that is taught informally in ways appropriate to children's previous learning, experience and interests. Now that the Early Years Foundation Stage applies to children from birth to rising 6, practitioners in

You can explore how to develop your knowledge and improve your practice for this age range in Chapters 4 and 5 as the authors examine babies, toddlers and young children up to the age of 6.

this area will need to extend their knowledge across the whole range of early years care and education, facilitating individualised play-based learning for children in the first six years of life. Such a wide age range encompassed under the umbrella of one specific (but unique) 'key stage' presents a challenging differentiation task to contemporary early years practitioners.

Socio-cultural perspectives emphasise that learning culture is also about participation. Children must be allowed to be active in the construction of their learning and it is important that they have a wealth of opportunities to be able to co-construct their own understandings and reflect on these with knowledgeable others. The Reggio Emilia approach (see later in this chapter, p. 73) allows the child to have an equal partnership with the educator by being involved in and directing their own learning. The emphasis is on the educator being a co-constructor of knowledge with children. However, it is important to examine cross-cultural diversity – how adults and children interact – to ensure equity for individual children, who will each have unique cultural values in accordance with their experiences in their personal families and communities. Educators need to engage with their pedagogy and reflect on what are the most appropriate methods of achieving

Ideas in action

A group of 4–5-year-old children in a Reception class are sitting on a carpet, facing the teacher. The teacher holds up baby photographs (of the children present) and asks, 'Who is this?' The children make a guess and the photographs are stuck on a collective board. Then, after sitting quietly for 20 minutes, the children return to their tables, find their names and copy down the sentence from the board for the information book they are to make. They had little opportunity to discuss, question or explore and have not even handled the photographs. Perhaps this teacher was under pressure to push the children into formal work, conscious of the fact they would soon be moving into Year 1 and National Curriculum work. The lesson was teacher directed. She asked mainly closed questions and, perhaps because of the need to 'move on quickly', she did not always respond to the children's answers.

Colleen, nursery nurse

Emotional intelligence
Level of awareness of one's own emotions and those of others, and using this to inform one's own behaviour and interaction patterns.

as their **emotional intelligence**. Her view of an appropriate pedagogy is matching the curriculum to individual children's needs, not matching the child to the 'expected' curriculum. The teacher in the scenario has not managed to initiate any 'sustained shared thinking' with the children, but talked 'at' them.

Stop and reflect

- How could you improve on the practice shown in the above scenario?

Improving practice

Compare the above activity with that used in the Ideas in action box in Chapter 2, Experiencing an unfamiliar community of practice. → Work with colleagues to develop children's sustained shared thinking in a similar activity.

Comment

This nursery nurse expresses her worries about some of the practices of those who do not seem to have an understanding of a pedagogy that pressurises children, as it can affect their attitude to learning at school as well

this equity for children. The next section examines a variety of international perspectives on curriculum and pedagogy. Interacting with these will broaden your knowledge and understanding of how/why different models aim to promote high-quality experiences for children.

International perspectives

There are a variety of curriculum models from around the world that have influenced educational practice and teaching and learning approaches internationally. Whilst this is particularly the case in early years education, it is also true for the primary years. The origins of these curriculum models addressed in this chapter

come from such diverse places as New Zealand, the United States, Italy, Denmark, Austria and the United Kingdom. Gammage (2006) views that the 'case histories' of High/Scope, Headstart and Reggio Emilia have become 'icons' affecting international policy, provision and beliefs. Curriculum models that have had specific impact on settings in England are High/Scope, Montessori, Reggio Emilia and Danish Forest Schools.

Montessori

Maria Montessori graduated from medical school in 1896 and her clinical observations led her to analyse how children learn. She believed that children could drive their own learning and were stimulated by their immediate environment. In 1906, she accepted the

Ideas in action

The Montessori approach (Practitioner observation)

Montessori viewed children as individuals and the approach is based on observation of the individual. Montessori doesn't rely on language to convey ideas, rather I'll show you then you repeat and work through it. I feel strongly that children need freedom to explore and play for longer than we allow them in the state system. In Montessori you train for the 3–6 age group, the early years first, before you do the primary, in order to gain a good understanding of children's development. Children don't fall into year groups or ability bands of a particular age.

Montessori favours the three-year mixed-age group. There are different levels of ability, which doesn't mean that the most able child is the 6 year old and the least able is the 3 year old, necessarily, but then they do learn from one another by having different ability levels.   Tanya, Montessori School head teacher

Stop and reflect

In what ways does your own philosophy reflect that of Tanya? Does that mean you agree with the Montessori approach?

challenge to work with a group of 60 children of working parents in Rome. There she founded the first Casa dei Bambini, or 'Children's House', and developed what ultimately became the Montessori method of education. This was based upon her scientific observations of these children's almost effortless ability to absorb knowledge from their surroundings and their tireless interest in manipulating materials. Her idea was to first train the senses through multi-sensory experiences and then develop children's intellect. She believed that children have innate characteristics, are naturally motivated to learn and that educators should conform to each child's natural patterns of learning.

Montessori developed a range of equipment, exercises and methods based on what she observed as children's natural accomplishments, unassisted by adults. Her educators act as facilitators, providing a specially prepared environment with the equipment, promoting independence, concentration and problem-solving skills. A particular emphasis of the Montessori Association is the structured training of its teachers. All Montessori teachers must first complete a validated Montessori course. However, Montessori's methods are sometimes considered to be at odds with 'notions of freedom, creativity, play, fantasy and self-expression' (Wood and Attfield, 1996, p. 17). The above quote in the 'Ideas in Action' observation from a Montessori head teacher demonstrates what she believes is important.

Figure 3.1   A Montessori school.
Source: Janine Wiedel Photolibrary/Alamy

High/Scope

The High/Scope curriculum is an approach to education used widely in the United States, but that has also been developed in 15 other countries including the United Kingom. The High/Scope programme was specifically designed in the 1960s by Weikart to improve intellectual performance for children in disadvantaged inner city areas. It is a cognitively oriented curriculum, based loosely on Piagetian theory with a pedagogy built upon a 'plan-do-review' sequence of activities. Children plan what they intend to do, carry the plan out and then reflect on what they have accomplished. This demands that they have direct personal interaction with reflection on their learning to increase understanding of the world around them. Children learn best when they have time to experience and explore the world for themselves and this curriculum is characterised by high-quality key learning experiences and promoting verbal interactions with children. Children are encouraged to make autonomous, independent decisions based on these active experiences, to develop confidence and reflection on personal learning (MacNaughton, 2003; www.highscopc.org.uk). High/Scope's 'plan-do-review' pedagogy may be especially effective in providing for both cognitive and socio-affective priorities, as the teaching and learning emphasises interaction, reasoning, reflection and responsibility for self-learning (Anning and Edwards, 1999). A longitudinal study of the effects of High/Scope demonstrated that children who had experienced the programme were more likely to

Ideas in action

Reflections in High/Scope (Practitioner observation)

We have had some excellent reports. In fact, the inspectors said that they don't know why more people don't use the High/Scope curriculum. We like it because it's a thinking person's curriculum. It's about making things fun for kids and all the time you're doing all this they're learning plenty. The children are involved with adults in a very different way from the teacher/child sort of perspective, we're friends. It's very often called 'upside-down teaching', because we give power to children, to decide what they're doing, with whom and how. We empower them to sort out their own conflicts and to empathise with other children when they're hurt. It's all about life skills, planning and thinking. What am I going to do this morning? Oh yes, I'm going to go in the sand area and make five sand castles with Sam, and then we're going to make some flags for the top and it's all about planning my day.

Jennie, manager, workplace nursery

Heuristic play
A type of play that offers children the opportunity to explore objects in a multisensory way.

Treasure baskets
A collection of everyday articles that can be used to stimulate a child or baby's senses (see chapter 4).

Multi-sensory
Relating to or involving several physiological senses, e.g. sight, sound, etc.

promoting **heuristic** play in the very youngest children in the setting through the use of **treasure baskets**, developing physical and creative learning. Children were encouraged to explore the natural side of materials through quality activities in **multi-sensory** ways and they found that children's attention span was 'lengthened to a very considerable amount'.

In this way her staff had to develop their professional knowledge of different but complementary curricula approaches to deliver an integrated and meaningful curriculum for the children in their care.

Comment

This manager offered the underpinning knowledge of the High/Scope curriculum that commenced with the 2-year-old children, starting the 'plan-do-review' questions such as, 'What are you going to do? Where are you going to play?' She cited this as being an excellent way of enabling the children to manage their own workload. Her setting operated the High/Scope curriculum combined with the Curriculum Guidance for the Foundation Stage. She had recently decided also to incorporate planning around core stories. In addition the staff were also

Stop and reflect

Go to Chapter 4 and find out more about treasure baskets. What would you include in a treasure basket that would support the multi-sensory experience promoted in this approach?

Improving practice

Do you employ 'plan-do-review' opportunities in your setting? If not then what action can you take to engage children in this metacognitive activity? If you do can this be enhanced and developed further?

achieve academically and vocationally, have greater self-esteem as adults and be less likely to be involved in drugs, crime, unemployment and teenage pregnancies (Sylva, 1994; Anning and Edwards, 1999). High/Scope established that high-quality early childhood education can produce lasting cognitive and social benefits throughout the later years of schooling for children (MacNaughton and Williams, 2004).

Reggio Emilia

Loris Malaguzzi established the Reggio Emilia approach immediately after World War II in the town of Reggio Emilia. He believed that children had rights rather than needs and could think and act for themselves (Malaguzzi, 1995). The Reggio Emilia model promotes a complex and changing version of the child as a competent learner who has the right and ability to construct and direct his/her own learning. It is based on Vygotskian theory – children learning through interaction, with modelling and support from others. The shape, tone, focus and content of the curriculum evolves through day-to-day experiences and the interests of children and adults, deepening children's enquiry and theory building (MacNaughton and Williams, 2004). Malaguzzi **reconceptualised** early childhood education, believing that children are rich in potential – strong, powerful and confident. He believed that children have '100 languages' through which they express themselves, such as words, movement, painting, building and playing, to name but a few (Edwards, 2002) and that children grow in competence communicatively and cognitively through these. However, he also believed that children lose part of their full capacity when they have to operate in a conformist formal school system, when their languages are lost one by one in many educational systems (Riley, 2003). The philosophy of the Reggio Emilia approach has creativity at the core of children's learning, working with artists and promoting artistic experiences in studios and other

---

Reconceptualised

To reframe a concept and subsequently attempt to communicate this effectively, usually done within teaching and learning to extend/improve a learner's grasp of the to-be-learned material.

---

creative learning environments. Reggio documentation is more than a record of the work with the children. It is part of the learning process and the educators are meticulous in recording the adult/child interactions. 'Many of the walls of the centres are hung with documentation panels tracing the development of the various projects undertaken by different groups of children (Abbot and Nutbrown, 2001, p. 3). The educators explore their own thinking and teaching styles as well as reflecting on children's learning and achievement. Reggio educators 'see themselves as a provocation and reference point, a way of engaging in dialogue starting from a strong and rich vision of the child' (Edwards, 2002). A criticism of the

Ideas in action

Reggio Emilia in action (Practitioner observation)

We now have 2 and 3 year olds who will paint for up to an hour and a half because they are allowed to paint anything they want. Previously if you offered them paint, spaghetti and cars, they would flit around like butterflies and get bored within ten minutes. It's something that people come to our practice to see. It flows partly out of the Reggio Emilia exhibition but we'd started before that. It's hard work but the benefits are huge for the children. Practitioners would say that children of that age group do not have a high attention span, but they're wrong. We are extending activities to work with the children on particular quality activities. For example – for the whole afternoon we might focus on water or sand to give them physical development in a multi-sensory way and the whole room will be full of different activities involving water. We've found that children's attention span is lengthened by a very considerable amount.   Amarjit, manager, private day nursery

Stop and reflect

Review the way your setting builds on the real experiences of the children in your care. In what ways could you make these experiences richer and more authentic?

Reggio Emilia curriculum has been that in the absence of a written curriculum there is a lack of accountability to the wider society. However, advocates of the Reggio Emilia approach argue that there is very detailed recording of the curriculum process, which opens their practice to criticism and scrutiny.

Steiner/Waldorf education

Rudolf Steiner (1861–1925) founded Waldorf education and opened his first school shortly after World War I in Stuttgart, Germany in 1919. He was a scientist and a philosophical thinker who integrated these two forms of understanding and experience in his schools. His desire was to produce young people who were intelligent, benevolent and socially aware. His theory of development was that learning occurred in three cycles of seven-year stages, with distinctive needs for learning in an ascending spiral of knowledge. Steiner's model emphasised the importance of unstructured play and that formal teaching should not commence until children reach the age of 7. Educators are important role models. Children learn through *imitation* and doing, with imaginary play being their most important work through which they grow physically, intellectually, and emotionally. The educational focus is on physical exploration, constructive and creative play, and oral (never written) language, story and song (Miller *et al.*, 2002). The curriculum promotes a strong emphasis on the Arts. Children are encouraged to become deeply engaged in the practical activities and so develop their powers of concentration and motivation. There are few Steiner schools in England, and those that offered early years education in the late 1990s suffered under Ofsted Inspections, because their ideology was strongly averse to promoting written language with young children and they could not achieve the **desirable learning outcomes** for language and literacy.

> **Desirable learning outcomes**
> A curriculum for pre-school children in England from 1996 to 1999.

Ideas in action

The Steiner/Waldorf approach (Practitioner observation)

As the children arrive at the Kindergarten, we help them prepare for the morning's activities. They can either join the activity at the tables, or begin their most important work: playing! Creative play is a time for the children to freely engage in imaginative play without adult direction. This is extremely important for their personal development. Imaginative play strengthens their independence, perseverance and social skills, while, of course, their creative expression is also enhanced. We provide them with toys such as natural resources that mean they have to be creative and use their imagination. The morning's activity is led by the adult who works with the child's capacity for learning through imitation. Monday is Baking Day, where we have time to watch the yeast rise in the bread, or grate, chop, squeeze and mix! We make food to eat at Snack Time for the rest of the week, birthday cakes or festival foods. Tuesday is Making Day, where we make a range of seasonal crafts, or continue with longer-term craft projects. Wednesday is Painting Day and we explore the different colours, textures and techniques of painting. Here, the emphasis is on the exploration of colour rather than form. Thursday is Sewing Day, where we introduce the children to initial hand–eye coordination and fine-motor skills, such as threading beads. As the child grows, we gradually build on their learning with other sewing techniques. Friday is Mending Day, where we take care of our equipment and help to keep it in good order, fostering care and respect for the world.

Renata, Kindergarten leader

Stop and reflect

Review the provision in your setting. Critically evaluate its effectiveness in light of the Steiner/Waldorf educational approach.

Danish Forest Schools

'Forest Schools' have been inspired by the ideas of Froebel, originating in Sweden in the 1950s when a retired soldier started to teach children about the natural environment through songs, stories and practical hands-on experiences. Gradually spreading to other countries, the idea of Forest Schools was adopted by Denmark where they have become an important part of the Danish educational programme. Forest Schools use the outdoors in a deliberate way as part of children's learning of practical and social skills with an independent approach to safety issues. The programme allows children to grow in confidence, independence and discover their abilities without fear of failure or criticism; through setting manageable tasks and giving genuine praise children gain a good foundation for future learning (www.foresteducation.org). The Forest Schools model promotes experiences where children can explore, be challenged and take risks, benefit from good health and physical development, as well as developing personal, social and emotional development and well-being. Since the concept of Forest Schools was brought to England by staff of Bridgewater College in 1993, 50 Forest Schools projects have been established across Britain. Maynard's (2007, p. 320) research suggests that whilst the

> significance of self-esteem and learning styles may be over-emphasised and, in some cases, the opportunities for environmental education under-emphasised, Forest schools fits well both with traditional views of 'good' early childhood education and more recent curriculum frameworks in England and Wales.

The importance of play in the outdoor environment for young children's optimum development was strongly valued in the MacMillan sisters' nursery

Ideas in action

Working in the Danish Forest School programme (Practitioner observation)

We became involved in the Forest programme because we were aware of the national emphasis on outdoor play and so included it in our school development plan. Over the past five years, we have created an outdoor area, planting 100 trees and shrubs. Twelve teachers from our authority are on the Forest Schools programme. One of the teachers and a nursery nurse from here went for training at a water centre in Wales for a week and then a weekend. It was quite in depth.

Jessica, head teacher, nursery school

> **Socio-cultural**
> Of, relating to, or involving a combination of social and cultural factors (Merriam Webster).

gained accreditation to run a programme for nursery nurses. The setting has a mixed catchment of families from different ethnic groups. It promotes a **socio-cultural** curriculum and policy and is keen to involve stakeholders in every stage of the development of the Forest programme. Parents were asked to complete a questionnaire giving their views and those of their children and the results were very positive.

Improving practice

This nursery head teacher's local authority wanted her centre to disseminate the aims and provision of the Forest Schools programme and so help promote the national emphasis on outdoor play. They ran the pilot and since they were highly regarded by the authority's early years inspector, they also received funding and

Stop and reflect

In which ways could a programme like this, and others you have met so far in this chapter, meet the range of learning needs and levels of development within the new EYFS?

schools in the early 1900s. The diminishment of outdoor play in school settings has been researched by Bilton (2002). Further contemporary concerns about the quality and time of children's outdoor play experiences are highlighted by the National Children's Society (2007) in The Good Childhood Inquiry and in the *Primary Review* (Alexander and Hargreaves, 2007).

See also
Chapters 7 and 9 ⇨

Te Whāriki

Te Whāriki is the early childhood National Curriculum of New Zealand developed by May and Carr in 1996. Te Whāriki translates from the Maori language as 'a woven mat for all to stand on'. As the first National Curriculum in the country, the aim was to regulate the hitherto diverse education programmes whilst at the same time providing space for cultural diversity. Providers of education are therefore extended the freedom to adapt the curriculum to their unique local setting. It is deemed equally important that the setting can cater for the interests, aspirations and skills of the children in attendance. The curriculum therefore provides a socio-cultural perspective on learning that both acknowledges and respects the rich cultural diversity of New Zealand. The fundamental basis of the Te Whāriki curriculum is the empowerment of children to grow up as competent and confident learners and communicators (Carr, 1999). It is a model which promotes that 'the context of a child's life is a critical factor in determining well-being, a sense of belonging, communication, a desire to explore, and contribution to society' (Nicholls, 2004). The principles of the curriculum are interwoven with five strands:

1   Well-being – the health and well-being of the child is promoted; their safety is of paramount importance.

2   Belonging – children are provided with an environment where the links to their family and wider society are affirmed and boundaries for acceptable behaviour are set.

3   Contribution – children are affirmed as individuals and know they can learn irrespective of age, gender or background – alone or alongside others.

4   Communication – children develop verbal and non-verbal ways of communicating; learn stories from their own and other cultures and can express themselves in a variety of ways.

5   Exploration – both directed and spontaneous play are given value as meaningful play; children become confident in their bodies; they develop strategies for learning about the world around them (Carr, 1999).

It can be seen how the Early Years Foundation Stage (DfES, 2007b) will parallel this international model. Furthermore Carr's (2001) learning story approach is being adopted by local authorities in their early years settings. This approach prompts practitioners to describe what children are doing, document it, discuss and make decisions about supporting each child's learning through to the evaluation of children's experiences.

A multitude of approaches

Many of these international models have been exported overseas – sometimes in their entirety, for example in traditional Montessori schools and Steiner/Waldorf schools; and sometimes different features of their structure and content have been combined or adapted to individual settings (Wood and Attfield, 1996, 2005).

> There has been much dissatisfaction with 'one size fits all' policy frameworks, with increasing interest in 'designer versions' of curriculum and pedagogy that are more in tune with children, local communities and the professional knowledge base within early childhood education.
>
> (Wood and Attfield, 2005, p. 123)

Educators need not only to have a good understanding of what, how and why these models are being adapted, but also need to be able to articulate this and be critically reflective and aware of their own personal values. All these models offer perspectives on aspects of both curriculum and pedagogy. The models prioritise them differently and the justification depends on the approach. The starting point for the Reggio Emilia model was giving children equity in planning their curriculum; Montessori planned a curriculum that first develops sensory then intellectual learning, and so on.

There are criticisms about elements of curriculum models (such as the aforementioned) adopted into different education systems, because when ideologies and/or practices are taken out of their cultural environment context and meaning can be lost. Protagonists and supporters need to examine which theories have importance and relevance to the children and their specific context and develop a deep understanding of the philosophies and pedagogies that underpin each approach. It is therefore important for educators to relate theory to practice and in so doing remain critical of their teaching practice. The next section explains the concepts surrounding curriculum, yet another complex area of education.

What is curriculum?

'Curriculum' can be defined in many different ways. In this chapter the approaches explored demonstrate that curriculum can mean any type of organised learning experience. Additionally, the definition and interpretation may even differ amongst educators. In a group of ten educators there may be ten different interpretations since it is a term that can encompass a whole range of meanings. It can consist of such dimensions as the educational curriculum, the total curriculum, the **hidden curriculum**, the planned and **received curriculum**, the **formal and informal curriculum** (Kelly, 2004). Can you determine aspects of these in the scenario on page 78?

What teachers think they are promoting is not necessarily what children perceive they are receiving. This teacher had probably planned an activity that promoted aspects of both physical

Hidden curriculum
Areas of the curriculum that are not necessarily directly taught but which are learned, such as codes of behaviour, unwritten social rules, or all the lessons that are indirectly taught by the school not necessarily in formal lessons; e.g. rules about time keeping, dress-code, etc.

Received curriculum
What children actually learn; what they actually take with them from the classroom and is remembered.

Formal and informal curriculum
The formal curriculum is the planned programme of objectives, content, learning experiences, resources and assessment offered by a school. It is sometimes called the 'official curriculum'. Informal curriculum is another term for hidden curriculum.

development for movement and gross motor control, how to participate in competitive games and how to work as part of a group, taking turns and sharing fairly – one of the early learning goal objectives in the Early Years Foundation Stage (DCSF, 2007a). Todd was enjoying the music and the dancing; he thought he was learning about freely expressing himself through movement. The hidden curriculum is to do with behaviour and children have to learn quickly what is expected and how to behave in educational settings. Children are at the heart of educational processes and educators need to be fully aware of all aspects of their provision. Cohen *et al.* (2004) propose that a full curriculum strategy addresses the following:

- context in relation to wider society
- purpose, priorities and principles
- breadth, balance and continuity
- progression, differentiation and relevance
- cross-curricular themes, dimensions, skills
- logic, sequence, organisation, resources
- indication of teaching and learning
- indication of assessment, evaluation and recording.

'Curriculum' has received many interpretations and definitions, and can encompass a whole range of meanings, which may differ from educator to educator. Curriculum models are socially constructed, composed by educators and politicians who have prescribed ideas and philosophies on how best to educate children at a particular moment in time. As Bruner (1974) indicates, knowledge about teaching, knowledge about learners and knowledge about knowledge itself need to be integrated at the point of delivery of the curriculum, since that is where the child and the subject matter converge. In planning a curriculum for young children from birth to 6

Ideas in action

Which curriculum?

Todd loved nursery, but one day he was subdued in the car on the way home and said in a very quiet voice, 'I was doing dancing and I like dancing and Mrs Kay told me to stop and sit down.' Grandma replied: 'Well, maybe it was just time to stop dancing'. Todd said: 'No, it was the music that stopped and we had to stop. And when she said stop I shouted NO [he whispered this quietly] and I was like Johnnie Smith – and I thought I'd have to go on the THINKING chair.' He had obviously enjoyed the dancing and had wanted to continue; he really did not understand musical statues. Grandma comforted Todd with, 'Children do get excited and sometimes shout out. Mrs Kay won't be cross with you.' Todd woke up the next morning worried about having to sit on the thinking chair. At age 4, he knew that this was a sanction for naughty behaviour. Todd wanted to conform, he didn't want to be in trouble or to sit on the thinking chair – it was a cause of concern to him.

Jean, grandmother and retired teacher

Stop and reflect

Try to imagine what it would be like if you were told to stop doing something you enjoyed without being given a reason. Is it possible that often our instructions to or our expectations of young children are misinterpreted? When working with young children try to empathise with them when identifying learning situations in your setting.

---

there needs to be consideration of its complex nature, and all of the experiences a child has as a result of the provision made should be taken into account (Kelly, 2004, p. 8).

Curriculum and pedagogy are by no means simple concepts and effective educators will develop professional knowledge about them through building theories, values and beliefs. Educators use their professional knowledge to mediate national policy frameworks and make informed choices about curriculum design and pedagogical approaches (Wood and Attfield, 2005). It is important that educators examine the beliefs and understandings about the curriculum and pedagogy they provide, whether it is the English National Curriculum, the English Early Years Foundation Stage or an international curriculum model. Just because educators subscribe to a particular model it does not necessarily mean that they are interpreting it appropriately. Critical thinking about curriculum and pedagogy can promote analysis and discourse, supporting a search for new understandings and self-awareness, allowing legitimate engagement with different perspectives (Kilderry, 2004).

It is the developmental curriculum model, underpinned by knowledge about psychological perspectives on children's development and learning that has been most favoured by early educators' provision in the UK (Alexander, 1995). This curriculum delivery has a **child-centred** perspective concerned with meeting individual children's needs through a **holistic** approach. It is based on knowledge and practice of how children develop, think and learn, which has been built upon principles and practice gained from the field of developmental psychology. There are many different interpretations of this complex and contentious concept of 'child centredness', for example whether it is child centred to let children drive their own learning, being allowed to choose what they want to do by following their interests through play; or catering for each child's individual needs or by the adult provision of 'developmentally appropriate' experiences. However, increasingly there are critiques of a curriculum based on **developmentally appropriate practice**

> **Holistic**
> Educating the whole person, i.e. not just the intellect but emotions and mind and body).
>
> **Developmentally appropriate practice**
> Practice based on what is known about how children develop taking account of age, social situation and emotional well-being.

(DAP) and whether the underpinning principles for DAP meet all children's needs. Many academics, researchers and professionals believe that DAP lacks a socio-cultural perspective, not least because it drives all children through the same stepping stones of development and also because it does not necessarily take their cultural experiences, family and community heritage into account. There are views that DAP can lead to educators forming a deficit view of children, if they cannot achieve according to statutory norms. The Early Years Foundation Stage (DCSF, 2007) attempts to avoid this in its central concept of a 'unique child', but the decision to extend an updated 'EYFS' profile to children from birth creates a concern amongst practitioners that once the guidelines are 'live' they may be forced into a situation where an outcome-based programme is applied to children from the earliest days of life. At the time of writing (late 2007) how the new guidelines will operate in practice remains to be seen.

You can see that there is more than one concept of 'curriculum' and so there are differing perspectives of what is appropriate for children's education. This can vary according to whether one takes the perspective of an educator, parent or policy maker; whether you are looking at the curriculum for early years, primary or secondary children; or even in which country you reside – be that a country within the United Kingdom, another European country, or a nation in Asia or Africa. As has been demonstrated, there definitely remains an ongoing debate about the form and content of the curriculum. The next section examines the debates that are ongoing about 'curriculum' in England.

The English context

A historical perspective – the Plowden Report

A brief review of history from 1967 will help you understand how education in England has arrived at the point it is today, show the direction in which it is heading and provide an explanation of why this is the case. Although 40 years have passed since the Plowden Report, it continues to receive mention in educational debates to this day. The Report is perceived to have had an impact on early years and primary education leading up to the Educational Reform Act in 1987. Alexander (2007: 194) reports that Plowden prompted changes that replaced the laissez-faire localism that has attended primary education in the 1960s England, with 'one of the most centralised education systems in the developed world, and since 1997, one of the most tightly policed'.

It was Plowden (1967) who coined the phrase 'at the heart of the educational process lies the child'. This gave rise to the affirmation of the child-centred approach. The report promoted play as the central activity in all nursery schools and said that it should be promoted in primary schools, as it 'is vital to children's learning and therefore vital in school' (Plowden, 1967, p. 193). The affirmation of play and of Piaget's work has had important implications for teachers and the Plowden Report relied heavily on Piagetian theories of children as active learners. Even though Piaget was not an educationalist, his observations on the sequence in the development of children's concepts were accepted. According to Jones *et al.* (2006, p. 44) 'it is undoubtedly Piaget's child development theories that gave play, particularly in the early years, its distinctive authority as a basis of evolution of learning'.

Whilst the Plowden Report promoted integrating the curriculum, using the environment, discovery learning and cross-subject teaching, it also criticised topics that did not address subject knowledge or were artificial or fragmented. Plowden was welcomed by many primary and early years educationalists with its advocating of child centredness, learning through play, first-hand experiences and collaborative working in groups. However, it has also been criticised for its reinforcement of Piagetian theories of developmental psychology and promotion of learning through stages that has underpinned early years and primary education in England. In Fleer's (2003) opinion this pedagogical practice of child centredness is a western view of childhood based on a historical inheritance of ideologies and taken-for-granted beliefs. 'Child centred' became an emotive phrase through media treatment in the early 1990s, implying inadequate, unfocused educational theories. Some politicians and the media suggested that the education of young children was in the hands of 'woolly-minded theorists' and 'post-Plowden progressives' (Blenkin and Kelly, 1994, p. 25).

However, it was rare for teachers in schools to provide a purely 'laissez-faire' approach or be 'radically progressive'. In Anning's (1998) opinion 'child centred' had often had an idealised interpretation; that many teachers of young children, in fact, taught a combination of cross-curricular work and discrete subjects. Several researchers found that Alexander's (1995) ideological category of 'liberal romanticism' was actually poles apart from many infant school teachers' practices, and that basic skills teaching occupied most of their time (Bennett *et al.*, 1984; Tizard *et al.*, 1988; Anning, 1991). Evidence from Tizard *et al.* (1988) and Bennett and Kell (1989) shows that children were sitting down to literacy and numeracy activities and that play-based and practical activity learning were perceived as having low status. Indeed, the extent to which play had ever become well established in reception settings was dubious (Broadhead, 2006b).

National Curriculum

The Education Reform Act in 1988 was the major driving force in the radical changes to primary education that have continued to the present day. The Government introduced a 'radical modernising agenda', which sought to impose a 'command and control' model of change, and introduced notions of 'performativity' in teaching and learning (Ball, 1999; cited in Wood, 2004). Robson and Smedley (1999) propose that the 'child-centred' approach had been interpreted as an idealised excuse for teachers to leave children to their own devices. Primary and early years teachers had determined their own curriculum to a large extent. Many taught knowledge through topic-based or thematic approaches, which would integrate a number of subjects. Policy makers believed that discovery-based active learning was an inefficient approach for children's learning and knowledge acquisition (Kelly, 2004). This concern formed part of the rationale for a more content-driven curriculum and the **National Curriculum** (NC) came into force in 1989 to offer the same education for all children in England irrespective of where they live. It was organised into four key age-related stages and had targets to be attained through level descriptors. It was intended to be a broad, balanced, coherent and continuous curriculum offering knowledge through core and foundation subjects (see Table 3.1 on pages 82–3). Whilst the content was prescribed for each of the subjects, the intention was to let teachers determine the pedagogy, that is, how to deliver the content. Gradually the subject-based structure replaced the **integrated topic approach**. In Brundrett's (2006, p. 99) view the NC, which at 'its inception was intended to be a general guide to the knowledge and skills required by pupils at different stages of their school career, rapidly became a complex set of directives about curriculum content'. The National Curriculum has been perceived as a '**technical rationalisation**' curriculum to create an educated, intelligent workforce that would encourage investment into the United Kingdom (Wrigley, 2003). In Kelly's (2004) opinion there was no theoretical or intellectual critique offered for the content-based curriculum. Unfortunately, whilst teachers in England affirmed the importance of play, they more often resorted to **didactic teaching** to deliver the subjects of the National Curriculum.

National Literacy and Numeracy Strategies

In the late 1990s the **National Literacy Strategy** (NLS) and **National Numeracy Strategy** (NNS) were introduced into primary schools. The Labour Government's

---

National Curriculum
The National Curriculum introduced in 1988 into state schools sets out the compulsory curriculum through the subjects and stages for children throughout primary and secondary schooling.

Integrated topic approach
Interconnecting several subjects within a curriculum into one topic to make cohesive 'human' sense to the learner.

Technical rationalisation
Reducing teaching and learning to specific skills and practices, so it becomes a technical process that teachers can be instructed to use on a national basis.

Didactic teaching
Teacher-led, direct instruction, where children are passive learners/simply take in information.

Ideas in action

When are we going to play? (Practitioner observation)

The transition from the early years Reception class in the Foundation Stage to Year 1 is huge. The children leave an environment where they can choose what they want to do, when they do it and how long they do it, where the activities are fun and can be lively. They then move into Year 1, where everything becomes formal. The children are given places to sit at desks and are discouraged from walking around. There are few play activities and children are encouraged to 'sit and listen'. Each school year, I hear the heartbreaking question, 'When are we going to play?' The pressure of achieving targets and results discourages many teachers from incorporating play into lessons. Some children have reached a maturity that, whilst they are not happy with this situation, they are able to cope, but many in the class have not yet reached that level. Some do not perform well and respond with hostility and confusion – they may be avoiding work. However, the issue is more that the method of teaching may be unsuited to their level of development. All too often I have heard adults observe, 'He/she is just ready to start in Reception'. This is often towards the end of the school year

when the child has been in Year 1 for a full year and reflects the child's yearning and need for play. Some of these children will be labelled as having special educational needs because they need extra help to complete the formal tasks set, but it is often because the teaching style is incompatible with their stage of development.   Selena, nursery nurse

Stop and reflect

Critically reflect on the transitions and learning experiences your students have on a daily, weekly, monthly or yearly basis. How much attention do you pay to the children's learning needs and in what ways do you promote play as you operate in the shadow of statutory guidance?

Transforming practice

Critically evaluate the provision in your setting, matching it to the stage of learning of the range of individuals in your setting. Identify areas where your practice and that of your colleagues could be improved to enrich the learning experience for each individual in your care.

National Literacy and Numeracy Strategies
Prescribed/structured teaching and learning activities aimed at instructing learning activities.

'education, education, education' pledge was the backdrop to these initiatives, 'aimed at raising achievement and highlighting the crucial importance of the knowledge, skills, attitudes and dispositions children have when they come into statutory schooling' (Taggert, 2004, p. 619). At this time England was near the bottom of the international studies/league tables for achievement and capability in mathematics. The aims of the strategies were to promote consistency, parity and equality for all children through improving the quality of teaching and learning, providing a

strong focus training and resources in order to raise achievement. They should have produced varied formats for delivery, yet actually restricted and narrowed educators' decision making. The strategies became part of every child's daily routine, imposing a single pedagogical formula on every primary school, classroom, teacher and child in England (Anning *et al.*, 2004). In Dadds' (2001) opinion this had a powerful national impact on teaching throughout all primary schools in England and radically changed many educators' pedagogical practices and children's learning experiences. Between them, the two subjects of English and mathematics had taken over nearly half of every school day and there was a concern that the Foundation subjects were receiving little attention, negating the broad and balanced vision of the NC.

Table 3.1 History and Continuum of Curriculum demonstrating the changes of Curriculum Models in England during the last 25 years

HMI areas of learning and experience (1980s)	National Curriculum (1988)	Curriculum Guidance for the Foundation Stage (2000)	Primary National Strategy (2003)	Birth to Three Matters (2003)	Early Years Foundation Stage (2008)
Aesthetic and creative Human and social Linguistic and literacy Mathematical Moral Physical Scientific Spiritual Technological	Core subjects • English • Mathematics • Science Foundation subjects • Art • Geography • Design technology • History • IT • Music • Physical education Religious education	Personal, social and emotional education Communication, language and literacy Mathematical development Knowledge and understanding of the world Physical development Creative development	The Primary National Strategy was to raise standards across the whole curriculum. It incorporated the National Curriculum; CGFS; 0–3 Matters; Every Child Matters; National Literacy and Numeracy Strategies. *Excellence and Enjoyment: A Strategy for Primary Schools* set out the vision for the future of primary education through a rich, varied and exciting curriculum	A Strong Child: me, myself and I; being acknowledged and affirmed; developing self-assurance; a sense of belonging. A Skilful Communicator: being together; finding a voice; listening and responding; making meaning. A Competent Learner: making connections; being imaginative and creative; representing. A Healthy Child: emotional well-being; growing and developing; keeping safe; healthy choices	*Early learning goals:* Personal, social and emotional education; Communication, language and literacy; Problem solving, reasoning and numeracy Knowledge and understanding of the world; Physical development; Creative development *Themes:* A unique child; Empowering relationships; Enabling environments; Holistic learning and developments

C O N T E N T

INTENTIONS					
These 9 areas defined by HMI (DfES, 1989) and endorsed by the Rumbold Report (1989) were widely adopted to inform curriculum planning in early years education. There was potential overlap between these areas and KS1 for continuity and to provide a breadth and balance of quality learning through play. It was a 'liberal' child-centred curriculum promoting a topic-based approach.	Introduced in 1988 after the ERA; revised by Dearing in 1995. Intended to provide a broad, balanced, coherent and continuous curriculum through statements of attainment and level descriptors. This subject-based structure replaced the integrated topic approach. It had specific principles for pedagogy to promote independent work, group/collaborative work, whole class interactive teaching. The intention was to let teachers decide how to deliver content.	The CGFS were developed from the desirable learning outcomes and were rewritten to early years educators' responses to a draft document. It firmly stated that the pedagogy was play-based and acknowledged parents, SEN, EAL. There were still six areas of learning, based on a programme of stepping stones leading to the achievement of early learning goals by the end of the Reception year. The Foundation Stage profile was to assess children's achievements of the goals.	Schools to develop their distinctive character, building on existing strengths, take ownership of the curriculum and develop excellence in teaching with enjoyment of learning through creative approaches. Tests, targets and tables to help every child develop their potential and measure school performance. A vision for 2020 was through personalising children's education.	*Birth to three* provides information on child development, effective practice, play and learning, planning and resourcing to meet diverse needs. The framework reflects the diversity of provision and promotes equal opportunities and relationships with parents. It recognises the contribution made to the development of very young children by the adults who care for them.	The EYFS (DCSF, 2007) brings together the 0–3 Matters framework, the CGFS and the *National Standards for under 8s Day Care and Childminding* in a single framework for children from birth to the end of the school Reception year. It is based on set principles and practitioners must ensure that the particular individual needs of all children are met.

Ideas in action

Issues of transition (Practitioner interview)

There is such a difference between what happens in the Foundation Stage and in KS1. In the Foundation Stage there is an emphasis on play, but in KS1 they have to do National Literacy and Numeracy Strategies and it's not a two-way magic door, they can't come in and out the other side once they've gone. The transition is so huge, to get to that point the children need more than being on holiday for six weeks. At the moment what happens is there's like a wall between us. We're protecting what we believe should happen to the children and on their side they're protecting what should happen for National Curriculum.   Marie, Foundation Stage coordinator

Stop and reflect

• How can knowledge about individual children be passed on effectively to other educators in your setting? In what ways do the systems support the intended purpose of such activity?

Transforming practice

• Think about children's profiles of learning: written observations, photographs of play experiences, samples of work, documentation of children's learning journeys, and so on, and how these can be passed on more effectively to parents or to the next setting or class.

The structured curriculum of NLS and NNS was perceived as the way for schools to achieve good scores in the SATs. Wood (2004, p. 361) argues that the strategies were policy driven, designed to challenge ideologies of progressivism, to 'radically change curriculum and pedagogy' and to 'drive up standards'. She describes them as 'high pressure policy levers' attempting to offer 'quick fix solutions'.

Curriculum Guidance for the Foundation Stage (CGFS)

In September 2000 the introduction of a Foundation Stage was described as a 'significant landmark in funded education in England', which 'gives this very important stage of education a distinctive identity' (QCA/DfES, 2000). The detailed curriculum planning guidance gave practical and illustrative examples of what might be expected of children at the different stages for children aged from 3 to the end of the Reception year. The curriculum was organised into six areas of learning achieved through developmental stepping stones (see Table 3.1). This QCA document clearly stated that

the quality of the aspects of teaching is informed by the practitioners' knowledge and understanding of what is to be taught and how young children learn; that teaching is a complex process and that there are different appropriate ways to teach young children.
(QCA, 2000, p. 6)

It promoted teaching and learning through a play-based pedagogy and was seen as reclaiming important principles and practice (Anning et al., 2004; Edgington, 2004). However, early years pedagogy is a complex phenomenon. Whilst the CGFS stated what a practitioner needed to do, most statements referred to the curriculum, and a number were actually pedagogically ambiguous (Moyles et al., 2002). The requirements of the CGFS were therefore over-optimistic for some early years educators, as there were expectations of them having a high level of subject and pedagogic knowledge (Siraj-Blatchford et al., 2002). This was because teaching in the Foundation Stage required educators to work in different ways and, if they had not been trained appropriately, it could be an 'unfamiliar and challenging territory' (Edgington, 2004, p. 81).

The CGFS was broadly welcomed because it emphasised the role and value of play in supporting learning at home and in educational settings (Lewis, 2002). It established the Foundation Stage of learning for 3–5 year olds. However, there were also criticisms of the Government's fragmented policy, which split primary education into three distinct phases and that was further compounded when the *Birth to Three Matters* (DfES/Sure Start Unit, 2002) guidelines was introduced in 2003. Moss (2006) voices many concerns, but particularly about the total of 68 goals in six areas of learning in a technical manual from which educators had to teach to and assess prescribed outcomes. In his opinion the language of the document was of formal education and preoccupied with what children can and will achieve, which was very different from what child care workers might have previously experienced.

In Moss and Petrie's (2002, p. 95) view the DfEE's mission statement 'investing in our future' on the front of the document implied a lack of distinction between care and education, which did not focus on children's and family needs. This specificity suggests a lack of confidence in practitioners knowing what to do, implying they have limited training for a curriculum that allows autonomy and decision making (Moss and Petrie, 2002).

Conferences held by the QCA during the early years of the implementation of the CGFS reported a number of concerns raised by educators delivering it in Reception classes. Early Years Development and Childcare Partnerships and teacher associations also had anxieties (Aubrey, 2004). In 2002 the DfES commissioned a telephone survey of 1551 head teachers and Reception teachers to investigate perspectives and challenges of the implementation of the Foundation Stage in Reception classes (Nelson Sofres *et al.*, 2002; cited in Aubrey, 2004). For this study professional telephone interviewers were employed and both quantitative and qualitative data collected. The study elicited respondents' knowledge, perspectives, experiences, attitudes and views about their practice and provision and found that the majority of head teachers and Reception teachers had a positive view of the Foundation Stage and the progress made in implementing it (Aubrey, 2004). The survey highlighted that the respondents' stressed the importance of staff qualification and training and a wide range of teaching strategies, based on children's diverse needs. Recent research by Tymms and Merrell (2007)

Ideas in action

Someone actually rang me up, doing a survey on behalf of the DfEE, all about the early learning goals. It was about half an hour over the phone. It was basically finding out how successful a Reception teacher thought the early learning goals are. I thought that was interesting. At least they want to find out what we think. Usually you find that teachers think this, you think, well hang on, nobody has ever asked me about it but they seem to be actually asking.   Uzma, Reception teacher

Improving practice

Use some of the web-based sources at the end of this chapter to investigate current research and development initiatives in your education system.

demonstrates that the 'best' teacher in a school should be placed in the Reception class, as this is the age that effective teaching has the most impact on children's learning.

Further studies at this time by Keating *et al.* (2002), Lewis (2002) and Garrick and Chilvers (2003) found that teachers welcomed the CGFS. The teachers in Keating *et al.*'s (2002) study were relieved that there was now a valuable and separate stage in children's education which acknowledged the importance and value of play. They felt they could return openly to what they felt to be sound early years practice, which some had felt had been undermined by previous curriculum guidance. Some teachers in the sample continued to express worries about the CGFS having so much curriculum content and that there were still too many constraints, but in conclusion the research team consider that the introduction of the Foundation Stage 'is the first step in what will undoubtedly be a long journey' (Keating *et al.*, 2002, p. 201). There are criticisms of the CGFS because of the way the guidance determines specifically the skills and knowledge to be learned and also makes assumptions that children's learning occurs in a straightforward sequential manner, which can be assessed and documented at pre-determined levels (Miller *et al.*, 2002, 2005). These issues may still be areas of concern with the new Early Years Foundation Stage.

The Primary National Strategy

The Primary National Strategy *Excellence and Enjoyment* was launched by the DfES in 2003 and renewed in 2006. It linked the Foundation Stage to this strategy to provide a continuum for both children and practitioners (Burgess and Miller, 2004). The aims are to raise standards by embedding the principles of both *Every Child Matters: Change for Children* (2004) and *Excellence and Enjoyment: Learning and Teaching in the Primary Years* (2004) for children aged from 3 to 11. 'The Primary Strategy encourages schools to use the freedoms they already have to suit their pupils and the context in which they work. The goal is for every primary school to combine excellence in teaching with enjoyment of learning' (DfES, 2007). The document focuses on the distinctive character of the school; excellent teaching; building on existing strengths; taking ownership of the curriculum; creativity and innovative teaching and leadership; using tests, targets and tables so every child can achieve their potential and school performance can be measured. The 2020 Vision Report of Teaching and Learning by the '2020 Review Group' (DfES, 2006) advocates the personalising of learning and teaching to take a highly structured and responsive approach to each child's and young person's learning. The aims are for all pupils to progress, achieve and participate through strengthening the link between learning and teaching by engaging pupils as partners in learning.

Building on the National Literacy/Numeracy Strategies, the Primary Framework for Literacy and Mathematics develops these further to 'reflect a significant development in teaching and learning in literacy and mathematics' (DfES, 2007). In Burgess's (2004) opinion the development of an integrated, whole curriculum is a complex matter that will require innovation and vision by primary school teachers. Teachers will need space and time to deliver a creative, broad and balanced curriculum, which was the original aim of the National Curriculum introduced in 1988. One problem could be

if teachers feel they have to pack even more into a busy school day and the pressures of working towards tests limits rather than broadens the curriculum. According to Burgess (2004) teachers have to address issues arising from the literacy and numeracy strategies before they can become innovative in their teaching. Furthermore, whilst teaching is felt to have greatly improved since the introduction of the strategies, there is less agreement about improved pupil learning. These concerns were supported by the evidence from research undertaken by Tymms and Merrell (2007) for an independent enquiry into standards of reading in English primary schools for The Primary Review (Alexander and Hargreaves, 2007).

In Chapter 6 you will see how Dodds, in her example 'A gift from Winklesea', demonstrates that an integrated approach is not only possible within a National Curriculum, but engaging for children.

Transition to Key Stage One

Early years educators sometimes have difficulty in convincing their primary school colleagues about their pedagogical approach to teaching in the early years. In Key Stages One and Two there are pressures to meet the demands of the National Curriculum, targets set by the local authority, SATs and the National Literacy and Numeracy Strategies. Keating *et al.*'s (2002) research determines that prior to the introduction of the Foundation Stage, which acknowledged the importance of play, many teachers had felt unable to justify learning through play due to the content-driven curriculum. Many local educational authorities are now tackling the issue and examining and reflecting on meeting the needs of 5 and 6 year olds through implementing a more play-based pedagogy and so making the transition between the Foundation Stage and Year 1 more fluent. However, whilst this is welcomed, it could be argued that educators face greater pressure to ensure that play is generic in their practice. Many teachers might not have received adequate training in appropriate play-led pedagogy, and may not be equipped to scaffold children's learning in ways that nurture their confidence and independence (Dowling, 2000).

Ideas in action

Case study: Katie's experiences from a trainee teacher perspective

Katie was a nervous child when she started in Year 1. Although she enjoyed playtime and ran around with other children, she was shy and timid in class, but could also be quite disruptive to children sitting near her. As part of my duties I supported Katie and three other children during their lessons – they all needed support and reassurance to complete the work set by the teacher. Sometimes the activities were laborious and I needed to adapt them to suit the children's individual needs, often by playing games. One week of lessons for the National Literacy hour was focused around the 'Farmer Duck' story and all the class had to contribute to making a book. The emphasis was on discussion rather than writing and the teacher was looking for teamwork and cooperation. I was concerned that Katie would not join in with the group discussions and I decided I needed a more play-based activity; so I created a small world farm for her group. Ideally I would have liked the children to create it, but unfortunately the pressure of 'fitting everything in' means that schools rarely involve children in creating play areas. The children were quite excited and immediately contributed ideas to create a story. I felt that it was important not to lead the play and I wanted them to support each other. I was ready to join in if necessary, using Pat the puppet, but as the children were playing well, all taking turns and storytelling, I did not interrupt them. They manipulated the small world objects, were actively involved and incorporated each other's ideas into the story to create their own version of 'Farmer Duck'. The children really enjoyed the activity and successfully 'published' three books.   Tessa, student teacher

Comment

Although I have always felt that play was an important feature in the learning process, I had not really recognised how few opportunities there were for 5 and 6 year olds to play in Year 1. With the pressure of school league tables and SATs results being published, schools have concentrated on the academic achievements of their pupils, often at the expense of personal, social and emotional development. I believe it is imperative that play opportunities are introduced as a means for learning in school.

Siobhan, nursery nurse

Stop and reflect

How are formal expectations being handled in your setting? How do these sit with the mission statement of your setting or your own personal philosophy?

Early Years Foundation Stage

In September 2008 the EYFS will become the new stage for Early Childhood Education and Care (ECEC) for children from birth to 5+. It is to be a single statutory framework for young children built upon established guidance in the *CGFS*, *Birth to Three Matters*, *Every Child Matters* and *Standards for Daycare* (DfES, 2007). Children's development is presented through six overlapping phases, acknowledging that there can be big differences between the development of children of similar ages (DfES, 2007). The emphasis is on understanding each child and their family as unique, with different needs and concerns. The *Key Elements of Effective Practice* (DFES, 2005) still underpin provision. The EYFS is built around four key themes: A unique child; Empowering relationships; Enabling environments; Holistic learning and development. Each of these is linked to a key principle, which is supported by four commitments. The statutory early learning goals establish expectations for most children to reach by the end of the EYFS and provide the basis for planning throughout the EYFS. 'All the areas must be delivered through planned, purposeful play, with a balance of adult-led and child-initiated activities' (QCA, 2007). Play is presented as developmental: at 16–24 months playing with other children; pretend play; playing with toys is presented as being important for learning; at 22–36 months physically active play with other children is emphasised and at 30–50 months children should have increased interest in joint play such as make-believe, construction and games with others.

Tensions about the policy documents continue. Moss (2006) finds the CGFS to be highly prescriptive and the EYFS even more so with 'over 1500 pieces of specific advice'. He views the EYFS as a technical manual with 'no democratic space' (Moss, 2006, p. 5), and believes that England has started a process of change in ECEC from a 'childcare discourse' to a 'pedagogical discourse'; 'the former representing a fragmented approach to services for children, the latter the sort of integrated and holistic approach to which the *Every Child Matters* policy aspires'. The DfES requested online consultation of the new EYFS and respondents had opportunities to make suggestions. Nevertheless, whilst many practitioners seem to be satisfied with the documents, discourse amongst researchers and academics seems to be less positive. All practitioners need to be knowledgeable and confident about the provision of play-based pedagogy, in order that they do not fall into the trap of becoming technicians, as suggested earlier by Moss (2006). This is why a depth of understanding is important, not only of knowledge of the principles, stepping stones and early learning goals of the EYFS, but also about the breadth and depth of play.

The Primary Review

The primary review was launched in October 2006 to answer questions about the impact of two decades of educational reform, analysing current practice and creating a vision for the future. It is an independent review, which published a series of 32 interim reports drawn from 'comprehensive surveys of published research' and on a range of evidence 'commissioned from 70 research consultants in 22 universities' (Alexander, 2008:1). In his keynote speech for a GTC conference, Alexander (2008:1), the Primary Review Director, reflects on the 'the larger issues' of 'wellbeing, equity, happiness, childhood, intervention, learning and empowerment' emanating from the Review. The Community Soundings reports (Alexander *et al.*, 2007) reveal the concerns of teachers, parents, children and communities and find

that 'today's children are under intense and perhaps excessive pressure from the policy-driven demands of their schools and the commercially-driven values of the wider society' and that the 'primary curriculum is too rigidly prescribed and, because of the pressure of SATs, too narrow' and that 'primary school children's educational careers are being distorted by the dominance of national tests' (Alexander and Hargreaves, 2007:1).

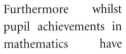 See also Chapter 11 Furthermore whilst pupil achievements in mathematics have shown moderately rising standards, research by Tymms and Merrell (2007) show that standards in reading have not improved since the 1950s. Positive moves forward in education determined by the Primary Review include personalised education, project work and listening to children.

The Primary Review challenges the view that an early school starting age is beneficial for later achievement, stating that it may actually be stressful for young children (Alexander and Hargreaves, 2007). The report compares the current state of English primary school curriculum and assessment with 22 other countries, including France, Norway, New Zealand and Japan. It determines that no other country appears to be so pre-occupied with standards, league tables and testing, which occurs more frequently and at a much younger age in England.

Critical reflection on curriculum and pedagogy

The curriculum needs to be continually scrutinised for both intended and unintended practices, in order to promote equity for all children. If such scrutiny lapses it is likely to become difficult to generalise when and which individual children may be advantaged or disadvantaged. As Kilderry

> **Critical pedagogy**
> An approach that attempts to help teachers or students question and challenge ideologies and practices that exist in education.

(2004) affirms, **critical pedagogy** promotes analysis and discourse, supporting a search for new understandings and self-awareness, allowing legitimate engagement with different perspectives. This is particularly the case with regard to play. You need to be

Ideas in action

I am keen for all my team to be involved in professional development. I give as much help as possible to allow them to follow their own interests, so that the children receive the best. I've come across people who are happy to do the same thing year after year and I don't think that's good for children. If people are being challenged and moving forward in ideas, then it's good for the children. We share our philosophy of how we're moving forward with parents and expect them to be involved too.

Joanne, nursery head teacher

Participating in ongoing and continuous professional development is important; this will be further explored in Chapter 5.

for the age range with whom you work or will work.

Look at the history and continuum of the curriculum in Table 3.1 and try to identify the key philosophies explored in this book so far and how these reflected government priorities at the time. If you were going to write a 'curriculum' for 2020 what would you include for children from 0–6?

Stop and reflect

Remember that you will never know everything about providing the most optimum curriculum and pedagogy

knowledgeable and articulate about justifying a curriculum and pedagogy that promotes play, not only to justify to parents and others that it is an optimum approach to learning but also to continually develop your understanding of the value of play. Educators need to engage with their curriculum and pedagogy and reflect on their practice through participating in ongoing professional development, as the head teacher affirms in the above interview extract.

A pedagogy of play

The value of play as a tool for learning has been challenging for teachers who have tried to link their beliefs about the importance of play with the reality of meeting curriculum demands (Keating *et al.*, 2002). There is doubt as to whether practitioners and policy makers sufficiently recognise and include play activities that capitalise on the complexity of learning potential in children (Broadhead, 2006). Broadhead (2004) argues that play is more than children's work, that it is their self-actualisation, a holistic exploration of who and what they are and know and of who and what they might become. Broadhead's (2004; 2006) research illustrates the complex learning processes children are

able to engage in through play. Her study resulted in the development of an observation-interpretation tool – the Social Play Continuum – a tool that can support the formative dimensions of observation and also detail children's progression in learning. The continuum informs the conversations and dialogues occurring between the adult and child and also supports practitioners' reflections on the observations that have taken place. Through using the domains as zones of proximal development it is possible for educators to examine children's language use, cognition and levels of cooperation. A key factor is therefore the quality of the educators' own knowledge, thinking and decision making (Bennett *et al.*, 1997; Broadhead, 2001, 2004, 2006). It is important that educators have flexibility to make their own professional decisions; many researchers and educators think that the National Curriculum and the strategies have discouraged flexibility. It is important that they examine their own participation, their part in the **co-construction** as well as children's contributions and the level of challenge being promoted.

Co-construction
When more than one individual is actively involved in the learning process.

Wood and Attfield (2005, p. 102) argue that children can learn and achieve in whole class, small groups and in individual situations through practitioners 'creating shared zones' for learning through employing 'pedagogical framing': '[which] involves making informed decisions about the structure and content of the curriculum and within this practitioners use a wide range of pedagogical techniques and strategies, supporting through teaching, playing, observing and assessing' (Wood and Attfield, 2005, p. 138).

The final section explores how play experiences can be capitalised upon to deepen children's thinking and understanding through promoting **self-regulation** and **meta-cognition**.

Self-regulation

Involves the individual child deliberately attending to, thinking about and reflecting on his or her actions.

Meta-cognition

The awareness of one's cognitive processes and the efficient use of this self-awareness to self-regulate thinking and understanding.

Self-regulation and meta-cognition in play

Play activities may help children to develop and refine their brain's **neural pathways**, through promoting cognition strategies when they memorise, organise and internalise their learning as they engage in problem-solving play (Meadows, 2005). Children can be taught facts and figures but they may not always remember or understand them. They are more likely to do so if they are embedded in meaningful activities, where they can be practised, applied and transferred to other contexts (Meadows, 1993, 2005; Wood, 1998; Wood and Attfield, 2005). In this way 'valuable formative play experiences may have some lasting effect on the ways in which the brain develops and the extent and efficiency of the neural networks' (Wood and Attfield, 2005, p. 68).

Neural pathways

The connection between one part of the nervous system and another.

Whitebread (2007) advocates that it is important to fully investigate what play is able to do. He is interested in the development of children's meta-cognition, their cognitive self-regulation and control. Guha (1987) reviewed examples from psychological research and suggested that such literature indicates that being in control is crucial for effective learning. This '**self-efficacy**' has a cognitive but also an **affective** component. Bruner's (1962) play experiments with 3–5 year olds suggest that 'instructed' children had limited ideas, failed tasks and gave up quickly, whereas children who directed their own play were more inventive, successful and persistent. As Parker-Rees (2000) argues, playfulness is fundamental to human learning and thinking. Whitebread's C.Ind.Le Project (2005) demonstrates how play, creativity and problem solving can be linked to meta-cognitive behaviour, through replicating Bruner's original experiment with taught and play groups using both closed and open problem-solving tasks. In play children create a zone of proximal development and establish a bridge between the real worlds of events and the symbolic world of thoughts and ideas (Vygotsky, 1978). Children can engage in '**meta-play**' as they define and orchestrate their activities (Wood and Attfield, 2005, p. 69).

If children are in highly structured situations there may be little opportunity to observe children in authentic free play, which raises implications for assessment. It is difficult to observe children's application of their knowledge and understanding if they are unable to demonstrate any independent learning (Chafel, 2003). Wood and Attfield (2005, p. 69) argue that 'a **transmission-acquisition model**' does not necessarily 'actively

---

Self-efficacy

Confidence to behave in a certain way – the belief that one has the ability to achieve.

Meta-play

Thinking about, communicating or reflecting on play experiences.

Transmission-acquisition model

A model of education that argues that the teacher needs to input knowledge in order for children to acquire knowledge.

Ideas in action

The development of these children as proactive learners and decision makers was certainly evident by the end of the project. They were now analysing and evaluating the events that occurred in the Forest. They told anecdotes and gave each other advice about what to do next. This stands in direct contrast to their performance at the beginning of the project when they were asking the teacher what to do next. We had to learn to take a step back to allow the children to formulate their own hypotheses and work strategies. This was not always easy . . . The children demonstrated that they could move on from the contextualised learning environment of the Forest and could discuss vocabulary and meaning in a decontextualised situation. They enjoyed engaging with the vocabulary and demonstrated their ability and desire to provide definitions.

(Brock, 1999, p. 46)

Improving practice

The research shows that we need to empower children's ability to make decisions, think things through collaboratively and reflect on their learning. It was not only a valuable learning experience for the children, but also for the teachers and students involved.

empower children to become self-conscious and self-regulating learners'. Brock's (1999) research in the 'Enchanted Forest' demonstrates the value of creating environments and experiences where children are allowed to be active problem solvers, required to negotiate meanings and then reflect on these with adults. This involves promoting children's meta-cognition about their learning and problem-solving activities, enabling them to develop knowledge and awareness about their learning processes.

There is a view that the over-emphasis on the importance of play in children's learning has led to some misunderstanding. Children are not just investments for the future. They have a right to freely chosen opportunities for play and self-directed exploration as well as structured play activities, rather than being made to follow a restricted or narrow curriculum (Gammage, 2006). Jarvis's (2006) research promotes the necessity of children having time to engage in rough and tumble play and voices concerns that the only regular chance many contemporary western children have to engage in interactive free play may be within the school playground. Jarvis's evidence from her bio-evolutionary theory and developmental research indicates there is a pressing need to provide opportunities for children to

You can find out more about this groundbreaking research in Chapter 7.

carry out collaborative free play activities within safe environments. She believes that such opportunities are as crucial to their healthy development and eventual adult competence as instruction in literacy and numeracy.

Play remains a contentious issue, namely the misunderstandings about the nature of play and its role in educational settings. These have evolved through political intervention, media perception, separation of care and education, as well as being a result of the different methods of training primary, early years teachers and nursery nurses. There are also ideological perspectives with polarised beliefs as to whether play should be freely chosen by children or structured to facilitate the delivery of knowledge and skills. Contemporary research and ongoing debates demonstrate how educators must continue to develop new knowledge and be able to articulate the complexity of curriculum and pedagogy. As can be seen they are by no means simplistic concepts. The child's education is seen as an interaction between the child and the environment, operating from a shared frame of reference between the educator, the child and his/her family (Moyles et al., 2002, p. 3). Childhood is important for its own sake, not just as a stage in the educational process – children contribute to society and add value by being children. Practitioners need to consider the importance of educating the 'whole child'.

Summary and review

There is international debate and reflection on the issues raised in this chapter through a socio-cultural perspective and the importance of theories in providing an equitable curriculum and pedagogy that meets all children's needs. This chapter should have provided you with an understanding of how children learn and why it is important to promote optimum learning experiences for learning through play. At the beginning of this chapter you were introduced to three key questions:

- What is meant by pedagogy and what do I need to know for practice?

Pedagogy encompasses practice and the principles, theories, perceptions and challenges that inform and shape teaching and learning and is a complex concept with varied contemporary definitions. As a practitioner analysing your own pedagogy you will examine your teaching and the methods, activities, materials and all other practical matters you provide to enrich the learning experiences of the children in your care.

This chapter suggested there is no single 'effective' pedagogy. Instead you must think in terms of a 'teaching toolkit' (your own knowledge of subject matter, the learner, the nature of social interaction and discourse, setting organisation and management, and how you monitor, assess and evaluate teaching and learning) that you draw from in your interactions with the stakeholders in your setting.

- How can international models influence my practice?

International models provide us with perspectives that we can draw upon to enhance our own provision. You have been introduced to several international models (Reggio Emilia, High/Scope; Montessori; Steiner Waldorf, Te Whãriki and the Danish Forest Schools) which will not only have offered you a fresh perspective on the learning of very young children but also some starting points for development in your own setting.

- What is meant by curriculum and what is the role of play within it?

You should have gained the following understanding:

- There are varied curriculum and pedagogical models that offer children varied learning experiences.
- Adults who work and play with children have an important role in making decisions about appropriate curriculum and pedagogy.
- Scaffolding children's learning is essential.
- Outcomes are built from experiences and process is crucial.
- Young learners' dispositions and self-esteem are inherent to learning.
- Cultural processes within families and communities play an important part.
- Children's diversity of heritage and experience need to be taken into account.

The centrality of play within education is key to these discussions. Wood and Attfield (1996; 2005), Anning et al. (2004), Moyles et al. (2002) and Edgington (2004) advocate that a child has a right to free play as well as structured learning and that this is of value in itself as part of the child's cognitive and creative development. It is therefore important to continue to examine the active debates that have arisen and still exist around the centrality of 'play' in a curriculum for children, not only for young children, but also for babies and children of primary school age. The next four chapters will examine these debates, taking you through a chronological journey of age phases from birth to 11.

Transforming thinking and practice: over to you!

This chapter has shown the complexity of the concepts of pedagogy and curriculum. Throughout modern history, many theories have been developed in an attempt to define the 'best' models for pedagogy and curriculum. Having read this chapter you will now be aware of how the English education system has developed, where it is now and the direction it is taking alongside international developments.

Questions for consideration

- Which curriculum models does your setting reflect? Can you identify one main approach or do you have a more 'eclectic' philosophy?

- In what areas could you transform practice and the thinking of others? Take your findings from one of the 'Stop and reflect' points in this chapter as your initial line of inquiry.

- How prepared are you to engage in the debates amongst early educators? How would you articulate this to parents, other educators and stakeholders?

Ideas for research

Practitioners need to ask the following questions to ensure relevancy to children's needs and the context of learning:

- In your setting how do you differentiate for a range of learning needs? Does this include taking account of the whole child (physical, emotional, gender and socio-cultural development)?

- Is there one element of the International perspectives explored in this chapter that you would like to develop in your setting? Develop your knowledge in your identified area by undertaking secondary research and then, working with colleagues, adopt an action research methodology by planning what it is you are trying to change, what you will do to make the changes, how you will implement them and how you will evaluate their effectiveness.

Further reading

Alexander, R. and Hargreaves, L. (2007) *Community Soundings: The Primary Review Regional Witness Sessions.* Cambridge: University of Cambridge Faculty of Education.

Broadhead, P. (2004) *Early Years Play and Learning: Developing Social Skills and Cooperation.* London: RoutledgeFalmer.

Bruce, T. (2004) *Developing Learning in Early Childhood 0–8 Series.* London: Paul Chapman.

Moyles, J. (2006) *The Excellence of Play.* Buckingham: Open University Press.

Siraj-Blatchford, I., Sylva, K., Muttock, S., Gilden, R. and Bell, D. (2002) *Researching Effective Pedagogy in the Early Years.* London: Institute of Education.

Soler, J. and Miller, L. (2003) The struggle for early childhood curricula: a comparison of the English Foundation Stage Curriculum, *Te Whāriki* and Reggio Emilia. *International Journal of Early Years Education.* Vol. 11, No. 1, 57–67.

Turner-Bisset, R. (2001) *Expert Teaching: Knowledge and Pedagogy to lead the Profession.* London: David Fulton.

Wood, E. and Attfield, J. (2005) *Play, Learning and the Early Childhood Curriculum.* London: Paul Chapman.

Websites – International approaches

www.highscope.org–High/Scope Educational Research Foundation
http://www.montessori.org.uk/Montessori St Nicholas Charity
www.foresteducation.org/Forest Schools Initiative
www.steinerwaldorf.org.uk Steiner/Waldorf
www.minedu.govt.nz/index. Te Whāriki
www.reggioinspired.com/Reggio Emilia
www.ltscotland.org.uk/earlyyears/resources/publications/ltscotland/reggioemilia

Websites – Policies

www.dfes.org.uk Department for Children, Schools and Families
www.**standards**.dfes.gov.uk The Nationals Standards Site including Primary National Strategy
www.**everychildmatters**.gov.uk/ Every Child Matters
www.ofsted.gov.uk/ **Ofsted – the official body for school inspection**
www.qca.org.uk Qualifications and Curriculum Authority
www.standards.dcsf.gov.uk/eyfs/ The Early Years Foundation Stage
www.aaac.org.uk National Assembly for Wales (2003) The Learning Country: Foundation Phase 3–7 years.
www.learning.wales.gov.uk/foundationphase

Born to Play: Babies and Toddlers Playing

JONATHAN DOHERTY, AVRIL BROCK, JACKIE BROCK

AND PAM JARVIS

I didn't realise children as young as Karla [2 years and 4 months] would be able to play with so much imagination. She makes endless pretend cups of tea, but the main thing is shopping. She puts something into your hand and when you ask where she is going, she replies, 'Shopping!' in a most indignant tone, as if you should understand what she is doing. She asks you what you want. You say, 'I'll have some bread' and she walks to the other end of the room, turns round, faces the wall, then turns round and comes back and puts something into your hand. She's into representation – using one object to represent something else.

(Freya, Grandmother, lecturer and teacher)

Introduction

Play, for the youngest children, is an important activity in which they make sense of the world around them, express themselves and form relationships with others. When children are playing, they are building the foundations of all future learning. However, whilst there is some acknowledgement by most parents, educationalists and policy makers of the importance of play for very young children's learning and development, there is sometimes a genuine lack of understanding of how it should be supported. This chapter offers both national and international evidence from eminent neuroscientists, developmental psychologists and early years researchers that demonstrate the richness of young children's play. Suggestions are made regarding how to provide enriching experiences for babies and young children in physical and social play, and why this is vitally important for early schema development. This chapter also questions how adults interact with babies – the appropriateness of the toys and resources that are offered, the language that is used and the attitudes that are displayed.

The human infant was historically viewed as *tabula rasa* – a blank slate that is vulnerable and dependent on others, driven by physical and emotional needs. Infants were perceived as passive learners shaped by the environment; however modern developmental and neurobiological research findings indicate that this is highly inaccurate. New technologies help us to observe, record and analyse the second-by-second behaviour of babies and new evidence has emerged from such research techniques, from neuroscience in particular, which provides startling insights that have gradually transformed the outdated view of the vulnerable, incompetent child to one of the infant and young child as a learning machine. Under-3s are active learners, equipped to make sense of the plethora of information that bombards their senses and, from the outset, they endeavour to become independent beings. A decade ago, Elinor Goldschmied's (Goldschmied and Jackson, 1994) reference to the youngest children as 'people under three' suggests that, from birth, we are people in our own right at a unique period in development, rather than occupying an entirely dependent stage, with the sole purpose of learning enough to move on to a 'better' lifestage in the future.

In recognising the very earliest years as a lifestage with its own integrity, the authors of this chapter aim to explore the competence and skill of under-3s as they enjoy experiences that also have the emergent effect of developing their physical, intellectual, social, emotional and linguistic skills. By the end of this chapter you should be able to answer these questions:

- How do we know that babies are fascinating, 'clever', active learners?

- What are the most positive, enjoyable and developmentally enriching environments and activities for babies and toddlers?

- Why are the first few years of life so important for cognitive, social, emotional, linguistic and physical development?

Children under 3 really do matter

These are exciting times to be involved in the education and care of young children. New research findings that recognise the child as an individual in his/her own right have had a significant impact on the creation of new legislation directly impacting upon children and

their families. There was no separate policy for children under 3 until 2003 in *Birth to Three Matters* (DfES, 2003), so it was particularly welcome that the Government's commitment to the under-3s was voiced as an assurance to 'develop a framework of best practice for supporting children between the ages of birth to 3' (DfES, 2001a, para. 2.19). This has now been superseded by a new set of guidelines which creates a new early years concept in England that combines care with education for the first time for children under 6: the Early Years Foundation Stage (DCFS, 2007) which 'goes live' in September 2008. This has created a new, very different 'key stage' for our youngest children, underpinned by an extensive framework recognising each child as a unique individual who has a right to enjoyment, play and individually appropriate learning experiences.

In 1994 the Carnegie Task Force Report specifically identified the 'critical importance of the first three years as being a crucial "starting point" on a child's educational journey' (1994, p. 4). Research informs us of the amazing capacity of young children (Trevarthen, 1992; Gardner, 1993) and how experiences in this brief window of time, conscious or otherwise, considerably influence later development (Eliot, 1999). Play is an effective medium for learning in the earliest years, since these are the years in which the foundation for later development is laid (Blakemore, 1998). With rapid advances in knowledge about this developmental period, the impact of the environment on this, alongside the quality of care and the play opportunities, it is proper that issues of education and care of our youngest children are properly discussed at the highest political levels.

Over the last ten years Government initiatives have set out to enhance quality provision for children. These have subsequently had considerable impact on children, families and the practitioners who work with them. The National Childcare Strategy, begun in 1998 in England, aimed to increase accessibility and quality of education and care in the early years. Early years development and childcare partnerships have been established to implement this in local authorities, and children's trusts were set up to integrate children's services across the various sectors. Early Excellence centres and over 900 neighbourhood nurseries were established in disadvantaged communities with the Government pledging to have a children's centre in every community in the country. There has been the creation of over 1 million child care places in the private sector and the provision of free part-time nursery education for 3 and 4 year olds. Sure Start programmes, now in all four UK countries, have the common aim of coordinating services to children and families and, in so doing, tackling poverty and social exclusion.

Over the past decade, a large increase in dual-income families has led to increased numbers in child care and nursery settings, which demands new knowledge and skills from practitioners working with this age group (Willan, Parker-Rees and Savage, 2004). Oberhaumer and Colberg-Schrader (1999) comment that:

Practitioners in today's early childhood institutions are maybe facing some of the most demanding challenges in the history of the profession . . . Profound and interrelated change in our social, economic, political and technological environments, combined with a fundamental shift in the nature of work and employment patterns, are impacting on the lives of children and families.
(Cited in Abbott and Hevey, 2001, p. 179)

The publication of the influential *Every Child Matters* (DES, 2003), the overarching document underpinning the Birth to Three Matters Framework, proposed a more coordinated approach to services, proposing that provision should be multi-agency and multi-disciplinary. The document's five outcomes are relevant to children of all ages (being healthy; staying safe; enjoying and achieving; making a positive contribution and economic well-being); however there is a special implication for children in the earliest years through the document's emphasis on early intervention, integration and improved support for parents and families. In England, the *Ten Year Strategy* (DES, 2004b) emphasised the need for a well-qualified workforce and high-quality services for young children and their families. The strategy raised the level of required qualification for those leading care and education settings for children under 3, with the aim that by 2015 all early years care and education settings will be led by graduate early years professionals. These aims were subsequently confirmed in the Children's Plan (DCSF, 2007c). In reviewing these and

other policy initiatives and a number of approaches to working with young children in this country and abroad, such as High-Scope (Hohmann *et al.*, 1979), Reggio Emilia (Edwards *et al.*, 1993) and Te Whäriki, (Ministry of Education, 1996), and from consultations with many groups and individuals, Abbott and Langston (2005) report the following findings from the research that led to the Birth to Three Matters Framework:

You can find out more about these international approaches in Chapter 3.

- Babies were found to be competent and skilful learners from birth.
- Early interactions with a knowledgeable, sensitive and responsive adult were central in early care and education.
- Anything that suggests a top-down model of early learning should be avoided, particularly the application of an outcome-based curriculum.
- Child-initiated, play-based activities should be at the heart of a combined care/education process between birth and 5+, promoting healthy social and emotional growth.

It is with due deference to the work of these authors and around these four important points that we structure our discussion on play and the under-3s in this chapter.

Play and learning for the under-3s

Throughout this book, as in many other texts, the benefits of play for children are quite rightly richly extolled. Yet it is only in recent times that its virtues have been researched and reported for very young children. Amongst many benefits, this has revealed a strong association with learning. Play allows babies and toddlers to learn about themselves and the world that surrounds them. They do not separate out playtimes from learning or other times. Their play *is* their learning and vice versa. Bruce writes of play as a 'learning mechanism' (2005, p. 131), one that fulfils a supporting role by helping children under 3 to develop, find out about safety

Ideas in action

The EYFS in action

Dawn is the coordinator of practice with under-3s in a children's centre that has recently been piloting the EYFS. She explains:

> Early years is like being involved in continual professional development. There is always change and you constantly have to rethink and examine what you are doing. We are informing parents about how the processes of exploring and learning through play are important – getting them to see that it is not the end product that is important. We are tuning into what the under-3s need. We have all areas of provision available for them that are appropriate for their interest and level. We are able to justify our practice but were a little worried about the generous amount of space we have and worried that Ofsted would think we had too much. However we got an 'outstanding' in our inspection so our provision feels well justified. Parents are children's first educators – it is so important to get them and the children's prime carers to support us, just as we need to support them and their children. We encourage parents to do different things. We piloted the EYFS and we like that there is continuous provision and principles throughout 0–5. We will be piloting the two-year-old grant – they will

> get funding for seven and a half hours of provisions per week, working with parents and visiting artists. The PICL – parents involved in children's learning – programme is about involving parents – they know their child far better than we do, so that we all tune into children's learning. We constantly review our practice.

Comment

The above description by the under-3s coordinator at an inner city children's centre demonstrates how she as a leader of a team of early years practitioners is able to articulate their provision. She has to do this for a wide audience of stakeholders – parents, staff, visiting students and teachers, as well as the manger of the centre and visiting Ofsted inspectors. Knowledge, professionalism and the ability to justify practice with underpinning reasons are so important in early years settings.

Stop and reflect

In your reading of the chapters in this book thus far, what professional development opportunities have you identified for yourself? How will the introduction of the EYFS impact on your future professional development needs?

and make healthy choices as part of living and learning. It helps them become competent learners who are able to make connections, be imaginative, creative and represent their experiences (Bruce, 2005, p. 131). There is a danger, however, that this association with learning may lead to over-zealous involvement from adults and an interpretation that play must always be planned and purposeful. However, tightly planned schedules for infants are highly likely to lead to narrow experiences that are at worst completely adult and outcome led, and conceptualised to provide ever earlier opportunities for assessment, in an anxious desire to measure adult-driven concepts of attainment. Clearly, in such a scenario, the child is invisible and it is the activity that dominates.

Manning-Morton and Thorp (2003) suggested that such a misguided view may have arisen from a lack of

understanding of early development. They cite Parten's classifications of play (1932), and the mid-twentieth-century model of young children's egocentricity, which gave rise to the view that young children are only able to play individually or alongside others and that they are incapable of cooperative play. Where exploratory play does occur, it was presumed that children were merely exploring objects and their properties, rather than developing any deep understanding of the world. This has resulted in the mistaken belief that babies do not play at all, and that toddlers cannot play 'properly'. Such a view inevitably causes problems and the setting up of inappropriate levels of expectation for the child.

Many practitioners report that the best examples of play with children under 3 are when there is a relaxed atmosphere of informality in which they as adults follow the interests of the children. There is of course an overall planned framework, but adult involvement is largely informed by a sound knowledge of development and a willingness to observe and listen to the child, interacting when appropriate, but allowing the child's own desire to explore and lead the play, an interaction that is referred to by the EYFS as 'sustained shared thinking'. **Playful learning** (Garvey, 1977) happens when children themselves select what they wish to play with and how they wish to play. An important feature of this is communicating that the mood is right to play. This might happen between an adult and child through the exchange of signals, commonly gesture and facial expressions (Trevarthen, 1998). It is not about intrusive adult intervention to move the child on to achieve a particular end product. There is no suggestion that when observing children playing their behaviours and development take place in any kind of set linear pattern or 'phases'. This very point is made by Rouse and Griffin, who tell us that 'such phases are not distinct, or an invariant sequence of play behaviour, they overlap and are part of a continuum of learning' (1992, p. 154). Related to this point is that children have individual learning needs according to the stage of their development. The needs of a 3-year-old child are different from those of an 18-month-old toddler. Holland (1997) gives a fine example of this from her observations in a day nursery describing how a leaf printing activity with children 3–5 years might be experienced quite differently by children under 2. Whereas the activity with the former age group might be set up to advance the children's understanding of the differing shapes of leaves, younger children will experience the same activity by putting their hands in the paint, dripping it off the brushes or floating the leaves off the table. Individual children also have highly individual development patterns within a broad window of 'normal' progress; in particular, it has been proposed that boys in general may typically be on a slower maturational trajectory than girls throughout the whole 0–18 year development period.

Playful learning

Having fun and enjoyment whilst learning. The experience is perceived as enjoyable by the learner.

Heuristic play

What does the play of children under 3 'look like'? This takes a variety of forms. Look for the 3-month-old baby contentedly watching the movements of the mobile at the side of her cot; the parent and 10-month-old infant enjoying a game of peek-a-boo together or boisterous 2½ year olds imitating each other bouncing on the sofa at home. One form of play very evident with the under-3s is heuristic play (Goldschmied, 1987), the term for the type of early exploratory play with objects such as boxes, jars and various types of containers. Here the children's focus is on discovery, finding out about the objects by manipulating them, filling and emptying them and putting things in and out of them. There is much 'natural' learning going on, much experimentation and no wrong responses to be measured. The adult's role in this play will be supportive and facilitatory – collecting a range of objects to stimulate the child, observing the play, and providing linguistic and practical support when requested by the child.

Eleanor Goldschmied pioneered treasure baskets and promoted heuristic play in response to her observations of babies playing with objects from the real world. She had noticed that everyday objects such as wooden spoons, saucepans, pegs and bottles particularly fascinated young children. In her research she discovered that babies could concentrate and persevere in their playing with these natural objects. She devised treasure baskets made normally from natural wicker containing functional objects easily found in the home environment, none of which were manufactured toys. Collectively the objects should promote a range of multi-sensory experiences through offering variety in size, shape, temperature, colour, texture, smell and taste. The objects can offer experiences contrasting concepts – hollow or solid, sweet or sour, rigid or flexible, full or empty, smooth or rough, and so on (Hughes, 2006). Goldschmied initially targeted babies from 6 months who were able to sit up without support.

There is much underpinning evidence for promoting treasure basket creation. Goldschmied and Jackson (2004) suggest that young children's concentration levels are higher when they play with the objects in a treasure basket than with manufactured toys. Babies should be allowed to choose which object they are interested in and encouraged to explore it in different ways – looking, touching, waving, banging, sucking (Goldschmied and Jackson, 2004). Sometimes their concentration would last for an hour, depending on the individual's curiosity. After reading Forbes' (2004) accounts of using treasure baskets with young children I was so fascinated that I created my own treasure basket the very next day. My basket contains a wooden spoon, fir cones, small glass bottle, wooden cotton reels, feather shuttlecock, large metal spoon, wooden rocking horse model, a dried lemon, metal potato masher, a cork coaster, ribbons, thick metal chain and plug.

Forbes (2004) demonstrates the challenge of offering treasure basket play, with observations gained through a video diary of the children's play over several weeks, and analysis based on the **Leuven Involvement Scale**. Heuristic play for toddlers offers an insight into how collections of objects can facilitate their first-hand experience of treasures from the real world, through exploring what they can and cannot do.

Once babies become mobile, the level of concentration in exploring objects in one place may diminish, as they begin to shuffle, crawl and toddle around the room exploring larger items, space and place. Heuristic play can also be promoted in this stage of development. Self-exploration is the key to heuristic play in which toddlers are able to engage in discovery about complex categorisation without any worry about success or failure. The resources can be organised into collections in small baskets, boxes or draw bags made of different materials – cardboard, cloth, unbreakable glass, metal, cork, and so on. Early experiences of exploring objects through multi-sensory play can advance children's thinking. Babies are the earliest scientists – they test and explore everything, often by putting every object in their mouths or by banging them on the floor. Through heuristic play a practitioner can explore the thinking and learning skills and the needs of young children (Hughes, 2006).

> **Leuven Involvement Scale**
>
> Ferre Laevers' Involvement Scale for Young Children is a process-oriented monitoring system – a tool for quality assessment of educational settings that looks at how 'involved' the children are in their work and their 'emotional well-being'.

Ideas in action

Alicia, a child development student, found that in her very small-scale research the majority of her 11 participant infants spent more time with the treasure basket that she had constructed than with a manufactured toy box. The contents of her treasure basket included items such as small metal candlesticks, feathers, wooden nailbrushes and chains. She recorded in her observations that one chain particularly fascinated 6 month old Harriet, as she passed it from one hand to another, putting it in her mouth, exploring it in a multi-sensory way for quite some time.

Figure 4.1   A treasure basket and its contents

The brain and neuronal development

The driving force for all development is the brain. Genes and the environment interact at all phases of brain development, and as increasing scientific discoveries have been made in this biological area the more evident it becomes that the experiences we have in

Ideas in action

We have a complete room dedicated to heuristic play. The room has lots of baskets, each containing collections of different objects made from natural resources – fir-cones, sponges, kitchen tools, glass bottles, wooden shapes. We look at what children are interested in. Children can spend a week in heuristic play with their key worker, who knows what they are interested in doing. The key worker can set up the room in advance with resources that the children are favouring at that time. If they have a particular schema they are exploring we can provide the objects and activities for them to do it. You don't need to say tidy up time to them, they just do it – they restore things to baskets and places as part of the play, they're tidying up, learning about sorting and categorisation, but to them it's just play.

Danielle, birth to 3 coordinator in a children's centre

Stop and reflect

If you were to create a treasure basket for your young learners what would you include? Carefully consider the rationale for the choices you make.

Improving practice

Consider ways in which you might integrate the use of treasure baskets into your existing provision. If you already use treasure baskets, evaluate their purpose and effectiveness.

---

infancy impact on our **neuronal** development. As Blakemore (2001) suggests, it can clearly be seen during early neuronal development that many examples can be found to support the proposal that nurture can mould nature. The phenomenal growth rate in the brain is unique to humans; the organ trebles in weight over the first year of life. At birth, simple brain structures are in place to meet the needs of the newborn, which are to feed, grow and bond with significant others. Higher order function improves rapidly after birth in what appears to be a genetically programmed sequence: neuronal connections are rapidly made in the **cerebellum**, which controls movement; in the limbic system, which is responsible for emotions and memory; and in the cerebral cortex, which is currently theorised to be the centre that controls purposive behaviour and rational thought (Eliot, 1999). The human cortex takes a long time to mature. Neuronal connection continues in human beings over the lifespan, but the most intense period of connection occurs over the first three years of life. The adult brain has over 100 billion brain cells called neurons, but it is the *connection* between such neurons, achieved by cells called **synapses** in what is

> **Plasticity/neuroplasticity**
> The lifelong ability of the brain to change as we learn or experience new things.

> **Cerebellum**
> The part of the brain that coordinates sensory perception and motor control. It integrates the pathways which cause the muscles to move.

> **Synapses**
> The junction between two neurons or brain cells over which information is transmitted.

> **Synaptogenesis**
> The formation of synapses that occurs throughout a person's life; it is greatest in early brain development.

known as **synaptogenesis** (Post, 2000) that occurs at such a fast pace during the early years. To use a computing analogy, babies are born with all the necessary hardware in place, but much of the connection ('software') is created via interaction with the environment during the 0–3 period. Babies are born with many more neurons than they need, and these are scrupulously pruned over the first years of life, with those that do not achieve connection dying back.

A good illustrative example of highly specific connection formation is that babies can discern every sound that it is possible for the human voice to make during their first 18 months. However, they gradually begin only to 'hear' the differences that they need to hear in order to decipher sounds within the language(s) in their immediate surroundings. This is why it is so difficult for those learning a new language after the age of 4 or 5 to speak it without an accent, as there are sound differences in the foreign language that we simply cannot 'hear'. Synaptic connection reaches a peak by the time children are between 2 and 3 years old, so much so that authors such as Gopnik *et al.* (1999) propose that the young child's brain is far more active and flexible than that of an adult. Rod Parker-Rees (2004) has a useful analogy for this, comparing the process to the development of paths and road networks across a landscape – the tracks most used are developed into roads or motorways, whilst unused routes become overgrown and fade. The destinations that are not visited become isolated and unconnected to other parts of the system, and as such they become shrivelled and redundant.

This sequence of neuronal development is determined by our genes, but the quality of development is shaped by what happens to us in our interactions with the environment. Every experience for babies – for example beginning to walk, talking, listening to stories, playing and enjoying being with others – excites the brain's neural circuitry and shapes the way the brain is wired and connected. Anxiety-provoking experiences early in life increase levels of the stress hormone **cortisol**, which can interact destructively with the biochemistry of the brain. Recent biological studies such as that undertaken by Sims *et al.* (2006) have shown the heavy impact that raised levels of anxiety have upon the developing human brain, via the raising of cortisol in the infant neuronal system. This has the potential to create ongoing problems for emotional regulation, by misaligning the biochemical mechanisms relating to emotion control in infancy.

> **Cortisol**
>
> One of several steroid hormones produced by the adrenal cortex, it is produced by mammals in situations of stress to increase metabolism of fats and carbohydrates in order to fuel the animal to run or fight.

Nature via nurture via play

Young children develop at a phenomenal rate in the years from birth to 3. This growth is interconnected and holistic – physical, social, emotional, cognitive and linguistic development advances at an individual rate, determined by a combination of **nature** (heredity) and **nurture** (environmental experiences). Play experiences provide gains in knowledge, skills and dispositions and enhance growth in all of these areas. There is unequivocal agreement from evidence from psychology, biology and recently from neuroscience that it is the interaction of heredity and environment that actively shapes who we are and who we will ultimately become. Genes provide the blueprint for

> **Nature**
>
> The inherited aspects of a creature's appearance, personality and intelligence.
>
> **Nurture**
>
> The environmentally created aspects of a creature's appearance, personality and intelligence. Theorists have continually debated the proportions of each of these qualities that are due to 'nature' and which proportions are due to 'nurture', with as yet no definitive agreement.

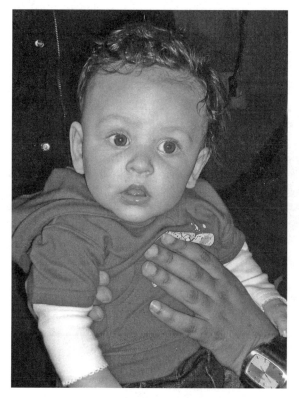

Figure 4.2 Mia (4 months) thinking

development through their role in the production of cell growth and in the development of the brain and the central nervous system. Genes underpin the **hard wiring** of the connections between the brain's regions, but the experiences we have fine tune these connections and allow us to adapt to our environment.

Factors in a child's environment influence how messages in the genes are put into action (Gottlieb, 1996); these include the family, peers, school and the wider community. Studying twins is an effective way of disentangling nature from nurture to some extent because the effects of genes and the environment cannot be separated for individuals, but they can be to some extent through twin studies (Doherty, 2008). It appears that there is almost an equal split between genes and environment in determining 'who we are', but there is much debate about exact percentages and some suggestion that percentages may vary according to different age groups (Petrill *et al.*, 2004). Identical or **monozygotic** twins (MZ) share 100

Hard wiring
The fixed inborn aspects of a creatures brain physiology

Monozygotic
Identical twins who share the same fertilised ovum and sperm, and therefore exactly the same DNA.

per cent genes, as both embryos develop from the same fertilised egg, which splits into two identical individuals, hence all identical twins are the same sex. Fraternal or **dizygotic** twins (DZ) are not identical as, in this case, the mother has released two eggs in one ovulation cycle, and both have been fertilised by separate sperm. The resulting individuals may be the same or different sex; in terms of genetics they are ordinary siblings, but the fact of being born together means that they share more experiences than different-aged siblings if they follow the typical developmental trajectory of being raised together in their natural family.

Dizygotic
Twins who begin life as two separate eggs fertilised by two separate sperm and therefore possess differing DNA.

What is revealed through twin studies can considerably advance our knowledge of the interplay between genes and environment. Identical twins tend to have very similar physical characteristics that go beyond the basic physical appearance (Plomin, 2002), for example speech and mannerisms are often similar (cited in Doherty, 2008). Personality traits such as sociability, attachment or anxiety can also be shared (McCrae *et al.*, 2000), and the biological evidence increasingly

Figure 4.3 Twins playing together

suggests that the basic 'setting' for such traits is biologically determined, although the environment then interacts with such 'raw material'. For example, the child who tends towards anxiety will become more anxious if s/he is raised in an unstable, stressful environment, but may become less anxious if raised in a calm, stable household.

Regardless of whether they are identical or non-identical, twins typically have a relationship that is rather more intense than the one that exists between different-aged siblings. This is particularly prevalent in the first years of life when they tend to be very much together, and such closeness gives rise to some very characteristic twin-shared play experiences, some of which can be used to illustrate the very competent and intelligent interactions of very young children at play.

Babies discovering and exploring

Peruse many early years textbooks that discuss learning and you are certain to read of the wisdom of early educators such as Piaget and Vygotsky proposing that children construct their understanding of the world around them through active engagement with their environment. In recent times, and mostly as a result of findings from 'new' sciences such as neuroscience, this same wisdom is applied to understanding how children under 3 years learn. Piaget proposed that thought develops from simple origins and eventually results in symbolic competence, which leads (amongst other things) to language. Vygotsky proposed that pre-linguistic thought was a very different type of thought (more like that of animals) and that the advent of linguistic ability created properly human thought. Babies *do* improve their knowledge, both theoretical and practical 'by doing', and if they don't get the chance to do this the potential can wither. It is now generally agreed that babies are already thinking about their experiences. Play becomes the vehicle to do this. Heuristic play provides many opportunities for problem solving, making choices and reaching decisions. Exploring the environment often takes place in a social/emotional context and, as we discuss later in the chapter, play behaviours help children learn about the contexts of social play.

Ideas in action

Baby twins at play

Charlotte is a teacher and parent to opposite sex twins and an older daughter. She was asked by the authors to reflect on memories of her twins at play when they were under 2 years old. Here are three of her memories.

When the twins were around 11 months old, we used to play the 'pointing game' with them – 'Where's doggy/daddy/mummy' etc. We were intrigued to find that when we asked where their older sister, Stephanie, was, they would both quite accurately point to her, but when Jon was asked 'Where is Jon?' he would point to Jessica, and when Jessica was asked 'Where is Jessica?' she would point to Jon. About six months later, when they began chattering, Jon used to call his older sister 'Stevvy' and Jessica 'the girl' (this didn't happen with Jessica, she first called her brother 'Don'). He did this until he was just

around his second birthday, then gradually began to drop 'the girl' and replace it with 'Jes-car'. We often wondered if he was seeing 'the girl' as some part of his own personality. Why it would happen with just him I still can't decide, unless it was something to do with a later (male) trajectory in social development.

When the twins were around 14 months I remember giving each of them a 'Fudge' finger while they were in their side-by-side twin buggy (old 'umbrella' design). Jon ate his quickly, while Jessica messed around with hers. At one point he turned to her and uttered a series of grunts. She uttered a louder series of grunts, while shaking her head briskly, and moved her bar of chocolate to the hand furthest away from Jon, and then extended her arm to its fullest extent over the edge of the buggy,

▶

holding the chocolate as far away from him as possible. They did used to grunt at one another from time to time, but I never got any clear example of a very abstract meaning being passed between these two babies except this once – it was fairly clear that he wanted some of her chocolate and she definitely was not going to agree to that!

About a year or so later, the twins were chattering quite happily (they were slightly earlier talkers than average, I think). I was at that point a home-based mum, as were quite a few of my neighbours, and the children in the street used to play together in each other's back gardens sometimes, while at least one mother watched over them. The little girl directly opposite had a father who was a building contractor, and at this point he was between jobs, so was out digging their front garden on a weekday morning. I seem to remember we had just returned from taking Stephanie to playgroup. Jessica looked out of the window and then said to Jon, 'Wot dat daddy doin'

home?' Jon went and looked, shook his head and made a tut-tutting noise, saying, 'Tut, tut, tut, dat daddy at home', and then they both started shaking their heads and tut-tutting. I thought at the time, maybe singletons *have* these sorts of thoughts, but they don't have a direct contemporary to share them with – that this two-way aspect of 'twinness' maybe opens a kind of 'window' in which adults can sometimes catch a brief glimpse of a small child's thoughts.

Stop and reflect

Have you had any experience or interactions with twins? Did you notice any unusual events or interactions? Perhaps you could organise a visit to a local setting that has some twins and observe their play.

Take a moment to ⏩ further explore the impact of sibling play explored by Jarvis in Chapter 11.

Ideas in action

Early role play (Parent's observation)

Rabia (aged 2) is really into role-playing mummy – she puts the dollies to bed, takes them for walks in the pushchair, undresses them, baths them and puts them on the potty. She's into role-playing mummy and family life. And drawing, she loves drawing; she's very creative. One thing I didn't realise that children so young as 2 could do this; she can actually identify things on a two-dimensional picture and she'll say 'shoes' and make marks over the shoes on the pictures. She draws endless pictures and draws lots of circles round and round. She does play with other children; she talks a lot about Danny and Ahmed with whom who she plays; a picture of a baby is always Sam. She can identify herself, Danny and Ahmed in photographs.

Sabila, Rabia's mother

Comment

The above scenario demonstrates how a 2 year old can undertake representation and role-play. Early years

practitioners should listen to parents as well as carrying out careful observations of the child and, by so doing, discover what the child is interested in at a particular time. In this way they can then support children's thinking and learning and discover which schemas they are currently exploring.

Improving practice

Examine the practices of your setting. Do you identify opportunities to talk to parents, both to share the experiences their children have explored in your setting as well as to find out what the children like to do at home?

Stop and reflect

In what ways is the approach outlined in this section 'good practice'?

Dispositions are frequently expressed patterns of behaviour and tendencies to respond in certain ways to situations (Katz, 1988). It is, for example, curiosity and the desire to find out that underpins exploratory play. Piaget called this 'intrinsic motivation'. The disposition to interact with other people and with tasks is indicative of long-term success as learners (Schweinhart and Weikart, 1993). Dispositions are linked to one's sense of likely effectiveness (Anning and Edwards, 1999). The challenge for adults who support young children's learning is to assist this development by connecting the *how* and the *what* to the *who* of learning and the relationships that support early learning.

There is evidence that learning takes place before birth and that children can recognise sounds they have heard in the womb; in particular, they show a clear preference for their mother's voice (DeCasper and Fifer, 1980). Memory, perception and attention are all cognitive processes, the bases of which exist at birth and before. Children are primed to explore their environments. This undertaking is a whole-body activity, using all the senses (sight, smell, sound, taste and touch) to find out about objects and people. Active interaction with the environment allows children to take in information and arrange it to form meaningful representations that are used to interpret experiences (Gopnik *et al.*, 1999). As they play, infants form expectations and theories of the world they test out first hand. Play provides many opportunities for them to ally previous experiences to current ones, to learn about cause and effect, spatial relationships, to plan outcomes and make predictions. Jennie Lindon (2005) believes that the behaviours of very young children show evidence of their thinking, planning and use of memory.

The play-driven development of schema-based thought

The pioneering work of Piaget that describes how children process information from their first-hand experiences underpins most constructivist perspectives on children as learners (Anning and Edwards, 1999). This section contains a brief overview of this area of theory. Piaget's notion of schema is a critically important concept in helping us understand just how our youngest children make sense of their world, although it must be stressed that his reporting on the ages in his stage theory are not completely accurate, and not fully culturally transferable. Schemas are concerned with the whole child, embracing the physical, mental and emotional aspects of development (Piaget, 1968). They are a mechanism for coordinating development and referred to later as 'biologically determined patterns in the way babies and young children behave' (Bruce, 2005, p. 70).

Sensorimotor development is the first Piagetian stage, and takes place between birth and 2 years. **Reflexive schemas** in the first month of this development are those unlearned, automatic responses to stimuli, such as a baby's grasping when the palm of the hand is touched. The primary circular reactions then follow in the period up to 4 months in which movement patterns, such as directing the hand to the mouth with some accuracy, are reproduced. Between 4 and 9 months, infants develop the secondary circular reactions where movements are initiated in order to make something happen, such as when a baby holds a rattle and by shaking it finds out that it makes a certain sound. Objects quickly become very significant for young children during this age phase. For example, the objects in treasure baskets (Goldschmied and Hughes, 1986) that were described earlier in this chapter encourage a variety of action responses in babies' play and early explorations. From 9 months to a year the coordination of secondary circular reactions emerges, when earlier actions are combined in new ways. Finally, from 12 to 18 months the tertiary circular reactions period begins, when we see much more playfulness appearing in the actions of the child, who is now able to be much more 'experimental' than before, and attend to the effects of what s/he is doing, rather than merely concentrating on each individual task separately itself as s/he did before. From 18 months on, a child is mentally able to attach labels to objects and events and thus to represent them internally. This heralds the beginning of what Piaget called the pre-operational stage, and is an important cognitive advance as internal models allow children to imagine what they might do, and

> **Reflexive schemas**
> How a baby assimilates stimuli in the environment.

105

to explore possible courses of action without actual movement (Parker-Rees, 2004). Symbols become very important to children at this age. Take, for instance, an infant copying the mother's expression of sadness. This act is more than merely repeating what is seen, the child is interpreting and reconstructing the facial expression and creating an internal image of what is observed. This type of imitation is frequently to be seen in pretend play too, for example pretending to feed or cuddle a doll. Everyday objects are used to represent others, say a hairbrush for a telephone. Children's imaginations and their actions are guided by the properties of the object. Under-3s need the extra prompt provided by objects, whereas in their pretend play 4 year olds can pretend with anything or indeed without any object. Symbols are also culturally specific, as can be seen when children kiss their parents goodnight, or wave goodbye to grandma when she leaves after a visit. As well as being a

rehearsal for future roles, such acts are also an initiation into a specific culture (Bruner, 1966).

In the United Kingdom, Chris Athey's work on schema, which she began in the 1970s, is especially significant. She emphasises how the biological (form) and the socio-cultural (content) paths combine in a unique way for each individual. (Readers are referred to Athey's seminal work, *Extending Thought in Young Children: A Parent–Teacher Partnership* (1990).) Building on Athey's work on schema development (1990), Nutbrown (1999) connects language and schema building in children's conversation, proposing that appropriate support from an adult can lead to deeper understanding and increased vocabulary. Bruce (1991) talks of schemas bringing order to the apparent disorder of a child's behaviour: an important point for parents and educators to understand is that there are underlying patterns beneath young children's apparently random actions. She also reminds her readers that past pioneers of childhood education knew about the concept of schemas. During earlier centuries, observations of young children by Froebel, Montessori and Steiner led to quality learning environments where schema-building play was central. Block play did and still does provide endless opportunities to arrange, rearrange, and create new combinations and new schemas. **Dynamic** and static configurations of vertical, horizontal, top, in/outside are enabled through such play. Heuristic play, including the use of treasure baskets (Goldschmied and Jackson, 2004) can very effectively support early schema development.

Ideas in action

Supporting early schema development

If children are interested in things turning round and round, we will provide different shapes and materials of wheels, cotton reels, slopes, etc. We very much believe in promoting positive behaviour – prevention is better than cure. We channel children's behaviour into something positive; we don't let it become a problem or disruptive to the other children. For example we had one little boy who was very into his trajectory schema and getting throwing things. We helped him to explore this in lots of ways, offering him challenges so that he did not become challenging. We gave him lots of things to throw safely in appropriate areas – soft balls, cotton wool, ping-pong balls, etc. We gave mum resources for him to play with at home and he worked through the trajectory schemas for several weeks then moved on to something else. We didn't have any tantrums, because we provide the right environment for him to naturally explore through play.   Chantal, early years practitioner

Dynamic systems
A system that works in interaction with other systems within the same organism or mechanism, each system regulating the other. For example the human body is a such an organism, and a car engine is such a mechanism.

Moving and doing: play and movement

The importance of movement for our youngest children is neatly captured in a quote by Hodgson who stated, 'Everything that we discover about life, we discover through movement' (2001, p. 172). A view of movement-based play as a way of children running off excess energy is to totally underestimate its potential for learning and establish a false separation between physical play that is active and learning that is sedentary (Parker-Rees, 2004). Physical development influences all other aspects of development: mobility, social and emotional relationships, self-concept on how one looks – communication with others, language, making friends, forming a sense of self. From their very first moments, babies communicate their needs and feelings and gain their first impressions of the world through movement. Movement in the womb provides information on the world and allows the exploration of that environment (Hannaford, 1995).

Movement enhances all aspects of young children's development. It contributes to physical development via strengthening heart and lung fitness and building strong bones; intellectually, it also contributes to the neuronal connections that are made in several regions of the learning brain – the basal ganglia, cerebellum and corpus callosum, as movement helps put ideas into action to accomplish a goal. Thus, when 14-month-old Ali sees the fluffy teddy bear in front of her she reaches out to grasp it. Her first attempt over-extends (the goal) and the second is too short, but on the third she successfully takes hold of the bear. Motivation combines with her current stage of perceptual, cognitive and physical development in her response to factors within the task, the individual and the environment that are essential to learning through movement (Doherty, 2008). Movement is also essential to the development of communication. Babies copy facial expressions and body movements of adults, and in so doing learn to connect with others and build strong relationships. Movement is an important part of the young child's emotional development, since it is a crucial way of shifting the brain's function from survival mode to higher order processing (Promislow, 1999).

In an interview for *Early Education*, Macintyre and McVitty (2004) discuss three reasons why it is important that children can move well. They propose, firstly, that moving underlies all kinds of learning. Whether this takes place in indoor or outdoor environments, learning involves knowledge of something or skill at something that was not possible before. Being able to show this new competence requires movement skill.

Being able to speak is a movement skill and it is the first piece of evidence used to assess children's development. Movement is also integral to later activities such as reading (that is, page turning that requires eye tracking, use of the pincer grip and crossing the body's midline) and early mathematics (that is, recognising, cutting out and manipulating shapes). Secondly, children want to be able to do what their peers can do, such as coping independently in the toilet and joining in imaginative games. The third reason is that if children are competent in their movement they are more likely to enjoy physical activity and will adopt healthy lifestyles and stay fit. That movement and physical activity are of central importance to children's lives is not disputed. Maude (2001) reports that 3-year-old children have the highest activity levels of any age in the human lifespan. They are constantly in motion, and to satisfy this need and to develop the large muscle groups of the arms and legs demands daily exercise. Physical activity has been found to reduce stress and anxiety (Dishman, 1986) and increase self-esteem (Gruber, 1986), as well as improve academic performance (Shephard *et al.*, 1984).

In order to survive, and for effective interaction with the world, infants must master three categories of movement or rudimentary movements (Gallahue and Ozmun, 1982). The first is **stability**, the relationship of the body with the force of gravity to achieve upright posture. Being able to balance is fundamental to many skills (Magill, 1988), is the first of our senses to develop and is vital for posture, movement and centring the body.

Stability
Relationship of the body with the force of gravity to achieve upright posture.

Secondly, the infant must develop abilities in locomotion as movement through space is dependent on this. Horizontal movement actions observed here include crawling (at 6 months on average) and creeping (at 9 months on average), through to achievement of upright gait and independent walking (between 10 and 15 months) and beyond. Standing is in itself a significant motor milestone but there is something unique about a baby's first steps and progress to the 'furniture walkabout' (Davies, 2003, p. 45) – a lovely way of describing the toddlers' route from one place to another with help, with strategically placed pieces of furniture that assist their locomotion. The third category is manipulation, which include the abilities to reach (at 4 months on average), grasp (from 3 months onwards) and release objects (from 12–18 months on average). This is also necessary preparation for fine motor and perceptual motor skills such as mark making, which has such significance when children begin formal education.

The first two years involves a high degree of adult handling as the baby alters from sleep to waking activity – picking up, putting down, holding upright and turning are just some daily movement experiences of babies. Movement researcher Mollie Davies believes this interaction with adults (parents) is a way of the latter passing on something of their own specific movement patterns and actions. She points out the mismatch between the levels of skill and variety of the adult movements and the unsophisticated movements of the children, but argues that this 'handling play' is an important part of the development of babies, giving them a 'rich vocabulary of movement' (2003, p. 34).

Piaget's work informs us that children's understanding of their world is grounded in sensory and motor experiences; in other words the very first pieces of external information that they need to take in and process from the external world in a direct way through the senses – tasting, seeing, hearing, smelling and feeling. Yet there are two other senses that connect with movement that are often overlooked but which are important to children's development and early learning. Firstly, **proprioception** is the sense that governs our knowledge of the body and body parts in relation to one another and, secondly, there is the vestibular sense, which is the sense of movement and our relationship to the ground. This provides reference points for where the body is in space. Movement can also reveal difficulties associated with learning. Poor foundations in proprioception reveal in children who fidget and are constantly on the move as if trying to get a better 'feel of themselves';

> **Proprioception**
> The ability to recognise movements in the joints that helps to assess where in the world the body is and how agile it moves.

while poor foundations in the vestibular sense result in poor balance and a dislike of movement activities or a tendency for excessive movement such as spinning (Greenland, 2006; cited in Bruce, 2006). Analysing competencies in early movement patterns such as in balance, coordination, body and spatial awareness, can form the basis for assessment that can indicate specific learning difficulties such as dyslexia (where there might be problems in sequencing movements), dyspraxia (where there are difficulties in organising motor output) or attention deficit hyperactivity disorder (ADHD) (where there are often problems with the inhibition of movement).

Physical activity play is the first and most frequent expression of play in infancy (Bailey, 1999). The phrase *infans ludens* meaning, literally, the child as a player, signifies the active, playful nature of young children's lives. Bruner expressed a similar view when he talked of play and physical activity constituting the 'culture of childhood'

> **Physical activity play**
> Play that incorporates physical vigour such as rhythmic play in infants, exercise play and rough and tumble.

(1983, p. 121). Bjorkvold (1989) warns that to disregard physical (and music) play in the lives of children creates a harmful and dispiriting tension. Play and active play is universal and bridges differences in social or cultural background and intelligence.

It is quite common for adults to work with young children to support their cognitive, social and language skills, but to subsequently be quite happy to send children off to play on a false assumption that their physical development will somehow look after itself. When adults do not respond or do not know how to respond to children's natural desire to move and play, huge opportunities for fun and learning are missed. In contrast, when adults value physical play and seek to provide for this, they open up a world of exciting possibilities where movement is central to progress in all areas of development. Active, exploratory inquiry into the environment can be readily seen in children's play. Learning to move and moving to learn are underpinning activities for the physical child and play provides a perfect medium. See the last section in this chapter on 'environments' for some ideas relating to the provision of exciting opportunities for physical play for children under 3.

Developmental movement play (DMP) is the term from the **Jabadao** National Centre for Movement, Learning and Health that describes an approach to physical learning in early years settings. This approach seeks to ensure that babies and young children establish the foundations for their futures by *playing* their bodies and brains into the best possible shape. The starting point of learning through the body by direct sensations and feelings acknowledges that sensory learning is the core learning experience between 0 and 3. It emphasises the importance of exploration to enhance neurological development; put another way: *being* a body and not just *having* a body. As children move and repeat movement patterns, the movements change until the pattern is complete. It is through their movement experiences that solid neurological foundations are built at the right level of functioning. Director Penny Greenland recommends (2006,

> **Developmental movement play**
> The Jabadao National Centre term for movement, learning and health.
>
> **Jabadao**
> A national charity that works in partnership with the education, health, arts and social care on developing natural movement for young children.

p. 164) a movement programme that includes the following:

- floor play – both on backs and tummies to increase the time in contact with floor surfaces;
- belly crawling – as the first self-determined travelling action;
- crawling – a combination of balance and travel;
- push, pull, stretch, hang and slide – as the foundations for proprioception, the sense that provides instant feedback on bodily actions;
- spinning, tipping, tilting, falling – to build the vestibular sense, that of balance and sense of space.

Findings from the Jabadao Centre's research (Greenland, 2006) projects have shown many settings now include child-led rather than adult led-movement play. Practitioner confidence has soared with many using movement play to build relationships with children; parents have been keen to become involved and gains in physical, emotional, social, language and cognitive development have been reported. This involvement of adults in early play was also observed by Davies (2003), who identified early **rhythmic play** taking place in the shared interactions between adult and child. In this type of play adults use various movement

> **Rhythmic play**
> Patterns of language or movement that are carried out in a rhythmic fashion.

Figure 4.4 Picture of floor play
Source: Bubbles Photolibrary/ Alamy

Impactive movement

Movement play between adult and baby in which movement starts away from the child and as the adult gets close the movement gathers speed and force, often culminating in the child being picked up by the adult.

Impulsive movement

Movement play between adult and baby in which movement starts strongly and gradually fades in speed and force to nothing, such as being lifted into the air and finishing being lowered to the adult's arms.

---

accents such as in games, for example where the adult is some way from the child and coming closer, gathers speed and force. The end result is a squeal of delight as the baby is picked up into the air. Such an example of **impactive movement** is often accompanied by nonsense word play. Another type of play Davies refers to is **impulsive movement** play – the opposite, which begins with the child held aloft in the air and movement gradually fades as the child is lowered by the adult with less speed and force. Children respond to this type of experience directly in a kinaesthetic sense and enjoy every minute of it.

Babies socialising and forming relationships

There is growing evidence from 'neuroscience, from longitudinal development studies and from population studies that the period of early childhood is crucial in establishing a child's self-identity, learning and achievement' (Gammage, 2006, p. 236). As outlined above, the past 20 years have seen exceptional developments in knowledge about how the brain develops, how genes and the environment interact to affect maturation (Shonkoff and Phillips, 2000, p. 182). A young child's early years are important, and language and physically active play are the keys to communicating, socialising, creating a self-identity as well as for learning about the world around them. One thing that really characterises children under 3 is their need to have close relationships with adults with whom they are familiar. They are born into a social world and are 'hard wired' to engage in activities that quickly develop their abilities to un-

derstand and respond to the feelings of other people. They need adults and other children to play with to develop their social competence. The ability to engage in social play is a key mechanism for early learning (Creasey et al., 1998; cited in Manning-Morton and Thorp, 2003). Such play experiences should be open ended to allow choice of playing alone or alongside another, as a key aspect of understanding others is extending one's understanding of oneself.

Although babies' language skills are limited, they can communicate quite well with others through the sounds they make, their gaze and by moving and touching. Their use of objects such as a rattle becomes a way of connecting to adults or peers near them and can form useful ways to introduce oneself to an as yet unfamiliar face, helping with confidence building, trust and social skills. The rate of their perceptual development equips them for our social world from an early stage. Surrounded by a host of other sounds, as outlined above, they are capable of recognising their mother's voice in the womb. Soon after birth, their developing sense of vision will allow them to track moving objects close to them and, importantly, to focus on features of the human face when held by a parent or carer. Young children are geared to be empathetic to the feelings of others and to communicate their emotions to others (Trevarthan, 1995). An ability to engage in social play is a key mechanism for early learning (Creasey et al., 1998; cited in Manning-Morton and Thorp, 2003). Rapid language development in the first three years provides them with an immediately powerful way to socialise with those around them.

Physical dependency is linked to emotional dependency. Adult–child relationships are an important consideration in the pursuit of providing high-quality play experiences. Babies build up an 'internal working model' (Bowlby, 1969) to understand their world and significant others in it. Schore (2001) emphasises how early face-to-face interactions assist here. Reduce anxiety and babies will feel secure; their view of the world as not a threatening place but as one of love and trust will support social competence, which in turn equips them to engage in social play (Creasey et al., 1998). Relationships are emotional bonds, and babies need to feel protected and safe. As stated earlier in this chapter, all the routines carers and babies are involved

Ideas in action

All introductory child development courses deal with the concept of object permanence, which was extensively studied by the psychologist Piaget. It is well known that he found that, until babies are around 6 months of age, they seem unable to comprehend that an object which is not in direct view has a permanent existence (for example Piaget and Inhelder, 1969). Babies' reactions to Piaget's tests indicated that once an object was gone from their visual field it ceased to exist in their thoughts. As babies move beyond the first six months, they are able to carry out a simple search for an object (such as lifting a cloth and looking underneath for an object they have seen an adult place there); but throughout the first year of life they can still be very easily confused into looking in the wrong place for an object that they have seen being hidden. Later research indicated that babies possibly have some innate ability to track the trajectory of a partially hidden, moving object (see Bower *et al.*, 1971), but the finding that infants clearly rapidly develop their schemas relating to the permanence of objects over the first year of life has been continually repeated over 50 years of developmental psychology research.

It is therefore interesting that adults and even older children seem to instinctively help to develop this skill in interactions with infants in a simple game that is played all over the world. In English-speaking countries the US name for this game now dominates – 'peek-a-boo' – but there are regional variations. For example, one of the authors remembers the Scottish members of her family referring to 'peep-bo'. As most readers will know, this is a very simple game where the adult hides her face in her hands, then the fingers are parted at variable speed so the adult can look through them and say 'peek-a-boo' to the baby, who will frequently smile or giggle, and when s/he is old enough, begin to imitate and play along, learning about the basic properties of a hidden object in an enjoyable social interaction.

Stop and reflect
Instinctive play? Peek-a-boo

Think about times when you have played peek-a-boo with young children. What are their reactions? Who wants the game to end first – you or them? When was your most successful peek-a-boo session and what made it so successful?

in – feeding, changing, dressing – are all opportunities for play activities and playfulness to occur. Physical and emotional dependency of children means the relationship of carer and child is central to any play experience (Manning-Morton and Thorp, 2003). Babies feel secure with someone who gives positive signals to them, is responsive to their needs and who tunes into the child's interests. This is the time to build the relationship and create trust, understand and respond to each other's motions. It is a time to share in the delights of everyday achievements or happenings and a time for the adult to get to know the child and vice versa. Most settings allocate a key worker to each young child in order to provide consistency in both care and in the forming of close relationships.

Whilst appreciating how important it is for adults to relate to young children for the reasons given, it is also important to appreciate that children relate to each

> **Attachment theory**
> A psychological and ethological theory describes how an infant can become attached to an individual with whom they spend prolonged periods of time, e.g. mother.

other. Strong early **attachment** influences the relationships that children have with other children. Friendship amongst peers is central to children's social development and competence (Doherty, 2008). Setting aside physical, cognitive and language limitations, babies are genuinely interested in others around them. Babies begin to form relationships with each other from an early age and they can recognise their friends, even look for them, when they go to day care or a neighbour's house where they expect to meet

See the box relating to twins' play above and the sibling play explored in Chapter 11.

another baby. The origins of social pretend play are present in the first year and children have the resulting abilities to share meaningful experiences with their peers from the earliest days of life. In the first year, this is seen by gesture, facial expression and mirroring of actions. Babies can connect in simple rule-based games such as peek-a-boo from a very young age, engaging in increasingly complex emotional and cognitive levels as they mature. This gradually develops into the ability to use symbolic representations and more complicated games with rules (Piaget, 1968).

Babies' communicative play

Language is crucial to young children's development and is not only important for communicating and building relationships with others, but also for enabling them to make sense of the world around them. Research in the field of developmental psychology shows that, from the earliest days of life, it is crucial to provide children with opportunities to engage in interactions, rich language environments and play experiences. The most important resources for young children learning to communicate are their 'caregivers', for example parents, other family members, paid or volunteer carers, key workers – as positive relationships foster self-esteem and confidence in talking and children are able to take risks and express their feelings (Manning-Morton and Thorp, 2003).

Children's understanding of language can be seen in the ways they learn to play with it in the early months and years of life. This language play is definitely seen in **infant direct speech** or **parentese**, which is the adaptation of simplified language by adults when communicating with very young children (Robsen, 2006). Adults adopt an adjusted way of speaking to the child, speaking in a high voice with slow, measured tones, which uses simple repetition and frequent questions to engage the child

> **Infant direct speech or parentese**
> The adaptation of simplified language by adults when communicating with very young children, which includes changing the tone of voice; altering words; using sounds; simple repetition and frequent questions.

more fully. They also respond to the babies' body language and physical cues (Selleck, 2001). Babies and children are active meaning makers, keen to make sense of the world around them, in fact they are impelled to interact through playful experiences (Wells, 1987).

Long before oral language begins, babies are using all their senses to play with us, to communicate with and to us (Forbes, 2004, p. 110). Language does not take place solely though talk and babies can and do communicate in many ways. Spoken language is actually very complicated, involving phonetics – the articulation of speech sounds through controlling air from the lungs via the larynx into the mouth, the movement and positioning of the lips, tongue, teeth, soft and hard palate. Whilst babies are listening and acquiring sounds and words, they will also be learning to communicate by using varied skills. Through observing and listening to what is happening in their immediate world they absorb patterns of non-verbal communication, which includes body language such as facial expression, eye contact, bending the head to listen, hand gesture and taking turns. They copy the facial expressions of adults and also mimic what they see and respond to the tone of adult voices. They wait their turn or, at times, take the lead in these interactions. 'These skills develop as babies and young children express their needs and feelings, interact with others and establish their own identities and personalities' (DfES, 2007b).

Bruner *et al.*'s (1976) research shows how a carer's role is important for a young child's language development through instigating games. Trevarthen (1998) goes further in suggesting that babies instigate the games and that adults mirror them, that the baby is in charge of play conversations and play without us being aware of it. They are pre-programmed to learn through all the means they have available. Conversation is actually a complex act of communication, but babies will be involved in turn taking in conversation from a very early age. Playing games such as peek-a-boo (see example above), where adult and child take turns, are important in learning about conversation strategies (Forbes, 2004). Adults scaffold their baby's language through interpreting what they might say or need. Throughout these early years parents and carers play games with the babies through repeating the sounds they make, and help to shape them. They model appropriate language,

Ideas in action

At 18 months, Ewan is the only child involved in the evening's celebration but he confidently engages in interactions with the adults in the room. No shyness here, in fact he held centre stage, not just because he could move at the speed of light to explore the familiar objects at his Nana's house, but also because he was requesting interaction from the adults. He is just at the stage of pointing to everything around – he is actually requesting the adult to supply the name of the object or person. He points to the lamp, the plant pot, a dragon, pictures in his book about a mouse hiding behind objects and to photographs on the wall of his daddy as a little boy, the dogs or his grandmother. This is all in the space of a few minutes. He seems inexhaustible, not only in his business, but also in his quest for new words and new understandings. Adults are there to answer his needs, and because he is so engaging and enjoying his 'word hunt' so much, they all oblige willingly.

Two weeks later Ewan was very excited when his baby brother was born, who at 2 days old was really fascinating for him. He pointed to his own nose, eyes, head and tummy and then his new brother's, comparing body parts as well as requesting the correct vocabulary labels.

Improving practice

Reflect on how you successfully scaffold the communication and language skills of the young learners in your care. In what ways could you make your practice even more effective?

Comment

Adults and other children are so important to scaffold young children's communication and language skills. They begin to 'soak' up the language and it is very important to provide them with a rich language environment. The box describing twins' play describes a common pre-linguistic pointing game that adults play with babies. When infants begin to speak they very quickly become able to convey a whole wealth of the meaning that they intend, with very few words.

providing words and extending the baby's contributions, offering them back in enhanced full sentences. Babies and young children listen avidly – collecting sounds and trialling these themselves (Brock and Rankin, 2008).

Everything practitioners do with babies and toddlers should involve conversation and non-verbal interactions, whether it is teatime, changing nappy time, going for a walk, shopping in the supermarket. Every activity provides rich opportunity for vocabulary to be

Ideas in action

Reflection point

Reread the scenario at the beginning of this chapter of Karla playing and the later one of Rabia and her friends. In light of your reading, can you identify why they are 'clever'?

Suggested activity

Carry out some observations of children under 3 talking and communicating in your setting, both to children and to adults, and then carefully analyse the language/communications they produce. Can you see how

they are also 'clever' in the same way that Karla and Rabia are, and how we could so easily miss such 'cleverness' if, because we are busy, we do not sufficiently focus upon what children are trying to say/communicate to us?

Improving practice

In light of your reflections, take stock of the practices in your setting. What opportunities and systems are there for a careful analysis of the language/communication of the children? How could these be improved?

modelled, for fun and humour to take place, for interactive and imaginative games to be played. Songs and rhymes accompanied by rough and tumble, body language, tickling, all send strong signals that verbal interactions are fun. Babies soon start to engage in vocal play – singing sounds, making engine and phone noises before they begin to be able to explicitly manipulate words (Crystal, 1998; Robsen, 2006). Garvey (1977, p. 69; in Robsen, 2006, p. 114) suggests 'three categories of spontaneous language play – rhyming and word play; fantasy and nonsense play; play with speech acts and discourse conventions'. Very young children begin to play games and cooperating in playing games can occur from 18 months. Dunn's (2004) research shows how friendships with other young children are seen through reciprocity, recognition and affection and that this occurs with very young children.

Babies also love **books**, and it is important they have access to them from an early age. Reading to babies and getting them involved in listening to stories and rhymes is one of the most effective ways of enhancing language development. Although the baby may not yet be able to understand the words or articulate formulated responses, clearly she is enjoying the experience. She is looking at the pictures and learning how to turn the pages. At times, looking at the book together may stimulate a response – gurgling or cooing sounds or an attempt to point at pictures on the page (Brock and Rankin, 2008).

> **Bookstart**
> Bookstart is the world's first national books-for-babies programmme, delivering free packs of books to babies and toddlers in the UK.

Environments for baby and toddler play

Indoor play

Environments reflect what we value for children. Goldschmied and Jackson (1994) suggest the idea of 'islands of intimacy' as a constant place of rugs and cushions where the key workers can give undivided attention to an individual or group of children. These areas promote physicality through organising resources at different levels to allow playing, sitting and standing, both indoors and outdoors, as well as time to practise skills. They also promote open-ended play experiences to allow exploration, attractive to both sexes and accessible for children with disabilities. This allows autonomy and choice, developing young children's self-concept, which affects their relationships with others and attitudes to new situations. A secure base provides both protection and safety with a child's desire need to explore. It balances inner trust and feelings of safety with a desire to be outgoing and independent (Liebermann, 1995).

Outdoor play

Outdoor play offers exciting opportunities for physical play and allows young children time and scope to acquire and refine their developing physical skills. Playing with wheeled toys is particularly helpful in the development of the stability, locomotion and manipulation skills outlined above. If children under 3 play with older children in such outdoor pursuits they can often usefully imitate their more highly proficient physical skills, and older children are frequently willing to provide usefully 'embedded' instruction in this area. Access to play spaces both indoors and outdoors are vital. Playing outdoors should not take place in the summer only – access to outdoor space needs to be year-round. What is experienced indoors can also be experienced outdoors. The early childhood educators of the past, for example Froebel, McMillan and Isaacs, were staunch advocates of outdoor provision. McMillan proposed that what children from age 1 to 7 years needed was ample space, 'to move, to run, to find things out by new movement, to feel one's life in every limb' (1930, p. 23). This point was taken up 71 years later by Perry when he proposed that 'outdoor play settings may be the one place where children can independently orchestrate their own negotiations with the physical and social environment and gain the clarity of selfhood necessary to navigate

You will find outdoor play examined in further detail in Chapter 7. In Chapter 6 you will also find examples of how children in the primary age range play outdoors when given the chance!

later in life' (2001, p. 118). One of the obvious benefits of play is how it can support children's physical development, as outlined above, yet this facet of such activity can become confused in some adult's minds with honing sports skills for competition.

The Pre-school Learning Alliance (1998) cautioned their play leaders that continually turning physical activity into competitive events is a risk for adults working with pre-school children. They propose that skill-based evaluations and competitiveness can easily undermine some children's self-confidence and spoil the pleasure in exploring physical development for its own sake. Elizabeth's story also gives us a further area of reflection: that such early experiences may set up a life-long dislike of such activities, which clearly has the potential to negatively impact on later lifestyles.

Ideas in action

Babies love stories

Josh was only four months old and was already having a wealth of story experiences. We were having lunch when I told him my own version of the story 'How much do I love you?' It is such an expressive story. Both the repetitive language and the way the story promotes a rise and fall of pitch and voice held his attention. Josh gazed at me intently with large eyes listening to the intonation of these phrases. I held his attention for quite a long time.

(Brock and Rankin, 2008, p. 26)

Stories at bedtime

Every night, when asked which story they wanted, the boys answered 'The Bear Hunt'. As I read it the two youngest boys act it out. They love the squelch, squelch, squelch part, and hide under the duvet at the end when the bear is coming after them. Even though they are just two and three they know the lines at the end where it says, 'We're not scared' and they anticipate and shout it out before I have chance to read it aloud.

(Brock and Rankin, 2008, p. 72)

Stop and reflect

Can you remember early favourite books or stories from when you were young? Why not collect favourite stories to tell and to read to babies and toddlers, or make up your own! What most simple songs and stories contain is a 'frame' (for example, 'Old MacDonald had a farm' or 'The wheels on the bus') that is repeated over and over, and a new 'nugget' of information inserted on each page or line. Once you have got the hang of this you can usually see that it is not so difficult to make up your own songs and stories.

Ideas in action

An indoor play environment for children under 3

The following idea in action takes the form of a journey around the provision for 0–3 with Holly, who is the coordinator for under-3s in this children's centre.

Our setting has a large space designated for them which is divided into large sections for rough and tumble, messy play, snack area, rough and tumble/movement area, role-play area. There is a multi-sensory room, with different lighting and soft furnishings. The sensory room is ideal for the under-3s, particularly if they are upset or missing mum. They can come into the sensory room and chill out. Children can choose when they want to come into this and we even allow them to be alone in here if they want – if they ask to be by themselves.

▶

The messy play area has a painting area, water trough and modelling cartons, and sand is on a tarpaulin. There is a natural materials tray for cornflour, dough, clay, gloop, soapsuds, cooked pasta, dry and wet sand. We explore the different vocabulary – slinky, silky, slimy, sticky, squeaky and swishy, and provide small utensils of sieves, pourers and ladles. Here is Kirsty, who has spent most of the morning painting – now she's painting on Sasha's (her key worker's) hands. Harris and Natalie have also been playing in here for quite a while with the bubbles in the water trough.

We have role-play, block-play, small world resources and home corner areas, all at young children's level and height, often with mirrors so they can observe themselves at play and what other children are doing.

We have a family playroom and a studio where we explore creativity with young children through a Reggio approach. You can see lots of creativity goes on here. There are bags of collections of materials, ribbons, feathers, tissues, streamers, wool, string, and lots of things hanging down from the ceiling. There is the mirror triangle where children can get inside and see themselves from different perspectives, as well as an overhead projector to both enlarge pictures and objects on the wall and to create shadows of the children themselves performing different movements. The laminated photos show lots of the activities that we have done with the children. Visiting artists come in often and work with children and families. We participated in the ART Project – this display shows the children having experiences with lycra and silk. We introduced the fabrics and asked them to imagine what it is like to be trapped inside ice. They drew with charcoal on large paper, describing it as being 'icy' 'cold' 'wet' and 'it's dripping'.

Holly, manager of under-3s in a children's centre

Comment

Forbes (2004) advocates that play spaces for babies and toddlers need to encourage physical movement and exploration. Tovey (2007) indicates that research evidence supports the close connection between design, use of space and young children's play. This children's centre demonstrates the excellent provision provided throughout all areas of the setting, promoting new artistic and creative experiences that challenge and excite the babies and toddlers, parents and the practitioners who work with them.

Improving practice

Take another look at ⬜▷ the international perspectives explored in Chapter 3 and identify ways in which you can promote the artistry and creativity above.

Review the provision in your setting. Do you employ the range of learning experiences that are evident in the children's centre above? What are the constraints you are under?

Ideas in action

Stop and reflect
The problem with physical activity as competition

I have always hated physical activity for as long as I can remember. I am what physiological research defines as an 'endomorph' [Budilovsy and Adamson, 2006], which means that my natural body shape is rather broad and unathletic, added to which I have

Endomorph
A heavy person with a soft and rounded body (dictionary.com)

an inherited type of near-sightedness that affects my eyes very unevenly (one has to have double the correction that is necessary for the other). This was not discovered until I was 7, by which time I had irretrievably poor depth perception. [This relates to the infant neuronal

▶

connection that you read about earlier in this chapter.] This makes me somewhat clumsy and very poor at ball games. I always did very well academically, so generally had high self-esteem in the classroom environment. However, this always plummeted rapidly during collective physical activities in childhood, both indoors and outdoors, because these events always seemed to be about who could run the fastest, climb or jump the highest, or excel at ball sports.

I still dislike physical activity to this day. However much I tell myself that yoga, aerobics or salsa dancing is not about competition, I inevitably seem to connect any issue relating to physical exercise to coming last in the egg and spoon race at nursery (and many other similar experiences in later childhood), or to being the one who missed the ball when our team was winning at rounders in primary school.

Elizabeth aged 42

How does physical activity make you feel? Do you share the opinions of Elizabeth or disagree? Is there a tension between what educators propose and the realities of life in the world outside educational provision?

Ideas in action

Creating outdoor play environments

Warren, a nursery nurse, talks about the outside area that he and his colleagues have created for their urban children's centre.

The outdoor area has provision that matches the indoor resources and experiences, but also particular areas for climbing, running and riding vehicles. The grassed area is on a slope so the 0–3s can gain experiences of running up and down hill. The concrete area has a dipped area that forms a natural paddling area when it has been raining. There is a landscaped area with tyres, tarpaulin, logs, autumn leaves and even puddles when it has been raining. The children can sit or climb on some old milk crates; we fitted steering wheels into them so the children can role-play driving. There are also garages with corrugated iron roll-down doors where the wheeled vehicles are kept, with parking bays outside. The children are able to select and return the vehicles. Today, Cameron aged 3 was in control of the roadway, driving round the group of adults in his vehicle, making engine noises and expecting to be taken notice of in a serious way. Some children were drawing on the floor on large cardboard pieces. Our concrete pathways have 20 different designs and textures, cat's eyes, dens, bamboo, willow weaving, obstacle course.

Improving practice

Both the above descriptions and the following observation on outdoor areas are examples of justifying provision to visitors to the setting. Bo-Foon, the under-2s cocoordinator at this setting, also talked about the outdoor provision:

We do not believe in confining our 2 year olds in small spaces. They need the space to run and explore. We have had a child who ran into a tree once, because her experiences of spatial awareness and freedom of expression had been so limited at home.

Do you feel confident you can justify your provision to stakeholders?

Comment

This early physical movement is so important for future development, not only with regard to physical fitness, but to knowledge and understanding of the world. A student who worked in an outdoor science project for primary school children recently told us that she dealt with children who had never got properly wet in the rain, or run until they were out of breath. One had told her that he was 'dying' because his breath was 'acting all funny' and was amazed to find out that it came back quite naturally when he sat down for a minute or so.

Summary and review

This chapter has introduced the complex and interesting arena of infant play, the importance of the first three years of life, and reflected upon how the quality of early experience can make such a difference to future development. Knowledge about very young children's development is crucial; it is the foundation of all learning, and the wealth of research and theory that has been referenced should have indicated both the importance and what is pertinent. You should now know about young children's brain development, the importance of appropriate resources including some useful arrangements of indoor and outdoor play areas, the crucial nature of communication and relationships, and how physical development fundamentally underpins a wide range of other developmental processes. The ideas in action examples have hopefully qualified the theories and given interesting examples of practice, demonstrating how theorists, writers, researchers, practitioners and parents, and even siblings, are all excited about their interesting and insightful infant learners.

Now we can reflect upon the questions raised at the beginning of the chapter.

- How do we know that babies are fascinating, 'clever' active learners?

We can see from the examples in the chapter that babies are interested and engaged learners from the start, learning quickly about the turn taking aspect of conversation, subsequently engaging in pre-linguistic interactions with their carers. Modern neurological research has shown us the rapid connections that are made in their physical brains, and we can see this in action in their behaviour through their rapid schema development, and how they gain understanding through interactive play with other people. The examples of play and communication between infant twins indicates that, beyond the crucial carer–child relationship in early infancy, there is also much to be gained in infant peer interaction. The 'lights are on' for human beings from the very first days of life, and it is crucial that carers recognise this and provide babies with rich resources and environments for their earliest play activities

- What are the most positive, enjoyable and developmentally enriching environments and activities for babies and toddlers?

The examples of activities and environments above should have given you some ideas that you can take forward into practice. The fast pace of neuro-physiological research will bring further insights as you move through your career, and as a professional in the field you should keep abreast of this, and try to incorporate new findings in your practice as innovatively as possible.

- Why are the first few years of life so important for cognitive, social, emotional, linguistic and physical development?

There is an old saying in English-speaking countries that 'first impressions count'. Those who care for babies are mediating these new human beings' first impressions of the world into which they were born. Such early experiences form the foundations upon which all subsequent development and learning are constructed; in this sense, the roles fulfilled by those who work with babies are the most important of all within the entire field of education and care. It has however been somewhat traditional in education and child care to presume that caring for babies is a fairly undemanding role that does not necessarily require professional knowledge, qualification or the insight to provide high-quality, varied experiences. We hope that this chapter might have created a very different picture for you, inspiring those who are just starting their careers to choose to work with infants and young children, and that it has provided accountability and professional acclaim for those of you already committed to working and playing with babies.

Transforming thinking and practice: over to you!

- Why not create your own treasure basket and, if possible, observe young children and babies play with the items in it. Engage in some reflective practice, evaluating the uses that they make of the items; then try a different range of items and note your reflections.

- Consider some other ways to support babies in heuristic play. One source of practice development lies in what is

termed 'messy play', the provision of safe tactile experiences for small children, for example supervising them in 'feely' play with, for example, cold jelly, 'crazy foam', a home-made gel created by mixing cornflour in water (you can add food colouring to add to the visual aspect). There are further examples in the indoor play Ideas in action box above, and/or you could add and test out your own ideas.

Remember, the task of the sensori-motor stage is to learn about the properties of objects within the world, and to develop the earliest physical competencies. There are so many potential play activities which can address these needs, that once you start thinking about this concept in earnest you will probably find it hard to select between different ideas rather than struggling to generate them!

Ideas for research

Designing and evaluating the contents of a treasure basket (as suggested above) comes into the arena of professional action research. You could also closely observe babies moving. Consider: how do they explore space? Observe their fine and gross motor movements, in particular, focus on how these rapidly develop over the first months and years of life. Relate what you observe to what you have learned about schema construction in the chapters of this book. You could also observe babies playing on their own, in their interactions with adults and other children. If you are able to watch twins or other 'multiples' in this type of play you will begin to understand how they sometimes 'mirror' each other's behaviour and appear to be more in tune with each other's presence than two singleton babies of the same age.

In terms of professional research activity, there is still much to be discovered about the developmental significance of early relationships between twins, triplets and other multiples, and this would be a very salient topic for a higher research degree.

Further reading

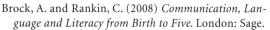

Brock, A. and Rankin, C. (2008) *Communication, Language and Literacy from Birth to Five*. London: Sage.

Bruce, T. (2002) *What to Look for in the Play of Children Birth To Three*. London: Hodder & Stoughton.

Doherty, J. (2008) *Right from the Start: An Introduction to Child Development*. Harlow: Pearson Education.

Forbes, R. (2004) *Beginning to Play: Young Children from Birth to Three*. Maidenhead: Open University Press.

Manning-Morton, J. and Thorpe, M. (2003) *Key Times for Play: The First Three Years*. Maidenhead: Open University Press.

Murray, L. and Andrews, L. (2000) *The Social Baby: Understanding Babies' Communication from Birth*. London: CP Publishing.

Websites

www.high-scope.org.uk.
www.ncb.org.uk.
www.childrensproject.co.uk

Playing in the Early Years: At Liberty to Play – Not only Legal but also Statutory!

AVRIL BROCK

As I entered the house, Grace asked, 'Have you come to play with me?' She asks this of every adult who visits. When I had to leave, she blocked the door so I couldn't get out – she wanted me to continue to play with her. Grace can't wait till her brother, aged 10 months, is old enough to play and communicate with her. Play is so important for her, and she takes it seriously.

Introduction

In Chapter 4 you were introduced to the importance of the first three years of life and the crucial role early experiences play in the development of very young children. In this chapter we consider children between the ages of 3 and 6 as we explore playing in the later years of the Early Years Foundation Stage in England. The key focus is on promoting play for learning purposes, not only to achieve the EYFS themes, but also to value play in its own right. The aim of this chapter is to encourage you to examine your perceptions of play for this group of children and, whilst the main focus is

embedded in educational early childhood education and care settings, readers are requested always to bear in mind the experiences, knowledge and values the children bring with them from home. This means not only having knowledge of children's individuality, culture, identity and diversity, but also valuing what new experiences children bring every day. Children do not only learn when they are in school or being directly taught by an adult; they have a wealth of valuable and interesting learning experiences during every evening, weekend and holiday.

The next premise is to acknowledge that young children are capable, confident learners and this chapter will ask you, as a professional, to reflect upon your own values, practice and underpinning knowledge. This is essential in order to promote rich and motivating play experiences that both you and the children will enjoy and value. The aim is to plant seeds of ideas that will become fertile and productive, resulting in you developing new and exciting challenges for play in your setting. As opposed to being presented into sections based on speci-

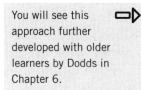

You will see this approach further developed with older learners by Dodds in Chapter 6.

fied areas of learning, this chapter promotes cross-curricular learning, drawing on authentic examples that have happened in settings. It

provides analysis from key theoretical perspectives with which you can 'grapple' in order to gain a critical understanding of this *simple* concept of play to balance alongside your own experiences. In so doing, you will be equipped to enter into contemporary debate about the complexity of play in the public forum. Many early years practitioners propose that the debates about the educational value of play derived from a lack of clarity about what is and what is not play (Riley, 2003). In order to understand why it is necessary to be knowledgeable of and an advocate for play, it is useful to have an understanding of the interconnection of care and education and why this has created contention about the early years of education. By the end of this chapter you should be able to answer the following questions:

- Do politics and national policy development really have an impact on the provision of play and why should this concern me?

- How do psychological theories influence my practice?

- What are children's languages of play?

- How can I create quality play opportunities for all children in the nursery and reception?

Early childhood education and care

Early childhood education and care is high on the political agenda. Yet, whilst there now seems to be international agreement that investment in ECEC is

important, the different approaches that countries have adopted means that, throughout the world, children's early education and care experiences can differ greatly (Gammage, 2006; Neuman, 2005). Some children attend full-day care from 6 months, some have state-provided pre-school, whereas others have no access to education or care experiences outside the home environment. Children therefore may attend different centres for different lengths of time at different ages and experience difference modes, quantities and qualities of ECEC. School starting age varies from 4 to 7 years across the world and children may be enrolled in school settings from the age of 3 or 4, whilst others do not commence official schooling until 6 or 7 years of age. Some in third world countries may never receive a school-based education, but may start work around their seventh birthday. Titles of provision embody a rich mix of traditions, values and understandings – *école maternelle*, *scoula dell'infanzia*, kindergarten, nursery, *förskola*, *crèche collectif* or children's centre.

Ideas in action

Stop and reflect

Do some internet research and determine the meanings and provision of these different early childhood settings.

Theorists, researchers and practitioners in the field of ECEC often define early childhood education from birth to 8 years, yet few early years settings in England would have children throughout this age range on roll. Most children experience at least two different settings over this period and possibly different educational and care practices (Saracho and Spodek, 2003). Young children may have their ECEC experiences in the private, voluntary or public sector in a combination of the following:

Childminder; children's centre; crèche; Early Excellence Centre; Foundation Stage unit; home environment; independent school; nursery class in school; nursery school; playgroup; private day care; Reception class; Special Needs school; SureStart setting (which may be situated in one of the other settings); workplace nursery.

Ideas in action

Vignette

The village playgroup is staffed by volunteers who either do it for love or 'because we are crackers!' Attendance is excellent and includes mums, dads, grandparents, babies, toddlers and young children, who all said it was the 'friendliest playgroup around. One grandmother came even though her grandchildren were on holiday that week! As it is in a rural area from which many people commute to work, families can be isolated, so the playgroup plays an important role in the community, offering support and advice, with strong links to the local authority's early years service. The coordinator observed how children feel more part of the community because the family is involved in the activities, and getting to know people in the village helps with the transition to school.

Definitions of child care settings, child care statistics and information on the number and type of child care providers registered in England can be accessed on the Ofsted website (www.ofsted.gov.uk).

Since 1997 parents have been able to access Ofsted inspection reports to determine the educational success of a setting, which can influence parents' selection. Parents choose their child's pre-school setting for a variety of reasons: children's happiness; the pre-school provider's reputation; proximity to home and opening hours; caring staff, good facilities; range of play activities; adult–child ratios; teaching of reading and mathematics; outdoor play area; or provision of information (Sharp, 1998). Foot *et al.*'s (2002, p. 189) research in Scotland about parents' choice of suitable provision for nursery-age children shows that they 'prioritise the safety and care of their children above all else' and that the type of provision can relate to 'education, setting, convenience and meeting parents' needs'. Similarly Dockett and Perry's (2005, p. 271) research in Australia indicates that there are 'some issues which seem to be of concern to most parents, regardless of their cultural or language background, such as parents' desire for children to be happy and confident at school'. Play does not seem to have an overly high profile in these studies and yet, perhaps it is implicit that this is what will make children happy? So what is important about children's early educational experiences?

Ideas in action

Children's observations

On returning home from school, Carys said, 'I left my concentrate at home, mummy.' She later said, 'School is boring, there's more work than play.'

'I haven't got time to go to school today, I'm too busy playing,' Rashid earnestly declared.

Jake had been so excited about going to school and joining his older brother Cameron. He loved school at first, but six months later he was crying that he couldn't do his writing, it was too hard to get it right. His mum said he set such high expectations for himself and he didn't like to fail.

Improving practice

Parents furnished me with the above examples of 4 year olds. All are very supportive of their young children's education. They know it's the key to success. Yet, first and foremost they want the children to be happy, and they expressed reservations about the demands being placed on these 4 year olds. As Anning and Edwards (1999) assert, children are unlikely to feel good about learning and to make academic progress if they are not happy and comfortable. In the week that I was writing the above, I heard that 60 children under 5 in England had been expelled from school!

Stop and reflect

Children's talk offers the practitioner a window into their thoughts and feelings. What messages do you receive from the children's observations reported above? Discuss with your colleagues or fellow students.

Early Education – a 'good start'

ECEC has become established in policy as advantageous for future educational achievement and employment, since a 'good start' in early education might be a way of compensating any negative effects of children's developmental context (Sylva *et al.*, 1994; Sylva *et al.*, 1997–2002; Villalón *et al.*, 2002). There is also growing evidence 'from neuroscience, from longitudinal development studies and from population studies that the period of early childhood is crucial in establishing a child's self identity, learning and achievement' (Gammage, 2006, p. 236). This, combined with the Labour Government's commitment to combat the number of young children living in poverty, led to it commissioning studies to examine effective provision. Very little large-scale longitudinal research on ECEC had occurred in Europe and the DfES-funded *Effective Provision of Preschool Education (EPPE) Project* (1997–ongoing) was the first notable study in the field. The project aims were to identify the following:

- What is the impact of pre-school on children's intellectual and social/behavioural development?

- Are some pre-schools more effective than others in promoting children's development?

- What are the characteristics of an effective pre-school setting?

- What is the impact of the home and child care history on children's development?

- Do the effects of pre-school continue through Key Stage One? (Sammons *et al.*, 2004)

Over 3000 children were involved from 141 different pre-school settings including playgroups, local authority or voluntary day nurseries, private day nurseries, nursery schools and classes and integrated educare centres in six English local authorities. They comprised advantaged, disadvantaged and ethnically diverse populations in urban, suburban and rural areas. Three hundred 'home' children, who had had no pre-school experience, were recruited on entry to Reception classes for a comparison sample. The EPPE research team studied the progress and development of children initially for four years using a range of standardised assessments and behavioural profiles until age 7

(Sylva *et al.*, 2002; Sammons *et al.*, 2004; Sylva *et al.*, 2004). The data were gathered through observations on children's experiences in pre-school, staff/child interaction, quality of settings and interviews with parents to determine home influences, health, education, occupation and the level of their involvement in their children's educational and play activities (Siraj-Blatchford *et al.*, 2006). The EPPE research team collected their data using a mixed methods approach including detailed statistical analyses of effectiveness and in-depth case studies (Siraj-Blatchford *et al.*, 2006). The study focused on areas relating to curriculum delivery, adult–child interaction, parental involvement, staff training and knowledge.

The key findings of EPPE indicate the importance and lasting effects of attending a pre-school; that the type, quality and duration of attending pre-school matters, as does the importance of parental involvement in young children's learning at home. EPPE stressed the importance of having well-qualified educators working in the early years and that this makes a strong difference to the quality of settings and achievements of the children. This parallels evidence from the longitudinal Competent Children project in New Zealand, which shows the continuing contribution of early childhood education to children's competencies at age 10, in that the children had higher average scores if they had three or more years of early childhood education (Wylie and Thompson, 2003).

EPPE was to be the first significant study in Europe to 'use an educational effectiveness design on sampling children in a range of different pre-school settings' (Sammons *et al.*, 2004, p. 691). The EPPE research team undertook observational assessments of pre-school practice and provision employing two research instruments as quality indicators: the Early Childhood Environment Rating Scale Revised (ECERS-R; Harms *et al.*, 1998) from the United States and the ECERS-E (E for English) scale (Sylva *et al.*, 2006), developed specifically in the EPPE study for an English context (Sammons *et al.*, 2004).

Since 1997, the government has made early education a high priority and a key objective is to develop children's readiness for school and so help them achieve educational success. As stated in Chapter 3, the Foundation Stage was introduced in 2000 for children from 3–5. Its aim was to promote high-quality early educational experiences through the play-based pedagogy promoted in the CGFS. In 2008 the EYFS framework will address provision for children from birth to 5 and aims to maintain and develop the education and care principles established in *Birth to Three Matters* and the CGFS. From where do these EYFS principles and commitments have their historical origins? In order to gain an understanding it will be useful to take a brief expedition into key psychological theories.

Ideas in action

Case study

Rating scales
Used to numerically quantify levels of attainment and/or environments, frequently in the form of 'scores'. In child assessment processes, this can mean comparing a child's actual level of attainment to a notional 'average level of attainment'.

Little Acorns Nursery uses the ECERS **rating scales** to evaluate the quality of their workplace nursery. The setting promotes a High/Scope curriculum and they actually find the ECERS-R more user friendly than the ECERS-E. They have high standards for all aspects of their setting and are hoping for 1s for their quality in all areas when the local authority inspects them. In contrast, Moretion Montessori school found ECERS-E to be rather limiting in their application, and that they do not take into account Montessori philosophy adequately and so miss important elements. The school found the results of applying ECERS-E produced quite different ones to those observed by Ofsted.

Influences of theoretical perspectives

Traditionally an understanding of early years practice has been developed through exploring the historical development of provision with reference to early years

pioneers such as Pestalozzi, Froebel, Montessori and the McMillan sisters. However, during the twentieth century the need for a scientific rationale for child-centred pedagogy drew on the study of developmental psychology. Throughout western societies provision has developed mainly from the theories of Piaget, Vygotsky, Bruner and Bronfenbrenner.

Piagetian accommodation and schema development

From the early 1950s there was a view, in both the United Kingdom and the United States, that Piaget was the principal contributor to the field of intellectual development. Piaget's study of psychological processes focused on the individual learner and his hierarchies of experience and knowledge were influential. The child as a scientist, researching the concrete world and coming to his/her own conclusions about its properties via the development of mental structures Piaget called 'schemas'. Piagetian theory proposes that cognitive development is the result of a child attempting to resolve conflicts to accommodate new understandings through building and refining schemas. In this way children can internally represent increasingly sophisticated understandings. Piaget saw the child as a hands-on experimenter in the concrete world.

Vygotskian 'zones of proximal development'

In contrast, for Vygotsky (1978) children's language and learning experiences develop through social interaction in cultural contexts, where their learning is guided, modelled and structured by adults or experienced peers. Vygotsky proposes that children's learning should take place in the 'zone of proximal development', which is the 'zone' or area that is actually beyond the level of the child's independent competence. A child is supported by knowledgeable others to move from their existing zone of actual development, eventually achieving within their future zone of development. An understanding of children's cultural and language experiences is essential for educators for

Olusoga examines ⇨ the ZPD in further detail in Chapter 2.
teaching and learning to be most effective. Vygotsky views language as the most powerful cultural tool possessed by young children, through which they not only talk and communicate, but also think and internalise their knowledge and understanding.

Brunerian 'scaffolding'

Bruner offers a synthesis of many aspects of both Piaget's and Vygotsky's theories (Harris and Butterworth, 2002). He further developed Vygotsky's ZPD through 'scaffolding', which describes the process of supporting children to become more competent (MacNaughton and Williams, 2004). Bruner's (1983) theory of learning is that young children learn by proceeding through three types of knowledge: **enactive representation**, **iconic knowledge** and **symbolic knowledge**. In other words, educators need to provide opportunities for children to broaden and deepen their **behavioural knowledge** through a variety of first-hand experiences. Similarly to Vygotsky he emphasises how culture shapes children's knowledge of themselves and that this is primarily transmitted through language (Harris and Butterworth, 2002). Bruner believes that play experiences provide opportunities for children to explore their world and engage in trial and error learning (MacNaughton, 2003).

Enactive representation
How a child stores memories from their past experience according to appropriate motor response, i.e. riding a bike – the actions are imprinted on our muscles.

Iconic knowledge
How the brain uses sensory images or icons to store knowledge.

Symbolic knowledge
Representing knowledge by ideas and concepts, symbolic knowledge provides an understanding of the interconnectedness of life experiences.

Behavioural knowledge
Enactive (physical) knowledge that is represented in the senses and is developed 'by doing'.

Bronfenbrenner's ecological theory

Bronfenbrenner's (1979, 1989) ecological theory provides a model for understanding human development – that children develop whilst interacting with their environment – socio-cultural context of the family, educational setting, community and broader society. Children act simultaneously within these different groups, the contexts are interrelated and all have an impact on the developing child (NAEYC, 1997). Bronfenbrenner's main concern has been how the settings surrounding the child operate and how the child is influenced by these systems. Bronfenbrenner (1979) saw children's own individual perceptions of their environments to be more important than what might be happening in reality. Teaching is developed through the adult endeavouring to interpret the learning situation from the child's perspective and consequently modifying their teaching approach (Fumoto et al., 2004). In this way there is shared co-constructing of knowledge rather than a one-sided transference of knowledge by adults.

Howard Gardner's multiple intelligences

Howard Gardner (1999) believes that the concept of intelligence is an outgrowth of accumulating knowledge about the brain and about human culture. Intelligence is a capacity that is geared to a specific construct in the world and draws on biological and psychological potentials and capacities. The intellect is the human mind in its cognitive aspects, which develops through constant and dynamic interaction between genetic and environmental factors. Gardner believes that education systems often limit the way children learn. He argues that children are not all the same and therefore cannot have the same kinds of minds. His theories are not an educational approach, but he argues that education works most effectively if these differences are taken into account rather than ignored. His multiple intelligences are kinaesthetic, interpersonal, intrapersonal, musical, spatial, logical-mathematical, linguistic. Some schools take account of children's intelligences when planning teaching and learning experiences. Planning for visual, auditory and kinaesthetic (VAK) enables children to learn and acquire knowledge, understanding and skills in multi-sensory ways, being actively involved in using seeing, hearing and doing to embed their learning.

Examining these theories will help you to gain your own perspective and understanding about what is important for young children's care and education. You can see that not only being involved with children from an educational perspective is required, there is also a need to listen to children and their families about what has importance for them.

Ideas in action

Stop and reflect

With a colleague or fellow student discuss some aspect raised in this section that is meaningful to you. Then select another aspect to discuss that you are having difficulty in either understanding or determining its relevance.

100 languages?

Children work hard at their play – this is what motivates them and they learn about the world through engaging in play, which is the context and vehicle that enables them to take ownership of that learning. You will need to promote a multitude of play experiences in order to engage children's interest, to promote active involvement and encourage experiential learning in both the cognitive and language domains. Children need an environment where they can practise, explore, think and talk aloud, with opportunities to talk in and beyond practical activities; where they are able to make mistakes and feel that their attempts and opinions are taken seriously (Brock and Power, 2006; in Conteh, 2006). Language is the key to developing young children's understanding, to enable learning to occur, so opportunities for talk are crucial. However, Malaguzzi purports that children have at least 100 languages through which they can communicate. Children express themselves in so many ways – through song, dance, music, art, socio-dramatic play,

Ideas in action

Jim would spend hours on one of his drawings at a very young age. As he got older they were always very complicated and highly detailed drawings of small people, creatures and weapons in landscapes of battlegrounds, chronologically moving from dinosaurs to knights in armour and then on to *Lord of the Rings* scenarios.

See Reggio Emilia in Chapter 3.
drawing, manipulating objects, climbing, modelling, constructing, and so on, and through play in all its forms.

Anning and Ring's (2005) research shows that boys prefer three-dimensional narrative play experiences featuring action, movement and speed, whereas girls immerse themselves in their mothers' stories about family life and histories.

Children's languages of play

Anning and Ring (2005) tend to lead us to rethink how what we do with young children reflects the communication systems for the future, that multi-modal communications, fluidity in thinking and acting are essential. We must not limit our expectations to the communication, language and literacy learning goals in guidance documents. In Flewitt's (2006) opinion there has been little focus on young children using non-verbal language in a systematic way to communicate their meaning and intentions. She opines that although EPPE used both verbal and non-verbal subscales as values for attainment, the non-verbal measures were considered to be useful only with reference to children's limitations with language. A socio-cultural perspective can offer more breadth and depth in valuing how children negotiate and construct their meaning in many and varied ways. Children use gesture, facial expressions, posture and eye contact in their communicative interactions. Flewitt (2006) advocates paying close attention to the multi-modal ways children can express themselves, for example: images, pictures and

Ideas in action

The following vignette shows how one trainee teacher's enthusiasm prompted a group of children in a nursery to take on the role of pirates – creating pirate outfits, designing treasure maps and going hunting for treasure. This dialogue demonstrates the thinking arising through talking about their drawings.

Sean: This is the pirate ship and I'm doing a shark behind the rock and the treasure. This monster is near the treasure, he's trying to dig and get it.

Jonas: I'm doing an octopus, 1, 2, 3, 4, 5, 6, 7, 8 octopus legs. Octopus is near the monster trying to attack and get the treasure.

Sean: I've done my map.

Megan: That's fantastic, Sean, can you tell me about it?

Sean: First you see the bear, then a giant, a whale, a shark, then a ghost and then you find the treasure.

Jonas: I've finished too.

Megan: Well done, can you tell me how to get to your treasure?

Sean: Go on here past the aeroplane and the monster and the octopus and the sun and the

moon with a hat on and the ghost and the treasure is where the purple cross is.

Comment

The children had been eager to create their maps and the boys in particular got very involved, showed a high level of concentration and were very focused. When Sean explained his map he got very enthusiastic; using hand gestures, body language and his voice was full of expression. We had attempted to promote activities that promoted equality of gender and diversity, but the children chose to be with same-sex partners and Summer told us, 'This is a boy's game.' Everyone had participated enthusiastically, but we reflected on this young girl's 'telling' comment. We would be more aware in future about making everyone feel inclusively involved.   Megan

Stop and reflect

Think of one activity where you have promoted equal gender interest and then another that you could have improved, and share them with a colleague.

diagrams (Kress, 1997); model making (Pahl, 1999); drawing (Anning and Ring, 2005); sign making and physical activity (Flewitt, 2006).

Pahl (1999) observed and recorded the meaning making of nursery children and recorded their story narratives in their socio-dramatic play and how they used a variety of objects for representation in their storytelling. She followed children's meaning making as they moved their play around the house and argues against children being told to tidy up, that they need the space to move fluidly and to weave in and out of adults' spaces. See the scenario on p. 128 – I know just what she means!

Broadhead (2003, p. 57) maintains that we need to elicit children's perspectives on play to gain more understanding of what they themselves hope to achieve

in their problem-solving activities. She raises concerns whether the Foundation Stage guidance and assessment documents 'can truly support educators in engaging with children's thinking and learning'. Her work demonstrates how difficult it is to clearly understand the complex social-psychological processes that are occurring and that educators often observe children's surface learning, get distracted by perceptions of 'messy play' and do not realise the depth of thinking in action.

Children can be creative in varied ways; they can approach play and learning differently and it is important that adults take this into account. It would be useful to read about Gardner's (1999) later research on multiple intelligences where he defines three further areas of naturalistic, spiritualistic/existential and moral; about Hannaford's (1995) brain gym and accelerated

Ideas in action

Scenario

Throughout my house I have quite a number of arte-facts – wooden jungle animals, rocking horses, ce-ramic creatures. This is unfortunate for dusting, but valuable for young children's play. Henrik and Kylie would normally collect them from all over the house and make corridors of animals that went in and out of the rooms. Matt created a jungle of animals and pot-pourri, Patrick a fantasy space scenario, Amy a Noah's Ark and Maya played and told fairy tales.

Stop and reflect

Observe children when they are engaged in their own problem-solving play. What can you do to gain under-standing of the complex processes? What are your views about '**messy play**'?

> **Messy play**
> Allows children to explore play involving different textures and resources without being labelled 'naughty', e.g. moulding clay and finger painting.

learning with children with special educational needs; and about promoting multi-sensory learning promoting learning in visual, auditory and kinaesthetic ways.

Creativity – what is it?

Many well-known educational thinkers and practition-ers such as Froebel, Montessori, Steiner, Dewey, Piaget and Bruner have strongly espoused the importance of creativity in education. The National Advisory Committee on Creative and Cultural Education (NAECCE) report (DfEE, 1999) entitled *All Our Futures: Creativity, Culture and Education* states that given the opportunity, to a greater or lesser degree we can all be creative. Recent thinking distinguishes between big 'c' and little 'c' creativity: big 'c' involves a break with current western cultural understanding such as Einstein's theory of relativity; in contrast little 'c'

enables individuals to find their own paths to travel, to be imaginative and innovative (Craft, 2000, 2002). In Duffy's (1998) view creativity means connecting the previously unconnected in ways that are new and meaningful to the individual; or as de Bono (1973) affirms, breaking out of conventional patterns to look at things differently. Creativity is fundamental to suc-cessful learning and is therefore important throughout life, not just in the early years. The CGFS and EYFS (QCA/DfES, 2000, DCSF, 2007a) reports show that creativity in young children enables them to make con-nections between one area of learning and another and so extends their understanding.

The problem with creativity, in Fisher's opinion (2004, p. 7; in Fisher and Williams, 2004) is that 'the concept is ethereal and elusive' and that people assume it is a 'type of thing' with essence or nature, but there are so many diverse definitions depending on the peo-ple, processes and products involved. What is clear to Fisher is that children need to develop both creative and critical thinking and that society needs children who will grow into adults who are capable of thinking and doing new things. Children who are encouraged to think creatively and independently become more interested in discovering things for themselves and are keen to explore ideas with other children and adults. In this way their sense of achievement and self-esteem de-velop. They require rich and varied contexts to acquire, develop and apply a broad range of concepts, skills and attitudes. Children should have opportunities through active engage-ment and problem solving. However, even after the investment in government-funded strategies such as *Excellence and Enjoyment* (DfES, 2003) there is still a widespread view that creativity is low on the agenda in England.

Look at how creativity is explored within curricular frameworks with older children in Chapter 6.

Developing metacognition

Anning and Ring (2005) believe that the kind of creative and imaginative play which was once a strong feature of UK nursery schools has been eroded and

Ideas in action

Scenarios about visiting artists

I couldn't immediately find the school where I was visiting a student on her second-year placement; it was in the middle of a large housing estate where it was easy to get lost. As I drove down a narrow street, there were some loud musical noises, which gradually got louder and louder and louder, as I approached the playground. The school had invited a musician, an African drummer, to come and work with all the children. They were having great fun beating out varied rhythms and tunes and demonstrating their aplomb at being burgeoning drummers! The staff joined in too and whilst there was a lot of noise, there was great concentration, fun and music evidenced.   Halle, lecturer in teacher training

In the next scenario Maggie Power, storyteller and dramatist, insists that World Book Day should be a must in all schools. She says, 'Just a little effort on the part of adults can open doors for all of the children.'

The children returned from lunch still in costume and some still in role. We again had spacemen, explorers and fairy-tale characters. One of the stories we dramatised was an Indian tale about a boy, Mahout, and his elephant. This was a story I had loved and used often over many years. I explained to the children that very special stories like this one, when read and re-read, live inside your head and your heart . . . They seemed impressed and could tell me stories! We constructed the story around the elephant's dilemma. He and his controller had been given a special job to lower a flagpole into a large deep hole, so that a flag could fly and celebrate the opening of a new temple. The elephant refused to follow instructions from the boy . . . even when threatened by a knife! He knew

something the others did not – at the bottom of the hole was a little kitten. He resisted all attempts to get him to act and the day was saved when a child came forward and looked down into the hole. There were so many children in various roles, but this time it was superman who was able to fly in and see that the kitten was trapped. The children were entranced and clearly enjoyed the telling.

Stop and reflect

- Have you ever been involved with an artist-in-residence or observed one working with children? What do you perceive to be the benefits?

- Explore, with colleagues, how you could initiate this in your setting.

Comment

Earlyarts is a professional development network for people working with under-5s across the north of England. It challenges practitioners to explore what good creative practice is and how to build it into daily practice. Smallsize is the European network for building knowledge about the performing arts for children aged 0–6 years. Its objectives are to share expertise and develop collaborative projects. Earlyarts and Smallsize collaborate in international conferences and exchange programmes bringing together community artists, education practitioners and policy makers. At the 2007 conference one nursery head teacher commented that settings often concentrate on meeting targets at the expense of creativity. The community artists' partnership project opened her eyes to relearn how to let the children lead!

that educators need to affirm the centrality of creativity in their thinking. Williams (2004; in Fisher and Williams, 2004) asks us to consider whether adult interventions are crucial to expanding creativity in play. He advocates stimulating children intellectually through one-to-one dialogues; probing questioning; getting them to analyse what works; engaging in philosophising and promoting their metacognition through reflecting on their thinking and learning. Through engaging in free-flowing exchanges children's

Ideas in action

Dad, an engineer, would take Sasha, aged 3, out on lots of trips and they took it in turns to ask questions. She would ask, 'Why does the tide go in and out? Why do the leaves fall off in winter? Why do the stars shine in the sky?' He would tell Sasha three or four times – this is what happens – and then ask her questions about it over the next few days. 'That steel in the harbour is called upper damming, the steel is corrugated and each piece interlocks with each other and it gets hammered down into the ground at the side of the canal. If boats go up and down the water pushes up against the embankment, but with the steel there it won't wear away.' The following day he would ask, 'What's that steel work called at the embankment? What does that do?' and support her burgeoning answers. He would then start on another topic that would arise through their shared experiences.

Stop and reflect

Sasha became a bio-chemist – how might these early conversations have influenced her choice of career?

Improving practice

Think about gender issues and play, don't undermine girls' interest in science and technology. Encourage them into the construction area by stimulating them with something they want to make. For example, get them to create village environments where story characters can live and inspire their constructions through providing problems. What suggestions do you have?

understanding is transformed, new insights develop and metacognition increases. Children need both free-flow self-initiated play and adult challenging interventions. As practitioners we need to understand how to resource, scaffold and discriminate between the opportunities children need for both self-initiated and adult-led play and to incorporate these in our provision for young learners (Anning and Ring, 2005).

At the age of 3 children start to ask questions; it's a natural stage in language development and they are active meaning makers (Wells, 1986). Children are curious, wanting to discover and make sense of the world around them. It is important to continue to develop children's 'enquiring minds' and to keep them questioning. Adults who ask closed questions often get short answers, so the use of skilful open questioning is crucial. What's happening? How does it look? What's going on? Children need their thinking skills continually challenged through their play, in everyday household activities and on visits. Developing memory is also key to learning about things and it increases capacity to learn about more things. Keep talking with children about general information in conversations and discussions. Don't underestimate children's capabilities.

Developing independent learning

Hendy and Whitebread's (2000) research findings demonstrate that whilst the young children in their study emerged as being capable of thought and judgement, the experience of schooling seemed to quickly dissuade them from independent action and towards dependency on teachers. In Hendy and Whitebread's view (2000, p. 251) 'when teachers are highly accountable for moving large groups of children through a predetermined set of narrow goals and targets – this is not conducive to developing independent learning, initiative and thinking'. They propose that helping children to learn how to learn is more likely to lead to higher educational attainment.

Play in the classroom

'Children do not make a distinction between "play" and "work" and neither should practitioners' (QCA, 2000, p. 11). This statement stands in contrast to Linklater's (2006) research, which showed that many young children in school contexts are situated in highly directed

Ideas in action

Case study

One Foundation Stage unit has a Developing Independent Learning (DIL) day every Friday to enable the children to be independent learners and thinkers. Previously, the staff had found that the children were always calling for help and found it difficult to make connections. The DIL day allowed the practitioners to work with children in smaller groups across the Reception and Year 1. Staff planned five key questions for literacy, numeracy, creativity, science and white board, staying with that activity all day whilst the children move around. All the basic provision activities are available and two of them are star activities that the children have to visit to be assessed for the Reception or Foundation Stage profile. The children develop independent learning through making choices about what they want to do. The main person is the 'negotiator', who monitors and directs everything. The children are always very engaged in their work and play, and there is a lot of socialising for both adults and children, which is not possible when you are teaching literacy hour or numeracy activities on a normal day.

Chloe, Foundation Stage coordinator

Stop and reflect

- Try to identify from your own experience contexts where developing independent learning is promoted. How is the success of such an approach ensured?
- In what ways can you plan how to provide this in your own practice?

teacher environments, where there is little time for deep interactive free play and 'there was little expectation that any learning achieved would be recognized and developed by the teacher or children' (Linklater, 2006, p. 75). Similarly, Murphy's (2004) research data suggests that, although the Irish early years curriculum of 1999 programme content and methodologies are explicitly child centred, senior infant pupils in Irish classrooms are given limited opportunities to be involved in play-based activities. Murphy's analysis of the patterns of interaction and activity show they generally remain teacher focused rather than child centred. This concern is also evident in school-based settings in England.

At the end of their training in university and teaching experiences in Foundation Stage and Key Stage One, groups of students in England created mind maps about the value placed on play they encountered in schools (see page 132). It can be seen that their observations of play in schools in their recent teaching practices bear out the points made previously. Often, both teachers and children do not think they are learning anything through engaging in play that is self-initiated by the children themselves. The belief seems to be that play is only generally valued when it occurs in a teacher-directed environment. This corresponds to Bennett *et al.*'s (1997) research that finds teachers' rhetoric about the provision of play in classrooms does not match the practice.

Use of observation for reflective practice

It is important to provide a supportive environment that offers children time and materials to engage in social play, to enable them to develop their 'social competence by allowing them the freedom, whenever possible, to construct their own social reality independently of teacher intervention' (Chafel, 2003). If children are in highly structured classes there may be little opportunity to observe them in authentic free play, which raises implications for assessment, as it can therefore be difficult to observe children's application of their knowledge and understanding without them demonstrating independent learning.

Figure 5.1 Ideas in action: students' observations

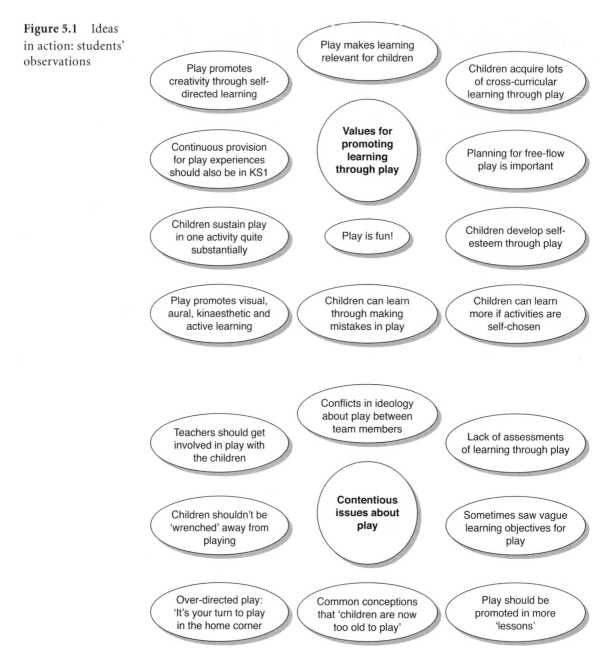

Play makes learning relevant for children

Play promotes creativity through self-directed learning

Children acquire lots of cross-curricular learning through play

Values for promoting learning through play

Continuous provision for play experiences should also be in KS1

Planning for free-flow play is important

Children sustain play in one activity quite substantially

Play is fun!

Children develop self-esteem through play

Play promotes visual, aural, kinaesthetic and active learning

Children can learn through making mistakes in play

Children can learn more if activities are self-chosen

Conflicts in ideology about play between team members

Teachers should get involved in play with the children

Lack of assessments of learning through play

Contentious issues about play

Children shouldn't be 'wrenched' away from playing

Sometimes saw vague learning objectives for play

Over-directed play: 'It's your turn to play in the home corner

Common conceptions that 'children are now too old to play'

Play should be promoted in more 'lessons'

Educators of young children acknowledge the importance of observing children and they believe ongoing assessments are a crucial part of their role that informs their practice and provision. When you really observe children playing what they are doing makes more sense, and appears more 'educational' in the broad sense of the word. Using video to observe children's learning can provide more depth of observation and assessment of what is really happening in children's play (Brock, 2004). It can 'reveal the multimodal dynamism of classroom interaction, giving new insights into how children and adults co-ordinate different modes as they negotiate and jointly construct meanings' (Flewitt, 2006, p. 29).

Ideas in action

This nursery nurse reflects on her Foundation Stage unit's provision in a video-reflective dialogue. The children have free choice first thing every morning for 20 minutes and she wanted to determine its effectiveness. You can see her analysis and enjoyment as she recounts the children's capabilities.

We realised that the children needed time for free play in the morning, so we set up the activities on each table with the sand, water and home corner. I filmed them to see in which areas they would choose to play. A group of boisterous boys went straight to the sand. They were talking to each other in their home language, discussing what they were doing, playing cooperatively and sharing the equipment. To my surprise, they included Sohail in their activities. He is a loner and his English is limited, which knocks his confidence. I thought the boys were cliquey, but they invited Sohail to join them in Punjabi. The children chose independently and appropriately, playing purposefully and completing one activity before they went on to the next. They did not find the activity of cutting out catalogue pictures stimulating enough and moved on

after only two minutes. We've obviously got to look more at what they do like and concentrate on that. It's good to see that our objective is working and that the children are on task and working at their play.

Nabeela, nursery nurse

Stop and reflect

The scenario is a very good example of the value of child-led versus adult-led practice. Can you identify a time when your thinking has ever been challenged and in what ways have you changed your mind about what children are doing and learning?

What have been your experiences of observing children? What might help you improve your ability to observe the learners in your own setting?

Improving practice

Why not undertake a series of observations that will help you to evaluate your practice. Enlist the help of a colleague so that you can 'moderate' your observations and discuss ways in which you can sharpen your practice.

Creating challenges through drama and role-play

Remember how little 'c' creativity enables individuals to be imaginative. It helps if children are put in a position of being confident to take on challenges and risks. Drama and socio-dramatic play offer enormous potential to get children to see things from another's viewpoint. Drama has always had the skills of critical and creative thinking – you cannot engage children in dilemmas and problems of the characters they take on in role-play and dramatic play without developing such skills (Hendy and Toon, 2001). Children willingly become involved in situations where anything is possible. Very young children are able to suspend disbelief in reality and move into pretend worlds. Children working in the narrative mode are quite happy to be made small by drinking potions, grow wings or fly on a magic

carpet (Hendy and Toon, 2001, p. 45). Parker-Rees (2000) demonstrates how children have resilient and playful dispositions, can live in imaginary worlds and immerse themselves in their play experiences.

In good drama play, children can often take on roles of adults or children three years older than themselves (Johnson, 2004; in Fisher and Williams, 2004). Heathcote and Bolton (1995) draw on Dorothy Heathcote's concept of the 'mantle of the expert', which allows children to assume a role as being experts in their actions and knowledge within the drama play. She uses the ideas children have about the world and builds upon the universality of their experience, allowing them to be in control and explore their thoughts through drama. The roles are reversed and the children are asked for their help, advice and support. Mantle of the expert allows children to look at a situation through special eyes (Morgan and Saxton, 1987). Tasks and challenges are set for the children in order to refine their thinking. Adults can create mantles of expertise for children to become experts in flying, catching giants or fighting fires (Hendy and Toon, 2001, p. 28). A third-year teacher-training student used the mantle of the expert technique with children aged 4 and 5 in a reception class.

Ideas in action

After a trip to the countryside the children told tales of seeing the woodcutter's cottage, signs about the wolf and Cinderella's castle. They found the world to be an enchanted and magic place to explore and enjoy. I decided to relax my authority as the teacher in charge in order to allow the children to become independent problem solvers and negotiators. I took on the role of Jack's friend and told them my tale of how I'd bought some magic beans from Bolton market, but the Giant had stolen them. I showed them his letter informing me he had hidden them in a dark forest. They were eager to fulfil their role as 'experts' when I asked them for help in retrieving the beans. The children had to negotiate how to cross a river, build an obstacle course, follow clues, advise and plant the magic beans and get back across the river without being caught by the Giant.
Nina, teacher-training student

Improving practice

This student had taken on the position of becoming an adult in role, stepping into *other* shoes to behave like someone else. This enables the children to focus on a character, pose an alternative view, and helps them come to collective agreements. Giving children problems to solve, empowering them to make decisions and work together, having to explain what to do next or what resources they need, is so important for developing children's creative thinking.

An assignment for teacher-training students was to plan, implement and reflect upon a programme to promote play and creativity with young children. The students went on a field trip to a small local museum located in a park, which had woods, gardens, a lake, an orienteering trail and a small environmental glasshouse run voluntarily by a local naturalist. The museum had been the home of a local philanthropist and stored several of his natural history collections, an Egyptian archaeological display, a tropical forest and a Victorian seaside. Settings could book times for children to handle artefacts with the museum educational team. The field trip was to stimulate and inspire students and they were also introduced to drama techniques such as mantle of the expert and adult in role. They had to work individually or in pairs, in an early years setting, in school or an after-school club and assume a role, for example as an anthropologist, apiarist, archaeologist, architect, historian, landscape gardener, museum curator, naturalist, ornithologist, park keeper or sculptor. As well as being provided with several possible 'mantle of the expert' scenarios many students identified their own:

- the Old Woman making gingerbread;
- a descendant of Blackbeard the Pirate finding treasure;
- a Giant getting old with failing eyesight;
- an archaeologist excavating to find ancient remains;
- an illustrator designing a children's book;
- the Billy Goats Gruff crossing a river after their bridge had been blown away in a storm;
- Red Riding Hood's Grandma was too frightened to walk to her cottage.

Case study

Marietta, an experienced Foundation Stage teacher, was inspired when she attended one of Ros Bayley's (author and early years consultant) courses and decided to create a 'provocation' for her children. One Monday morning when they entered the classroom, they spied a strange object hanging down from the ceiling.

See the 'Cocoon Planning' on p. 136.

Chas: What's that up there?

Shula & Janie: A cocoon, a cocoon. It's a cocoon.

Ravinder: It's fake, because cocoons don't have square patterns on.

Julie: Yeah, but inside there's real eggs.

Nicki: Put your hand up if you say it's pretend.

Gavin: Put your hand up if you think it's real.

Hari: It's a chrysalis.

Mrs M: Where is it from?

Leanne: I think a fairy came and did some magic and an egg came.

Leah: A wizard might have put it there.

Hari: It's pretend.

Piotr: Gandalf put it there. It's a squirrel inside.

Floele: There is a caterpillar about to turn into a butterfly.

Paris: It might be fake with loads of fake caterpillars inside.

Syd: It is fake. It's got little plastic bits holding it up on the ceiling.

Lara: It's hanging. A fairy waved a magic wand and put it there.

The children are excited about the object's appearance and it promotes much discussion that they can lead themselves without any prompting from an adult. They draw on their previous experiences from home and school, from film, story and natural history. Some of the children had initially been very sceptical about the object's origin, but soon entered into guessing and reasoning. They were very willing to suspend their disbelief (Heathcoate and Bolton, 1995) and the excitement mounts until they spot a change in the object the following week.

Kemi: It's got a crack in it. I think one of the teachers has ripped it open.

Mira: I wonder what's inside?

Sammy: Maybe it's come out!

Alex: There's a spider in it like in the *Lord of the Rings*.

Levi: Some air might be in there . . . loads and loads and it's cracked open.

Jack: I think someone's blown into the bag. When it's got bigger it's burst open.

Cody: It might be magic.

Lori: Maybe it's getting too big for it's old skin and getting a new one.

Two weeks after the strange object first appeared . . .

Lori: Look, something's happening in there! It's a butterfly coming out!

Zack: There's legs coming out of it. They've purple legs. It's got wings with purple bits inside.

Mira: It's horrid. It's a spider.

Hari: It could be the spider from the *Lord of the Rings*.

Piotr: It's a tarantula. The legs are so big.

The whole class sat in silence as Mrs S. climbed the ladder, reached up and picked the creature out of the 'cocoon'. There was much discussion about the colour and body shape of the creature. It looked like an ant. Cody and Mira were convinced they had seen something like it in a film. The creature sat quietly all afternoon. The children inspected the new arrival. Some went to the mark-making area and started to draw pictures, others picked up clipboards, sat on the floor and drew still-life pictures.

In Chapter 6 you will ⇨ see how literature-based integration has the same engaging effect with older children.

Improving practice
Some ideas for 'provocations'

- Why not write a letter to the children saying that Baby Bear needs help to mend his chair?

- Send a message by email on the class computer to invite the children to plan a teddy bear's picnic.

- Bring a puppet into the setting who is shy and needs a friend.

- Wear a hat and be Topiwalo who needs help with the monkeys.

- Wear an apron and be Mrs Wishy Washy who is having trouble with the washing.

- Wear a chef's hat and ask for help for a surprise birthday party.

- Wear a cap and be Percy the park keeper whose shed has blown down.

▶

- Discover a map showing lost treasure.
- Show a magic lantern that needs cleaning.
- Find enchanted cloaks that turn children invisible when they want to help someone.

- Ask for help searching for a lost dog (see *Into the Enchanted Forest*, Brock, 1999).
- Display an advert for a scientist to work in a laboratory.

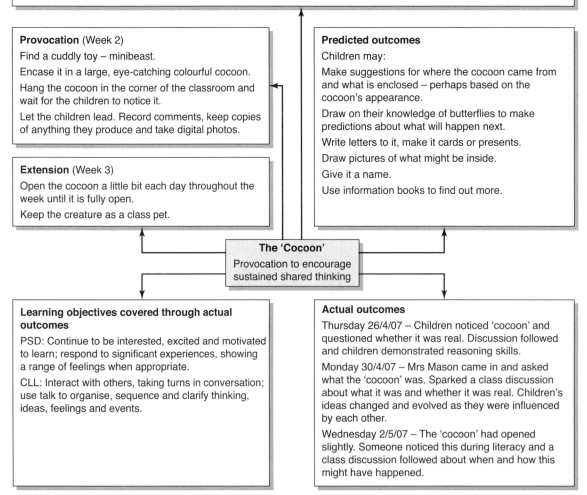

Learning intentions

PSD: Continue to be interested, excited and motivated to learn; respond to significant experiences, showing a range of feelings when appropriate.

CLL: Interact with others, taking turns in conversation; speak clearly and audibly with confidence and control and show awareness of the listener; use talk to organise, sequence and clarify thinking, ideas, feelings and events.

KUW: Investigate objects and materials by using all of their senses as appropriate; find out about and identify some features of living things, objects and events they observe; ask questions about why things happen and how things work; observe, find out about and identify features in the place they live and the natural world.

CD: Explore colour, shape and form in three dimensions; use their imagination in imaginative and role-play; respond in a variety of ways to what they see, hear and feel; express and communicate their ideas, thoughts and feelings by using a widening range of imaginative and role-play.

Provocation (Week 2)

Find a cuddly toy – minibeast.

Encase it in a large, eye-catching colourful cocoon.

Hang the cocoon in the corner of the classroom and wait for the children to notice it.

Let the children lead. Record comments, keep copies of anything they produce and take digital photos.

Extension (Week 3)

Open the cocoon a little bit each day throughout the week until it is fully open.

Keep the creature as a class pet.

Predicted outcomes

Children may:

Make suggestions for where the cocoon came from and what is enclosed – perhaps based on the cocoon's appearance.

Draw on their knowledge of butterflies to make predictions about what will happen next.

Write letters to it, make it cards or presents.

Draw pictures of what might be inside.

Give it a name.

Use information books to find out more.

The 'Cocoon'

Provocation to encourage sustained shared thinking

Learning objectives covered through actual outcomes

PSD: Continue to be interested, excited and motivated to learn; respond to significant experiences, showing a range of feelings when appropriate.

CLL: Interact with others, taking turns in conversation; use talk to organise, sequence and clarify thinking, ideas, feelings and events.

Actual outcomes

Thursday 26/4/07 – Children noticed 'cocoon' and questioned whether it was real. Discussion followed and children demonstrated reasoning skills.

Monday 30/4/07 – Mrs Mason came in and asked what the 'cocoon' was. Sparked a class discussion about what it was and whether it was real. Children's ideas changed and evolved as they were influenced by each other.

Wednesday 2/5/07 – The 'cocoon' had opened slightly. Someone noticed this during literacy and a class discussion followed about when and how this might have happened.

Figure 5.2 Cocoon activity planning sheet

Creating environments

Ask adults what they remember about playing when they were little and a common answer will be about the dens they created – under tables, in a hen hut, using wooden frames known as clothes-horses or 'maidens'. They are more likely to talk about their own instigated play experiences than anything they have played at school. One Steiner nursery had a total of eight clothes-horses, which the children themselves arranged into different areas for varied scenarios, helping themselves to materials and natural resources as part of their collaborative role-play. A teacher in Broadhead's (2004) research commented on how the large construction and sand offered the most open-ended play for the children. These areas seemed to promote social and collaborative play and allowed the children to determine their own play themes. The teachers in the research decided to establish a non-themed, open-ended role-play area in each of their classrooms. They provided fabric, empty boxes, clothes-horses, hats, cushions, seats and buckets. Using the continuum of social play to assess the quality of children's play they found much of it to be in the Highly Social or the Cooperative domains. One child named it the 'whatever you want it to be place, because it can be whatever you want it to be' (Broadhead, 2004, p. 73).

There is a complex balance between adult-led and child-led activities. Many adult-led activities (such as provocation) can have a very high creativity value. Children can be much more imaginative than adults, but they do require countless opportunities and experiences to stimulate their creativity and imagination. The creation and use of role-play scenarios are valuable for promoting cross-curricular learning opportunities. They also fulfil many of the early learning objectives, which more than merits the time spent. It is important to create surprises for children with ready erected scenarios, as well as to invite them to participate in planning and organising their own role-play area, which could be based on a story, topic or the children's own interests. Teachers often comment how, when they have spent time setting up the role-play, the children could become over-excited and demolish it. This is quite a natural process and may need to be factored in if children are not used to differently resourced environments. Once children have explored and handled the role-play resources, they will normally begin to play effectively and more calmly. However, they need ownership and should be involved in negotiating and organising the role-play and be able to adopt different roles (Bennett *et al.*, 1997). Giving role-play areas status is important and adults can model how to play, use language and handle resources. Use children who may be accomplished role-players to be the scaffolders for other children. To keep the role-play areas interesting intermittently add small resources and create problems for the role-play, for example, the pet shop has no food left for the rabbit; the dishwasher is broken in the café; there are several cars waiting to be repaired; a flood has damaged the flower garden.

> Two very different mid-twentieth-century childhoods, in Chapter 11, provide such examples.

Childhood 'spaces'

Dixon and Day (2004, p. 93; in Cooper, 2004) also reflect on fond memories of dens and secret places in their childhoods and investigated nursery children's secret places. These researchers endured 'prickles, insect bites and bad backs' in the exploration of the children's 'willow wigwam, tree house, animal hide, wooden cottage, wooden rowing-boat and a grass-covered hummock with tunnel entrance'. They found a distinct difference in gender play – the boys spent much time running to and from their hiding-places, whereas the girls used them for sociable play. The boys talked about 'dangerous things such as robbers or houses on fire', engaging in sustained cooperative fantasy and superhero play with lots of action and movement, whereas the girls often played at families and domestic play. Dixon and Day (2004) advise the importance of staff being enthusiastic about outdoor play, getting involved and adding layers of language of stories, place and time.

> You will find further examination of the impact of gender roles in Chapters 2 and 7.

Ideas in action

Dramatic environments

Successful holistic dramatic environments observed in West Yorkshire Foundation Stage settings include a fairy-tale cottage; tropical world; airport; space laboratory with rocket; police station; ice world; caves; library; travel agent; veterinary surgery; art gallery. One nursery created their own exhibition area after a visit with parents to Bretton Hall Sculpture Park. Over the next few weeks the parents came into the nursery to work with the children to create sculptures using clay, natural and manufactured resources. The works of art were displayed and the opening ceremony, attended by the Lord Mayor, made local news. Staff in several nurseries and schools were stimulated by Brock's (1999) Enchanted Forest, which demonstrated how a holistic environment can be created for free imaginative play and cross-curricular learning. It particularly focused on drama, language and science, supporting children's bilingualism, problem solving and creativity. Children, students, teachers and lecturers provide ideas and reflections on practice and analysis of the children's responses. One child had really suspended her disbelief: 'I don't know whether it is a real or just a very good story.' The children who worked and played in the Forest remembered it years later, not only their drama experiences, but also the scientific and technological concepts.

According to Bilton (1998, 2002) the need for outdoor experiences is crucial and the whole curriculum can be accessed outdoors and should be planned for in as much detail as the indoor experiences. She views that children can be more free and independent, taking more risks in exploring and collaborating more effectively, as there are normally less constraints of space, noise and adult direction.

Stop and reflect

Most young children prefer to be outside than inside, so how can you create valuable learning experiences such as those outlined above outside?

Improving practice

Children may gravitate towards the bicycles, as these are often the prime resources for outdoor play. Whilst the physical act of cycling, manoeuvring and turn taking are extremely valuable, if these are the only activities that are provided in the outdoor environment then the children's experiences will be limited. Use the larger toys to the best advantage in a role-play activity. Get them to think about space, environments, resources and about road safety, transport, buildings and occupations. Encourage children to socialise, collaborate and solve problems through block making their own role-play areas. Provide opportunities for building:

- garages
- houses
- car parks or bike parks
- restaurants
- farms
- supermarkets
- ships
- aeroplanes
- trains
- builder's merchants
- laundries
- baby clinic
- estate agents
- pirate ship
- garden centre.

Den making is coming back into fashion and can now be found as a key feature in many Foundation Stage settings. You can even engage community artists to stimulate the den building with children. Dens are ideal for promoting cross-curricular learning and imaginative language. Children can be encouraged to be creative in their designs and envision an end result. Gross motor skills of stretching, reaching and holding promote physical manipulation. If you cannot find suitable clothes-horses, try garden canes fastened to chairs with masking tape or use washing lines tied to outdoor fences. Fasten materials with plastic clamps (as cheap as 4 for £1) and use pegs to hang heavy wool and chiffon fabrics, duvets, net curtains, cotton sheets, shawls, scarves, etc.

Den making

Making dens offers more scope and challenge than always providing large vehicular toys. It prompts problem solving: 'How do we make this?'; 'How do

▶

we get his piece to stay there?' It's great for conflict resolution – they have to agree and negotiate designs – 'You hold this and I'll do that'. Shazia spent all day in the den. Although joined intermittently by other children, she persisted in completing it in order to take her dolls in and tell them a story. In so doing, she fulfilled so many stepping stones and cross-curricular areas.

Carlotta, Foundation Stage coordinator

Stop and reflect

- Next time you are working in the outdoor area reflect on how much you get involved in the children's play.
- What can you do to improve your practice?

Ideas in action

Stop and reflect

What message does this give you about gender play and provision?

- Plan how to stimulate den making.
- What challenges could you introduce?
- What resources can you collect?

Case study: Concept boxes

The idea of concept boxes originated from a desire to encourage students to make resources for children. At the time of their inception, many teachers in schools were finding they had little time to create their own teaching resources. Manufactured resources were becoming more abundant and lesson plans readily available on QCA websites. Yet, creating personal resources is important for determining how we can support and scaffold children's learning. Concept boxes were introduced as part of an assessment for students following an advanced study of early years specialism. The aim was to enable students to produce a collection of resources that would contextualise a specific concept for children through promoting play experiences. The contents of the box could be student designed and created or a

Figure 5.3 Photo case study: Concept box contents for a theme of journeys

collection of manufactured objects that were multi-sensory and stimulating for children. The students also had to write academic rationales to explain and justify their boxes and activities. Over the years some of the boxes grew to be very imaginative, with the exterior 'box' taking the form of a sunflower, an egg, an appliqué village playmat, teddy's wardrobe, a shoe shop, farm, theatre, hamster's cage, pond or badger's set – the list is endless. Students selected a concept; created or organised appropriate resources; planned learning activities and potential play experiences, sometimes selecting a specific group to target, at other times promoting a range of activities that could be experienced in family groups or across age ranges. Some examples were:

- ourselves
- size
- growth
- directions/mapping
- habitats
- seasons
- healthy eating
- pairs
- water
- minibeasts
- seashore
- shapes.

Improving practice

Creating resources

Making time for creating resources for children's play experiences is valuable, and not purely because of the end result of the product. The actual constructing of resources engages you in a process of creativity, it develops critical thinking about purpose and potential of children's play and supports planning and meeting curriculum demands. What is really important about creating your own resources is that this enables you to think about your particular groups of children and supporting their particular individual needs through:

- contextualising thinking, learning and linguistic processes;
- facilitating differentiation through practical activities and play experiences;
- promoting English as an additional language and supporting bilingualism (see Brock and Power, 2006; in Conteh, 2006 for further ideas);
- offering experiences and language related to refugee and asylum seekers' heritage culture and language;
- supporting specific special educational needs;
- encouraging non-gender specific play: girls to play with construction and boys to role-play;
- allow the genders to play out playtexts that appear important to them, even if these are highly gendered;
- developing particular concepts, skills, dispositions and attitudes;
- consolidating concepts through varied and diverse activities upon a similar theme.

Suggested activity

Why don't you create your own concept box and trial it with a group of children? What should you consider when identifying your theme?

Playscapes

Brock and Power (2006; in Conteh, 2006) demonstrate how builders' trays (large rectangular or square trays that builders use to mix cement on) provide small world role-play environments for children to explore their knowledge and understanding of the world. Key questions, sentence starts and lines of exploration are offered to help adults develop children's vocabulary and concepts. Repeating and using language gives both familiarity and confidence to children. Posing problems and challenges then helps children to use their imagination and problem-solving skills. Playscapes extend the concepts of builder's trays, through pro-viding landscapes and environments that can extend children's storytelling and problem solving.

1 Tell or read a story or introduce an idea.
2 Introduce the playscape – discuss the landscape and layout; ask open questions and offer prompts. What is it? What do you think this is? Where do these go?
3 Provide small world resources.
4 Introduce new vocabulary.
5 Offer further and regular challenges, through introducing new resources or posing a problem.
6 Provide prompts for storytelling.

Ideas in action

Playscapes

A Foundation Stage unit coordinator and a lecturer in teacher education compare notes and discuss how they create playscapes to promote imaginative small world role-play for children.

> An important part of our continuous provision is the weekly builder's trays. What started with a plastic mat in the bottom of the tray has developed into the real thing. We have wood, sawdust and wood chippings, but the best one is the forest and the jungle toys. The science coordinator and I are going to develop it into a dinosaur land. We will build mounds with chicken wire and papier mâché, and sprinkle grass seeds on a mound of compost so that it grows into a hill.
>
> Penny, Foundation Stage teacher

> I made my playscape with four boys aged between 3 and 6. On a solid wood base, we moulded mountain ranges from papier mâché; created arid and luscious moorland; forest, mossy and grassy areas; rocky, rough and arid terrains with varied materials from a garden centre; a river with rapids, shallows, pebbles, shells, sand and gravel. So far we have played the Billy Goats Gruff story, *Lord of the Rings* and Mr Mole's adventures.
>
> Abigail, Grandmother and ex-teacher

Improving practice

Further ideas/themes for playscapes are:

- industrial urbanisation
- cultivated farmland
- marine and coastline seascape

Figure 5.4   Playing with the 3 Billy Goats Gruff on a playscape

- fantasy environment
- outer space playscape.

Comment

Playscapes such as these provide a landscape of different terrains not only to contextualise the play but also to encourage problem-solving skills. Talking about what is happening enables children not only to articulate their thinking but also to consolidate and further develop their ideas. Playing with other children provides a forum for ideas to be shared as children cooperate in their play. True partnership can be seen when children take each other's ideas and work together in their play, not necessarily to achieve an end result, but to keep the play moving forward and developing. See the long-term planning sheet for small world provision (Figure 5.5).

Reflecting on practice

Professional knowledge, understanding and expertise have an important place in providing effective pedagogy. Moyles *et al.* (2002, p. 2) consider pedagogy to be not only the actual practice of teaching, but also being able to talk about and reflect on teaching. They believed that defining 'pedagogy' and 'effectiveness' is vital to achieving 'valuable professional dialogue and understanding amongst and between professionals'. Educators therefore need to be skilled, knowledgeable and sensitive to an appropriate pedagogy and curriculum for the children they teach. Not only do they need to make everything meaningful for children, they also have to explain effective teaching and learning practices. Moyles and Adams (2001) suggest educators need to articulate the implicit differences in pedagogy in early years education and other phases of education to a not always knowledgeable group of outsiders. This has traditionally been very difficult for several reasons – lack of status for those working with children; a mainly female profession compared to a majority of male policy makers and Government requirements for achievements of set targets and quantitative evidence of improvements.

In the following reflections these educators demonstrate that they are not only knowledgeable and passionate about their work, but that they also need to explain to parents and education managers why the children are playing, and defend both their provision and pedagogy to policy makers. Over the years, they have needed to justify their practice to a critical audience of Ofsted inspectors, local authority advisers, head teachers and parents. Continuing professional development (CPD) is important for all practitioners to further develop their knowledge and understanding of the most effective provision and pedagogy for the children they are educating. CPD can occur through many varied activities and is important to build self-confidence in the effectiveness of your practice.

Ideas in action

Practitioner reflections

We need to justify what it is we do, to people who don't have the knowledge about early years.

Denise, manager, workplace nursery

When the children go home and say they've played all day, parents need to understand that they have engaged in directed play and undertaken valuable activities. I think we don't explain to parents enough exactly what the value of these activities is. I think that's partly our fault and partly a misunderstanding of early years.

Riari, Reception teacher

I think people do have the perception about early years, that it's all playing. I also get the impression that that's the way Government thinks as well.

Steve, nursery nurse

So I'm not only playing with children and alongside them, I'm actually teaching as well.

Shagufta, nursery nurse

Ideas in action

Improving practice

Continuing professional development

Here are some examples of how to be involved in CPD:

- Talk to colleagues in your own and other settings.
- Visit diverse settings and varied provision to gain new and different ideas.
- Read educational magazines and journals to acquire practical ideas, resources and new thinking and practice.
- Read textbooks to further develop professional knowledge.
- Attend local educational authority in-service settings; meet like-minded colleagues and gain up-to-date ideas.
- Enrol on professional development courses at colleges and universities and acquire further qualifications.
- Travel internationally to observe different curriculum models and ideologies.

Stop and reflect

Can you think of any other ways in which you can develop your understanding and expertise as an early years practitioner? Talk to colleagues and identify opportunities for CPD relevant to you and your setting.

LONG-TERM PLANNING			
EARLY YEARS UNIT			
Continuous provision – Small world role-play			

Key learning opportunities

- To build on personal individual experiences from home and the outside world (PSED/KUW)
- To cooperate and negotiate through play in small groups (PSED)
- To empathise, respect and listen to others' ideas (PSED)
- To extend vocabulary, particularly the language of storytelling (CLL)
- To promote use of non-fiction to move knowledge further (CLL)
- To investigate materials, objects and varied resources in different environments (KUW)
- To sort and classify for different criteria (MD)
- To develop fine motor skill through manipulation and design (PD)
- To use imagination and solve real-life problems through play (CD)

Permanent resources (changed according to current topic)	**Resource provision**	**Intended experiences** (cross-curricular dimensions)	**Key vocabulary and questions**
Builder's tray environments Jungle/zoo Farm Builder's yard Under the sea Arctic Dinosaur land Dolls' houses Playground Mini beasts Small world topic boxes Pictures of scenes on interactive white board to encourage the children to talk and create stories Photos of children playing in small world area Emergent literacy opportunities	Distinctive small area Adults to listen, share, observe and monitor Model role-play engaging the children, but also allow them to make decisions and to direct the play Regular addition of tactile materials – sand, water, pebbles, soil, grass seed, bark chippings, leaves Intermittent introductions of additional small world resources Introduce challenges, cause problems and promote creative thinking Fiction and non-fiction books related to the topic Scribing materials: paper, pencils, clipboards	Use increasing imagination in their play, through listening and responding to ideas from adults and other children Planning and creating small world play activities; explaining, reflecting on and sharing these with peers and adults Further develop vocabulary related to knowledge and understanding of the world Promote storytelling and story writing related to the topic and activities through manipulating small world resources Problem solve, reason and categorise through play activities	Frequent adult support to model, promote language and problem solving **Key vocabulary** Naming and labelling objects and resources Use adjectives of properties and appearance – colour, size, shape Promote adverbs of speed and position **Key questions** Who? What? How? Why? When? Where? What is happening to this creature? How could we build . . . ? What if there was a flood? What are we going to do now? Where is the problem? Who can be responsible for doing that?

Figure 5.5   Long-term planning sheet, small world play

Summary and review

You will now have an understanding of why development and learning are so complex and that no one theory is sufficient to explain them. At the beginning of this chapter we set out to explore four key questions:

- Do politics and national policy development really have an impact on the provision of play and why should this concern me?

Contemporary research during the last decade demands educators and policy makers critically reflect on the status quo with regard to what their theories are predicated upon. They need to examine what is considered established practice in education systems and the traditional ideologies that might have informed philosophies which underpin provision. The impact of national policy developments should be carefully considered by all early years and care professionals to ensure provision not only meets nationally agreed expectations but, more importantly, the developing needs of the child.

- How do psychological theories influence my practice?

As research theories are examined and new thinking is offered, so the demands intensify and increased professional knowledge is required. It is therefore important that question and debate amongst professionals occur in order to stimulate the growth of professional knowledge (NAEYC, 1997).

- What are children's languages of play?

This chapter has offered a multitude of play experiences that can be employed to engage children's interest, promote active involvement and encourage experiential learning in both the cognitive and language domains. Children need environments where they can feel safe and secure to use a full range of ways to express themselves through play.

- How can I create quality play opportunities for all children in the Foundation Stage?

This chapter should have demonstrated why your professional knowledge and understanding of the complexity of play in all its facets is crucial. The context of the professional knowledge base of early childhood education and care is distinguished by the continuing arguments about the achievement of young children, which focus on what is necessary and effective for their development and learning. The field of knowledge continues to move forward and the debates about the care of young children are still ongoing. Questioning and debate among early childhood professionals is necessary for growth of professional knowledge in the field (NAEYC, 1997). Therefore you need to be a part of a knowledgeable, highly qualified and articulate workforce, able to define and demonstrate your own professional knowledge and put this into practice. The ability to reflect on and evaluate your professional role with regard to play is key to your professionalism. Whilst you have stopped to reflect in this chapter you will have identified a plethora of starting points for quality play opportunities for all children in the Foundation Stage.

Transforming thinking and practice: over to you!

This chapter has highlighted the importance of play in early childhood education and care and suggested that there needs to be renewed emphasis placed on the role of play in the Early Years Foundation Stage not only as a tool to achieve the EYFS learning goals, but also as an end in itself. Play can stimulate creativity, inspire children's imagination, help them learn how to resolve conflict, improve their self-confidence and strengthen their sense of self-identity. There is a need for greater adult–child interaction through both adult-directed and child-directed play. Adult-led play can enhance the child's scope of creativity in play through probing questions and eliciting responses, and one-to-one conversations can encourage children to reflect upon what they are learning, challenge their thinking and aid their understanding. Child-led play promotes creativity through self-directed learning and makes learning relevant for the child. Free choice play broadens the range activities in which the child will participate and can encourage the child to sustain play on one activity for a considerable length of time.

Questions for consideration

This chapter has presented many different ways in which you can stimulate play scenarios in the early years. Consider the following questions:

- Can you articulate to stakeholders why it is important that play receives a central role in nursery and reception?

- What are the advantages of adult-directed and child-directed play? Do you make provision for both in your teaching?

- What are children's languages of play?

- Which of the suggestions for encouraging opportunities for play mentioned in this chapter can you import into your work and play with children?

Further reading

Brock, A. and Rankin, C. (2008) *Communication, Language and Literacy from Birth to Five.* London: Sage.

Casey, T. (2007) *Environments for Outdoor Play: A Practical Guide to Making Space for Children.* London: Sage.

Conteh, J. (2006) *Promoting Learning for Bilingual Pupils 3–11.* London: Paul Chapman.

Edgington, M. (2004) *The Foundation Stage Teacher in Action.* London: Paul Chapman.

Flewitt, R. (2006) Using video to investigate preschool interaction: educational research assumptions and methodological practices. *Visual Communication.* Vol. 5, No. 1, 25–50.

Riley, J. (ed.) (2003) *Learning in the Early Years.* London: Paul Chapman.

Scaarlett, W., Naudeau, S., Salonius-Pasternak and Ponte, I. (2004) *Children's Play.* London: Sage.

Tucker, K. (2005) *Mathematics Through Play in the Early Years: Activities and Ideas.* London: Sage.

Chapter 6

'We Want to Play': Primary Children at Play in the Classroom

SYLVIA DODDS

The best time we ever had was way back when we were in Reception. ['Yeah', Kerry agrees.] They had these, like, little tubes and nails and we made a tower over 5m tall and it was so strong you could stand on it. We all ran on it, do you remember, and then I jumped on it and it collapsed [laughter]. It was really fun. Now we're older we just have to work all the time. I'd prefer it if we could still do all the learning but then have time to practise what we'd learned in a fun way. I'd just love it if we could play and experiment more!

Alex and Kerry, aged 11, reflect on their experiences of 'playing' at primary school

Introduction

Children of all ages, as seen in the chapters of this book, whatever their background, culture, religion or gender, pursue and enjoy opportunities to play imaginatively, creatively and independently. Play can serve many important purposes, can be both directed and undirected and is an essential part of child development and **social interaction** – 'Oh, we're just playing'. With increasing parental anxiety about the safety of our children playing outside the home, in a world that may appear more dangerous than ever before, many young people are denied the freedom they need to simply 'go out and play' with their friends. Indeed the first of several inquiries to be

> **Social interaction**
> A dynamic sequence of social actions between individuals or groups who modify their own actions in response to the interaction with others.

published in 2008 by the Children's Society, *The Good Childhood Inquiry* has already found parents regularly deny their children the same freedom to go out unsupervised that they had when they themselves were growing up.

Meanwhile in school you may hear the woeful moans of children, 'I have finished my work so can I go and play now?' This is intermittently reward focused, token gesture 'free time' or **'golden time'** where children pursue independent activity or learning from a

Golden time

A short period, often in the afternoon or at the end of the week, where children and their teachers either sit down together and celebrate achievement or children are offered a range of activities in which to engage. It is often used as a method for modification of inappropriate behaviours and rewarding children who behave well.

Governed by 'golden rules' it is an opportunity, at its best, for self- and peer reflection.

predetermined selection (for example the Lego on the carpet or reading a book in the book corner). Occasionally the opportunity to play is relegated to a Friday afternoon when the class teacher is absent and a teaching assistant 'looks after' the class! Primary school educators have come to believe that 'playfulness' is only an acceptable trait of the learner in the early years, that learning opportunities *have* to be driven by a recognised statutory curricular purpose (objectives and outcomes, play for 'play's sake' is not enough) or as we are often reminded, 'There is so much to cover these days, we don't have time to play!'

The reality then for many primary-age learners is that play is a non-existent element of their everyday classroom-based lives. Thus the challenge, for schools and societies of today and the future, is to find ways for children to experience, even learn how to play, providing the freedom to develop the range of skills fundamental for learning and adulthood. With this in mind this chapter sets out to explore starting points for practitioners to provide play opportunities to meet and enhance the demands of a prescribed curriculum and support the development of key skills. It will explore:

- The climate for play – what can be learned through play in the primary phase? Has the opportunity for play-based learning and personal development been squeezed out of the curriculum in the hunt for academic excellence and achievement?

- Opportunities for play in the classroom – how can play-based experiences be utilised to encourage learners to take *ownership* of learning and develop their key and thinking skills within the constraints of a formal curriculum?

The climate for play: what is the difference between work and play?

In Figure 6.1 Mark, Lucy and Jason spontaneously re-enact a scene from *Teenage Mutant Ninja Turtles* that they all watched on TV that morning. Each takes turns to be the 'baddie'. Interestingly, Jason (on the right and the youngest) steers the ferocity of the play and is central in assigning roles to each player. In order to become Donatello, Leonardo and the baddie they use props – the sofa is the 'base' and a toy cutlass and some wooden dowelling that Jason found in the shed become 'weapons'.

Consider the ideas around gender, identity and aggressive play explored by Olusoga in Chapter 2.

For the young child it is often asserted that there is no distinction between work and play and that children learn by being active, organising their own learning experiences using language and interacting with others (Fisher, 1996). Through play youngsters are motivated to experience their world, grow, develop and learn (Drake, 2001). Many authors and researchers, including those in this book, would agree that to try and explain the difference between work and play, to try and define the notion of play or even categorise different forms of play, is nearly impossible. Indeed Janet

Figure 6.1   Play or work?

Moyles (2002, p. 5) suggests that:

> Grappling with the concept of play can be analogized to trying to seize bubbles, for every time there appears to be something to hold on to, its ephemeral nature disallows it being grasped! Because of its diversity, it continues to defy attempts at quantification . . . It makes more sense to consider play as a process, which, in itself, will subsume a range of behaviours, motivations, opportunities, practices, skills and understandings.

Wider-ranging studies of children's own perceptions of play reflect the varying responses about what it means to play given here (see Ideas in Action below). Karrby (1989), in a study of 15 5 and 6-year-old Swedish children, found that they also associated play with activities involving **pretend fantasy play**, agreed by themselves, based on a theme such as a robbery or partying. Pellegrini and Galda (1993), on reviewing a range of studies, concluded that older chil-

---

Pretend fantasy play
Where children either enact or create imaginary situations within their own play. This type of play emerges when an environment sparks or allows the freedom for imagination and creativity.

---

dren (9–11 year olds) may focus on the fantasy or imaginative link that is often socially planned and structured, adhering to rules and utilising learning influenced by the media. The small group interviewed here had clear ideas of what 'play' meant to them. It is interesting that all the children included game play in their own definitions and that these games involved high levels of physical activity. Play was also the social activity found in the studies – pursued with 'friends'. The creative element of fantasy play seemed to be more prevalent in the younger children interviewed. What is clear is that play, even

A view supported by ⇨ Jarvis and George in Chapter 11.

Ideas in action

Case study: What do 'tweenies' say about play?

A mixed group of 7–11 year olds (**tweenies**), both boys and girls, were asked what the phrase 'play' meant to them. They were encouraged to add examples of their explanations for clarity. They were also asked if they played imaginative or fantasy games (the word 'pretend' was used to ensure understanding) and if they did examples were sought, and if they did not then who did?

Tweenies
A phrase used to describe children between the toddler and teenage phase of development.

The responses were as follows.

Play means to have fun! Play is doing games [like tag, Monopoly, Mousetrap], pretending to be someone [like Superman or Spiderman and you act like them, pretending to save people from evil villains]. It's all about playing nicely, enjoying yourself, not cheating so that that makes it a fun time. When I have played I have pretended to be Spiderman before. I played with my friend Max, we played it outside school by the wall [which was our base] and we got other people to play too. They were the villains and we had to capture them – they ran about trying not to be caught. And we sang the song 'Spiderman, Spiderman, does whatever a spider can' (you know it?) while we were doing it. It was a fun game actually. **I like to play games where I pretend to be someone from a movie or off the telly all the time – it's really good fun.**

Mark, aged 7

Playing is having fun! I like to play with my friends or play on my own, I don't mind. The best thing I like to play is with my toy horses; I love horses. I pretend I am one of the rides and I go around a pretend ground and jump and stuff. **I like to play games too – some I make up and some that are real** (like Monopoly). You

▶

don't have to win either – it's about joining in and having fun. We don't play at school though . . . well only outside when it is PE!

Lauren, aged 8

It means like playing games like sports [like rugby], and games when you have to take turns and there are rules and playing games with my friends like 'it' [one person is 'on' and they have to chase the rest of us and then when they catch us we are 'it']. **Play, like pretending to be cops and robbers, is for the little kids!**

Charlie, aged 9

Like playing in the ground [like playing bulldog, that game where you have two teams, one team runs and the other one catches. You have to run from one side of the playground to the other without getting caught but it has been banned 'cos too many people are getting hurt – it is a bit rough! We also play 'it', the Year 7 and 8s get to play netball and basket ball, it also brings to mind playacting [like arguments and other role-play] like pretend playing [like we pretend to act out real situations and our friends join in and we all pretend together]. **We don't do fantasy play – that's for Reception and Year 2.**

Jessica, aged 10

Play means doing things like running, playing soccer and lots of other sports. You can play at playtime in school and you get to practise sports like football and basketball. We also play games like tag or man hunt [you have a person who is 'it', they run around and try to touch one of the others and as soon as

they do they are 'it'], capture the flag [you have two teams and they both have a flag, which is an object, and both teams have to try and capture the other team's flag without being touched on the opponent's side of the field. If you get caught you go to jail and someone has to free you]. **We don't play pretend games any more, it's babyish; it's for Reception kids, those types of games!**

Alex, aged 11

Look back at the emboldened statements made by the tweenies above. Would you agree that there is a developmental issue in the way play is viewed by the individuals here as they get older? Why might this be the case?

Perhaps use children's ideas about play as a starting point to help them invent a new game or adaptation of an activity they enjoy doing.

Consider how you can plan for play in the learning environment, both inside and outside the building, that complements the formal learning requirements of a standard curriculum.

Stop and reflect

Have you ever asked the children you work with what they think play is? Do you think children have an insight into how play might help them learn more effectively?

Do the children you work with have the opportunity to experience a variety of play activities that extend their development in a range of areas? Do we, as practitioners, promote the notion that play is only appropriate for 'little kids'?

enjoyment in their culture, according to the tweenies, is connected with sport, or activity outside the classroom and absolutely nothing to do with school.

Play and the developing learner

Purposeful learning has to be linked to the active acquisition of knowledge, the solution of practical problems, joint social participation and engagement in the process of learning.

Many classroom-based practitioners argue that the ever-increasing quantity of information and skills that children are expected to acquire require direct teacher

instruction to meet the specific goals and objectives. Perhaps this view is underpinned by a National Curriculum that itself does not explicitly lay down play opportunities in the subject orders, and is perpetuated by those practitioners who misinterpret this as a pedagogical framework and thus find their artistry limited. However, a recent inquiry commissioned by the National Association of Head Teachers and collecting evidence from a range of organisations, academics and writers, reported in the *Independent* (13 November 2007) suggests the blame lies with ministers who have presided over the 'death of fun and play in the primary school curriculum', suggesting that end-of-term National Curriculum tests and primary school league tables should be scrapped as children have been put off learning, their education has been damaged by too much repetitive teaching for tests and children have been robbed by the testing, targets and tables regime in schools. More alarming are those schools that find they are squeezing out 'unplanned playtime' as they try to keep up with a worldwide educational culture that demands higher standards, increasing targets and improved performance (www.cmslive.curriculum.edu.au).

But play is, in fact, one of the most efficient, powerful, and productive ways to learn the information we might need (Whardle, 2007). One has only to look to the earlier chapters of this book (Olusoga, Chapter 2 and Brock, Chapters 3 and 5) to see how this is the case from both theoretical and practitioner perspectives.

Reflecting on knowledge

For educationalists the notion of knowledge is difficult to define. One could argue that knowledge is the awareness or possession of information, facts, ideas, truths or principles of situations learned throughout time. Scheffler (1999, p. 1; in McCormick and Paechter, 1999) suggests:

the range of the everyday concept of knowing is very wide, including familiarity with things, places, persons, and subjects, competence in a variety of learned performances, and possession of ostensible truths on matters of fact as well as faith . . . It is closely associated with notions of understanding and controlling . . . of contemplation, absorption, appreciation.

Computational view of mind
An individualised view of mind that involves the simple transmission of knowledge without interaction with one's surroundings, either biological, psychological or sociological.

In considering knowledge, it is useful to briefly explore concepts of knowledge and how, in contrasting theories of learning, these differ. In a **'computational' view of mind** knowledge is transmitted in a process independent of interactions with

Radical Constructivism
A view of learning whereby individual meaning is constructed from individual experiences within reality.

the environment (Bredo, 1999). In this 'frame' the building of knowledge is therefore an inner process within the individual as the mind operates independently from biological, psychological and sociological influences (Roth, 1999). This is developed in the more **Radical Constructivist** approach that suggests, 'intelligence organises the world by organising itself', or as Goodman (1978, p. 22) in Roth (1999, p. 8) suggested, 'Comprehension and creation go together' – meaning is constructed from experience and reality. Practitioners who endorse current educational approaches that encourage interaction, discourse and shared learning rather than isolated, individualised activity may regard these views of knowledge acquisition

Constructivists
Researchers who adhere to the notion that meaning is individually constructed from one's own perceptions and experiences, through interaction with the environment in which one exists.

Social constructivists
Researchers who adhere to the notion that meaning is socially constructed from joint perceptions and experiences, through interactions with the wider environment and everything within it.

as limited in their application. As Reay and Williams (1999) point out, this contradicts the way children are assessed within the highly structured and individualised English National Curriculum testing system.

In contrast to the computational view, **constructivists** and **social constructivists** emphasise the impact of social and intellectual interactions in the acquisition of knowledge. Learners of all ages need a range of opportunities to play, work and learn; within different groups, in cooperation with peers, through interaction, sharing, exploring, questioning, discussing, reflecting, internalisation, application and so on. As Olusoga explores in Chapter 2, Bruner and Vygotsky regarded social interaction as crucial at all stages of cognitive development, the former emphasising the

Olusoga explores scaffolding in Chapter 2. ⇨

importance of language in 'scaffolding' the learning process whilst Vygotsky added the key role played by a more experienced partner (either peer or adult) in taking the learner into the zone of proximal development. More recent theories, including those of Lave and Wenger (1999) go on to suggest the notion of **learning communities** (where a more experienced other nurtures and guides the learner to knowledge acquisition), **Legitimate Peripheral Participation** (LPP) (where the support of a 'community of learners' facilitates the development of appropriate levels of knowledge, skills and understanding) and **apprenticeship** (where the learner observes, participates in learning, adopts and rehearses essential knowledge to become part of the community). This model identifies how the learner experiences learning in a variety of contexts, which in turn sees their role shift and change until they, the learner, are ultimately accepted as a full member of the community. Learning communities that reflect such a model might include doctors, tailors or indeed teachers, where substantial amounts of time are spent by trainees observing more experienced colleagues, where practice of the novice is guided by interaction with senior colleagues and workplace experience until a level of proficiency is attained.

As we can see, social interaction in this type of play can have an important role in cognitive development. Let us not forget that this type of learning can also facilitate an individual process of learning too, as chance discoveries are made – just like an individual scientist making a new discovery! The challenge for practitioners is to embrace provision of opportunity whilst working within the constraints of a curricular 'straitjacket'.

Children are keen to learn new information and are hungry to master new tasks (such as learning to ride a bike or moving to the next level of an electronic game) and, because they hate to be bored, children self-diagnose what they know, can do and what they can learn next. Play provides the ultimate curriculum for social, physical and cognitive advancement (Whardle, 2007). By using materials, interactions with others and mastery of tasks and skills to progress through levels of play, children develop a sense of control of their environment and a feeling of competence and enjoyment that they can learn. Could this be due to the way in which play provides an instinctive method of assimilation for brain function and the fields of learning that are not easily achieved in discrete teaching? Brain research shows that this integration is very important to development (Shore, 1997). Whardle (2007) also identifies that play is a very effective way for children to accumulate a vast amount of basic knowledge about the world around them – knowledge needed for later learning in language, mathematics, science, social studies, art and medicine. It is important to remember that learning through play is not exclusive to children in the early years but is an important vehicle for human learning all the way into adulthood.

Reflecting on history and the time for change

For over a century the nature and purpose of education has constantly been reviewed, deliberated and revised. As explored in the early chapters of this book, early years educators have actively argued the place and importance of play in the formative years of learning, innovative philosophies and curricular freedom have been applauded, as in the Plowden Report's vision for a wider curriculum. One of the key goals for education has always been the desire to inspire children, whilst motivating them to learn.

Learning communities

A group of persons who share a set of relations, expectations and opportunities to ensure full participation and a positive learning environment.

Legitimate Peripheral Participation

The actions of a newcomer into a community of practice that lead him or her to full participation of that community; e.g. a trainee doctor enters the community of doctors (e.g. hospital).

Apprenticeship

The period of Legitimate Peripheral Participation where learners are engaged in the active process of acquiring the knowledge and skills of a community of practice until they are deemed sufficiently knowledgeable to practice on their own, e.g. apprentice bricklayer, community nurse, dentist, etc.

Ideas in action

I'm forever blowing bubbles! (Author observation of undirected play)

This observation was noted at a local museum that promotes an environment where children can 'learn through play' and explore a range of phenomena from the natural and human-made world. A group of nine children, from ages 3–11, and their accompanying adults are amongst a range of visitors actively engaged in an area called 'Kidspark'. The focus of current activities is exploring liquids. The observed group is attempting to blow bubbles. They have a large sink full of 'gloopy' liquid (this was discovered to be simply water, washing-up liquid and glycerine) that magically allows the children to blow gigantic bubbles with only their hands.

All the children attempt the activity by forming circles with a thumb and forefinger on one hand. The youngest children have limited success to begin with – they either fail to form the necessary shape with their fingers to hold the liquid or, as they begin to blow, the liquid film bursts before it has time to form into a bubble. After a short while they begin to notice Gareth (10 years old) is having much more success – to the point that he is not only blowing huge bubbles (sometimes they are in excess of 40cm in diameter!) but he is also managing to keep them up high in the air. He does this by blowing the bubble above his head to launch it upwards then positions himself underneath it, blowing gently, changing the direction of the blast of breath from his mouth, moving his body to ensure the best position to do this as well as keeping his eye on the trajectory of the bubble so as to limit the chance of it colliding with either another bubble or an object, and bursting.

One of the biggest bubbles is aloft and by this stage he has an audience – everyone is watching *him*! He glances around, taking his eye off the giant, floating bubble for just a second, and then continues to tease the bubble with breaths of air. As he manages to blow the bubble higher in the air (by now it is bouncing around more than 3m above everyone) you hear 'Ooh', 'Aah' and the 'Wow!'s of the group. Then suddenly the bubble is no more and a fine mist showers the onlookers. Everyone laughs and then there's a flurry of activity as everyone dives into the sink. Then come the questions: 'How do you do that?', 'Can you show me how to get it that high?',

'Mine won't get that big – how do you get it that big?', 'Can you make one even bigger?' 'What's the biggest you have made?' 'How high did it go?'

The boy, now the expert, goes on to give elaborate explanations that encompass not only the physical make-up of the bubble and its potential expansion rate but also the aerodynamic and physical processes that are required to keep the bubble afloat. And of course the show continues.

Stop and reflect

From a theoretical standpoint, how is knowledge acquisition evident in this vignette? Do you see evidence of the different standpoints outlined above? Is the notion of a 'learning community' present, and how powerful is it for the children in the vignette?

Improving practice

Does your setting provide opportunities for learning within a community-style setting? What are the advantages and disadvantages of working in this way?

Comment

In this example, what starts off as exploratory 'free' play quickly develops into more intellectual play as Gareth figures out the best way to form the bubble, what needs to be done to get it aloft and how to keep it there! (That is, development of knowledge.) During the experience he constantly tests possibilities, makes decisions, uses prior knowledge and learning and applies ideas, notions and hypotheses to the developing situation. Cognitive development is evident as each new attempt results in bigger bubbles, greater time in the air before they burst, and so on. Whether there is a positive or negative outcome, understanding and thus learning occur. There is also clear evidence of cognitive development through the social interaction of the group as the novices (the onlookers) look to the expert (Gareth) for guidance that helps them, in turn, solve the problems they experience. In conclusion we can observe clear evidence of Gareth and the novices ZPDs, and the context supports the notion of participation within a learning community.

Recurring themes such as individual learning, flexibility in the curriculum, a stimulating environment, ownership of learning, enquiring minds, the ability to question and argue rationally, reminiscent of the messages of over a century ago in the Plowden Report (1967) continue today to challenge educational thinking. However, it is the demand for improving standards and ensuring the acquisition of basic skills that has gathered more speed (Beardsley and Harnett, 1998). In the last two decades political forces worldwide have been observed increasingly steering and shaping curriculum thinking and development in the race to raise educational standards. With the advent of statutory guidance (for example *The National Curriculum* for England and Wales (DfEE, 1989; DfES, 2000 or Provincial level programmes of study in Canada), strategies and frameworks to develop literacy and numeracy (e.g. The Primary National Strategy: Primary Framework for Literacy and Numeracy, DfES, 2006), and schemes of work and published lesson plans in hard and increasingly electronic forms, teaching has become standards based, highly structured and continually scrutinised. Predetermined and nationally assessed goals – skills, concepts, bodies of knowledge, delivered through highly structured, whole-class lesson teaching such as the UK mathematics three-part daily lesson and literacy hour are, for many, hailed as the key elements for effective teaching and learning. However it could be suggested that original ideologies, including the place of play for older learners, have been lost to learning experiences in primary childhood that are narrow, often teacher-driven **transmission learning**, steered by formal assessment purposes, and make little impact on life-skill development.

However the new millennium may herald the time for change. As you will have seen demonstrated by Brock in Chapter 5, the introduction of *Excellence and Enjoyment* (DfES, 2003c), the key aims for youngsters in *Every Child Matters* (DfES, 2003b), the Primary Framework for Literacy and Mathematics

(DfES, 2006a) and 20/20 Vision (DfES, 2006b) new guidance promotes greater flexibility, more emphasis on personalised learning and brings educational thinking up to date with current research findings that stress the importance of how one learns. Naturally the thrust of recent developments continues to focus on the 'basics' (literacy and numeracy), standards and ensuring every child reaches their full potential. However, coupled with new thinking on how one learns, there is now greater scope for practitioners to explore avenues for learning, in which play and thematic approaches have once again become more widely acceptable. For primary-aged children we see practitioners offering more active learning experiences and, in the most creative classrooms, exposure to experiential learning opportunities that meet the needs of **multiple intelligences**. It is now widely accepted that high standards can be obtained through a rich, varied and engaging curriculum where primary schools take control of their curriculum and are more innovative in developing their own character (*Excellence and Enjoyment*, DfES, 2003b).

> **Multiple intelligences**
> A theory developed in 1983 by Dr Howard Gardner that challenges the traditional IQ test-based notion of intelligence. Gardner suggests there is a broad range of different intelligences to describe adult and child potential and that these exist in different combinations within an individual. Thus a teacher must use a range of different teaching methods or pathways to reach a learner effectively.

> **Transmission learning**
> Where the learning experience is inactive and consists of didactic teaching, where information is conveyed to the student and the student is simply expected to remember it.

Opportunities for play in the classroom: any time, any place, anywhere!

Learning through play is for anyone, any time, any place, anywhere! As seen throughout this book, play provides the vehicle for experiential learning at a range of levels – intellectual, creative, physical, emotional, social and cultural. So much of what is learned in the primary years of schooling is planned by educationalists and yet some of the most powerful learning can come from spontaneous, even unsupervised, play. This has long been accepted and supported by theoretical perspectives yet often fails to manifest in everyday practice in primary classrooms. Furthermore, when adults continually drive learning experiences, as Fisher (2002, p. 119) explains, sometimes 'golden opportunities for learning are missed'. Claxton (1997) warns that to rely on experiences that focus on quick questions, slick answers and explanation rather than time to simply observe, deny the mind the opportunity to dwell, reflect, consider and roam. Reminiscent of Bruner's **perturbations**, the natural moments in a learning experience where we momentarily feel confused, bemused or just need 'time to think' and organise our thoughts, Claxton (1997) proposes that learning emerges from uncertainty and learning environments need to provide the time and space for such uncertainty 'to act as a seed bed in which ideas germinate and responses form'.

> **Perturbations**
>
> A term coined by Jerome Bruner to describe the moments in learning, where one might feel unsettled, uneasy or anxious, that should be an expected and accepted part of cognition.

Take, for example, planned learning at the local pond where the expectation is to learn about the cycle of life and the pond environment and concepts related to water safety and drowning. It is also highly likely that a child, given the time and space, will observe the properties of water including sinking, floating and surface tension and the effect of cold water on the body's thermal system. An older group of learners who debate the development of the local area traffic improvement scheme and the impact it will have on local people and the environment are emulating a more adult-oriented world. As they begin to consider the social impact – the winners and the potential losers and the impact of human development on the natural and physical environment, so the socio-dramatic role-play, in the form of a debate between the developers and the locals, is a way of exploring opinion, point of view and cultural norms and values. Whilst practitioners are able to take learning to identifiable objectives and curricular targets, which objective do we mark against as 'achieved' for the individuals who become impassioned and emo-

tional, or who demonstrate empathy and compassion? Perhaps we have become so focused on meeting standardised expectations we forget that there are much 'softer' areas of learning, the hidden curriculum, that are just as important in lifelong learning.

In contrast, spontaneous, unsupervised play such as digging around the roots of a tree, mounding and re-mounding the excavated soil, introducing stones and removing unwanted debris not only allows a child to explore the properties of soil (and apply it to similar materials such as sand) but, depending on how the play develops, s/he might experience basic building techniques (inserting sticks to stand up), the way materials must be retained from rivers, roads and mountainsides (banking the removed debris), the effect of moisture on materials (moister soil as the hole is dug deeper, the nature of gravity (as the mounded soil collapses), and ways of creating patterns, shapes and lines by drawing in solids made up of small particles. With skilled scaffolding by and shared thinking with an adult, whatever the focus of play for any age of child, there is potential for powerful learning.

Naturally the primary practitioner is in a difficult position – just how much undirected play can I incorporate in the curriculum? Can I justify the time I spend allowing my learners exploration, observation, time to muse? How can I cover the expected curriculum and provide opportunities for experiential learning? How can I respond to every child in my class as and when I need to? Will my learners be safe when they play? The answers lie in one's own creativity, belief in the power of play-based learning and ability to engage flexibly with a variety of learners. Many opportunities will have to start from planned beginnings (if only to justify the insatiable need for paperwork from curriculum managers and inspectors) but where possible there need to be activities in every lesson that allow developing learners to have time to reflect and explore ideas, take control of their learning and utilise their toolkit of knowledge, skills and understanding to not only advance through the prescribed curriculum but develop those skills that are essential for lifelong learning. Additionally, as a practitioner cannot be working with everyone all of the time, the minutes spent with individuals or groups have to be high quality and purposeful. It is with this in mind that the following sections

Ideas in action

A large group of children (ranging from 7–12 years old) and their teachers attended a local track meeting and due to the delayed arrival of the bus for the return to school found themselves engaged in self-directed activities whilst waiting for the bus to arrive. The children initially broke into smaller groups, some chatting, some practising athletics skills and some playing in the sand in the long jump pit. After a while the group came together and started an adapted game of leapfrog. The group were observed working together, supporting the less athletic, offering advice and guidance and simply having a 'good time'! The participants were totally absorbed in the activity and protested loudly when they were told it was time to go home as the bus had arrived.

Improving practice

Should learning always have a formalised plan with expected outcomes or are there times when, as educationalists, we can justify 'going with the flow'. How do current developments and initiatives provide scope for practitioner autonomy?

Figure 6.2   At the athletics track (Undirected play)

examine how play-like opportunities can be used to satisfy curricular objectives and enhance the acquisition of some of the universal skills for lifelong learning (communication, teamwork and creativity, problem solving and enquiry and, most importantly, self-evaluation to improve one's own performance for future learning).

Play to develop communication skills

Communication skills, being able to communicate and exchange information clearly and in a variety of ways, are fundamental elements of one's personal, social and academic life. In simple terms, communication can take many forms (for example verbal and non-verbal), be through a variety of media (such as human interaction, electronic, the media) and can be both an individual or reciprocal activity.

Role-play is a perfect vehicle for learners to explore many aspects of verbal communication. Role-play is used here to describe any type of pretend, imaginative, fantasy or socio-dramatic play and forms part of epistemic play (see Chapter 1). This includes imitation of real or imaginary events that allows a child or group of children to act out situations and experiment with events, language and emotions. (Notice in the Ideas in Action on page 156 the incorrect use of the word 'extinct' – here an opening arises for a practitioner to clarify meaning and advance learning that may otherwise not have occurred). The play might be spontaneous or more planned.

Ideas in action

Impromptu imaginary play on the school field at lunchtime (Author observation of undirected play)

A mixed-age group of children (three girls and two boys ranging in age from 7–9 years) were observed during a play period at lunch break. They had demarcated a large square with freshly mown grass that represented their house. When asked, 'What are you guys up to?' they replied excitedly that they were taking on the role of a group of adult friends 'hanging out' at home. The play was observed for more than 15 minutes with the following talk concluding their play before they decided it was time to go and have a game of tig.

Boy 2: I think I will have to mow the lawn – it's getting a bit long.

Girl 1: Well I don't know if I have got everything to go on this vacation.

Girl 2: Well I have my stuff in this *bag [showing an imaginary bag represented by a clump of grass cuttings].*

Boy 1: Sick! The main thing you need is your passport, like they say on the TV.

Boy 2: Yeah, my mum 'n' dad thought they had lost mine and then they found it. Good job as we were going to Florida. They said I would have had to stay at home if they hadn't found it!

Girl 1: Here's my passport.

Boy 2: Let's see.

Girl 1: I'm not showing you *[she runs to the corner of the house and pretends to hide it in her pocket].* It's a bad photo!

Girl 2: Help me tidy up the house will you . . . the taxi will be here in a minute.

Boy 1: I'm not tidying up – my mum does that, not me!

Boy 2: I'm fed up with this. Look – there's Sam and the others. Let's go and play with them.

[Boys leave.]

Girl 2: *[Going over to Girl 1 and pretending to look at her passport]* Oh no!

Girl 1: What is it?

Girl 2: You can't go to the airport!

Girl 1: Why not?

Girl 2: Well, look at the date on your passport.

Girl 1: Where? There's nothing wrong with it!

Girl 2: Here. Look. Look at the date. It's extinct!

Improving practice

How could you provide opportunities for your learners to engage in such activity within the formal curriculum and confines of the classroom? Discuss your ideas with colleagues.

In the early years the role-play area provides the environment for such activity but there are ways in which such learning can be accessed by primary children. It is possible to set up role-play areas in classrooms of older children (see 'Southowram Village Garage' later in this chapter), but one can also plan dedicated drama lessons within language or indeed draw opportunities from other curricular areas to enhance learning. Also remember that often the most powerful learning comes from experiences where the children take the lead rather than being driven by the practitioner and their intended outcomes!

Stop and reflect

Children naturally engage in imaginative play when in actual fact they are role-playing experiences from a more adult world. How does this sort of play encourage communication amongst learners?

Francis Whardle (2007) suggests this type of play enables children of all ages:

> To develop flexible thinking; learn to create beyond the here and now; stretch their imaginations; use new words and word combinations in a risk-free environment; and use numbers and words to express ideas, concepts, dreams, and histories. In an ever-more technological society, lots of practice with all forms of abstraction – time, place, amount, symbols, words, and ideas is essential.

In the school environment it is the role of the practitioner to focus on the *four* language modes – listening, speaking, reading and writing – and use these in an integral way to not only acquire knowledge of language structure and usage but also to ensure continuous understanding across the curriculum. For example, whilst reading a poem or extract from fiction, to develop a response to its tone or mood, one must have a sense of the overall flow of the passage rather than focus on word-by-word analysis. However, to understand or be able to solve a mathematical problem or algebraic equation one must pay attention to each word or individual unit to be able to find the clues that lead to solution.

Thus, whatever the curriculum, subject teaching should, at the very least, focus on the language demands of each subject in terms of talk, the way language is recorded, the subject-specific vocabulary and the structures used to express ideas. You will also observe in the sections that follow how communication underpins learning both of a range of other key skills and subject-specific experiences (see Figure 6.3 on page 159).

Play to encourage teamwork and creativity

Schools play a key role in the socialisation of children of all ages as learners engage in social play, playing together with an agreed purpose. This type of play, also described as **ludic play** (see Chapter 1), is often seen in playgrounds

Ludic play
Play activities that are either engaged in, or have the outcome of, pleasure.

where children engage in traditional or modified games, as part of a small or large group, as well as in other areas of their life in and outside of school. Sluckin (1981) carried out a substantial observational study of the playground activities of 8–10 year olds, which led him to propose that children build numerous specific skills in outdoor free play, often learning much more than is immediately obvious.

Social play allows children to explore, for example, the conventions of interaction with others, taking turns, cooperation, reciprocity, sharing, leading and being led, developing ideas and utilising norms, values and morals. Social play also facilitates networking with peers, children of similar and varying levels of socialisation experience, within and outside of an immediate friendship group as well as across the age phases – the 'buddy system' often used in schools works on this latter premise, where a more experienced other supports the least experienced individual. Add an environment that contextualises learning and stimulates curiosity, motivation and willingness to learn and social play impacts on life skill development as it allows children to explore and refine the ability to survive in the socially complex environments we experience as adults.

Preparing children for a world of the future is to prepare them for life in a new millennium that may well be unpredictable. The rate of change that blankets our world almost certainly means that in ten years from now many individuals will not recognise their job description today and some may even experience career extinction. Indeed it is believed that the workforce of the twenty-first century will be a transient one and that uncertainty where jobs may be will mean that the worker of the future may have as many as 19 different jobs in their lifetime and may retrain more than three times, as half the careers in 20 years from now may not exist today (City & Guilds, 2004). Therefore we need to ensure, if nothing else, that our children are taught transferable skills and have the capacity to be creative, alongside being numerate and literate, so that they can adapt and change to the demands of whatever life may hold in the future. All children have the capacity to be creative, and yet one could argue that education systems have failed to recognise individual talents and nurture this creativity.

Ideas in action

Case study: *The Gift from Winklesea* (Directed play: language focus)

The Gift from Winklesea, a novel by Helen Cresswell, was used as the key resource for thematically planned work for a group of 10 year olds over a period of seven weeks. The story revolves around two children who, after a visit to a local seaside town when they purchase a gift in the form of an egg, become the custodians of a Loch Ness monster type pet and their valiant attempts to keep it from harm.

Each week a new chapter of the book would reveal events that would be taken as starting points for lessons across the curriculum. Thus whilst an outline structure for planning existed the nature and focus of learning evolved as the story unfolded, as did subject-specific lessons. For instance, after reading how the children had purchased the egg in the story, the next morning, as the children entered class, there was great excitement. Overnight a series of strange footprints had been left on the floor (the creature had obviously stepped in the paint from an overturned paint pot found at the same time). The footprints started at the egg that had miraculously appeared the week before (and had been left near a radiator as the children thought that the heat would help it to hatch) and had now cracked open and its contents vanished! When the footprints were followed they disappeared through a dislodged tile in the classroom ceiling! What had come from the egg? It had to be an animal as it left prints that were not like ours! How would it stay alive? Did it need someone to look after it? Where was it now? What if it grew fast like in that film where a monster has babies and . . . Should we tell the caretaker in case he saw it? Would it need capture? Should we contact a local zoo? We need to make some posters to tell everyone it is lost! Can we keep it?

These were some of the responses that inspired a lengthy debate and follow-up activity as to the whereabouts of the contents of the egg and what should be done about it. Children split into equal groups and were asked to discuss and record what they could do to: (a) find out what the creature could be; and (b) report their findings to the school community and public at large.

Fantasy, speaking, listening, interviewing, reporting (including IT – TV, newspaper, newsroom, etc.), wanted posters, investigation – using the internet to explore possible creatures from the footprints – were some of the group activities that followed, culminating in the preparation of a short TV broadcast and then group presentation which would form the basis for a debate at the end of the week.

Additionally, a range of learning activities based around eggs was discussed at class level, identified in collaboration with the children and then focused by class teacher planning. For example, the patterns on different types of eggs provided the starting point for exploring marbling techniques in art; the work of Fabergé was examined in history and led to report writing about the discovery of a lost Fabergé egg; technology and mathematics lessons saw the creation of egg boxes from only limited materials including newspaper (incorporating multiplication tables, measurement, nets, strong structures, etc.) – the work for the week!

Improving practice

Observe the 'learning map' shown in Figure 6.3. Identify the links between different areas of study and how learning opportunities provide embedded experiences for the children. Take an area of your practice and attempt to create a web similar to this. (It is interesting to note that 'mind maps' work in this way and can be used as powerful tools to clarify thinking and improve study skills for your learners too.)

Stop and reflect

How does this learning experience fit within the remit of play? Which elements of communication could be explored over a series of lessons from a starting point such as this?

How does working in this way have an impact on the planning that is expected by managers and inspectors?

▶

LANGUAGE

Speaking and listening:
Discussion, debate, re-telling, instructions, role-play, problem-solving chapter events, prediction, inference, deduction, compare and contrast, etc.

Reading: shared reading of text, guided reading of text extracts. Epilogue creation.

Writing:
Narrative: own journeys on holiday or visit to the seaside (Ch. 1)
Creative writing: the gift decides – Winkie leaves and where his journey takes him (Ch. 9)
Newspaper/report writing: newsflash (Ch. 9)   My pet is a...It needs...(Ch. 3)
Advertising poster: Church Bazaar Children's Show (Ch. 5)
Poetry: With my found I could buy....(Ch. 1)
    The egg hatches...(Ch. 3)
    The tale of Winkie (Chs 3–7)
    Acrostics – various (Chs 6–9)
Class compositions: Winkie Doubles (based on Hungry Caterpillar? Ch. 5)
Instructional writing: to keep Winkie healthy
Letterwriting: to the zookeeper (Ch. 4)
Animal-based sayings: 'Every dog has it's day'

MUSIC
Sea-shanties/seaside songs (Ch. 1)
Compositions – 'the egg hatches' – tempo, mood, dynamics (Ch. 3)
Class composition (lang) – lyrics and melody

GEOGRAPHY/HISTORY
Seaside towns – past and present (Ch.1)
Packing for a holiday (problem solving) (Ch. 2)
Loch Ness monster and other sea creatures (Ch. 4) or 'salty seadog tales'

DRAMA/PE
Role-play of story elements
Dance – Winkie moves

The Gift from Winklesea

Potential curriculum starting points for study (but don't forget to go with the children's ideas)

MATHEMATICS
Number: Purse/piggybank money problems (Ch. 1)
At the refreshment stand/ice cream shop (Ch. 1)
At the church bazaar – money problems (Ch. 5)
Winkie's journey home (Ch. 8)

Measurement: Calculating journey distances/times (Ch. 1)
Bucket and spade problems/containers for Winkie (Chs 1 & 3)

ROLE-PLAY
Travel agent, Ice cream van (Ch. 1), Fish and chip shop (Ch. 3), Pet shop/vet/animal hospital (Ch. 6)

COMMUNITY LINKS
Visit by local animal charity or veterinary staff, visit to animal hospital visit to local animal sanctuary/zoo and talk from a zookeeper

SCIENCE
Life processes and living things
Animals/creatures that hatch from eggs (Ch. 2)
Observing processes in the classroom (chicks/frogspawn)
Exploring what animals need to stay alive/healthy (Chs 3 & 6)
Amphibian study (Ch. 4)

Materials and their properties
Insulators and conductors – which stay warm longest (Ch. 2)

Scientific processes
Fair tests, inquiry, prediction, variables, hypotheses, etc.

ICT
Design a magical egg (Ch. 2)
Amphibian data collection (Ch. 4)
Research – domestic/wild animals – what should we/could we/do we keep as pets? Why? Should wild animals be kept as pets? (Chs 6 & 7)
PDSA and other animal charities

HEALTH/PSE
Keeping Winkie healthy (Chs 5 & 6)
Keeping ourselves healthy – compare and contrast
Animal activism – the pros and cons of keeping animals debate

Figure 6.3   *The Gift from Winklesea* (learning map)

We need to ensure that we value the things that our learners are good at and provide learning environments which are interactive, encompass learner diversity and reflect how we experience learning (visually, auditorially and kinaesthetically). Pupils who are creative will then be prepared for a rapidly changing world, where they may have to adapt to several careers in a lifetime. Ken Robinson (2006) reiterates that employers want people who see connections, have bright ideas, are innovative, communicate and work well with others and are able to solve problems, emphasising:

> We must see our creative capacities for the gift that they are and see our children for the hope that they are. Our task is to educate their whole being so that they can face the future. We may not see this future but they will. It is our job to help them make something of it.

Ideas in action

Case study: *Into the Enchanted Forest* (Directed play)

The Enchanted Forest, as introduced in Chapter 3, was created by a group of practitioners from everyday materials in an inner city school in Bradford, West Yorkshire, England. An agreed space was darkened and lighting adapted to create a 'greenish woodland hue' with giant leaves, creepers, vines, a cave-like grotto and all manner of woodland creatures, enhanced with 'mysterious magical chimes'. A variety of activities exposed the children to collaborative problem solving (storytelling then clues led to tasks that would lead the children to search for Kaliya the dog who had been stolen by the Forest Jinns), exploration of scientific learning during their journey (building bridges, boat construction, sending a signal using an electrical circuit and choosing materials to protect the magic key), as well as language acquisition, development and role play.

> The children had a wonderful time in the Enchanted Forest . . . the children could easily become actively involved in the story. They quickly learned the procedures and realised they needed to collaborate to try out the tasks . . . they became self-sufficient – supporting and scaffolding each other's learning and understanding. Many children had the chance to assume leadership and demonstrate personal expertise. They were eager to participate . . . organise themselves and allot roles in order to solve the problems.   (Brock, 1999, p. 10)

Improving practice

Some ways in which you can encourage creativity in your setting:

- Actively encourage pupils to question, make connections, envisage what might be and explore ideas. Promote and reward imagination and originality. Ask open-ended questions such as 'What if . . . ?' and 'How might you . . . ?' to help pupils see things from different perspectives.

- Value and praise what pupils do and say. Establish an atmosphere in which they feel safe to say things, take risks and respond creatively.

- Create a fun, relaxed working environment if you want to encourage pupils to be adventurous and explore ideas freely.

- Create conditions for quiet reflection and concentration if you want to encourage pupils to work imaginatively.

- Make the most of unexpected events. When appropriate, put aside your lesson plan and 'go with the moment', but never lose sight of your overall learning objectives.

- Be willing to stand back and let pupils take the lead. However, make sure that you are always on hand to provide prompts and support as needed.

▶

- Join in with activities and model creative thinking and behaviour. Showing the pupils that you are a learner too can help to create an open, constructive learning environment.
- Give pupils opportunities to work with others from their class, year group and different age groups.

http://www.ncaction.org.uk/creativity/

Visit the National Curriculum website (http://www.ncaction.org.uk) and take a look at the new 'Creativity in Action' examples that can be used with pupils from Year 1 to Year 9.

Stop and reflect

Are there opportunities for your learners to engage in creative learning experiences where they can develop a range of academic and social skills? Do you provide opportunities for them to explore ideas, be creative in their thinking and encounter moments when they can make their own decisions (whether right or wrong) – even take chances? Do children need to be creative all of the time? Scrutinise your planning and identify openings where you and the children can take a more creative approach to learning.

Improving practice

'Imagination is more important than knowledge. Knowledge is limited. Imagination encircles the world' (Calaprice, 1996, quoting Einstein, 1929).

How do you encourage your learners to use their imagination? How do you respond to the child who answers your questions with what are seemingly 'ridiculous' or 'incredible' answers? What opportunities are there in your setting for learners to really develop and use their imaginations?

Ideas in action

Case study: Pens for Hens (Mathematics focus)

In the main part of a mathematics lesson, 9–10-year-old children were asked to solve a problem for Farmer Brown. The children were clustered around 'discussion tables' (we had already rearranged the classroom furniture) to encourage a positive and purposeful working atmosphere. This also facilitated social play, talk, collaboration, problem solving, exploration and communication of ideas. Resources (matchsticks for pens, plasticine for hens, different types of paper, scissors, glue, etc. were provided to 'try out' ideas and the children were expected to play and work together. By the plenary we hoped to be able to tell Farmer Brown exactly how to calculate the number of pens he would need for any number of hens!

The activities started from an embedded, experiential base as the children were asked to assume the role of Farmer Brown, and discuss and explore how they might create pens for the hens. The children were encouraged to use any resources available in the classroom as well as the small images of hens; matchsticks to represent the pen sides.

After our discussion the play really began as children manoeuvred their resources, discussed and modified their ideas, reconsidered their thinking and engaged with the challenges of the activity. Different groups shared their ideas informally with those in close proximity – some individuals consequently changed their plans whilst others acknowledged the 'good idea' but continued with their own strategy. It was not long before explorations developed into intellectual play. Here procedural learning was developed as correct operations or symbols were used (making formal jottings, tables, and so on), then summarising/generalising evolved, culminating in algebraic notation in the plenary.

▶

Maths	Curriculum Area: NC U&A POS Ma 2.1a,d, f,g h,i,j,k	Time: 9.00–10.30am	Age group: Year 4	Context/past experiences: Prior lesson explored multiplication patterns and how to create simple generalisation.
Learning objectives: i) to take a problem and explore different ways to solve it; ii) to make, justify and record thinking and then a generalisation as a solution to a given problem.	**Assessment: Level 3–4 Criteria:** Children can make a reasoned generalisation in response to an investigation. Children can present results, using a range of methods, to communicate information. **Evidence:** Discussion and recordings.		**Resources:** Self-chosen but could include: play animals, plasticine, wooden sticks, pens, plain/lined/ graph paper, scissors. Provide whiteboards, worksheets.	**Key vocabulary:** Pattern, calculate, method, jottings, what could we try next? How did you work it out? Sign, symbol, equation. **(Key vocab NNS Y4)**

	Teacher/Teaching activity (including key questions)	Pupil/Learning activity (including key questions)
Oral/ mental starter **15 mins**	Share objectives with children and clarify understanding. Recap previous lesson learning considering number patterns – finding the pattern and detecting the link between numbers (generalisation). Use OHT to practise examples. Can we spot the link? How? Explain. Cover repeating patterns, e.g. 1, 2, 4, 1, 2, 4 or with shapes. Ask ch for ideas. Growing patterns: 3, 6, 9, 12; 1, 3, 6, 10 (triangle nos). Ask ch for ideas. Link to examples from real life – boxes of eggs, multipack crisps, etc.	Recall previous patterns - adding five, the ten times table, square and triangle numbers, etc. Children need to look for the pattern in the differences and try different operations (detectives). Use white boards to provide the product of inputs but also the starting numbers from given products (differentiated).
Main teaching activity **15 mins** **Group activities** **35 mins**	Going to look at a problem and solve it eventually with a generalisation. Introduce Farmer Giles and his hen pens! Think, pair share ideas how to start. What will you need? What is your strategy? How will you know when you have succeeded? Work an example drawing on the OHP. Can we see any patterns? What do we notice? Can we guess what might come next? How can we check? Groups (self-identified) to identify and gather resources. Children work from given starting points (differentiated) to explore the activity. Teacher to focus work with Group 1 who will be encouraged to try different sizes and arrangements of pens. Children will be encouraged to reflect on learning. Colleague to follow observation schedule.	Children listen to the information. Groups 1 and 2 (average and above average) are given free choice as to how to tackle the activity – working in pairs or individually. Can choose the shape and orientation of pens but must justify choices. Can 'build' the pens and explore the problem. Teacher to support explorations and recordings. Groups 3 and 4 (below average ability) advised to use rectangular pens as per class example and instructions and will need to record, predict and check their findings.
Plenary **15 mins**	What have we found out? Groups to lead the discussion: What have they learned? How did they do this? What helped them so far? Could they have tackled the problem in a different way? Ask the rest of the class to comment and evaluate. Mention that tomorrow we will be continuing with this work and exploring further possibilities.	Group 1 given thinking time prior to plenary. Reflect on what they have learned and how they did so, what helped/hindered them. Receive comments and feedback from the other class members.

Figure 6.4   Problem solving and enquiry: Lesson plan for Pens for Hens   ▶

Stop and reflect

Look at the lesson plan for this learning experience in Figure 6.4. Imagine taking this sort of approach to organising activities in your learning environment. Take a closer look at the ways the children demonstrated their thinking in Figure 6.5. How would you plan and assess such an activity? How does it fulfil set objectives from a given curriculum? Can you identify what the key learning objective was for this activity? What role does the teacher play in this approach to learning? How does your intervention enable the learner to take their learning on to a higher level or even ZPD?

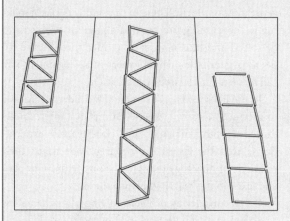

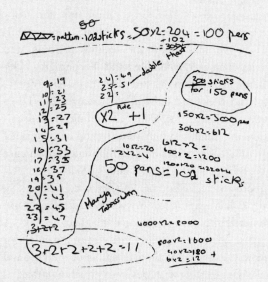

(a) The learners were able to make their own choices regarding the materials they wanted to use to help them in their problem solving. Choices ranged from using card/paper to cut or draw (including miniature chickens.), small world farm animals borrowed from an early years class, Lego, etc. In example 6.5(a) we see how they used matchsticks and glued these to record their ideas.

(b) The activities started from an embedded, experiential base (as in 6.5(a)), developing for some of the children into procedural learning through the use of correct operations or symbols by making informal jottings, lists, tables, summarising/generalising with algebraic notation as seen in 6.5(b). These ideas were explored further in the plenary of several later lessons.

Figure 6.5   Children use self-regulated methods to record thinking

Play to facilitate problem solving and enquiry

Problem solving and enquiry or 'intellectual play' (a term I have used to mean any play activity that encourages higher levels of thinking, such as problem solving and investigation) requires strategy, a structured approach, assimilation of given information, exploration of possibilities, and thinking creatively about solutions, logic and hypothesis. Here ideas are explored with an identified purpose and a range of solutions evolve that are then analysed for feasibility and acceptability. The earlier example of the Enchanted Forest as well as investigations in science and mathematics are examples of this category of play. It differs from role-play in that accepted notions and ideas are explored (rather than just fantasy or adaptation of role). Problem solving can be an individual or group activity but the ultimate goal is to further skill, knowledge or understanding. It can have exploratory beginnings but will often end in a heightened understanding of a concept and an increase in skill or application of knowledge, as described earlier in this chapter.

Transferable skills
These encompass communication research and planning interpersonal skills; organisation, management and leadership.

Children need stimulating practical problem-solving experiences (which allow them to make the connections between procedural and conceptual understanding) to be meaningful for lifelong learning and development of **transferable skills**. Encouraging older children to engage in this sort of play is extremely powerful and goes hand in hand with many of the DFES (2000, and online) Key Skills (Communication, Application of number, Information technology, Working with others, Improving own learning and performance and problem solving) and Thinking Skills (Information processing, Reasoning, Enquiry, Creative thinking and Evaluation) (http://www.standards.dfes.gov.uk) promoted in current educational thinking.

Close observation, timely intervention, open-ended questions encouraging the articulation of thinking and challenging existing strategies are key teaching strategies when learners are engaged in problem-solving activities. As practitioners, we need to take time to analyse where they are. Pupils need to engage in reflective enquiry during play and activity, treating mathematics as problematic and exciting, to fully experience a problem-solving approach. The 'plenary' or conclusion of a lesson is the perfect opportunity for the children to listen and discuss what has been learned, share their approaches to solving the problem, question, and try to prove their own

hypotheses. Children need help to recognise intangible strengths such as memory, imagination and persistence, but also the security to not give up too soon before the right and bright ideas come along (Fisher, 2005).

When learners are engaged in activities similar to Pens for Hens learning reflects those expressed experiential learning cycles as seen in Kolb (1984). Kolb's model is underpinned by the idea that learning is rooted in a concrete experience. From this a learner makes observations and reflections from which concepts and generalisations form. These in turn guide decision making in the learning process that allows for problems to be solved and thus new learning identified. Figure 6.6 demonstrates how such an experiential learning model can be seen in a classroom context.

In the Pens for Hens example the children were able to produce their own generalisations that interestingly exceeded both curricular and class teacher expectations. After the lesson the children were asked their opinions of how they thought the opportunity to play, and learn in this way, had helped them.

When considering problem solving in mathematics, a curriculum that both teaches knowledge and skills and develops learning through understanding, i.e. a situated context is favoured. All learners have to develop knowledge, understanding, concepts, notions and ideas in order to acquire the 'tools' to begin to address a problem. Then by using operations or symbols, presenting information in a range of formal and informal ways and recognising patterns and sequences an 'intuition' develops as approaches are adapted to new situations

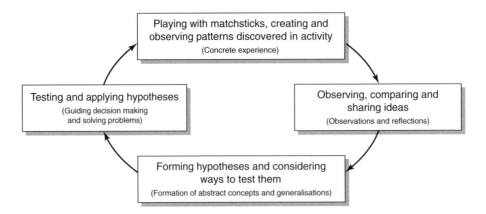

Figure 6.6 Kolb's experimental learning model, adapted for Pens for Hens
Source: Wallace, 1999, p. 235.

and routines. At the same time, knowledge can be shaped and developed through interaction with others. In Pens for Hens, discussions clarified thinking and purpose – what did we need to do? Did we need to record our thoughts? How would we do this? What was important to remember? We also agreed rules for the activity – we wanted to make as few pens as possible – we didn't want the farmer wasting resources! Also we only had our lesson to get our ideas presented – the farmer would have time targets to meet too!

Problem-solving play is not only limited to learning with a mathematical focus. Problem solving can be evident across the curriculum – from manipulating their environment or objects in it (science) to creating entirely new inventions modelled on an artefact they have seen, heard, touched, and so on in their environment or simply exploring ideas (technology). The importance of stimulating the learners' interest and curiosity should not be underestimated.

Children engage in problem-solving play from a very young age, for example making sandcastles on the beach, building towers with blocks (until the tower falls down!), building with kits such as Lego, K-nex and other modular apparatus or simply using everyday waste objects (cardboard boxes, toilet roll tubes, paper, pieces of wood) or household objects and so on to create structures or elaborate complexes. As children advance through primary education their opportunities for such activity often become limited to specific subjects (for example creating a moving car in technology or designing an energy-efficient home in science), and the chance to use true creativity and problem solving diminishes as products duplicate predetermined examples given by teachers or curriculum documents. Yet, when given the chance, learners seize the opportunity to work hard and for longer to create more adventurous and imaginative approaches to learning.

The inability of adults to solve everyday problems was certainly criticised in the Cockroft Report (DES, 1982) two and a half decades ago and is still of central concern (Thompson, 1999). The importance of exploring ideas through practical, embedded learning

Ideas in action

Feedback: What the children said about Pens for Hens

It was fun . . . I liked it because I got that question right and Miss let me tell everyone else. I liked playing with the sticks 'cos they helped you to see what you were doing. Miss's sheet was good, that box one, 'cos I didn't have to make it myself. I liked working with M. It was fun.

It was fun . . . I enjoyed it . . . I liked sticking the matches down.

Playing with the matchsticks and talking to M. [was the best bit] we helped each other and Miss was nice . . . she told us we were brilliant! I liked sticking the picture – so we can use it again. I want to do some more. It's maths but its also like art!

I learned how to be a detective to spot a pattern a g . . . g . . . generalation . . . to get the difference . . . the numbers between the numbers. I didn't think play could do it like that!

That if you know then you can make the patterns . . . in my pattern you get the triangle and then you added more sticks . . . two more sticks, yeah . . . you make a gen . . . er . . . a . . . lisation . . . It's a bit like a rule. And that you can learn when you are playing!

Improving practice

Identify an area of your practice where you could adopt a similar approach, or even develop an original activity, to that used in Pens for Hens.

Consider how you will introduce the activity to your learners, what organisational issues need consideration, the nature of the resources required to facilitate the learning experience, how your role will advance learning and how you will know when learning has been achieved.

Analyse the appropriate curriculum expectations to identify what should be learned and what could or would be learned if sufficient 'freedom' was offered in the learning experience.

Ideas in action

Case study: Conservation – saving energy in the home (A homework activity)

For homework, a class of 10 year olds were asked to consider ways in which a home could be made to use energy more efficiently. The teacher gave the class an open-ended brief so that they could respond in a variety of different ways – oral, written, pictorical, electronic. Two boys decided that they would like to 'build' their ideas in the form of a Lego model. However they did not stop with just Lego – they included cotton wool to represent wall cladding and roof insulation, cardboard solar panels provided the energy source for electricity, specific Lego transparent pieces represented low-energy bulbs,

amongst the many features. The flat roof comprised a green baseboard that in reality could be planted with grasses and alpines – a living, insulating roof!

Stop and reflect

What opportunities are there for your children to have flexibility in the way they tackle activities? What ways are available for you to give your learners 'choice' in their responses and thus encourage creativity and independence in learning? Remember, you are often only limited by your own imagination.

Agentive

Active participation in the social creation of meaning (within a constructivist learning model).

is not a new idea (see, for example, Wallace, 1999) and by focusing on a 'child-centred' learning environment we can encourage **'agentive'** (Bruner, 1999) learners. Furthermore, the processes outlined in this section of the chapter, as Glaser suggests, may guide future problem-solving activity, but more importantly develop an 'intuition' to respond and adapt to new situations. This is surely a key approach in adulthood and a vital trait of the lifelong learner.

Self-evaluation to improve one's own performance for future learning

Of key importance in learning is the need to reflect, evaluate and self-regulate one's own performance. Young's (1999) analysis shows we are faced with the reality of a learning culture that is individualised, abstract and written, based on high-status knowledge assessed through high-stakes testing, rather than collaborative, discourse-driven, practical learning environments rooted in everyday-life contexts. In all the examples seen in this chapter, there is a collaborative and reflective

approach where feedback, praise and encouragement are crucial elements in encouraging groups, and more particularly individuals, to self-evaluate. Focusing on effort as well as outcome is as important – getting the 'right answer' was only one part of being successful in Pens for hens, for instance. By their very nature, open-ended activities suggest there were many ways to approach learning and thus a range of solutions possible and valued. What we have to do as practitioners is provide opportunities for learners to not only engage actively and creatively with the prescribed curriculum but also have the time and space to reflect on learning, and individuals' capacity to take learning to a higher level.

Alongside simply reflecting on learning we also need pupils to become 'critical' thinkers. Robert Paul (in Fisher, 1996) divides critical thinking into interdependent categories of affective strategies (fostering independent thinking); macro-abilities (the processes involved in thinking and organising thinking – reasoning, identifying purposes and criteria, evaluating outcomes, making judgements); and micro-abilities. Some of the most important of these are being able to ask the right questions, using time to think effectively, being able to reason when invited, apply logic and meaning coherently and, perhaps most importantly, understand others and oneself. Through critical thinking we can encourage children to be reasonable, fair-minded, skilled and creative thinkers.

Ideas in action

Case study: Glitter bugs (Directed exploration)

A class of 11 year olds are expected to explore the concept of germs as part of a unit of study on micro-organisms within the science curriculum. They are expected to recognise that diseases can be passed on by very small organisms and that this idea is based on scientific evidence. Formal guidance suggests teachers introduce the topic by finding out children's ideas about what makes them ill. Follow up children's ideas by discussing some ideas people used to have about illness. Ask children to use secondary sources such as CD-ROMs, reference books to find out about scientists, for example Jenner, Pasteur and others who developed the 'germ' theory of diseases. Explain that 'germ' is an everyday term for the very small living organisms called micro-organisms that cause disease.

A creative practitioner decided to go one step further in providing a first-hand embedded experience of germs. She asked some of them to coat their hands with glitter (usually used for decorating cards at Christmas) and then proceeded with a series of tasks where the glitter was transported to different locations (just as germs are!) Then the learners without glitter had to go about their normal classroom routines and observe their hands, at intervals. It was a huge surprise to the pupils that they were picking up the glitter left behind by their peers as well as finding glitter in all sorts of strange places! The use of a torch added further evidence as to how the glitter 'bugs' had spread! Of course eradicating the glitter bugs was an even trickier proposition. Contextualise the experience as a pandemic and learners suddenly grasp the importance of why some germs are deadly!

(You could also do this by giving learners several different kinds of liquid and then asking them to continually change partners and tip a bit of their liquid into someone else's glass, followed by a simple chemical analysis that looks at the composition of the resulting mixtures).

Improving practice

Look more closely at an area of learning that you will be exploring with your learners. Try to think 'outside the box' in the way you might present the experience to your learners. Perhaps you can use an internet source to give you ideas or use an interactive resource such as a smart board or white board. Remember to pay attention to any health and safety issues!

Stop and reflect

As a practitioner, how have you responded when faced with a learning objective that is problematic to deliver? Do you take the 'easy' or 'safe' option of simple research, chalk and talk or do you choose a more creative option, as did the practitioner above? How is such an approach more meaningful and powerful for learning?

Ideas in action

Case study: Village Garage (11 year olds use role-play to explore life skills)

As an end-of-year project a class of Year 6 children had the opportunity to focus on the learning they had acquired in primary school before leaving for secondary education and forging links with the local community.

The aim of the project was to encourage a sense of citizenship and develop key skills as the pupils entered this important transition phase in their lives and also to give them opportunities to experience life in the 'real world'.

▶

As part of the project the class teacher organised for the pupils to visit local businesses, spending time 'on the job' and finding out about different occupations in the village, and then drew these together in the class-based learning activities under the theme of a garage.

The garage had several departments. Throughout each week groups of children were rotated through different roles and departments and each week concluded with a board meeting at which one representative from each department presented a report of activity (compiled by the group). After the reporting session time was utilised for self-reflection at an individual, group and class level where affective learning took place. The pupils were encouraged to reflect critically and empathetically. In light of discussion the director, the class teacher, set targets for each department for the following week and negotiated individual learning skill targets – these had to be completed and presented to the board for discussion the following Friday. At the end of the term, based on the data collected from meetings, the most successful departments would be identified (by the class) and rewarded! Some of the weekly tasks included:

Sales: calculating production costs and profit margins from a given design of new vehicle or solving supplier problems.

Design: new peripherals (for example a mobile phone holder and earpiece for Madonna and personalised hubcaps for David Beckham!).

Marketing: design and implementation campaigns for the company or the design team peripherals.

Accounts: several customer profiles were introduced and repayment plans were to be calculated with 'good deals' included ensuring a sale! Also dealing with a customer defaulting on payment – recalculating, etc.

Personnel: dealing with specific issues and problem solving to reach agreement – the employee who has turned up late for the last month – what is our course of action?

Improving practice

When providing opportunities for and encouraging self-reflection and improvement, it is useful to remember that self-reflection:

- depends upon meta-cognition, which in itself depends upon the stage of learning;
- can be seen as a way to reinforce learning (constructivism);
- encourages higher levels of self-awareness and empathy of others;
- can be highly charged and emotional – the process has to be carefully managed as memories of feelings and thoughts come into play;
- allows children to think through the stages of or their journey through the learning process – and it takes practice;
- reiterates the importance of self and the child's sense of self;
- requires logical reasoning and sequencing – these skills have to be taught too;
- can be written, drawn and oral, and individuals may have their own preferences (for example smiley/sad faces, thumbs up/down, short written comments, and so on);
- will need to be modelled and scaffolded in the early stages of development;
- takes time to improve.

Stop and reflect

What opportunities are there for such a thematic approach to learning that not only delivers key learning objectives but which also develops skills for lifelong learning? How much time do you allow children for self-reflection? Should you or could you create more time? Identify opportunities in your teaching timetable that you could utilise to facilitate the development of reflective learners.

Summary and review

This chapter has helped you explore the place for play in the primary phase of learning and now returns to the original questions set out in the Introduction.

- The climate for play – what can be learned through play in the primary phase? Has the opportunity for play-based learning and personal development been squeezed out of the curriculum in the hunt for academic excellence and achievement?

Practitioners in primary settings can and should provide a play-based environment where play can be used as a vehicle to facilitate learning not only for academic achievement but for personal, social, spiritual, moral and cultural development. This chapter has demonstrated that experiences in the curriculum such as investigation in science, problem solving in mathematics, communication and role play in language, imaginative and thematic work, are all examples of how 'play-based roots' may already exist in primary teaching. Formal curriculum expectations may well be 'squeezing out' opportunities for play in some settings but creative practitioners can still provide educational starting points that facilitate a rich and authentic learning experience and prove to be valid in both meeting and exceeding targets for academic excellence and achievement. Play is not necessarily subject specific nor is it unique to the early years phase. Indeed the examples provided in this chapter have not only demonstrated how children across the primary phase might engage in meaningful activity but also the cross-curricular nature of the approach itself.

- Opportunities for play in the classroom – how can play-based experiences be utilised to encourage learners to take *ownership* of learning and develop their key and thinking skills within the constraints of a formal curriculum?

This chapter has provided a plethora of examples from practice that have demonstrated how practitioners can meet and enhance the demands of a prescribed curriculum as well as support the development of the transferable skills vital to the lifelong learner. The ability of learners themselves to take a more active learning role, develop the capacity to be reflective and take ownership of their learning is of central focus in current educational debates. Indeed, where integrated approaches to practice are adopted learners themselves become excited, engaged and enthused and, most importantly, have the opportunity to develop their own imagination and creativity. Most of this chapter has provided you, the practitioner, with starting points to fire your own imagination and creativity and provide the foundation for empowering your learners. It has been argued that children need to become more fully involved in the processes of learning – to be able to explore their own concepts in an environment in which they have the opportunity to really question, even disagree. Surely expert mathematicians, scientists, artists, are engaged in this type of activity and we therefore have a duty to teach our children how to do so too? This would allow us to explore with children what helps and hinders them in learning, offer purpose in learning and perhaps go some way to meet individual learning styles. We need to foster and encourage the lively enquiring minds we observe in the young child all the way through primary schooling and beyond, so that we continue to see the engaged, developing learner ask, 'Why?'

Naturally, as practitioners, we are unable to have complete autonomy on what is and is not taught in a classroom. Every school has targets to meet and statutorily there is a curriculum to adhere to. Yet when a little imagination is applied to the objectives to be achieved, rich and highly contextualised learning opportunities are possible. Furthermore where flexibility is applied to the *way* in which learning is possible, we pave the way to incorporate more playful, active learning experiences for youngsters in our schools.

As we stand at the gates of a new millennium, we need to take stock of our educational values and be accountable for the practice in our settings. Now, more than ever before, we have the chance to put the child back at the centre of learning. As the boundaries between work and play become increasingly more evident as children progress into adulthood, we need to promote the notion that children who are engaged in play-oriented activities work hard, sustain high levels of motivation and concentration and demonstrate high levels of learning and achievement. We have the opportunity to re-engage learners in exciting and challenging learning that incorporates play-based approaches and ensures pupils experience the joy and desire to learn in and beyond the classroom. Practitioners need to rekindle their intuition and their own creative talents, be committed to the inspired use of sustained shared thinking and scaffolding and not be afraid of knowing when or how to move learners forward in their development. Perhaps the most important changes we make to our settings are not in the organisation of resources and furniture but in our own abilities to listen to and observe our learners in a range of contexts. After all we are only limited by our *own* imaginations!

Transforming thinking and practice: over to you!

Practitioners in a **pedagogic setting** must consider intentions, actions, **metacognition** and knowledge. You will need to determine the nature and purpose of learning, identify educational goals, identify assessment activities, organise resourcing and facilitate discourse and reflection. Your complex social setting should encourage knowledge that is jointly constructed through activity and collaboration and promote learning that encompasses the needs of the whole child. You need to ensure your learners are active participants in learning processes where they are agentive, reflective and able to work collaboratively. Play, as seen in this chapter, can be a central and effective vehicle for learning if you are willing to be creative in the management of your setting and imaginative in the delivery of your learning intentions.

> **Pedagogic setting**
> The practice that a teacher, together with the particular group of learners, creates, enacts and experiences.
>
> **Metacognition**
> Reflection or analysis of one's own process of learning and thinking.

Questions for consideration

One could argue that the current educational climate places greater emphasis on the absorption of curriculum content and demonstration of nationally agreed expectations, with an emphasis on the development of acceptable literate and numerate individuals. But is this enough? How do we encourage our learners to be agentive and active problem solvers rather than simply vessels of knowledge?

The challenge for practitioners is *how* we build upon children's prior knowledge, experience and interest and engage and motivate learners in a curriculum that makes human sense, engenders motivation and explores real-life scenarios. Let's encourage children to play! Take another look through the scenarios in this chapter and you will see how many of the examples are rooted in real-life experiences (for example I'm forever blowing bubbles; Village Garage) and children leading the learning experience (see Hens and pens; *The Gift from Winklesea*).

How can we develop approaches to assessing learning that enable us to focus on process as well as product and the learners' ability to contribute to broader learner environments? When reconsidering what we value to be of impor-tance in the learning experience, we now need to shift the focus on to the needs of the child, not just attainment of the curriculum. Instead of assessing elementary skills, facts and concepts (one could argue this is the current approach of Standard Assessment Tests), could we assess children's strategies, schema and indeed metacognition (Greeno *et al.*, 1999) in the primary years? In this way can we guide children in 'how to think'? Children must not only be encouraged to articulate and share their ideas within formalised learning situations but should be steered to make links with real-life situations that reflect the here and now, and possibilities in the world of the future.

Ideas for research

As a committed practitioner:

Review your own ethos! Take stock of who you are and the type of practitioner you want to be. Think about what life could be like in an 'ideal world' and what you consider your own core values and how your provision can be more play based. As a lifelong learner yourself, who or what has influenced your values and norms and how did play have an integral role in your own development?

How do you role model the notion of lifelong learning to your learners? Do you demonstrate risk taking, creativity and imagination, and encourage your learners to do the same?

To what extent are you able to reconcile the thinking you may have developed engaging with this chapter with the external demands exerted upon you by parents, your colleagues and managers, or even political forces?

As a facilitator of learning:

Think about the ways in which you encourage independence, self-directed learning or play-focused activities in your own learning environment. In your setting, do you gather the necessary resources and make these readily available for your learners as part of your own organisational approach? Could you manage your learning environment in such a way that it puts the learner in a position to have to choose what, how and when they access the resources they need to scaffold their learning? At a higher level, where are the opportunities for your learners to direct their own learning or engage in play-oriented experiences? What are the pros and cons of such an approach? What can be realistically achieved?

To what extent are you tailoring the curriculum to the needs of your learners? Analyse your current educational plans and try to identify the extent to which the learning experiences you provide are product (for example knowledge, skill) or process driven. Can you be more explicit in identifying the key and thinking skills, identified within this chapter, and ensuring balance between predetermined outcomes and self-directed learning?

In what ways do you encourage and foster positive attitudes towards play the transferable skills that your students will find so valuable in their lifelong learning in the world of the future?

As a curriculum manager:

With colleagues, review the curriculum in its current form and anlayse how much time is available to pursue the interests of the children or to incorporate the flexibility to offer children the lead in learning that is central in a play-based pedagogy.

Take a fresh look at the initiatives that are driving your phase or subject in the current educational climate. To what extent do these contribute to the development of the view of learning proposed in this chapter? Critically analyse the pros and cons of these and other questions you feel this chapter has raised for both your setting and the learners in your care.

For the central educational agenda and further consideration:

Given curriculum constraints, government targets, high-stakes testing and close monitoring of performance of pupils and teachers, how can settings at all phases of education organise to teach learners to become active and agentive problem solvers? As practitioners, how do we engage in the accurate assessment of the development of such complex cognitive operations?

Further reading

Beardsley, G. and Harnett, P. (1998) *Exploring Play in the Primary Classroom*. London: David Fulton.

Craft, A. (2000) *Creativity Across the Primary Curriculum: Framing and Developing Practice*. London: Routledge.

Fisher, J. (2005) *The Foundations of Learning*. Buckingham: Open University Press.

Peturson, R. and Asselstine, L. (2001) *Creating the Curious Classroom*. Toronto: Harcourt Canada.

Websites

http://www.ncaction.org.uk.
http://www.standards.dfes.gov.uk

Supporting Children's Play

Building 'Social Hardiness' for Life: Rough and Tumble Play in the Early Years of Primary School

PAM JARVIS

Five children, four girls and one boy, are chasing one another around a school playground. The boy catches one of the girls and wrestles her to the ground, whilst the other three girls run around them; the whole group are screaming and laughing. The boy releases the girl, briefly chases the other three girls, then runs off to play with another group of boys. The girls immediately get into a huddle, talking and giggling. The researcher observing the children has placed a microphone on one of the girls. When she transcribes the tape, she discovers that one of the girls was directing the boy, shouting instructions to him about who he should be 'catching' at different points in the game. When the boy ignores her instructions and leaves the group, the girls huddle together to discuss the chasing play. The content of their conversation focuses upon who has been 'kissed' (which, as the researcher has seen no kissing, seems to equate to being touched or grabbed) and how disgusting boys are, each girl impressing upon the others how much she has personally been chased, while sympathising with her friends' concerns about the 'over-eager' behaviour of the boy.

Introduction

'Kiss-catch' activities such as these can be observed in any primary school playground. They are one version of the generic chasing and catching game known to generations of British children as 'he', 'tig' or 'tag', depending on regional origin, and which has also been observed internationally, for example as 'El Dimoni' in Spain and 'Oni' in Japan (Opie and Opie, 1969, p. 20). This chapter focuses upon the developmental role of rough and tumble (R&T) play with particular attention to the narratives that children use to underpin such activities.

> **Empirical**
> Based on observation or experience.
>
> **Gendered**
> Reflecting or involving gender differences or stereotypical gender roles (Merriam Webster).

In outlining a wide range of theory and **empirical** research findings, it will seek to explore the following questions:

- What is 'rough and tumble' play?

- What are the typical narratives underpinning such play, what level of social complexity do they reach, and how might they become '**gendered**'?

- What developmental learning may occur within such free play activities?

Introducing rough and tumble play

> **Reciprocal**
> A return in kind, mutually corresponding (Merriam Webster).
>
> **Anthropologist**
> One who studies human beings and their ancestors through time and space and in relation to physical character, environmental and social relations, and culture (Merriam Webster).

R&T play can be defined as a physically vigorous set of behaviours, for example chase, jump and play fight, accompanied by positive feelings from the players towards one another. R&T also involves **reciprocal** behaviour, which is often observed in role change, such as chasing and being chased. The play type was first formally named as such by the **anthropologist** Karl Groos in his books *Play of Animals* (1896) and *Play of Man* (1901).

The first modern **ethological** study of human R&T was undertaken by Neil Blurton Jones, in 1967. He transferred observation techniques used by Harlow and Harlow (1965) in monkey R&T studies into human developmental research, carrying out pilot studies of children's R&T play within several London nursery schools. He reported a pattern of running, chasing and play fighting occurring amongst the children that reflected

> **Ethological**
> The scientific and objective study of animal behaviour, especially under natural conditions (Merriam Webster).

behaviours previously observed by animal ethologists among juvenile apes and monkeys. Subsequent studies were carried out in non-western cultures and made similar findings. Konner (1972) undertook an ethological study of the Zhun-Twa (!Kung) people, and Fry (1987) studied children in Oaxaca, Mexico. Both of these researchers found that the children in the cultures that they studied engaged in R&T play which appeared very similar to the R&T of western children, with common behaviours observed including chasing, fleeing, laughing, jumping, play noise and a particular facial expression, also found in young apes and monkeys, that animal ethologists had already named as the 'play face'. The play face is a wide, open mouthed smile with the top teeth covered (see Figures 7.1 and 7.2). The fact that it is not only found in human beings but also in non-human primates and monkeys suggests that it is a natural, evolved behaviour, rather than one that is socially learned in childhood by observing other people.

Figure 7.1   Human play face 1

Figure 7.2   Human play face 2

What is rough and tumble play?

In human beings, R&T appears to be a cross-generational and cross-cultural phenomenon, particularly prevalent amongst young males. However, the term 'rough and tumble' can be an unsatisfactorily vague description of a diverse set of play behaviours. As more

research data was gathered, following Blurton Jones's (1967) initial observation studies, several taxonomies of movements in R&T emerged. Some of the movements identified appeared to be common across primate species; others, mainly those involving language and/or fantasy components, were identified as particular to human play.

One immediate question with respect to developing a taxonomy of R&T is whether to include the non-contact aspects of the behaviour or to narrow down the behaviour to actual play fighting. However, this could lead to breaking down the behaviour into very artificial 'slices'. As such, modern researchers have tried to study R&T as a complex and composite behaviour, incorporating some elements of social exercise play (such as chasing) and some elements of play fighting (for example wrestling).

A pressing question for practitioners is whether the individuals engaged in what appears to be R&T are carrying out such actions in fun or in anger. This was also a question studied by animal ethologists, including Loizos (1976), who undertook an ethological study of chimpanzee play, proposing that although social play and aggressive behaviour share some of their

Figure 7.3   Bonobo play face
Source: Frans B.M. de Waal

motor patterns, social play differs from aggressive behaviour in three specific ways:

1 It has its own set of signal patterns that indicate 'I'm only playing', including play face and role reversal.

2 It does not end in the separation of the participating animals.

3 The reaction of the recipient of social play is to respond with similar behaviour rather than a different set of patterns altogether. For example, an animal that is aggressively attacked will often seek to gain an advantage by attempting to surprise the attacker with a different type of aggressive response, or may attempt to run away.

In his studies of human R&T, Boulton (1988, 1993a and 1993b) found that groups of children of all ages could broadly agree whether a behaviour was R&T or aggression, and that they used similar criteria to do so. Boulton used these children's definitions to guide his own creation of a taxonomy of R&T. Costabile et al. (1991) carried out a cross-national investigation of how children differentiate R&T from aggression. These researchers found that although older children showed slightly higher competence, children of all ages used similar criteria to judge physical interaction incidents.

The study was carried out by videoing children in schools in England and Italy, and it was subsequently found that not only did children in both countries apply similar criteria to R&T definition; they also judged incidents to nearly the same standard of consensus when they were shown the tapes of children speaking a foreign language. This indicates that such judgements may be made on the basis of non-verbal signalling, including subconscious recognition of the human play face, possibly indicating that human beings use similar judgement systems to those used by non-human primates.

The criteria proposed by Costabile et al. (1991) and Boulton (1988) differentiating R&T from aggression were later synthesised by Power (1999), and added to his own criteria, mainly drawn from work with non-human animals. A composite of the information contained in Power (1999), Costabile et al. (1991) and Boulton (1988) differentiating R&T from aggression is summarised and presented in Table 7.2.

It would therefore seem clear that R&T is a specific, universal play behaviour, easily recognised by children across language barriers, and that separating such behaviour from the serious fighting it enacts can be achieved relatively easily, by using mainly behavioural indicators.

Table 7.1 Typical Movements Identified in Human R&T Play

Play-fighting movements (contact or mock contact mimicking aggression)		General R&T movements
Hit/kick at	Colliding	Chase
Light blow	Butt	Carry other child
Pounce	Hit and run	Spinning and swinging
Pile on	Play bite	Tease/taunt
Hold/grab/restrain other child	Wrestle/pin	Sneak up
Push	Trip	
Grappling (brief struggle whilst standing)	'Shoot'	
Kung fu/karate	Boxing (series of light clenched fist punches, may hit lightly or 'stage fight')	

Source: Jarvis, 2007, p. 173 (Synthesised from: Humphreys and Smith, 1987; Boulton and Smith, 1989; Pellegrini, 1996; Power, 1999).

Table 7.2 Differentiating R&T and Aggression

Length of episode	R&T lasts longer than 'real' fighting.
Stay together or separate	R&T partners tend to stay together when the R&T episode is over, combatants almost never do.
Facial expression	R&T partners smile and laugh, combatants frown and possibly cry.
Physical acts	Were blows actually landed or 'staged'?
Crowd	A real fight will typically draw other children, standing in a crowd to watch. Children conversely tend to show little interest in other children's R&T unless they are actively attempting to join in.
Threats	Where language is used it may be quite easy to differentiate real threats from play threats.
Intensity	Real aggression will result in higher intensity action than play aggression.
Tactics	Real fighting will involve tactics where each partner tries to gain the upper hand, making attempts to really hurt the opponent; play fighting will involve role reversals and restrained, stylised 'aggression'.
Targets	Play fighting opponents are likely to be friends. Real fighting opponents are likely to be children who dislike one another.
Consequences	Injury is rare in play fighting, but likely in real fighting.
Age group	Increasing age is positively correlated with an increasing likelihood that a fight is real rather than in play. Fights between children of high-school age are likely to involve some real aggression.

Source: Jarvis, 2007, p. 175

Ideas in action

Observations of 'monkey play'

Monkey play involves much rough and tumble, with some play actions that are very similar to those used by human beings. The animals frequently play fight, which involves play biting, role reversal and pretending to be injured; they also play 'tag', where one monkey approaches another with a play face, hits it and runs away, inviting the other animal to chase.

Improving practice

R&T 'spotting' on playground duty

On one of my own playground duties I saw three 11-year-old boys play wrestling, and realised by noting their facial expressions that whilst two of them were enjoying the activity the other was not. I asked them to stop, and then asked the boy who was frowning if he

was OK. He said that he was, but used the resulting stoppage to remove himself from the game without 'losing face'. I made no further comment, and the other two boys continued with their game. R&T/aggression taxonomies can have a very practical use, in this way.

Stop and reflect

How long would you have allowed this type of play to proceed? Would you have noted the children's facial expressions before deciding how to respond?

Comment

Might current ideas of 'best practice' encourage practitioners to intervene in such play too quickly and punitively?

Ideas in action

Girls' R&T (Author's observation notes)

Girls-only R&T play seems very rare, based on the findings of my own observational study of children's R&T play between the ages of 4½ and 6, as during the 18 months of observations, just four focal child observations of a total of 33 containing R&T play involved girls only. One of these generated an intriguing, highly original narrative of a witch and a magic rabbit, invented by the three players. Madelaine played a magic rabbit, whilst Emily took the role of a witch who wanted to turn her into wood. Cheryl played a rescuer who was trying to save the rabbit from the witch. Another girls-only R&T game was quite lively and involved a large amount of physical contact. It involved spinning quickly around a signpost and then lying on the grass, which at one point involved a gentle pile on as the girls laid on top of one another, giggling and hugging. The underlying story appeared to be 'putting baby to bed', in that baby gets up, goes and plays (spins around the post) and then gets tired and fractious so has to go to bed again.

Stop and reflect

What sorts of play do you expect to see all-girl groups engaged in during free playtime? Why not carry out a focal child observation to see if you can discover at least one all-girl play narrative.

Boys' R&T (Author's observation notes)

Fifteen episodes of boys-only play were observed; ten of these involved highly active R&T. In single-gender R&T the boys tended to rely on current media for their play narratives. Beyblades, a Japanese fantasy cartoon about spinning warriors, was very popular at the time of my observations, and I observed several boys' spinning activities where they pretended to be the 'Beyblades', sometimes taking on the names of the characters. The game involved spinning while karate chopping at one's opponents, the aim being to knock the other player out of a 'ring'. When a player was knocked 'out' he generally collected himself and went straight back into play; there did not seem to be any concept of being 'out' for any length of time. It was this higher level of energy in boys'-only play that separated the genders most distinctly.

Stop and reflect

What sorts of play do you expect to see all-boy groups engaged in during free playtime? Why not carry out a focal child observation to see if you can discover at least one all-boy play narrative.

Comment
Differences between boys' and girls' R&T (Author's observation notes)

To a casual observer both the girls' and boys' play described above would fit the broad category of chasing and catching play. However the pace, roughness and particularly the nature of the contact between the boy players indicated subtly different gender orientations to chasing activity. There were many play-fighting actions that occurred in the Beyblades game which were not present in the story of the witch and the magic rabbit, and a boys' Robot Wars game involved Adam continually play punching at Chris with sound effects (pow, pow), whilst Chris aimed play karate chops at Adam. Later, when I asked the boys to tell me about this game, they proposed that the chopping motion was 'Mr Psycho's hammer'. In contrast, the girls' game involved a lot of hugging, with Cheryl hugging Madelaine as they ran to protect her from Emily's 'evil' touch. When Emily stopped chasing, Madelaine would turn around to face her, putting her hands up by the side of her head to

▶

mimic 'rabbit ears'. At times, Cheryl and Madelaine would allow Emily (who was the younger, smaller player) to get nearly close enough to touch them, but then they would laugh and pull back. I also observed a tendency to hug and cuddle in the brief and gentle girls' pile on, the underlying narrative for this being rather caring/maternal: 'putting baby to sleep'. The more common boys' pile ons I observed, for example connected to a cheetahs and leopards narrative, were conversely related to brawling and play strength competition. There was more direct physical confrontation in most of the boys' games observed, and less coherent vocalisation than was observed in girls' play.

Improving practice
When does R&T become aggression? (Author's observation notes)

At times a clear hierarchy seemed to be in operation within the boys' play that did not appear so obvious within girls' or mixed-gender groups. There was also sometimes evidence of boys 'passing on' feelings of subordination to other, often physically smaller boys, usually in more overbearing play fighting behaviour with particular individuals. I noted that neither Rory nor Chris pushed Grant, but Chris pushed Rory quite hard, whilst Rory was quite rough with Leon. I wondered if this indicated an underlying dominance hierarchy. Chris always exhibited the play face whilst he was

pushing Rory, but the level of energy in the pushing seemed quite high to me.

However, I had to remember that I was judging the interaction of young males from a female point of view, so came to no firm conclusion on this point. During one of my observations, such play fighting behaviour developed into serious aggression, where a boy excluded from play by a group of boys joined another friendship group of younger, smaller boys and was subsequently admonished by the supervising adults for deliberately bumping two of these children's heads together.

Stop and reflect

What might have been different if the adult on duty had noticed the exclusion of the child from play, and dealt with the situation at that point, rather than after he had joined a different group of younger children, and redirected his frustrations on to them?

Improving practice

Having gathered one all-girl and one all-boy play narrative for the activities above, compare them and see if you come to the same conclusions outlined above. If not, consider what aspects may be different, and why.

What might be the problems for judging when to intervene for an adult supervising many young children engaged in free play in a school playground? What changes in policy might improve the situation, without curtailing the children's ability to engage in such play?

Gender differences in rough and tumble play

One of the clearest differentiations in all aspects of R&T play appears to be the different amounts of such behaviour found between the genders. In terms of performance of such play, a common finding in both human and non-human animal research appears to be that young females carry out less R&T than young males, and the overall female play style is less physically oriented. Many researchers have concluded that R&T is more important in the development of males, in both human and non-human animals. Pellegrini and Smith

(1998) noted that males of all playing species, including humans of all cultures, exceed females in frequency of R&T. The suggestion is, therefore, that this gender difference relates to evolved differences between males and females in many mammalian species, including human beings. This introduces the concept of **sexual selection**: that girls and boys have a natural tendency to play differently in order to prepare them for different roles in reproduction.

Sexual selection
A theory which proposes that the genders evolved slightly different attributes, due to the different roles that they play in parenting.

How are girls and boys different?

Support for the greater prevalence of R&T play in males across primate species was found by Braggio *et al.* (1978) in the data gathered in their observational study comparing the behaviour of children, juvenile chimpanzees and juvenile orang-utans. They found that in all three species males undertook a higher frequency of R&T than females. The reason the researchers suggested for this difference was hormonal: the evolved effect of the hormone **testosterone** within male bodies. There is a surge of testosterone in mammalian male bodies in early infanthood (the priming or 'organising' effect), then again at puberty (the activating effect). If the priming effect is absent in males, there seem to be corresponding behaviour changes; in particular, reduced R&T has been observed in rats and monkeys. Introduction of testosterone to young females correspondingly creates more R&T play.

> **Testosterone**
> A hormone produced by the testes that creates male sex characteristics.

There have also been studies which indicate that the same processes occur in human beings. There is a condition called Congenital Adrenal Hyperplasia (CAH) that occurs in children if their mothers are accidentally exposed to high levels of testosterone (via medical treatment) whilst the children are still in the womb. Berenbaum and Snyder (1995) found that girls with CAH showed a significantly greater preference for boys' toys and activities; whilst boys with the condition did not appear to differ from non-CAH boys in any way. Additionally, Hines *et al.* (2002) calculated the amount of testosterone present in human expectant mothers' blood and, when they studied the behaviour of the resulting child at age 3½, they found that higher than average levels of maternal testosterone during pregnancy resulted in higher than average rates of physically active play undertaken by female children. Again, there seemed to be no effect on boys. Both of these studies suggest that even slightly higher amounts of testosterone than is normal in human beings' pre-birth environment will trigger a mild priming effect, eventually resulting in more male-type behaviour in female children. The overall conclusion drawn from both human and non-human animal studies is that testosterone has an important effect upon the expressed play behaviour of young mammals. To understand why this might happen, we need to consider the evolutionary theory of sexual selection.

Why are girls and boys different? Evolution and sexual selection

A theory originated by the evolutionist Trivers (1972) proposed that males and females in each species have evolved slightly differently, due to the different parenting roles that they undertake in adulthood in a **natural environment**. This theory of sexual selection suggests that female mammals have to give far more of their own biological resources to each child than males (for example, in pregnancy and **lactation**). The instincts that are related to mating and child rearing have consequently evolved along a different pathway in each gender, hence males and females of every species have slightly different characteristic behaviours.

> **Natural environment**
> The environment that a creature evolved within; for people this is a world of animals to hunt and plants to gather, not a world of farms and cities, which have been made by people.

Bjorklund and Pellegrini (2002) proposed a theory of **evolutionary developmental psychology**, which suggests that evolution has pre-programmed human infants with a specific human and gendered behaviour 'template', which is primed to undergo much further development in interaction with the child's specific environment during the early years of life. This means that free

> **Lactation**
> Literally, to secrete milk, refers to the period that a mother is breast feeding an infant.
>
> **Evolutionary developmental psychology**
> A theory that proposes that children are born with a basic set of evolved features, which need to be further developed in interaction with the environment.

Ideas in action

Mixed gender R&T (Author's observation notes)

During my 18-month study of children's R&T play, I found that the mixed gender R&T of 4½–6 year olds usually began when two or three girls sought out a boy to offer an invitation to chase them. This invitation was typically a 'touch and run' action. When I asked the children what they were playing in mixed groups the uniform response was 'kiss-catch', if I got a response at all. They seemed quite reluctant to talk about this to me. The narrative underlying mixed gender chasing seemed to be quite predictable; boys pretended to be some kind of powerful, frightening creature and girls ran away from them. There was, however, quite wide variation in the specific story created, which seemed to be influenced to some extent by the weather-mediated play environment.

In the winter months, the child chaser would often pretend to be some kind of 'monster'. There was a particular stance for this, an expression that can best be described as a grimace, teeth showing, hands up in a clawed position and a slow lumbering walk in the style of an actor playing Frankenstein's monster. In all the games of 'monsters' I observed, I only observed a girl acting as 'the monster' once, in an all-girl play cohort for a short time before the group went to invite a boy to play. He immediately took over the role of 'monster' and chased them.

Other play narratives observed underpinning chasing between the genders included a summer grass-based activity I described as the 'poison touch' game, where girls touched by the boy chaser laid down and 'played dead' until another girl's touch 'revived' them. On damp summer playtimes, I subsequently observed games with similar narratives, for example 'capturers and captives', where boys and girls collaborated in a game where boys pretended to tie girls to a wall with imaginary ropes, where they had to stay until released by another girl, and a 'dodge and catch' game where girls ran past a line of boys whilst the boys tried to catch them as they ran.

Improving practice

Carry out some focal child observations of children playing 'kiss-catch' (also known as 'kissy-catch' 'kiss 'n' catch' or 'kiss-chase', depending on the regional area). What types of narrative/stories do they appear to be using? Repeat your observation in a different season/different weather conditions and see if the basic narrative has remained the same whilst the specific story has subtly changed.

Adapted
A species that has undergone evolutionary changes that have enabled it to fit neatly into the environment which it naturally inhabits.

play experiences are of vital importance within this process, particularly in preparing children for complex social aspects of adult life. Evolutionary developmental psychology proposes that children's play styles have been **adapted** by **evolutionary forces** to prepare them to seek out the correct practice experiences to gather skills and knowledge in preparation for the often gendered roles that they would undertake in adulthood in a hunter–gatherer environment. So what do we observe when the genders interact in active free play?

Balancing culture, biology and evolution

Whilst there is good evidence for the contribution of evolution to children's play styles, it is also clear that human behaviour is not 'programmed' by nature to the extent that the behaviour of less complicated organisms (for example, bacteria and insects) seems to be. This leaves us with the question of how culture and biology may interact in developmental processes on the journey to the production of adult human beings. Human beings are psychologically very flexible, which means that they are able to learn many different ways of coping with their environments. Philosophers Mallon

Evolutionary forces
Forces that shape creatures, creating a situation where creatures with a specific set of features are more likely to survive to mate and have offspring than those who do not possess such features.

Bioculturalism
A theory that suggests that people are constructed equally by their biology and their cultural surroundings.

and Stich (2000) proposed the concept of '**bioculturalism**', highlighting the complementary roles of biology, evolution and culture in the production of human behaviour.

Given that human beings are such a complex species, we have to attend to many different aspects to make sense of children's behaviour in R&T play. Whilst the basic occurrence of R&T play in human children can be shown to have a biological cause via the action of testosterone in the body, and clear evolutionary roots in the non-verbal play of earlier species, such play in human beings is likely to show greater variability and complexity than that observed in less complex animals, due to the greater psychological flexibility of the human being.

The biological and evolutionary evidence thus suggests that we are provided by nature with a very basic set of instinctive behaviours, some of which vary between males and females. We now have to consider what effect this may have upon the skill that separates us most sharply from all other species on earth: that of language. Tomasello (1999) proposed that, because human beings can so successfully share such complicated and abstract ideas via language, we are able to understand other people as creatures with internal thoughts and motivations like ourselves – we can begin to understand what it might be like to 'stand in their shoes'. This in turn underpins a form of **cultural evolution** that is unique to the human species, as ideas and stories are passed from person to person. The ability to read and write hugely extends this ability, as it allows us to share our thoughts

Cultural evolution
The unfolding of cultural practices to fit the environment in which a population live, e.g. for example the cultural norm of very swift disposal of the newly dead in hot countries.

with many more people, even those who are born long after we die.

Lyle (2000) described human beings as 'storying animals', making sense of their environments via stories and narratives, meaning that human beings live in a world that is largely created through the stories we tell about it. An emergent question is therefore: do the genders construct rather different stories, originating from their evolved psychology? Carol Gilligan (1993) proposed that the genders speak with 'a different voice' and that, when adult, men and women tell stories rather differently and take different attitudes to many aspects of human life. She argued that the genders approach moral decisions differently, with women putting more emphasis on caring than men. She suggested that this explains why women of all cultures are more inclined than men to consider the motivations and circumstances of others before coming to a conclusion on a specific situation. Empirical support for Gilligan's theory emerges from Marder's (1987) review of courtroom-based research. Marder outlined a clear gender-related finding: whilst male jurors tend to be 'verdict driven', female jurors are more likely to be 'evidence driven'; that is, more inclined than men to carefully consider different points of view contributed by different members of the jury before coming to their own decision.

The earlier sections of this chapter have described studies of play that have found males of several primate species to be more involved with physically active play which revolves around issues of dominance and status, whilst females prefer more sedentary play exploring more symmetrical, co-operative relationships. In order to initially investigate the correspondence between **linguistic** and behavioural gender differentiation in human beings, we now need to consider whether there are matching correspondences in the different types of play undertaken by girls and boys, and the 'voices' they use to narrate and describe it.

Linguistic
Relating to language.

The current early years gendered language research evidence can be summarised as follows: girls build a sense of community in their language. Their conversation indicates that they are concerned with being nice, and creating intimacy and solidarity within their friendship groups, wishing to be seen by their friends as moral and lovable. People who are perceived to be mean are excluded from the group. Boys are concerned with being adventurous, risk taking and flouting authority outside the friendship group. They do not seek to appear nice, but they do have underlying concerns about the cohesion/solidarity of the group. People who are weak are seen as not worthy of male group membership.

How girls and boys use language to cooperate and compete

On the basis of their classroom experiences, many teachers would propose that issues arising in the classroom and playground relating to competition tend to mainly revolve around boys. This was the position taken by Sheldon (1990), who proposed that boys' groups are adversarial and girls' groups affiliative. However, Kyratzis (2000, 2001) firmly disagreed with this position, proposing that the reason that researchers had not perceived girls' competition was because the type of assertion that girls engaged in was far more subtle than that found amongst boys. Crick (1996) similarly argued that the reason for some researchers proposing that girls are not aggressive is because they are focusing on the wrong type of aggression in their research methodologies! Kyratzis (2000, 2001) proposed that both genders vie for position in the peer group, boys seeking to be the most dominant, and girls the nicest. She described a juvenile form of Gilligan's (1993) 'different voice', proposing that girls tell stories to indicate and consolidate alliances, whilst boys' stories are designed to emphasise to one another how naughty (authority flouting/dominant) they can be. Whilst girls do not typically engage in direct physical or verbal aggression, they do employ relational aggression, undermining other children's relationships within the peer group. Roy and Benenson (2002) linked this gender difference to a sexual selection explanation: adult males can achieve their maximum chance to produce **offspring** by directly competing with other males for status and resources, which enhances their

Offspring
The product of reproduction, the young produced by an organism.

Kin groups
Groups of people who are genetically related.

attractiveness to females as superior providers. However, the adult female can produce less offspring and must invest far more of her physical resources in each child than the male parent. In the natural environment, primate females typically care for their children within female **kin groups**; as such, the pathway to successful child rearing for the female is through building and maintaining strong relationships with the other females in her kin group. Consequently, covertly undermining other females within a peer group whilst simultaneously maintaining a pleasant façade would appear to be a highly adaptive strategy for females, allowing them to undermine specific competitors whilst maintaining good relationships with the majority of the group.

It appears that whilst both genders compete, males use an openly competitive style in their conversations, depicting a world in which individuals are engaged in contest, whilst women and girls are more likely to use the conversational style of 'double voice **discourse**' (Kyratzis, 2000, 2001), a highly assertive conflict-speaking style, which nevertheless uses mitigating language content in an apparent attempt to quell discordance amongst the social group; for example issuing instructions to other children to stop engaging in mischievous behaviour. Girls' talk thus has a cooperative surface structure but provides a framework where they can compete for emotional dominance within their social group, whilst boys' talk has a competitive surface structure but provides a framework for companionship and group solidarity. It can therefore be proposed that cooperation can become a very effective form of competition amongst female groups, and that within each gender cohort, power relations, social ranking and disagreements can be routinely managed through narrative rather than ongoing physical competition.

Discourse
Literally a conversation, but frequently used by social scientists to describe an ongoing theoretical debate.

Empirical evidence for the 'gendered competition styles' hypothesis include the work of Charlesworth and Dzur (1987), who found evidence of cooperation mixed with manipulation amongst 4–5-year-old female, but not male groups. This study of single-gender interaction found that girl groups tended to form under the control of a single, dominant female who used relational

Ideas in action

Gendered competition styles (Author's observation notes)

I noted that when boys took on roles in fantasy play based on current television programmes that the largest and 'toughest' characters were most popular; for example two boys chose the role of 'Mr Psycho' (the newest, 'toughest' house robot) in the Robot Wars chasing game. Similarly, during football play, Ben proposed that he was 'one boy, but I can tackle a thousand men'. Rory, who was significantly smaller, replied rather uncertainly 'I can tackle lots of men.' Additionally, when Chris scored a goal he would typically say 'like Beckham', accompanying this utterance with a well-observed imitation of Beckham's characteristic 'victory wiggle'. After one game, he tapped Rory on the shoulder as they were walking towards their class lines, saying 'winners . . . we're the winners, 85-nil. We won, 85-100.' By contrast, the girls seemed more concerned to appear caring. In the witch and magic rabbit narrative, the youngest player was allocated to the most powerful but most villainous role, that of the witch, by the two other players who were several months older and recognised 'best' friends.

Improving practice

How do boys and girls compete in the playground? One way to consider this is to keep a brief 'log' of the complaints that children bring to you when you are on playground duty, organised in 'boys' and 'girls' categories. Once you have done this for at least one half-term, collate your data to see if there are any clear pattern differences between the genders.

aggression to retain her authority, whilst male interaction tended to involve dominance behaviours from the majority of group members. Whilst some boys are inevitably more successful than others in their dominance attempts, these researchers noted that all-male groups did not typically fall under the control of a single boy to such a great extent. Additionally, Marsh (2000) invited children within a nursery setting to undertake active, fantasy play within a 'Batcave' role-play area, emphasising that both boys and girls could play and be 'Batmen' or 'Batwomen'. It was clear throughout her research period that there were distinct differences between the gendered superhero discourses. Batwomen were more likely to rescue often clearly vulnerable victims, such as small children, whilst maintaining good relationships with the other Batwomen; the Batmen chased and apprehended 'bad guys'.

Boys and the 'warrior' discourse

An evolved, gendered psychology certainly appears to be reflected in the voices described in this chapter, girls creating imaginary narratives where good relationships are maintained, while protecting their own place in the group hierarchy by emphasising their own 'niceness' compared to other girls, whilst boys create scenarios in which they explore their own and others' potential for physical dominance and 'daring'. The discourses created by each group focus upon these different hierarchical structures. Jordan (1995) identified a strong 'warrior' discourse amongst boys in her primary classroom, which she found problematic within the teaching and learning environment. She reflected that she had been unable to find any explanation of how or why such a narrative seemed so important to the little boys in her care, but that research evidence strongly suggested that the male fascination with physical competition has been present for many generations, represented in the discourses of both historical and contemporary human cultures. It is suggested that the missing explanation she seeks may be the evolved, gendered human psychology described above, due to the body of empirical evidence to suggest that the genders are influenced by their underlying bio-psychology to build gendered play narratives in active free play; biology and culture playing complementary roles in this process.

Ideas in action

Girls' talk in kiss-catch (Author's observation notes)

Whilst the children described mixed gender chasing and catching play as 'kiss-catch', I never saw one kiss occur during any observation. There was an incidence of 'kiss-catch' described in dialogue from one of my radio microphone transcripts, generating a description of 'kissing' incidents that I did not observe in my simultaneous focal child observation. This was very much managed by Felicity, the girl wearing the microphone, who called the boy back into play several times, issuing instructions relating to the specific girl that he should be chasing at specific times.

Speech transcript:

Felicity: What? No. What? (*Another child talking, indistinct.*) It's her . . . with the friends . . . What? What did you say, Kayleigh? Kayleigh. JAMIE! JAMIE! (*Very loudly.*) Stop.

Child: Come out!

Felicity: Jamie! Jamie! Jamie! Oh-oh. No, you've got to get her and Francisca now.

Child: Stop . . . no . . . op run off.

Child 2: He tried to get Francisca.

Felicity: You can try to get Francisca now.

Child (*Boy?*): Come on, over there.

Felicity: I'm here! We're not talking.

Child: Not playing? You're not playing.

Felicity (*Breathless? Running*): Mmm, mmm, Kayleigh, you've got a kiss. Got (*?name's*) catched (*?*) game, Kayleigh's a kiss! I've already got a kiss twice. (*Breathless.*) I've already got a kiss, have to catch to get a kiss. Jenny is playing. You gotta get Jenny. Jenny, run!

Child: Jenny, it's kiss-catch!

Felicity: It's kiss-catch, Jenny! Run, run, run, run run! (*Heavy breathing.*) Come on, Jenny, run!

Child: I'm staying out here . . .

Felicity: Jamie! JAMIE! Umm, umm, umm. La, la. (*Singing.*)

Child: No, you've gotta?

Felicity: Kayleigh. Kayleigh's not . . .

Child (*Simultaneously, indistinct.*)

Felicity: Jamie . . . Uh-oh. (*Breathless, running.*) Ah! Got a kiss. Not time now! Oh, man, I got a kiss all over the place. Got kiss on my cheeks, kiss on my head. Oh, man. Kayleigh! (*Calls.*) I just got kissed!

Child: Have yer?

Felicity: Yeah, and it were right there, it all went over (*?*).

Child: He kissed Kayleigh right there.

Felicity: And mine went all over!

Child: Oh, no! (*Indistinct.*)

My simultaneous observation recorded that what had actually happened was that the boy had chased Kayleigh, wrestled her to the ground and had then run off, following which he had been called back into play by Felicity, and had unsuccessfully chased the other girls in the group for a brief period before going to join an all-male group playing a different game. The sophistication of Felicity's behaviour in her false claims of getting 'a kiss all over the place' and clear organisation of the chasing process, coupled with the overtones of disgust when discussing the resulting male behaviour, and the appalled 'Oh, no!' response from her female playmate indicates that the children involved in this game were practising complex social skills, simultaneously competing and cooperating within a highly gendered, independently directed activity.

Improving practice

As children tend to be rather secretive about their 'kiss-catch' play, it can be difficult for adults to collect data relating to such activities. When I was trying to make sense of this area of my data I found it very helpful to talk to teenagers about their memories of, and insights into 'kiss-catch'. If you have some young friends or relatives in this age bracket, you may also find it useful to do the same.

The complexity of gender roles in kiss-catch

The female initiation and organisation of mixed-gender chasing games observed within my R&T research possibly indicates a more assertive role for human females than is generally proposed by researchers to be present in the behaviour of mammalian species. The observational data suggests that female choice is an important human initialiser of male–female pursuit – at least in this early period of development. It may be that the girl-to-boy touch and run invitation foreshadows the female choice and organisational aspect of adult human mating described by evolutionary researchers. Geary et al. (2004) carried out a review of research on human courtship behaviour. They proposed that adult courtship begins when females make it clear to males that they are available, signalling to the man that he may 'chase'. Hrdy's (1999) review of female primate behaviour also indicated that typical female primate behaviour is far from passive in courtship and mating activities, with females of several primate species appearing to take an organisational role.

It would therefore seem that both adult and child mixed-gender interactions begin with a negotiation of availability. The highly gendered 'tag and chase' narratives for mixed-gender play appeared to be a simplified physical mirror of more abstract, linguistic adult 'flirting' behaviour, the play activities created by these children in mixed-gender chasing mirroring and simplifying aspects of the adult social world. Carroll (2004) suggested that by far the largest proportion of stories created by adults that are not related to survival in a difficult situation are organised around mating issues. This was also clearly evident in the mixed-gender play undertaken by my sample of children. The human capacity for linguistic interaction creates more varied and sophisticated R&T play activities than those observed between non-human primates; within human R&T play, children use (and further develop) language to create their first independently mediated gendered narratives which, at this point in development, underpin physical activities that are comprised of basic motor actions which can be traced back to more primitive evolutionary roots. Such physical interaction has been observed within the juvenile R&T behaviour of non-human animal species; for example the 'touch and run' aspect of 'kiss-catch' uses a basic action found in the play of 'monkey tag' games described by Bertrand (1976). My research participants' kiss-catch play can therefore be proposed to use physical behaviour that can be observed in other primate species, whilst also being underpinned by the linguistic **bio-psychology** of specifically human sexual selection.

> **Bio-psychology**
> In full, biological psychology, a branch of psychology that is based on the physical properties of the brain.

Ideas in Action

Exploring the 'warrior discourse' (Author's observation notes)

Where a boy took an injury or a heavy fall and did not make a fuss, or dealt with a play-fighting incident that injured another child in a responsible way, boys had a very subtle but obvious way of showing approval and solidarity; a light touch in passing to the boy who had shown resilience in a difficult situation, often offered by another boy who both individuals within the interaction would see as having a more 'senior' role. For example, 4½-year-old Rory received a hefty shove in the back during a football game from one of the larger, older players. He fell quite heavily, but got up and ran back into the football crowd, smiling. An older, Year 1 boy ran past and gently patted him on the back.

Stop and reflect

Does current advised 'best practice' allow children sufficient time to attempt to sort out their own problems and disputes? Or are adults encouraged to become too quickly involved, not allowing children to develop their own solutions?

There appeared to be an intricate web of inter- and intra-gender cooperation and competition unfolding within mixed gender chasing, the boys forming a 'hunting party' that might engage in protection of its members, but with the underlying competitive purpose of individual recognition as a 'good chaser' by peers of both genders and possibly supervising adults. The girls usually initiated the chasing games and subsequently competed to be 'most chased', whilst collaborating to protect one another from the boys' attention when it became too energetic, marshalling adult assistance when necessary. The basic underlying understanding of 5 year olds of both genders appeared to be that boys are 'tougher' and more dangerous than girls. However, on further examination, the girls appeared to be far from powerless within mixed-gender chasing activities, particularly when it is considered that they were most often the initiators and organisers of such games, using verbal admonitions and adult support very skilfully to control male behaviour.

Several researchers have proposed that male single-sex R&T play forms the basis for male socialisation, in that boys who successfully engage in the mock fighting involved in such play are creating **neuronal pathways** that will later be developed in rule-based sporting activities and language-based competition, whilst those who are unable to grasp concepts of play fighting in early childhood are at risk of becoming less socially successful, more aggressive adolescents (Pellegrini, 1993a, 1993b; Orobio de Castro et al., 2002; Sax, 2005). Pellegrini and Blatchford (2000) concluded that for 5½-year-old boys, the amount of time spent in R&T play with other boys can directly predict their level of success in social problem solving one year later. There is as yet no data to suggest what adolescence may bring for children of either gender who do not successfully engage in mixed-gender R&T play,

Neuronal pathways
The pathways along which thought occurs in human and animal minds, involving an electro-chemical reaction between cells in the brain called 'neurons'.

but this would certainly be an interesting focus for future research.

The 'adult's role in play' debate

The evidence cited so far suggests that the outcomes of active free play, whilst subtle and slow acting, are more numerous than is generally perceived. Physical fitness is a clear and obvious result, but it can also be proposed, based on the evidence above, that subtle, highly gendered social interaction skills are also developed in R&T play, particularly in the early years of primary education. However, Sylva et al. (1980) proposed that adult-defined, structured tasks are superior to all others because they alone stretch the child's intellectual capacity and provide a definite goal structure. These researchers designated R&T as 'low-challenge play', proposing that it is carried out in a careless fashion that involves little mental effort, resulting in few opportunities for planning, feedback or correction. Bishop and Curtis (2001, p. 34) quoted the superintendent (education director) of schools in Atlanta outlining a similar view: 'we are intent on improving performance. You don't do that by having kids hanging on monkey bars'. Such points of view fail to recognise that within a complex organic social environment, social feedback emerges from the reactions of the other players, giving children opportunities to independently problem solve and autonomously self-correct in order to remain within the group activities. Sluckin (1981) carried out a substantial observational study of the playground activities of 8–10 year olds, which led him to propose that children build numerous specific skills in outdoor free play, learning much more than is immediately obvious, principally social and problem-solving skills that can be transferred and generalised to other, non-playground situations.

Whilst it may be possible for a human adult to directly 'teach' ideas relating to social and physical interaction skills via linguistic communication and closely directed activity, it is unlikely that the second-hand nature of such an experience will be internalised to the extent that a child will internalise the first-hand lessons of the playground. R&T play puts children

Ideas in action

What is the adult role in kiss-catch? (Author's observation notes)

Girls' complex orientations to kiss-catch involved a clear role for adults within such play. This was explicitly raised by one of the children, when I talked to a group of girls, following their initiation of a mixed-gender chasing game:

Researcher: Will you be playing at chasing again with Ben at lunchtime?

Celia: Yes, if he tries to catch me.

Researcher: If they catch you, do you try to catch them?

Celia: Yes.

Researcher: What do you do when you catch them?

Celia: You tell the teacher.

Additionally, during a summer game of kiss-catch, I observed Elliot hit Francisca on the head with his cap. I thought that the energy with which he did this was rather over-eager, and this was confirmed when she yelled and held her head. Kayleigh immediately snapped, 'I'm telling,' and stalked off; the boys running behind her saying, 'No, no'. This was a game where Kayleigh had been the principal organiser, and had called the boys back into play several times before this incident occurred.

Where I observed adults dealing with situations relating to girls' routine complaints about boys, I got the impression that this was often part of the fun for both boys and girls, the adult reinforcing the girls' pretended outrage, and the boys being marked in public by the adult remonstration as a successful 'chaser' in front of both male and female peers. These behaviours seemed designed to ensure that the adult provided a mild admonishment to mark boys out as rule breakers. The female role in this process revolved around 'telling' behaviour, drawing adult attention to perceived male transgressions. Girls exerted a certain amount of power over boys in this respect, in that their construction of the 'telling' process could be a deciding factor in whether a mild (desired) admonishment was administered, or a more severe admonishment and punishment (undesired) was the eventual adult response. There was a tendency for the behaviours of both genders to direct adult attention towards boys' behaviour. This seemed to create a 'risky benefit' situation for boys, in which they clearly did not enjoy serious reprimands from adults, but appeared to use mild admonishments in passing to enhance their status.

Improving practice

It is much easier for a **non-participant** observer to note children's manipulation of adult attention in the playground than it is for a supervising adult. Children may also try to 'draw in' a person they know as a teacher or 'helper' with some disciplinary responsibility who is trying to act as an observer during a 'non-duty' playtime. Perhaps carrying out short interviews with the children of friends and family members would be more likely to produce some useful data about the 'telling' conventions in their playgrounds.

> **Non-participant [research]**
> A piece of research (most frequently observation) where the researcher does not interact with the participants, but collects data relating to their behaviour/interactions.

into situations where they can simultaneously practise independently directed competition and cooperation – both vital skills for primate adult life. R&T is a natural, evolved juvenile behaviour that creates a vital socialising experience for all young primates, especially the linguistic human being, serving a vital purpose within children's development by allowing them to operate spontaneously within a forum which facilitates learning about complex physical and linguistic responses from other children of both genders. As organic,

Ideas in action

The problem of adult intervention in football play (Author's observation notes)

Over the course of the 18-month period during which my observations were undertaken, it became increasingly clear to me that a huge amount of social skills development was taking place within these playground games, as children learned to independently negotiate their positions within various social groups, both mixed and single gender. This was particularly prominent in the R&T and simple football-play games that took place amongst groups of boys. However, the children's self-directed 'scripting' of these games was always vulnerable to adult intervention, which frequently appeared to be poorly judged. For example, when Rory took a heavy fall during football play, a lunchtime supervisor intervened and started to organise the children into teams. First of all, she designated two Year 1 'team captains' and helped them to undertake a 'team-picking' exercise. The Reception boys subsequently begin to wander off, but the lunchtime supervisor called them back. The usual practice in the Reception/Year 1 football play was for boys to join and leave the ongoing football games as and when they felt like it, taking turns to be 'goalie'; there was no concept of opposing teams. As such, when they were left to play in these adult-directed teams, the game began to break down as new entrants attempted to join in, and several of the original players took 'time out'. The ball play quickly stopped as the designated captains attempted to marshal their 'players' back on to the 'field' and remove those who had not been allocated to a team. After a short time, the Year 1 and Reception boys split into two separate groups, whilst the Year 1 captains attempted to draw them back into increasingly fragmented negotiations that the Reception boys in particular seemed to have problems concluding successfully. Eventually, the Year 1 boy who was the first to be picked as team captain tucked the ball firmly under his arm, and walked from boy to boy trying to direct each one separately. The football play never effectively restarted during that play period, and the next play period (afternoon playtime) opened with the boys back to playing 'football' in their customary haphazard, non-team-based fashion.

Improving practice

Have you ever intervened in children's play and tried to help them to solve what you saw as a problem, only to find that they found it hard to grasp your suggested solution? Visit the High/Scope website (www.highscope.org) and try to apply their conflict resolution strategy the next time you are called upon to adjudicate in this way:

- Approach calmly, stopping any hurtful actions or language.
- Acknowledge feelings.
- Gather information.
- Restate the problem.
- Ask for ideas for solutions and choose one together.
- Give follow-up support as needed.

evolved creatures it is surely necessary for human beings to thoroughly explore attributes of our human (and gendered) physiological and psychological biology, and use our huge capacity for learned behaviour to build most successfully upon these, whether we are male or female.

The need to recognise **dynamic relationships** between the individual and the group within such an environment is also an important factor that has

Dynamic relationships
A relationship where one part complements (but is not the same) as the other(s), and when one part changes, the others also change to continue the complementary relationship.

emerged from R&T research investigation. This is particularly found within the work of Jarvis (2006), which suggests that evolved, gendered behaviour is expressed and further developed by young children in active free play, and that such activities may underlie the development of a 'social hardiness' that is needed for the successful development of later adolescent and adult social skills. As such, it can be proposed that one of the most pressing duties for contemporary early years and primary practitioners is to consider how to satisfactorily reset the balance of children's learning opportunities, focusing upon more holistic practice which continues to address the development of academic skills, but within a much broader curriculum that equally nurtures the physical, social and emotional development of the child.

Summary and review

This chapter has outlined theory and research relating to R&T play in children and other juvenile mammalian species, and children's play-based linguistic interaction, using a biocultural model of human children, which suggests that they are evolved primates growing up within a complex human social environment that is highly dependent upon the use of language and narrative. We are now in a position to propose some tentative answers to the questions posed at the beginning of the chapter:

- What is 'rough and tumble' play?

R&T is a physically active, socially interactive play style in which we clearly see evolved physical behaviour and language interacting in the play of human children. It comprises a physical play structure that can be clearly traced back to earlier mammalian species, and uniquely human narratives which children invent to underpin and 'script' their R&T activities.

- What are the typical narratives underpinning such play, what level of social complexity do they reach, and how might they become 'gendered'?

Narratives underpinning R&T play are socially complex, particularly those occurring within mixed-gender chasing, where we can observe children collaborating and competing in same-gender groups to achieve social competence. The narratives are gendered both in single-gender play, where subtly different scenarios are explored, and in mixed-gender play, where the genders create variations on a chasing and catching narrative that has a common core of girls seeking out male playmates to act as 'chasers'.

- What developmental learning may occur within such free-play activities?

It is concluded that much social and gendered learning takes place within the play structures that children use in their outdoor free-play activities. It is further suggested that such learning may help to instil a level of 'social hardiness', a collection of complex social skills which may underpin coping strategies used in later interactions within adolescent and adult relationships.

This outline of R&T play, in particular the implication that children must independently construct their knowledge of social skills, following the evolved patterns of all primate species, raises the key issue that children need adult support, rather than direction and/or interference in their free-play activities. Within a twenty-first-century post-industrial society, such support should include the facilitation of safe outdoor play areas and non-directive but engaged adult supervision, so that children can undertake such developmental activities within suitable environments. Bishop and Curtis (2001) proposed that the principle role for adults within early years and primary education should be to foster play by providing quality time, sufficient space and low-key supervision to allow children to undertake self-directed activities.

Given our current national obsession with tightly defined and clearly measurable educational targets imposed upon children who lack opportunities for spontaneous out-of-school social free play, we are in danger of depriving our children of the vital learning that occurs when young primates engage in such play. This chapter proposes that the playground is an important, but much neglected forum for essential early years developmental activities. It is therefore suggested that outdoor free play is an activity area in vital need of regeneration within early years, using the biocultural model of human development to underpin both practice and research, and that early years and primary practitioners should be in the forefront in pressing for commensurate developments within nationally recommended practice.

Transforming thinking and practice: over to you!

Questions for consideration

- How might early years and primary school outdoor environments be transformed to support children's outdoor social free play?

- How can we best provide the non-directive but vigilant supervision advocated by Bishop and Curtis (2001) during free-play supervision, balancing health and safety requirements with activities that involve acceptable risk-taking behaviours, and avoiding the temptation to intervene excessively within children's free-play activities?

- How might early years and primary school practitioners most effectively act as advocates for a change in focus within their areas of practice, providing sufficient time, safe areas and non-directive supervision for nursery and primary school children to engage in the natural, evolved primate free-play process?

- How can early years and primary school practitioners most effectively initiate discussion that explores carefully balancing health and safety practice requirements with children's rights to innovate, discover and engage in an acceptable level of risk taking, whilst gently encouraging parents and colleagues to recognise the difference between helpful, facilitative responses and unhelpful, directive intervention in children's free play activities?

Such initiatives can build on the most recent, promising developments in English early years policy embodied in the Early Years Foundation Stage, due to come into force in 2008, with a play-friendly emphasis on 'fun, relevant and motivating activities' (DfES, 2007b).

Ideas for research

The biocultural model of human development is a new approach within the field of early years play-based research, one which is currently ripe for future researchers and practitioners to expand and refine, initially by enthusiastically engaging with the child-led, play-based learning promoted by the Early Years Foundation Stage proposals. The model of the child derived from the biocultural perspective is best described as a young 'storying animal' (Lyle, 2000), with very basic evolved characteristics, some of which are gendered, that need to be thoroughly explored and developed in the types of social free play in which children naturally engage, alongside adult-directed classroom-based teaching, balanced in amounts carefully tailored to each child's individual developmental stage.

Basing our understanding of children's developmental needs upon such a model allows us to comprehend how the developing child can be perceived as both evolved and **socially constructed**. However, the biocultural model of the child is very new, and thus underpins an exciting research arena, encompassing many poorly addressed research topics with the consequent potential for new researchers to generate original insights. Areas for research could include:

> **Socially constructed**
> An attribute, behaviour or belief developed through social interaction with others.

- the nature of single- and mixed-gender narratives underlying active free play;

- an analysis of ways in which the outdoor play environment can be developed to maximise children's engagement and enjoyment.

Further reading

Bjorklund, D. and Pellegrini, A. (2002) *The Origins of Human Nature*. Washington, DC: American Psychological Association.

DfES Standards, Early Years Foundation Stage website: http://www.standards.dfes.gov.uk/primary/faqs/foundation_stage/eyfs/?subject=S_953489.

Holland, P. (2003) *We Don't Play with Guns Here*. Maidenhead: Open University Press.

Laland, K. and Brown, G. (2002) *Sense and Nonsense: Evolutionary Perspectives on Human Behaviour*. Oxford: Oxford University Press.

Pellegrini, A. (2005) *Recess: Its Role in Education and Development*. Mahwah, NJ: Lawrence Erlbaum.

Chapter 8

Play for Children with Special Educational Needs

JONATHAN DOHERTY

Play is a need of every child. Children virtually overflow with all the prerequisites for play . . . a vast reservoir of energy and curiosity, excitingly new experiences, ripe ideas, and a rich supply of imagination that pours forth freely as a constant stream of activity ... play is an important childhood activity that helps children master all developmental needs.

Maxim, 1997, p. 261

Introduction

This chapter begins by acknowledging that children everywhere are growing up in a world of rapid change and increasing **diversity**. Societies now recognise and celebrate diversity and difference. Cultural changes have occurred in almost every aspect of society: urbanisation, new technologies, adult work patterns, social stratification and family organisation. Human rights and entitlements are continually evolving, and place enormous expectations upon children in terms of their development, dispositions and skills. **Inclusion** is a process of including young people (and adults) with disabilities and/or learning difficulties in mainstream society predicated on a belief that including all children is a basic human right. This implies that, because we are human, we will all have particular needs at one time or another – not that we are different. It follows then that we aim to provide for the individual needs of all children so that each child can attain his or her full potential as a human

> **Inclusion**
> Allowing all children to be able to fully participate in mainstream institutions whatever their individual needs or abilities.

> **Diversity**
> Recognises the uniqueness of individuals in terms of needs, aspirations, abilities, weaknesses and strengths.

Inclusive education
Ensuring that all children have access to appropriate and effective education irrespective of physical disabilities.

Play
A dynamic, active and constructive behaviour. An essential and integral part of all children's healthy growth, development and learning across all ages, domains and cultures.

Special educational needs
Refers to children with learning difficulties or disabilities that can hinder their ability to learn or to have access to education.

being. There is a changing situation in schools to parallel this, and any drive towards **inclusive education** must be viewed in a wider societal context: that of social inclusion. Pressures on academic attainment for all children alongside a narrowing view of learning and overly competitive, results-driven curricula are leaving many children behind with a danger of making learning exclusive and inaccessible for many – and for many children with particular individual needs this is certainly the case.

As a consequence of such changes, in school settings, at home and in their wider communities, there is less opportunity and time available for children to **play**. Through the opportunities it provides children in free choice and more structured activities, play is an effective means to tackle poverty and social exclusion. The play cultures of children have seriously altered, with an adverse effect on childhood. Many authors comment on the disappearance of childhood and how as a concept it is under threat. Characterising childhood as time for playing, exploring, enjoying, and learning is for many children now not happening. This book presents a wealth of evidence on the value of children's play and of the central place it needs to occupy in children's lives. In this chapter I argue that it is central to the experiences of childhood, with particular emphasis for children with **special educational needs**, and in it I seek to explore the following questions:

- What do we understand about 'inclusion' and 'inclusive education'?

- Why are child, family and curriculum sometimes referred to as the cornerstones of SEN?

- What is the particular significance of play for children with special educational needs and how can we best support inclusive play?

The context of inclusion

Although not the first to do so, I want to help the reader understand the term 'inclusion' by introducing it through the metaphor of a journey. Twenty years ago Baroness Warnock elegantly stated,

> If I am to walk along a road, I need shoes; but there are those who need a wheelchair, or a pair of crutches, or a guide dog, or other things beside. These needs could be identified and met, and then off we could all go together. (1986)

Implied strongly in this statement is that inclusion is about bringing people together and helping them to move on in a unified way. At its core is an assertion that inclusion is about basic human rights and, as we shall see in the next section, this is increasingly echoed in legislation across the world. So what is inclusion? It is not about separation and is more than integration.

Separation
Placing children of particular difficulties and similar needs together, but separated from other children of their age.

Special schools
Provide education for children whose needs cannot be catered for in mainstream institutes of education.

Impairment
To be damaged or diminished in strength or ability.

The former term, **separation**, is concerned with placing children with particular difficulties and similar needs together but separated from others of their own age. Writers such as Herbert (1998) argue that there can be no justification for placing children in **special schools** and separating them purely on the grounds that they have **impairment**. Separation from peers can result in feelings of marginalisation and stigmatisation through perceptions of being 'different' to other children. A counter argument is that for *some* children the provision of special schools is an appropriate setting to meet individual needs. They play a vital role in the continuum of provision to support all children, giving access to an inclusive education and a curriculum in which every child can flourish and achieve enjoyment and success. Special schools are a tremendous source of practitioner expertise and resources but are increasingly catering for children with severe and complex needs, placing heavy burdens upon them. The latter term, **integration**, is concerned with mainstream (educational) settings not making deep philosophical or indeed structural changes, but making arrangements and adaptations to accommodate pupils with particular needs. Such a distinction between the two terms is made by Farrell (2005) who interprets the term inclusion to mean approaches (by schools) to reconsider how their structures, pedagogical approaches, pupil groupings and support mechanisms are designed to respond to the perceived needs of all pupils. Integral to this is the notion of collaboration and the processes of reflecting and experimentation to provide opportunities to involve pupils and plan a broad and balanced curriculum that is accessible to all (p. 91). Inclusion in this sense is about being included and making each individual feel part of a school or community and welcomed by it, and as Ainscow (1995) reminds us, demands more radical change but change that can develop a much richer mainstream learning experience for pupils.

Other definitions of inclusion point to a much wider conceptualisation. The definition provided by the Centre for Studies on Inclusive Education (www. inclusion.uwe.ac.uk/csie) defines inclusion as 'the process of increasing the participation of students in, and reducing their exclusion from, the cultures, curricula and communities of local schools'. **Exclusion**, not confined to schools, is very much part of society as a whole. Social inclusion (Acheson, 1998) and educational inclu-

> **Integration**
> The inclusion of disabled children in the mainstream education system.

> **Exclusion**
> When a pupil is prohibited from attending school on the grounds of a serious offence.

sion are linked and relate to wider issues in society such as health, poverty and disadvantage. Lingard links it across issues of social justice, equity and citizenship (2000). The idea of barriers to inclusion (which I return to later in the chapter when discussing inclusive play for children) is reflected in the definition from the Early Childhood Forum, which defines inclusion as 'a process of identifying, understanding and breaking down the barriers to participation and belonging' (2003, p. 89).

The **social model of disability** argues that it is environmental barriers which disable people. The model is useful in promoting understanding of how disability affects not only the individual but the community to which we all belong. It aims to empower individuals by emphasising the right to be independent and to make choices. Reiser and Mason (1992) suggest that for this to happen requires change at community level which transcends the notion of integration. In this way, the social model prompts a challenge to society to become inclusive. Booth (2000) writes of inclusion as a process, taking the view that it is not a finite state but one affected by both cultural and historical differences resulting in an evolving understanding of it. Daniels and Garner (1999) argue that inclusion can have cultural agreement, but individual countries need to interpret it within their own national systems. Although very much a part of the recent agenda of the UK Government, inclusion has historically had its focus on children with special educational needs in school settings – which is the focus for this chapter with specific reference to children's play. In order to understand the current status of inclusion and SEN, it is necessary to have knowledge of how the intertwining of politics, history and culture over the last 30 years, characterised in the early days by separation and difference, has provided the definitions of special

> **Social model of disability**
> Seeks to reduce the barriers that hinder a disabled person from being an equal participant in society.

education needs we have today and the thrust towards a truly inclusive society.

The emergence of an inclusion agenda – national and international

The vagary of language around special educational needs has been identified by writers such as Wolfendale (2000), who rightly comments that this is not only at policy level, but has also affected practice. Corker (2002) disputes even the term's existence, arguing that its associated labels are dehumanising to children. In chronicling special educational needs in the United Kingdom, it is clear that prior to 1981 attaching labels to certain types of individual needs was very much normal practice. Prior to 1981 in the United Kingdom it was perfectly acceptable to refer to categories of handicap using words such as 'maladjusted' and 'educationally subnormal', since these were the categories set out in the regulations of the Education Act of 1944. Frederickson and Cline (2002), in their comprehensive and informed text *Special Education Needs: Inclusion and Diversity,* tabulate official categories of SEN in the latter part of the last century and present labels such as 'multi-handicapped' (England and Wales); 'mentally retarded' (United States); 'severely maladjusted' (the Netherlands) and 'backward pupils' (New Zealand). Surely such terms appear almost medieval in tone to readers in the early twenty-first century and as lacking in sensitivity towards the recipients of these labels. Even in the last decade of the last century the issue of using or not using labels to categorise particular needs was hotly debated amongst many, not least because of its associations with funding. In describing the relationship between disability and language, Corbett (1998) argues that a term such as 'special' is prejudicial to our view of disability and has negative connotations of inadequacy and dependency. A brief trawl through the legislation with particular emphasis on England and Wales from this time until the present day, and drawing in relevant legislation from other countries, will illuminate the changes in ideology that present us with the concept of inclusion and the definition(s) of special educational needs

which are currently in vogue. It also strikingly reveals a lack of references to play as a means of supporting SEN children.

Defining special educational needs

The definition of SEN within the SEN *Code of Practice* (DfES, 2001b) is not particularly clear. It states that children have special educational needs if they have a learning difficulty that calls for special provision to be made for them. This means that they experience greater difficulty in learning than the majority of their peers. (The association with learning is the very essence of the definition). They can also have learning difficulties if they possess a disability that prevents them from attending a local school which provides a curriculum and facilities generally available to their peer group. Finally, the definition applies to children who are below school age and who come under one or both of the above two definitions. The actual term 'special educational needs' came into use with the advent of the Warnock Report (DES, 1978) where, following its recommendations, the Education Act of 1981 (DES, 1981) replaced the then existing 'categories of need'. The Report acknowledged that the needs of individuals change with time, and subsequently proposed that provision should accommodate the changes in a flexible manner. It set out that children with special educational needs should be assessed, their needs identified through detailed profiles and that provision be made applicable to more children. It was this piece of legislation that was to dramatically change the face of special needs. It was also the first time in which special needs provision was seen as a continuum of need, a significant departure from the earlier position of polarity where provision was either within special schools or mainstream schools. Definitions of special educational needs within the Act clarified terms such as 'learning difficulty' and 'disability'. To muddy the waters even further, the term **special needs** also exists. This

> **Special needs**
> Those with a particular need different or extra to those children in the same social situation.

rcfcrs to those from a social group with background or circumstances that are different from those of most of the school population. Robson (1989) suggests this might well include language, where the need is in having support with English; culture, so that references are made to a child's cultural heritage; racism, where there is a need to oppose overt racist behaviours and socio-economic disadvantage to combat its effects on academic achievement. Often the two terms are confused with negative consequences for the child. Special educational needs is concerned predominantly with learning difficulties; special needs are group phenomena shared by children in the same social situation (Frederickson and Cline, 2002).

Evans (2000) comments that the influence of Warnock and the 1981 Education Act remains strong, despite significant changes that have since taken place in education, originating in the latter years of the 1980s. The early 1980s signalled a broad commitment to inclusion and promised movement towards social justice, both in the United Kingdom and globally. The year 1981 was designated International Year of Disabled Persons, and 1983 to 1992 the Decade of Disabled Persons. In the United Kingdom, the 1981 Act established a major forward step: it offered children with special educational needs the same equality of opportunity as children without special educational needs. Yet in the current increasing climate of national testing and school league tables; of increased numbers of children labelled as having special educational needs of some description in mainstream schools; of continued pleas to local authorities and Government for guidance on clear criteria on deciding this; and now the existence of an education marketplace in which parents compete for the best education for their child, it is difficult to see how the messages of the Report and the 1981 Act can be realised. There is as yet still no mention of play in British legislation, with regard to education in general, let alone with relationship to special needs/special educational needs.

The *Education Reform Act* (DfEE, 1988) established a National Curriculum for children from the age of 5+. Its rhetoric talked of accommodating the learning needs of children with special educational needs and specified that all children had equality of access to a broad and balanced curriculum. The Children's Act (DoH 1989) defined children's needs in a broader context and emphasised how this terminology differed from educational terminology, specifically special educational needs. The Act highlighted the importance of multi-agency working on behalf of children – which is very much at the core of current thinking and provision. Clarification was given with regard to terms of 'family' and 'development'. In this definition, 'need' referred to a significant impairment in health or development, and a child was deemed to be in need if unlikely to achieve, maintain or have opportunity to achieve, or maintain a reasonable standard of health or development without provision by services outside the family and mainstream education system (DoH, 1991). It is interesting that the term 'development' was used and encompassed physical, intellectual, emotional, social and behavioural development which are (alongside language) the main components of child development as well as being the broad areas of need recognised today. It is timely to report here that the Rumbold Report (DES, 1990) made mention of children's need to talk, play and have first-hand experiences, and viewed these as essential elements of child development.

The 1993 Education Act strengthened the case for early identification and assessment and of parental involvement and partnership. There was further progress the following year with the publication of a *Code of Practice* (DfEE, 1994), which again emphasised multi-agency working and introduced the role of the **special needs coordinator** (SENCO) in schools. The notion of differentiating work in classes within a common curriculum framework was introduced so that schools could meet the learning needs of all their pupils. Guidance was produced for practitioners and local authorities on early identification and assessment of SEN involving five stages, beginning at birth, with the final stage requiring information gathered and shared between practitioners, other professionals and parents. Recurring in its

> **Special needs coordinator (SENCO)**
> The teacher with overall responsibility for ensuring that the requirements of children with special needs are met and for monitoring childrens' progress.

Figure 8.1 Inclusive classrooms

Source: John Callan/reportdigital.co.uk

revision in 2001, the later Revised Code of Practice shows the increased emphasis now being placed on early identification of need and of early intervention to meet those needs.

In the context of international moves towards inclusion, articles contained in the UN *Convention on the Rights of the Child* (United Nations, 1989) to which 177 countries signed up, upheld 'the right of disabled children to enjoy a full and decent life, in conditions which ensure dignity, promote self-reliance, and facilitate the child's active participation in the community' (Article 23) and signalled a drive to keep the rights and entitlement of children with disabilities high on the global agenda. The Framework of Action proclaimed that 'inclusion and participation are essential to human dignity and to the enjoyment and exercise of human rights' (UNESCO, 1994). Shortly afterwards, in what is more commonly known as the Salamanca Statement, came a statement urgently calling for the provision of education for *all* children within the regular education system and the adoption as a matter of law or policy of the principle of inclusive education. Significant too was the recognition that inclusive schools were deemed to be the most effective type of schools in uniting children with special needs and their peers. Two years later the

publication of a worldwide survey (UNESCO, 1996) reported that 92 per cent (amounting to 48 countries) had laws relating to special educational needs. An important finding of the survey was that most countries favoured an integrated approach to special educational needs/disability in schools and this was accomplished in different ways. Spain, for example, required schools to adjust their curricula to accommodate the interests, aptitudes and abilities of pupils; whilst in Chile a phased approach is preferred, where pupils with sensory or motor deficits attend classes in parallel to regular classes or attend integration workshops. In all the countries segregation into special schools was considered only where a pupil's needs could not be met in mainstream schools.

Messages within the international arena were reflected in England and Wales around this time. The 1996 Education Act (DfEE, 1996) imposed a duty on local education authorities to identify and assess children from the age of 2 who were deemed to require separate statements about their particular needs. Parents with children who had statements of need were able to choose which maintained school they wished their children to attend and the rights of appeal against LEA decisions on assessment were extended. The definition of SEN contained in this Act stated that 'a child has special educational needs . . . if he has a learning difficulty which calls for special educational provision to be made for him' (DfEE, 1996, section 312), which was instrumental in shaping the definitions we use today. The Labour Government's green paper *Excellence for All Children: Meeting Special Educational Needs* (DfEE, 1997) supported the Salamanca Statement calling for the adoption of the principles of inclusive education and an extension of mainstream schools to extend their capacity to accommodate children with a wide range of needs. Subsequent legislation has reflected this move. An inclusion statement is contained within the revised National Curriculum (DfEE/QCA, 1999). The Special Educational Needs and Disability Discrimination Act (DfEE, 2001) has strengthened the right of children with statements of SEN to be educated in mainstream schools and the accompanying *Code of Practice* (DfES, 2001b) places more emphasis than the previous version on teaching and learning responses to pupil needs, as well as on parent and pupil involvement in assessment and decision making.

The current situation: inclusion today and where is play?

Nowadays, the status of and interest in inclusion continues to rank very highly on the political agenda of the United Kingdom, and it has recently enjoyed an elevated profile in the early years. A plethora of governmental initiatives such as SureStart, Early Excellence Centre programmes, **Portage**, Children's Centres, Excellence in Cities, and behaviour improvement programmes as part of the National Behaviour and

> **Portage**
> A home-visiting service for those who have special needs.

Attendance Strategy (DfES, 2002), *The Five Year Strategy for Children and Learners* (DfES, 2004b) and *The Ten Year Strategy for Children and Learners* (DfES, 2004c) reflect this interest. These share common aims of decreasing disadvantage and improving the life chances of children through family support interventions, increased services for children and families and emphasis on professional and inter-agency working. The message that

> **Every Child Matters**
> The English government's new approach to ensuring the well-being of children from birth to age 19, encompassing five main areas.

the needs of very young children are not forgotten rings clear, and underpins much of the hugely influential publication *Every Child Matters* (DfES, 2003c) (ECM). The five outcomes of *ECM* (Be healthy; Stay safe; Enjoy and achieve; Make a positive outcome; and Achieve economic well-being), given legal standing in the Children's Act (DfES, 2004),

> show the important relationship between educational achievement and well-being. Children and young people learn to thrive when they are healthy, safeguarded from harm and engaged. The evidence shows clearly that educational achievement is the most effective way to improve outcomes for poor children and break cycles of deprivation.
> (ECM, p. 8)

An analysis of ECM and other policy initiatives in England, Wales, Scotland and Northern Ireland reveals they are unmistakably needs centred and that they are inter-dependent. In the documents these needs are expressed as 'outcomes' and individual practitioners and extended services are tasked with working towards better outcomes for children. Multidisciplinary team systems have been championed to meet the needs of parents and children in aiming towards a seamless service of provision. The notion of a fundamental entitlement for all children is clear in legislation and also in policy initiatives. The document *Improving the Life Chances of Disabled People* speaks of providing disabled people with full opportunities and respecting them as equal members of society. *Every Disabled Child Matters* (2003) speaks of the rights of disabled children being too low on the agenda and reminds of poor outcomes for disabled children, urging action for services to support them. The report *Special Educational Needs and Disability – Towards Inclusive Schools* (Ofsted, 2004) set out a vision of inclusion as a reality in schools. But where is play?

Professional standards to award Qualified Teacher Status (Teacher Training Agency (TTA), 2003) contained SEN competencies aimed at raising the professional knowledge and skills of new entrants into teaching. A similar expectation is included in the professional standards for Higher Level Teaching Assistants (TTA, 2005a). The accompanying handbook of guidance for those training to teach in Foundation Stage stated that trainees 'support and extend children's play, learning and development' (TTA, 2005b, p. 15) but failed to expand on how this might be put into practice. It is worrying that, in their revision of the standards for initial teacher training (TDA, 2007), the links to diversity and learning are explicit, as are those to *Every Child Matters*, but references to play are conspicuous by their absence. Play has been associated with 'quality provision', particularly in relation to child care, whilst in other documents terms such as 'purposeful' and 'structured' are used. Thus there is confusion – on the one hand there is a strong message that play is important and something to be fostered with young children, and on the other there is a lack of clarity about what constitutes play that is planned and set up by adults and free play, which is child initiated. Research findings (for example Hendy and Whitebread, 2000) describe a similar division – celebrating the role of play but reporting some confusion about the term and anxieties from practitioners about where play fits into a curriculum context of testing, targets and results. Where does this lead us? Have we come full circle? Before going on to discuss the three most important stakeholders in relation to inclusion, let us remind ourselves of the principles of inclusion presented so far:

- Inclusion is not a fixed state. It is a process.

- It is a basic human right for all children to learn together.

- Inclusion is about mutual respect and valuing everyone equally.

- All cultures need to consider how their policies and practices respond to the diversity of children (and adults).

- Barriers to inclusion must be addressed and discriminatory practices eradicated.

- Every child should have access to a curriculum that meets individual needs and allows each individual to achieve their personal potential.

- Early identification is vital so that children's individual needs can be maximally supported.

Ideas in action

Perceptions of inclusion (Practitioner observation)

Speaking personally, I very much want to make sure that everything I do in my work is aimed at the experience of every child. It isn't just because of documents like *Every Child Matters*. I have been teaching young children for a lot longer than this has been around and I always aim to include children regardless of any difficulties they might have. It isn't easy though and there is so much to know but I think if you want to do your best for a child you will make it work.   Reception class teacher

Perceptions of inclusion (Student observation)

In college we were told how important inclusion was, but it was really only when I went into school that I saw it for myself. What it really meant. I want to try and include all the children, but it is not easy. I feel I have so much more to learn. Our SENCO in school has a lot of knowledge and I know she tries hard to include everyone too. I think all students should know about this work and a lot more about special educational needs.   Newly qualified teacher, Year 1

- Play is accepted as being something valuable to promote, but there is some confusion as to how it is understood and how it exists in the current curriculum.

Specific areas of special educational need

Findings from Clough and Corbett (2000) suggest that the number of children with special educational needs in mainstream education is increasing. In 1978 the Warnock Report (DES, 1978) stated that 20 per cent of all children will have special educational needs or experience a learning difficulty at some time in their school career. In 2007 *Statistical First Releases*

SEN statement
A statement of special educational needs sets out the help required by a child with learning difficulties that falls outside of the regular provision of the education system.

published figures that showed a trend decrease in the number of children with **SEN statements** and an increase in the number with SEN without statements. An interpretation of these figures is that, through improved systems of support and early intervention, a wider range of children have had their needs met without requiring statements. This is one interpretation, but what does this look like in real terms? In 2007, there were 1,333,440 pupils with SEN without statements in schools in England, a figure representing 16.4 per cent of all pupils and an increase on the previous year. In the same year, 229,100 pupils in England in all schools had statements of SEN, a fall on the previous year (ibid). The incidence of boys with SEN with and without statements is greater than for girls. If Warnock's estimations hold true, this amounts to a considerable number of children, approximately 6 in a class of 30 pupils. The *Code of Practice* (DfES, 2001) has identified 12 categories of difficulty that a child may be experiencing to warrant a special educational need. These may conveniently be categorised into four broad groups:

1   *Cognition and learning needs*   This group includes specific difficulties with learning such as dyslexia and dyspraxia (DCD); moderate learning difficulties where attainment is below expected levels and profound and multiple learning difficulties that are complex and severe (such as physical disabilities) and warrant a high level of support.

2   *Emotional, behavioural and social needs*   This group covers behaviours and emotional disorders that hinder learning such as attention deficit disorder (ADD) and attention deficit hyperactivity disorder, and Tourette's syndrome.

3   *Communication needs*   This group covers the spectrum of speech, language and communication needs (including autistic spectrum disorders).

4   *Physical/sensory needs*   In this group physical disabilities are included, regardless of there being no special educational needs. It includes conditions such as cerebral palsy, spina bifida and muscular dystrophy. Sensory impairments include visual, auditory and multi-sensory and any that are a combination of these.

Play and the child, the family, the curriculum

The three cornerstones of special educational needs are the child, the family and the curriculum. This is easily shown in diagrammatic form as in Figure 8.2. Note that play is at the centre of the triangle. This is significant because play is central to every child's experiences in childhood.

Why is play important for a child with a special educational need? Quite simply for the same, myriad reasons that it is so important for any child, as outlined in all the chapters of this book. Childhood should be a time for children to play, and playing freely is an essential part of being a child. It was Hughes (1990) who described childhood as a journey into an unknown place where play was a means for a child to discover and forge a relationship with the environment. Being able to play freely should be so much a part of children's lives and is hugely important for children with special educational needs. SEN children engage in play like those without disabilities, but can require adult support and modifications to attain variety and depth from these experiences. Their need to play is no different. Quoting from *Birth to Three Matters* (DfES, 2002), 'all children have from birth a need to develop, learning through interaction with people and exploration of the world around them'. Play admirably provides such opportunities.

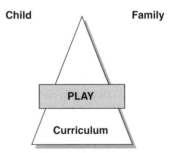

Figure 8.2   The three cornerstones of SEN

Ideas in action

Case study: Categories of need

Example 1
Cognition and learning needs

Daljit is 2 years old, and approaching his third birthday. His parents suspect that he may be showing early signs of learning difficulties. In his play he seems unable to form concepts or make connections between events. Cognitive skills such as memory and problem solving are still to mature but already he has perceptual problems that result in him not taking in relevant information from his surroundings via his senses. General cognitive skills are low. In his play he fails to recognise basic shapes or have the language skills to accompany recognition. In later years, Daljit might also display difficulties in remembering and following instructions and with sequencing activities. This could also result in frustration and low self-esteem.

Example 2
Emotional, behavioural and social needs

From the time Sonya was born her parents recognised that she was an extremely active baby. She had difficulty sleeping and her parents reported that it was as if she always wanted to be awake and involved in whatever was happening around her. She had some difficulties in sustaining attention, instead preferring to try something new and different. Now aged 2, she seems to be always on the move and constantly mobile. When alone she appears restless. She finds it difficult to follow instructions, and she is impulsive and constantly fidgeting. Whilst not professionally diagnosed as yet, she may be displaying early symptoms of attention deficit hyperactivity disorder (ADHD). Further signs of this condition include displays of unpredictable behaviour and behaviours that are not socially acceptable. She may become introverted and withdrawn or show physical aggression to other children or adults.

Example 3
Communication needs

When Ben was only a few months old his parents noticed that he rarely made eye contact with them or indeed with anyone else. He seemed reluctant to follow pointing or respond with interest when his parents, Karen and Thomas, tried to encourage him to look at things of interest around him or introduce someone new to him. Karen felt that he might have a delay in normal language development because, now that Ben is 18 months old, he has words but is reluctant to engage in discourse with other people. He has never engaged in the common parent–baby interactions that rely so importantly on shared meanings and early dialogue. At this rate, Ben is likely to develop an as yet unpredictable level of communication and have language difficulties. He also may be diagnosed at some position on the Asperger/autistic spectrum.

Example 4
Physical/sensory needs

Ali is a 5-year-old boy who has cerebral palsy. Motor cortex damage from birth means his physical mobility is significantly impaired. He is able to walk but requires callipers on both legs for extra support. His motor control is very limited, which makes the manipulation of toys and other objects difficult when he plays. He is a happy and sociable child but his impairment presents some difficulties when playing with peers. He needs considerable support from parents and other adults. In the classroom he finds difficulty in table-top activities where there is a practical and group element such as in 'design and make' activities, since the control of his fine motor skills are noticeably below his peers.

Play has been explained in an extensive literature, through sociological, psychological, anthropological and pedagogical perspectives, and has been defined by many. Its benefits such as having fun, providing contexts for choice, assisting in decision making, educating about rules, helping children learn about themselves and as a rehearsal for later life, and many other positive benefits, are threaded throughout this book.

I emphasise the point that play is vital as a context for the development of all children. The Qualifications and Curriculum Authority has this to say about it:

> Well-planned play, both indoors and outdoors, is a key in which young children learn with enjoyment and challenge. In playing, they behave in different ways: sometimes their play will be boisterous, sometimes they will describe and discuss what they are doing, sometimes they will be quiet and reflect as they play. (QCA/DfES, 2000, p. 25)

Play and child development complement each other admirably since the former involves the use of skills in all domains providing information on how children move, how they manipulate objects, how they express emotions and language and the quality of their social interactions with peers and adults. Academic benefits for all children include the enhancement of number and spatial understanding, language skills, causal reasoning, persistence and a sense of mastery. Play, simply, is the best vehicle for the advancement of children's learning (Hanline and Fox, 1993).

Culture and environment also influence the ways in which young children play. Play allows us to come into contact with our environment and our culture in a very direct way. Early work by Singer (1973) showed that children need to have privacy as well as space, props and adults around them to model and encourage play behaviours. Yet not only does culture affect play, it also serves to express that culture. In this way, home and school are part of any culture and serve to shape children's play experiences. More later; let us now consider the first of these three stakeholders: the child.

Beginning with the child

What adults may think a child's understanding of their play is can be different from the reality of the child's perceptions (Scott, 2000). A useful way to be able to understand children's needs (and hence support these needs), is for adults to try to see things through the eyes of a child. As Cohen and Stern state, it is 'only by learning to see children as they see themselves, we will get our clues' (1983, p. 4). Valuable research carried out by Langsted on kindergarten children (1994) reported that children felt adults made too many decisions about the play activities they engaged in and this was

most apparent with regard to outdoor play. Central to understanding the world from a child's perspective is the importance of listening to the views of children. It is vital that children's voices are heard in order that their opinions are recognised as valuable in an educational system which is more democratic and inclusive (Mortimer, 2001). In the history of SEN in the United Kingdom, children's voices have often been overshadowed by those of other stakeholders. What children have to say should be actively sought out and acted upon because they have much to say and we have much to learn from them. The 1989 Children Act specifically emphasised that children's feelings must be taken into account when decisions are being made that involve them. Rose *et al.* (1999) tell us of the developments in our understanding of how children with severe learning difficulties participate in decision making. This is in line with encouragement within *The Code of Practice* (DfES, 2001) that encourages children to make choices and share their feelings and wishes with adults. It states simply, 'the principle of seeking and taking account the ascertainable views of the child or young person is an important one' (DfES, 2001, section 3.3).

A first principle of The Code of Practice is that the special educational needs of children must be met. Meeting a child's particular needs begins with a positive disposition to view each child as *competent*. The term, as defined by Thurman (1997) is the ability to perform a task or activity and implies a degree of proficiency for a single skill or set of skills on the part of the individual (for example writing, drawing, riding a bike and so on). Disposition is a desire on the part of others, normally interpreted as parents or practitioners, to view the child as a 'can-do' individual. This is a view that each child inherently possesses certain skills and abilities to bring to any situation. This notion is supported in *Birth to Three Matters* (DfES, 2002), which talks about children being viewed as capable from birth. It proposes that all children are capable; not in terms of attaining milestones at identical ages, but at undertaking an individual journey where individual development is varied and uneven. Parents and practitioners need to identify the areas of competence within every child (for example thinking skills, movement capacity, language or social skills) and then foster these to allow each child to attain his or her full potential. Factors impacting upon a child's competency include temperament, culture and the experiences and the opportunities a child has in the formative years in the home and school environments; as do age, gender and motivation. From robust research evidence linking learning difficulties and academic achievement with low self-esteem and social and emotional problems, practitioners need to acknowledge and address the affective needs of individual children (Wall, 2006). Needs in this context are those related to a child's social development, like the differing expectations that families and society place on us according to different situations. Emotional needs in the early years are those in connection with expressions of happiness, sadness, anger, disgust, surprise and fear. Psychologist H. Rudolph Shaffer uses the term 'emotional competence' (2006, p. 148) to refer to the skills we use to interpret others' emotions and respond appropriately and sees it as an essential part of our social lives. Affective needs are also linked to the child's sense of self by being able to separate the self from other people and from the environment, their view of themselves (self-concept) and the value they place on themselves and their capabilities (self-esteem).

Families

Families provide the second cornerstone of SEN explored in this chapter. Parents have been referred to as a child's first educators (Atkins and Bastani, 1988) because they are the people who create the environment for their child and who provide that first and crucial input. They are the ones who are with that child from birth and know their own child better than anyone else. They know what the child likes and dislikes, his or her interests, the child's health and the development progress made. Over the last 30 years there has been a steady increase in the emphasis placed upon the value of involving parents in a child's education and the roles they play in this. Including parents in children's care and education is based on parents' legal rights to be involved and the many benefits for children that result from this (Powell, 1994). Partnerships with parents in such aspects as decision making and service delivery are central to the Code of Practice and *Every Child Matters* (DfES, 2003) frameworks. Clearly it is of benefit to all parties if collaboration between home and setting is led by a mutual desire to do the best for the child. Writers such as Cook *et al.* (2000) view parental involvement in a child's programme as the main factor allowing early gains in intervention to be maintained over a longer time frame. A useful model put forward by Rennie (1996) illustrates progression in home-setting partnerships, moving forward from confidence building in the initial stage to a position of parents as co-educators in the final stage. Parents know their own child better than anyone else, and partnerships that identify and respond to the needs of parents (through such aspects as communication, information and support) and the contributions of parents (such as information about the child's likes/dislikes and strengths/weaknesses) are crucial in achieving positive outcomes for children. **Play plans** (Drifte, 2005) offer an effective method for parents to support a child in the home environment by sharing information about a child's individual progress within an early years setting. These plans complement activities in settings and incorporate games and play activities to reinforce what is happening in educational settings and are a fine example of collaborative partnership.

> **Play plans**
> The planning of a range of activities for parents to support their children at home.

Having a child with special educational needs affects not only parents but the entire family – which for the purposes of this discussion includes single-parent families, foster, extended and same-sex families. The family is an important context for understanding a child with SEN. Kieff and Wellhousen (2000) comment on the positive impact on achievement that comes from involving families in children's education. Increasingly, through changing patterns of work, grandparents are often closely involved with children and can have a major input into the child's care from an early age. A child with a special educational need brings enormous richness to a family, and yet can cause tensions not only for parents or grandparents but for siblings – the latter experiencing negative feelings of rejection or jealousy towards that child. (For more detailed information on the issues for siblings, readers are referred to Carpenter's useful review (1997).) In the guidance alongside the Common Core of Skills and Knowledge for the Children's Workforce in *Every Child Matters* (DfES, 2007) *skills* (being

Ideas in action

Supporting inclusive play in the home

Here is a completed Play plan for Cindy, who has Down's Syndrome and learning difficulties.

Play Plan for Cindy . . . and her mother

Cindy . . . will play these games to help her recognise red and green and say their names:

- Sorting and naming all the red things she can find, followed by green things when she knows red very well.

> **Feely bag**
> A bag in which items can be placed so that pupils can guess the contents through touch or by asking questions.

- Painting and potato printing using red first, then green when she knows red.
- Sorting and matching all the red shapes, then the green ones.
- Naming red things that she takes out of the **feely bag**; then the green ones.

Begin by

Looking at lots of red things; help Cindy to sort out her red clothes; say the word each time for her to repeat.

What Cindy did

- She spotted her dad's red shirt and said the word 'red'.
- She pointed to a green cup and said 'green'.
- She could tell what was red and what was green every time.

Time to move on to more colours. Drifte, 2005

Improving practice

Use this example of a play plan for a child you are familiar with in a home setting with a different category of need.

Stop and reflect

Discuss with your colleagues/peers in college how such play plans might be adapted for use in an educational setting. What value do you see in such a plan?

able to support children and young people with a developmental difficulty or disability, and understanding that their families, parents and carers will also need support and reassurance) and *knowledge* (knowing how to interact with children in ways that support the development of their ability to think and learn) illustrate the importance of practitioners having knowledge of child development and understanding of how developmental changes affect behaviour.

A curriculum to meet individual needs

Education for all children is integral to the government's drive for social inclusion in society and, as we have seen, legislation has been one means to achieve this. Wording in the Special Educational Needs and Disability Act (DfES, 2001) makes it clear that it is the right of every child to be educated in mainstream schools. The words of the DfEE reflect this, saying that 'the education of children with special needs is a key challenge for the nation. It is vital to the creation of a fully inclusive society' (DfEE, 1999, p. 1). The introduction of citizenship into the curriculum in primary and secondary schools is part of that same drive to educate children to be responsible members of society. Naturally there are hurdles to overcome in developing inclusive educational practices. This is an inevitable situation operationally as the inclusion agenda moves and broadens. Barriers to an inclusive curriculum might include the stability of the family, gender and ethnicity, challenging behaviours, transition, mobility and disaffection. Despite these barriers, there is much to celebrate in early childhood. Considerable progress has been made lately to elevate the state and status of inclusive early education, nationally and internationally. It is embedded into the ethos and curriculum of Reggio Emilia in Italy and Te Whākiri in New Zealand, which is more fully outlined in this book by Brock in Chapter 5. The new curricular framework within the English Early Years Foundation Stage has a strong commitment to inclusive and anti-discriminatory practice explored through six headings of children's entitlements: Equality and diversity, Early support, Effective practice, Challenges and dilemmas and Reflecting on practice. Other national initiatives such as the Every Child Matters programme, *The Five Year Strategy for Children and Learners* (DfES, 2004b) and *Choice for parents, the best start for children: a ten-year strategy for child care* and legislation such as the Children Act (2003) and the Childcare Bill (expected to be in operation in 2008), offer firm foundations upon which to really build inclusive educational practice for children. But what do we mean then by a curriculum that is inclusive?

Inclusive education

Earlier in this chapter inclusion was introduced as a process and, returning to that idea, the term inclusive education can be thought of as a process in which educational settings structure or indeed restructure themselves, their curriculum and resources to optimise opportunities for each individual child. But as Barton (1998) reminds us, inclusive education is much more than schools making minor changes; neither is it about becoming a repository for children from segregated provision into mainstream school. Reflecting the Warnock Report (DES, 1978), Barton states it is an entitlement for every child and reflects a basic human right. It is about 'the participation of all children and young people and the removal of all forms of exclusionary practice' (1998, p. 85). Inclusive education does and must reflect contemporary society and, in the rapid changes taking place in society and the implications of these for young children, this can mean radical shifts to schools and other settings. Amongst the many benefits of an inclusive education system can be listed increased opportunities for friendship with normally developing peers, opportunities to interact with

competent peers that promote social and communication skills and realistic life experiences which provide opportunities for skill application in activities typical of early childhood (Hull *et al.*, 2002). Important, too, that peers without special educational needs gain from interactions with peers who have needs – such as in the development of positive attitudes and altruistic behaviours. It means giving serious consideration to how pupils are taught and where play fits into the curriculum and respecting children's right to play and free time, how the existing curriculum might need to be modified, implementing changes to traditional modes of assessment and a focus on the diversity and individualisation of pupils' needs. In this way, inclusive education becomes education where all pupils can learn successfully together. Inclusive education has, I believe, two significant implications for early years practitioners. Firstly, it presupposes the existence of the core values in the curriculum about diversity which are embraced by educators and responded to positively by them, and secondly, that the principles behind inclusive education practice can be enabled through certain pedagogical approaches; play being a highly effective approach.

Models of organisation that are inclusive and value the role of play are important considerations in early years settings and issues of strategic planning, ownership and evaluation (McQuail and Pugh, 1995) need to be addressed as much as the specifics of programme individualisation. A *bottom-up* approach to the curriculum is child originated and views children already as competent learners, actively engages and responds to the interests and skills of children and parents and, with play integral to it, takes the view that over-demanding content can harm children's dispositions to learning and inhibit understanding. In contrast a *top-down* approach has the content and skills determined by adults and has educators framing the content in the light of learning theories and their own personal philosophies of education according to parental values and preferences and guided by policy directions from governing authorities (Porter, 2002).

Research findings agree that the quality of the inclusive programme is critical (Scruggs and Mastropieri, 1994; McLaughlin, 1995). In identifying some of the

Figure 8.3 Providing resources for inclusive play
Source: Jim West/Alamy

factors for successful inclusion in classrooms, those of Ainscow (1995) are lucid. He lists them as the following:

- effective leadership
- whole school involvement
- collaborative planning
- coordination
- reflection
- school policy.

Children with SEN should engage in learning programmes that are guided by the same key principles as those underpinning quality early years curricula where play occupies a central place and practitioners acknowledge that it may be necessary to make changes to curriculum content and to teaching approaches so that programmes are differentiated and individualised to best meet the needs of each child.

Inclusive play

Combining the terms 'play' and 'inclusion' into **'inclusive play'**, seems to suggest particular types of experiences that are available to all children. Sadly, this is often not the case. There might be barriers existing in a child's culture that might discourage playing with others or barriers in the social environment such as children who display aggressive behaviours or those too

> **Inclusive play**
> Providing equipment and apparatus in school and in out-of-school activities that allow disabled children to participate.

shy to join in social play. Barriers in terms of perceptual-motor difficulties that mean a child cannot remain still easily, clumsiness or problems in organising oneself or the play resources, cognitive difficulties such as poor short-term memory or inability to follow rules or emotional difficulties such as poor concentration or unwillingness to help others, mean that full participation in play may not always be possible for all children at all times. Children who for many reasons can be excluded from play include travellers, children in care, disabled children, those from ethnic groups and children who display the kind of anti-social behaviours that bar them from participating in play with their peers, including shyness (sometimes not considered in the range of anti-social behaviour). Yet when play is truly inclusive it has so much to offer children and has benefits for each of the three stakeholders outlined in the previous section. The *child* benefits first hand from play experiences that help with problem-solving skills, assessment of risk, increased learning, language and social development. It helps develop attitudes of tolerance and respect and fosters independence, confidence and self-esteem. *Family and the wider community* benefit from friendships that

Ideas in action

Scenario: Principles behind inclusive education

The DfES set out the principles of inclusive education in its publication *Inclusive Schooling: Children with Special Educational Needs* (DfES, 2002c) in this way:

- Inclusion is a process by which schools, local education authorities and others develop their cultures, policies and practices to include pupils.

- With the right training, strategies and support, nearly all children with special educational needs can be successfully included in mainstream education.

- An inclusive education service offers excellence and choice and incorporates the views of parents and children.

- The interests of all pupils must be safeguarded.

- Schools, local education authorities and others should actively seek to remove barriers to learning and participation.

- All children should have access to an appropriate education that affords them the opportunity to achieve their personal potential.

- Mainstream education will not always be right for every child all of the time. Equally, just because mainstream education may not be right at a particular stage does not prevent the child from being included successfully at an earlier or later stage.

Improving practice

The ideas contained in this document are very worthy indeed, at policy level. Carry out some research to consider how they are realised in practice in your local authority area.

Stop and reflect

Reflect on the practice in your own setting. Do the above principles accurately reflect what you see on a daily basis? If they don't, what needs to change to enable these to become a reality? Discuss this with your colleagues or peers at college and make a list of your ideas.

begin and grow in social networks centred around play in homes and community play spaces. A sense of belonging to a community is fostered, which in turn increases social cohesion. Communication helps build feelings of being connected and taking an active part in a family or community group. It builds an appreciation of the diversity that is a part of every society. Schools and other settings benefit in providing a *curriculum* that is matched to individual needs of children, it adheres to well-established principles of good practice in early years and is delivered by reflective practitioners who care for children and reflect upon how best to meet children's changing needs.

Acknowledging these benefits, how can the principles that underpin play experiences be put into practice to support children with SEN? Opportunities for play must be open to all children and this made explicit to everyone. To really be inclusive, play must be accessible. This means, for example, consideration has to be given to the type of paths in a play space and where these paths are located. Transport should be considered if this is needed for the child to participate in the play experience. Choices about what play children would like to engage in must be made and any adaptations to games and activities made to accommodate the changing needs of children. Play experiences must be safe but this does not mean they have to lack challenge. They should when necessary extend the challenge, not deny it. Play features, whether these are natural or artificially constructed, should offer children variety and stimulate their interest. Adults need to address the skills of children and their dispositions to play in their planning. Inclusive play means children with special educational needs interacting with able-bodied children on an equal footing, playing together.

Ideas in action

Perceptions of play in the curriculum (Practitioner observation)

I think that play is really important for all children. It has so much to offer but I think that we are so squeezed nowadays to fit everything else into the curriculum that it can be overlooked. That's not to say that it isn't important – any early years teacher will tell you it is. But there are difficulties in where it is in the curriculum. I suppose being in early years we are lucky. It is a natural part of what we offer children each day. It isn't something that is offered once other work is done. I believe it is something that is central to any early years curriculum. Look at my classroom!

Jessica, Foundation Stage teacher

Improving practice

Look around your setting and consider potential barriers to play for children with different types of SEN, and then think how you could best address these.

Stop and reflect

Are the messages in this extract reflected in the setting you are currently working in? What are the barriers to including play as this teacher suggests for you and/or your colleagues? How can these barriers be lessened? You might consider cost implications, any solutions currently viable, and so on.

Supporting Play for SEN Children

In school settings, approaches to inclusive play should be aimed at providing the sort of experiences that allow each child as full participation as possible. Recent studies point to the role of the responsive adult/practitioner in enabling this. Hestenes and Carroll (2000), for example, found that a key feature in supporting play was the understanding the practitioner had of the children and skills associated with pre-empting difficulties the child might encounter by engaging in the play. In this study, developmentally delayed children selected play activities that required predominantly **gross motor** or sensory **skills** often in solitary play, whilst normally developing children opted for more solitary play activities. The teacher was seen as a key element in the play through his/her role in supporting and extending and seen by the researchers as a key element in effective inclusion programmes.

> **Gross motor skills**
> Involve the movement of the muscles in larger actions such as running, jumping or riding a bike.

As I have already stressed, all children have the same need to play, so formal teaching methods are not always relevant to the needs of young children with special educational needs. Research shows direct formal teaching can show some short-term gains but has negative results in consolidating deep learning and skill generalisation (Mahoney et al., 1992). Children can lessen their involvement in what is happening and become passive rather than active participants in the experiences, becoming reliant upon the adult to direct them. As children get older and move from the child-centred experiences in early childhood to more formal structures in the later primary years, children who have had too much formal instruction early in life retain a reliance on adults that is in contrast to aims of developing independent and autonomous learners. This is not to deny that formal teaching has a place in education practice for SEN children, but a more naturalistic approach with a strong play emphasis is certainly to be preferred. Wilson's idea of 'teachable moments' (1998), where practitioners make the most of opportunities that arise naturally in unstructured or semi-structured situations to teach a particular concept or skill, seems an eminently more sensible approach to adopt with SEN children than formal didactic teaching. Differentiation is a critical aspect of meeting individual needs in the classroom and involves teachers and children collaborating to develop the best learning strategies in what Corbett (2001) referred to as a connective pedagogy that bridges curricular demands with a child's needs.

Sayeed and Guerin (2000) remind us that young children with SEN may have physical difficulties accessing activities, understanding instructions from adults, responding verbally and coping with unfamiliar materials. Play overcomes such hindrances. They propose four areas of consideration in supporting inclusive play for children with SEN:

1 Expectations of the child should be high and this requires some accurate background information about the individual child (that is, home circumstances, medical history, and so on).

2 Planning should support the needs and short- as well as long-term targets identified.

3 The play environment should allow for safe but challenging activities but also permit opportunities for risk taking and exploration.

4 The roles played by adults in providing play plans (they call this indirect involvement) and gathering information about an individual child in order to plan for specific needs (direct involvement).

This last point refers to assessment, which is pivotal to supporting children's inclusive play.

Garvey's definition of play as 'the spontaneous voluntary behaviour of a child' (1991, p. 10) seems to invite opportunities for adult interaction to support children's learning and development and to respond to individual needs. (In this case this means practitioners, parents, health and other professionals.) Observation-informed assessment is now a familiar feature of early years practice. Play settings provide a natural environment for assessment in interactive experiences between adult and child. Such assessment can take place over time and can provide a comprehensive picture of an individual child's strengths and weaknesses. Pugh described the importance of assessment neatly when she said,

Ideas in action

Play-based assessment (PBA) model

Stage 1 Pre-play (preparation)

- Be specific about the information to gather.
- Decide on the number of sessions, duration and time.
- Negotiate timing and type of activities.
- Decide the location.
- Consider cultural and linguistic factors.
- Familiarise yourself with the child and the environment.
- Decide on group or individual focus.

Stage 2 (adult–child interaction)

- Consider proximity to the child.
- Where possible allow the child to initiate the play but lead when necessary (flexibility).
- Share the agenda, making the interaction as pleasurable as possible.
- Be aware of the child's basic needs.

Stage 3 Post-play (completion)

- Phase out gradually.
- Structure the information gathered.
- Feed back to other relevant adults.
- Plan the next step.

From Sayeed and Guerin, 2001

Improving practice

Select a child in advance and try out the PBA model in your setting.

Stop and reflect

Afterwards evaluate the effectiveness of the tool. How useful was the information it provided to you about the child? How easy was it to administer? Was it more/less effective than other diagnostic tools your setting uses? Why was this?

'Observation and assessment are the essential tools of watching and learning by which we can both establish the progress that has already been made and explore the future' (2001, p. 70). Observing children at play can alert practitioners to patterns of atypical development that can then help specialists respond early to concerns expressed about developmental or behavioural changes. Play-based assessment (Sayeed and Guerin, 2001) combines observation and adult participation and allows assessments to be made in familiar play situations. (Readers are referred to the text *Early Years Play* by these authors for further information.) The assessment has three stages and its component of participatory play, when the assessor interacts with the child in a play situation, is given in the accompanying Ideas in action box.

Creating environments for inclusive play

The environment is critical to supporting inclusive play. Casey (2005) believes that improvements to play environments can actually result in new possibilities being created for more inclusive play. She writes that rich play environments offer opportunities to explore and discover open-ended destinations whilst dull or neglected environments decrease the opportunities for children to play together, resulting in frustration or destruction. Play allows children to come into contact with their environment and culture in a very immediate way. Children's environments are better predictors of developmental outcomes than the existence of disabling conditions, and the way in which children interact with the environment and the people in it is crucial. What happens in the environment influences the ways in which young children play and the perceived importance of play; for example how parents choose one toy over another or the encouragement they give to their children to play. Play permeates all cultures and allows us to come into contact with the environment and culture in an immediate way and to express that culture. In this way, the home is a vital part of a culture and serves to shape children's play experiences and, later, so do schools. But it is not always such a rosy picture. A child's environment can cause social, emotional and physical challenges and be far from inclusive.

Marginalisation of a child with SEN can impede developing social skills through lack of contact and play-times with peers. Children with physical disabilities can quickly become frustrated in the absence of ramps or lifts and the existence of steps or narrow doorways that impede their mobility, just two examples of how the environment can also be a barrier to inclusion.

The research literature has much to tell us about the positive influence of the environment on learning and development. Hull *et al.* (2002), in their book *Opening Doors: An Introduction to Inclusive Early Childhood Education*, describe four attributes of the environment to be considered when supporting SEN: physical; temporal and social and affective.

Physical attributes refer to aspects such as group size, and these authors cite research indicating that smaller groups are preferable where smaller groups are more likely to engage in pretend play (Smith and Connolly, 1980). They also say that large play space invites more

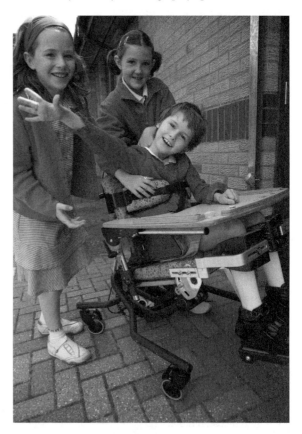

Figure 8.4 Forming playful friendships
Source: Paul Box/reportdigital.co.uk

active physical play and pretend play is more likely with large play equipment. Resources are important for quality inclusive play and the appropriateness of activities and materials is vital and confirmed more recently (Fromberg, 2002). Adequate physical space is linked positively to developmental gains. Opportunities for children to move around freely, group games, exercises for large muscle groups (such as skipping and throwing and catching balls) are linked to outcomes in learning and behaviour (Jensen, 2000).

The *temporal environment:* children with SEN need sustained time to engage meaningfully in play and derive the maximum advantage from it. Christie and Wardle (1992) in a study of 5 year olds observed that children were more engaged in various types of play in 30-minute periods than in 15-minute blocks.

What children think about themselves and how they behave are bound up in the *social* and *affective environments* they experience. Making friends, risk taking and resolving conflict are part of 'emotional literacy', and

being able to play out these roles may reduce the risks of mental health problems in later life (Mental Health Foundation, 1999). This facet is about warmth, feeling secure and belonging, and how the environments communicate these messages, whether this is in the home, in school or in the playground.

The Play Inclusive Research Report (Casey, 2004) identified five features of quality inclusive play environments that are described in the accompanying Ideas in action box with examples of how these appear in practice.

The traditional working areas (often known as zones) that exist in many early years settings allow much support to be given to meeting a variety of needs through play. The home corner can quite easily be transformed into a hospital, café or shop to stimulate children's imaginative play. Here children can be involved in dressing up, perhaps talking on the telephone, caring for a baby or preparing meals for peers. Or the '**whatever you want it to be place**' (Broadhead, 2007a) might particularly help SEN children in that

Ideas in action

Features of quality inclusive play environments

Flexibility. Any spaces should have open-ended opportunities for play. These need to be varied and interesting to engage children. What will this look like in practice? Play spaces should have slides to use with running water, have trees to make into dens. Wooden planks to use as bridges, balancing beams or diving boards are useful. There should be safe zones and sheltered areas for storytelling.

Shelters may be permanent or temporary. Ideally these are constructed by children out of natural materials. They offer privacy and safety. What will this look like in practice? Ground-level dens offering shelter from the elements; tree huts, tunnels and below-ground spaces.

Centres of interest can be permanent or changing and made by children. What will this look like in practice? Sensory gardens, paddling pools or mazes as permanent features and tents or even a pile of earth as a temporary one.

Natural elements for children to play in and with. What will this look like in practice? The list might

include trees, caves, long grass or rushes. Also stones, logs and water.

An *atmosphere* that exudes warmth, welcome and accommodates difference. It is a child's space. What will this look like in practice? Sculptures or paintings and images in soil.

After Casey, 2005

Stop and reflect

In auditing the setting where you work or one that you are familiar with, are the features described integral to the play experiences offered to children there?

Improving practice

If your audit indicates that the play areas in your setting do not meet the standards described above, discuss with your colleagues how you could make improvements.

Whatever you want it to be place

An area where children are provided with materials that encourage them to use their imagination and engage in free play.

Fine motor skills

Involve the movement of the muscles in smaller actions such as holding a pen or wriggling the toes in sand.

there is no adult-imposed agenda into which they may not 'fit' due to their SEN. Sand and water play promotes valuable **fine motor skills** through activities such as pouring and filling beakers; it can assist with language development where children use phrases such as 'more than' or 'less than', and cognitive skills can be enhanced through measuring and counting or acting out roles using toys such

Hand–eye coordination

Is the ability of the vision system to control and guide the hand to perform tasks such as catching a ball or writing a letter.

as diggers in sand. In the music corner, musical instruments are available that can be used for individual self-expression which might not be in evidence so easily in other areas of the setting.

The book or story corner allows children time to sit quietly and browse through a variety of books individually or to share a story read to a small group by a practitioner. Play activities in an art and craft area can help build cooperation skills, language skills by sharing ideas with others and important fine motor skills and **hand–eye coordination** whilst large apparatus in or outdoors helps children to develop gross motor skills

Ideas in action

Case study: Meeting needs of a child with dyspraxia through play

Karl, aged 6, has dyspraxia, a condition that affects four times more boys than girls. He has difficulty with many everyday tasks in school because of poor planning and organisational skills. Hanging up his coat on the right peg and returning to it later, arriving at the dining hall in time for lunch, getting changed for PE all present him with problems. Although a bright boy, he struggles with academic tasks – poor short-term memory means that facts remembered one day do not guarantee recall the next day. He finds written tasks difficult due to lack of control in his fine motor skills. He reads slowly and needs to use his finger to guide him to orient him to the next line of the text. Socially, he finds the activities that his friends engage in after school a challenge. To him, swimming or riding his bike are major hurdles and, at times, the clumsiness associated with his condition does not help him make new friends easily. Throughout his school life and recreation time Karl displays the classic symptoms of dyspraxia.

Improving practice

When Karl was a baby, he never crawled. This meant that activities such as reading that involve crossing the midline of his body present difficulties. Similarly a sport such as swimming that involves coordinated use of all four limbs is also a major challenge for him. At 6 years old, time spent using large and small apparatus such as in a PE lesson will be essential for him to educate his brain to send the correct messages to his muscles that will help with overall balance, sequence his movements and coordinate them more efficiently. In his classroom, providing role-play opportunities for him to dress up, giving him time to thread beads and play with sand and water will help strengthen important motor skills. Play in this case is integral to his classroom and out of school life in a non-threatening but positive way.

Improving practice

What other ways can you think of to support children such as Karl in the classroom? What other types of play experiences do you think would help him with his difficulties?

Ask some colleagues in your setting to help you to make a short-term play plan for a child like Karl.

and work alongside others, to take turns and facilitate confidence in meeting challenge.

By understanding the needs of the child and planning to accommodate those needs in the indoor and outdoor classroom, play occupies a central place in meeting an individual child's needs. In the Ideas in action box you can see this exemplified for Karl, who has dyspraxia.

Summary and review

This chapter began by taking you on a journey. It was a journey that proposed, paraphrasing Baroness Warnock's words, that if certain needs could be identified and met, then we could go on it together. Yet in undertaking the journey we needed to consider certain important things. The chapter posed three initial questions:

- What do we understand about 'inclusion' and 'inclusive education'?

A trawl through the legislation over the past 30 years has seen huge progress, not least in giving clarification to the terminology associated with special educational needs in this country, but significant changes in legislation, UK policy statements and in the wider international context, and to practice. There is much to celebrate in that policy and provision for children with all kinds of special educational needs has moved on considerably during this time. I have argued the importance of this, since inclusion is about much more than what happens in a school or any type of educational setting – it is about how societies fundamentally perceive the concept of special needs and special educational needs. Inclusion is a basic human right for *all* children.

- Why are child, family and curriculum sometimes referred to as the cornerstones of SEN?

Beginning with the child, it was argued that the starting point must be with the child and serious consideration given to his or her needs and competencies. Parents as first educators and family create the first environment a child encounters and their influence is significant. The school extends this influence to peers, other adults and to a curriculum that must aim to cater for individual needs. Recent legislation such as *Every Child Matters* and the Code of Practice reflect this drive and provide the justification for practitioners to move the agenda forward.

- What is the particular significance of play for children with special educational needs and how can we best support inclusive play?

Against a backdrop of an ever-changing world placing enormous demands on children and increased pressures about pupil attainment and the achievement of even higher standards, I argued that play has so much to offer the lives of all children that it must be defended robustly by educators and by parents. Play is, in short, essential for every child. It is a currency for the present and, importantly, for the future in this world of change, which takes us back to what is important in the curriculum, and in our lives. We all need to play and have a right to play.

Transforming thinking and practice: over to you!

The chapter concluded by offering some practical ways to make play more inclusive for children so that our natural desire to play (as adults as well as children) balances with the enormous benefits to development and learning that play offers, especially for children with special educational needs. The nature of pretend or imaginative play, for example, has so much to offer a disabled child by way of a release from a physical disability if the environment was arranged to support this. This is my message for parents, practitioners and policy makers. The journey continues.

Questions for consideration

- Is there a gap between rhetoric and reality? Does legislation suggest certain rights and entitlements for children that are not apparent in practice?
- Are the voices of children, parents and practitioners equally heard and responded to?
- Are school league tables in mainstream schools jeopardising experiences for children with special needs?
- Recent reports suggest that SEN children are being let down by an under-funded system that is not 'fit for purpose'. Do you agree?

Ideas for research

Examine your setting and explore some practical ways that have been highlighted in this chapter to make play more inclusive for children. Critically examine their impact both in the short and longer term.

The nature of pretend or imaginative play has so much to offer a disabled child by way of a release from a physical disability if the environment is arranged to support this. What considerations would you need to explore to ensure your environment supported such a vision?

Further reading

Casey, T. (2005) *Inclusive Play: Practical Strategies for Working with Children aged 3 to 8*. London: Paul Chapman.

Frederickson, N. and Cline, T. (2002) *Special Education Needs, Inclusion and Diversity: A Textbook*. Buckingham: Open University Press.

MacIntyre, C. (2001) *Enhancing Learning through Play: A Developmental Perspective for Early Years Settings*. London: David Fulton.

Porter, L. (2002) *Educating Young Children with Special Needs*. London: Paul Chapman.

Wall, K. (2006) *Special Needs and Early Years: A Practitioner's Guide*. London: Paul Chapman.

Websites

www.surestart.gov.uk
www.nasen.org.uk
www.unicef.org.uk
www.kidsactive.org.uk

Chapter 9

Playwork

FRASER BROWN

The opposite of play – if redefined in terms which stress its reinforcing optimism and excitement – is not work, it is depression. Players come out of their ludic paradoxes . . . with renewed belief in the worth-whileness of merely living.

Sutton-Smith, 1999, p. 254

Introduction

Although it is possible to identify supervised out-of-school provision for play towards the end of the nine-teenth century (Cranwell, 2003), most commentators would accept that the seeds of the modern-day play-work profession were planted soon after World War II. In the 1950s and 1960s, largely in response to the ideas of Sorensen (a Danish architect), a number of adven-ture playgrounds appeared in the United Kingdom. Sorensen envisaged 'junk' playgrounds where children could imagine, shape and create their own reality. In *Planning for Play* (1968, p. 55) Lady Allen of Hurtwood quotes correspondence between herself and Sorensen from 1947, which provides some clues to his thinking:

> The object must be to give the children of the city a
> substitute for the rich possibilities for play which

> **Ludic paradox**
> Ludic refers to play, and a paradox is a strange contradiction that might not be expected, but nevertheless exists, so 'ludic paradox' refers to a complex contradiction relating to play behaviour.

children in the country possess . . . It is opportune to warn against too much supervision . . . children ought to be free and by themselves to the greatest possible extent . . . one ought to be exceedingly careful when interfering in the lives and activities of children.

These ideas shaped the thinking of many of the early playwork pioneers (Abernethy, 1968; Benjamin, 1974; Hughes, 1975). In this short quote it is possible to iden-tify the early germ of ideas now taken for granted by the playwork profession: children being in control of their own play places (Hughes, 1996); the dangers of adulteration (Else and Sturrock, 1998); the value of providing enriched play environments (Brown, 2003). The last ten years has seen both a consolidation of that early thinking and the development of a number of new ideas, with the result that modern playwork practice is now informed by a substantial body of underpinning theory. Having dealt with most of the classical playwork theories in Chapter 1, by the end of this chapter you will be able to answer the following questions:

- What do more recent theories of playwork and the ideas of Brian Sutton-Smith tell us about the nature and purpose of playwork?

- What are the implications for playwork practice?

Ambiguity and beyond

Sutton-Smith's classic text, *The Ambiguity of Play* (1977) contains the most comprehensive examination of play theory that has yet been attempted. Sutton-Smith identifies over 100 theories, which he groups under generic headings (rhetorics). Some are respected, others ridiculous. They have one thing in common: they all fall short of providing a full explanation of play. Via an exhilarating sweep of humour, research, children's folklore and cutting edge theory, he reaches the conclusion that trying to define play is virtually impossible. A definition of play would have to be extremely wide ranging. It would have to apply to animals as well as humans, adults as well as children, and could not be restricted to the values of western civilisation. It would have to cover all manner of participant forms, from daydreaming and jokes to sports and festivals. He says 'play is like language: a system of communication and expression, not in itself either good or bad' (1997, p. 219). He expresses concern about the modern western tendency to idealise play, which he says leads us to accept untenable definitions – for example that play is intrinsically positive, voluntary and free. He then goes on to introduce a new approach, suggesting that play has evolutionary impact, because it is the means by which human beings adapt to all aspects of historical

> **Potentiation of adaptive variability**
> A potential for a player to carry out/practise varied behaviours that will help him/her adapt to life beyond the play situation.

> **Individual development and species 'evolution'**
> Play creates situations which do not simply help the individual to develop skills, but help whole groups of players to develop skills that they can then teach other people, which in turn helps the whole human race to progress.

change. Play is characterised by the **'potentiation of adaptive variability'** (1997, p. 231). Sutton-Smith suggests that play activity stimulates the brain in such a way that brain cells retain their 'plasticity'. In other words, the very act of playing enables us to retain, and even develop, our flexibility of thought. This clearly has substantial impact on both **individual development and species 'evolution'**.

In his most recent work, *Beyond Ambiguity* (2008), Sutton-Smith reveals that in recent years he has become more and more interested in both the paradox and the duality of play. Play is paradoxical because it is not always what it seems: for example, a fight

> Jarvis, in Chapter 7, takes an in-depth look at rough and tumble play.

is sometimes not a fight, but simply rough and tumble play. The 'duality' refers specifically to a link that he has identified between the primary emotions identified by Damasio (1994) (shock, fear, anger, sadness, happiness and disgust), and certain fundamental aspects of play. Thus,

shock is ever-present in games of teasing and hazing; fear is the key in risk taking; anger dominates all forms of contest; loneliness accounts for festivals of all shapes and sizes, happiness is the best label for our

> **Peak experiences**
> A peak experience is one where the individual feels intense joy and sense of purpose.

modern consumer play subjectivities known as **peak experiences**, and disgust fits all forms of nonsense and profanity.

He has now taken this one stage further, and suggests that within these different forms of play performance there is always also a duality, and that there are elements in our informal play behaviour that may be seen to prepare us for the trials and tribulations of real life. Thus:

- Teasing involves harassment that when met with player resilience may be seen to prepare us for initiation procedures in later life.

- Risks involve dangers being confronted with courage, which prepares us for the chances we take with our physical and economic fate.

- Contests involve attacks rebutted by vigilance and defence, which in many ways can be seen to prepare us for combat, war and predation.

- Festivals involve loneliness sometimes confronted with inebriation, which helps to develop the coping mechanisms for when we are confronted with the absence of membership identity.

> **Individualistic consumer subjectivity**
> The excessive amount of choice created by a modern consumer society means that people constantly have to choose between which items to buy, such as clothes, food, furnishings, in a subjective fashion on the basis of trivial factors; hence consumption becomes highly subjective and individualistic.
>
> **Iconoclast**
> One who destroys culturally important symbols and monuments; in the sense the chapter uses this term, it is suggesting that play might enable a player to experiment with ideas that are unconventional in his/her culture.

- Flow experiences describe narcissisms met by fame, which prepares us for the central role of **individualistic consumer subjectivity** in modern life.

- And finally, profanities involve deviance rebutted by wit, which prepares us to be rebellious **iconoclasts**.

All this leads him to the conclusion that play has evolved as the mechanism that enables human beings to cope with a rapidly changing world. Our biological genetic

> **Play 'gene'**
> A concept proposing that the desire to play is encoded in human beings' biology. The reference to 'a gene' is a figure of speech, as what we know of genetics indicates that the need for play would be the result of complex interactions between many genes.

make-up is generally unable to keep pace with our rapidly changing social world, but the presence of a **'play gene'** enables us to overcome the problem.

The concept of risk in play and playwork

In a letter to the *Daily Telegraph*, dated 10 September 2007, headed 'Let our children play', concern was expressed about the 'marked decline over the past 15 years in children's play'. The letter was notable for the fact that it was signed by 270 senior figures from a wide range of professional backgrounds. The authors highlighted a wide range of features of modern life that have eroded children's play, including a 'pervasive cultural anxiety which, when uncontained by the policy-making process, routinely contaminates the space needed for authentic play to flourish'.

This is a theme reflected in Tim Gill's *No Fear: Growing Up in a Risk Averse Society* (2007). Gill draws attention to developments that have taken place in UK society during the last 25 years that have had a negative impact on children's play, and especially on children's opportunities to experience risk. These include: greater amounts of traffic on the roads; increased regulatory frameworks; media scare stories about paedophiles; and a growing fear of litigation on the part of professionals who work with children. The result is that children are far less visible in our local communities than they once were. This is potentially dangerous because, as Chilton (2003) suggests, children need to experience all aspects of their local environment in order to understand the community in which they live. Nor will it be easy for the community to accept them as having a legitimate presence if they are rarely seen. It is also dangerous in the longer term because it means children will have far fewer opportunities to take risks.

Ideas in action

Practitioner observation

The following sequence took place in an early years setting, and illustrates many of the preceding points – especially the paradoxical nature of play; the role of free-flowing play; the complexity of play; and the duality of the experience. (I am grateful to Katherine Fisher for permission to use this story.)

It is snack time, and picking up on the relaxed atmosphere, I lie on the floor in the middle of the children whilst they have their snacks.

Gerry: 'Look – Katherine has fallen asleep!'

I open one eye and look at Gerry.

He laughs and runs back to his seat.

Martin: 'That's not Katherine – it's a troll.'

I then start to snore: zzzzzzz. . . .

The children laugh and start to get excited.

Two children come over with their apples and put them on my tummy.

As I move to get the apples the children run back to their seats.

I pretend to eat the apples but sit up and start to sniff.

'I think there must be children moving around!,

I can smell children when they move close to me! Yum yum!'

They all scream and run back to their seats.

Lisa creeps into the home corner.

'Let's get some pretend food for the troll.'

She puts the food on a plate and pushes it towards me.

I sniff again . . . 'Oh yuck that's not my food.'

Lisa laughs.

Then Jodie gets a teddy from the cuddly toy box.

She creeps up to me with the toy and puts it by my head.

'Here you go Mr Troll, I got you a teddy.'

She sits back.

I slowly start to stroke the teddy.

I start to smile and cuddle the teddy bear.

I sit up slowly and cuddling the teddy I walk out of the classroom.

I come back in as Katherine.

'Hello everyone. I just saw a really funny troll holding a teddy, did you?'

The children start to tell me about their adventure with the troll and how he could smell them and wanted to eat them if they moved! Not one single child said that the troll was me.

Comment

This short story illustrates not only the power of play but also the potential impact of a sensitive playworker. To begin with, the playworker relaxes with the children, and is not at all intrusive into their experience. However, she is imaginative enough to respond to the children's cues; going with the flow of their play. The playworker is clearly not a troll, and would not eat the children. All the children know that, and yet none of them break out of the fantasy. Presumably they feel safe with their playworker in the dangerous world of trolls. One of the children appears intuitively to understand the power of **transitional objects** (Winnicott, 1971), and in particular teddy bears – so much so that she is able to take the heat out of the situation

> **Transitional object**
> A transitional object is created in a child's belief that one object can 'stand for' something else in the sense of a fantasy experience.

with her peace offering to the troll. Perhaps the most remarkable thing is the final duality; the discussion about the troll with the very person who was pretending to be the troll. These are quite small children, and yet they are clearly able to separate the complex and powerful imagery of their play experience from the subsequent discussion about that experience.

Gill (2007, p. 16) summarises the case for enabling children to engage with risk as being fourfold:

1 Encounters with certain types of risk help children learn how to manage those risks.

2 If the child's appetite for risk taking is not satisfied s/he may seek out situations that carry even greater risks.

3 Undertaking risky activities carries beneficial side-effects for children's health and development.

4 Overcoming challenging situations is an essential part of living a meaningful and satisfying life.

The problem exposed by Ball (2002) is that the positive outcomes from play are hard to measure; whereas the negative outcomes – accidents, costs, litigation – can be measured by science and other qualitative tools, and are all too real. Faced with this situation, and children's lack of political muscle, the tendency will be for benefits to be undervalued and play provision to lose out.

However, the letter to the *Daily Telegraph* is an indication of a growing understanding that things have gone too far, and that we need to redress the balance. This is something playworkers have been saying for many years. Hughes (2001) has suggested playwork is essentially evolutionary in nature, and that risk and challenge are at the very heart of what the profession is all about. For him the child's opportunity to experience risk should be seen as part of the right to play, which is enshrined in the UN Convention on the Rights of the Child (UNICEF, 1991). Hence Hughes (2001, p. 10) sees this element of the work as compensatory in nature. The role of playwork is to offer children environments and experiences that whilst 'providing challenge, do not expose children to unknown dangers, fears or feelings of failure'.

The key to this approach is the need to differentiate between risk (which is assessable) and hazard (which is unpredictable). Gladwin (2005) says risk assessment requires two separate judgements: firstly, what is the potential for something to happen; and, secondly, what are the likely consequences if it does? Evolutionary playwork accepts that children are capable of their own risk assessment. Furthermore, it is the human being's inclination to take risks that sets us apart and makes us the dominant species on the planet.

The theory of loose parts

Bengtsson (1974), speaks of play as taking place wherever 'something turns up to move the imagination'. This can be anything, 'but preferably something that can be manipulated and influenced' (1974, p. 49). It also reflects the optimistic view of creativity touched on by Nicholson and Schreiner (1973) when they suggest that children should be empowered to structure their own play environment, because human beings are inherently creative, and there is no reason to believe we lose that talent as we grow older. This view is supported by Hart's (1995) observation that children are only excited about playgrounds when they are being built. He suggested there was a link between their interest and the availability of 'materials for them to work with' (Hart, 1995, p. 21). Why should that be? We know already that play is more about process than product. Nicholson (1971, p. 30), in developing his 'theory of loose parts', explains it thus: 'In any environment both the degree of inventiveness and creativity, and the possibility of discovery, are directly proportional to the number and kind of variables in it.'

Nicholson is using the word 'environment' in the holistic sense: 'a system of interactive parts that affect us' (Nicholson and Schreiner, 1973, p. 19). Thus, a loose part environment includes everything from the perimeter walls of a building, to the flotsam and jetsam that lie within. He suggests the beach is a good example of a loose part environment. Here the sand is constantly shifting, the sea is fluid, even the rock pools change with the tides. The debris of past holidaymakers is left on the beach for future children to play with. Thus, the form and structure of a loose part environment is the result of 'community generated forms' (1973, p. 20). However, Nicholson is not of the opinion that this is an entirely random process. Instead he describes a loose part environment as having 'the form of highly ordered disorder – where every part has its place' (1973, p. 20). The value and popularity of loose part environments is

Ideas in action

Author's observational notes

Once, when my wife was away in France, I collected my 5-year-old grandson from school. As a special treat we went to Rowntrees Park where there is a variety of brightly coloured adventurous play equipment. He went straight to the top of the 'spider's web (about 10 metres off the ground). Admiring his agility, I sent a text message to my wife telling her of our grandson's feat. Almost immediately I received a reply saying, 'Are you mad? Get him down!' In an instant my whole perspective on the situation changed, and I began to encourage him to come down. He was half-way down when a girl, at least three years his senior, passed him on the way up. Of course, he turned round and followed the girl back to the top. When she reached the top, the girl leant through the ropes, grabbed the central pole and slid down to the ground. My grandson started to copy what he had seen (and I started to panic!). Reaching through the ropes he placed his hands on the central pole, but on surveying the scene, he pulled back and climbed back down the net (much to my relief).

Comment

The lesson from this story is that, even at the age of 5,

my grandson was perfectly capable of his own risk assessment. He was able to judge what he could and could not manage. The irony is that if he had not been out of my reach I would have intervened. Such intervention would have had purely personal motives, and would not really have been in the best interests of the child. In the words of Bob Hughes (2001, p. 54),

> Most children are neither stupid nor suicidal. They are not going to deliberately go beyond the limits of their known skills. But to evolve at all they must take much of what they do to that limit and test it. When we see a child engaged in something 'dangerous', we are making that judgement from our standpoint, not from theirs.

Stop and reflect

Are there moments in your own practice where you have intervened in (what you consider to be) a potentially dangerous situation when you could have let events unfold? To what extent do you agree that our assessment of what is 'dangerous' is indeed a judgement from our standpoint, not theirs?

confirmed throughout the literature. Norén-Björn says 'loose materials are of crucial significance in enriching play' (1982, p. 166). Numerous researchers have shown that children prefer sandpits and paddling pools to most other items of equipment (Blakely and Hart, 1987). Moore (1974) found this was especially true of the under-5s. Berry (1993, p. 129) stated that dramatic play is stimulated by the introduction of loose parts, and that the 'amount of time spent increased considerably when loose parts were added'. Parkinson (1987) even suggested loose parts are one of the factors governing the extent of a child's play range.

Nevertheless, it is important not to give the impression that loose materials are all that is needed to stimulate children's play. Chiang (1985) found that whilst 'portable' materials are used during group dramatic and group constructive play, fixed equipment comes to

the fore with group functional play. Nicholson (1971) himself makes the point that a loose part environment is a holistic concept, which includes the solid structures such as walls and fences, as well as the creative materials within. He would not suggest climbing frames should be demolished, but it should be possible to combine them with loose resources in order to facilitate creative possibilities.

The play cycle and the play stage

In their excellent conference paper, 'The playground as therapeutic space: playwork as healing' (1998), Perry Else and Gordon Sturrock put forward a strong argument for playworkers to be regarded as potential healers.

Ideas in action

Loose parts stimulate the imagination

The book *The Venture: A Case Study of an Adventure Playground* (Brown, 2007, pp. 40–2) contains an excellent example of the way in which loose parts can stimulate the imaginations of children who might otherwise not be expected to be creative. Ex-playworker Ben Tawil recounts a tale about a lorry-load of old furniture that was dumped at the entrance to the adventure playground. In his (slightly abridged) words:

As the children arrived for the evening session they took immediate interest in the furniture. A group of about seven children, aged eight to twelve, both boys and girls, started to sift through it. At first their search seemed indiscriminate, almost chaotic, with very little communication between them . . . the children seemed to have concurrent ideas that stemmed from one person's initial placing down of a piece of furniture. Two leaders emerged – the eldest girl of about twelve, and one of the younger boys of about eight. They seemed to be taking on the role of interior designers – telling the rest of the group where to position the furniture. These instructions were followed to the letter with great seriousness. Together they created a home environment . . .

Straight away a boy of about eleven sat down at the bureau and exclaimed, 'Can you keep the noise down? I'm trying to write a letter to the council,' and without question or hesitation the oldest girl (until this point the chief interior designer) addressed the other children in a sharp authoritarian voice, 'Your Dad's told you to keep the noise down. Now go and play quietly.' Immediately the rest of the group took on roles as brothers and sisters, grandparents, daughter and visiting boyfriend . . .

This play . . . continued for *two weeks* – every evening and for full eight-hour days at the weekend. Different groups of children used the materials and altered the environment and the narrative to suit their needs . . . Eventually the children's interest waned: perhaps they had played out their need for this type of play for the time being, they had certainly worn out the already dilapidated furniture. The play began to morph once more as the children found uses for panels from the furniture in construction play, and the remnants were put to good use fuelling our nightly campfire."

Comment

Tawil says

the value of this wagon load of tatty cast-offs was immeasurable . . . the new materials available that evening stimulated an evolving idea that the children controlled – they had complete ownership of their play, and it was developed naturally without the need for me to intervene or entertain or provide diversion.

At one point he alludes to the idea that the children were not just engaged in dramatic play, but rather in socio-dramatic play (Smilansky, 1968). They could clearly be seen to be acting out roles of importance to their everyday lives. There was an easy mix of ages and genders, with children 'showing compassion, consideration, encouragement, and support – experiencing sympathy and empathy (Brown and Webb, 2005)'. He also speaks of how the narrative appeared to take on a life of its own, 'unhindered by the intermittent comings and goings of players'.

Taylor (2008) suggests the theory of loose parts has relevance in a number of areas of playwork theory and practice, including play types (Hughes, 2006), compound flexibility (Brown, 2003), transitional phenomena (Winnicott, 1951), values and assumptions (SkillsActive, 2002), playwork principles (PPSG, 2005), and quality assurance (Conway and Farley, 1999).

Stop and reflect

How could you explore the theory of loose parts in your setting?

They argue that playwork has so far failed to flourish because of a lack of theoretical clarity, political naivety, conflicting claims on scarce resources, and a lack of in-house research. As a consequence, the last 30 years has seen a reduction in open access playwork provision.

Else and Sturrock focus on the study of the mind or psyche at play, and to describe this they have coined the term **psycholudics**. Their thesis rests on the proposition that 'prior to each act of creativity . . . lies an imaginal realm or zone that is playful *(ludic)* and symbolically con-

> **Psycholudics**
>
> Psyche – of the mind; ludic – relating to play; psycholudics is therefore the study of the mind at play.

stituted. The playworker joins and works with this *emergent material* and content'. Thus, they argue, playwork is not about control or management, but rather its value rests in the richness of response that a play exchange, setting or artefact generates (1998, pp. 4–5). For Else and Sturrock playwork takes place on two levels: firstly the obvious level of playing; and secondly at a deeper layer of unconscious, but emerging content. They reject the commonly held view that sees play as indefinable. Instead they suggest the purpose of play is to act as a prefiguring element to creativity, which might be seen as the source of all mental health. Therein lies a means of healing trauma, neurosis and psychic ill (through play).

Like Bateson (1955) they suggest the play drive takes place in a *frame*, and that players issue signals which are contained and reflected back to the player. They use Sutton-Smith's (1984) concept of the *play cue* to describe these signals. They introduce the concept of a *play cycle*, which in an ideal world satisfies the child's immediate desire to play, and which holds the meaning of that play. Else and Sturrock focus on the idea that playworkers are in a unique position to respond to the child's play cues, and they highlight the importance of ensuring those responses are appropriate. From these interactive experiences playworkers may be able to 'develop insights and interpretative responses, aiding further, and perhaps deepening, expressions of this *ludic content*' (1998, p. 5).

However, this occurs only in the ideal play cycle. Sometimes that ideal process breaks down. Else and Sturrock call this *dys-play*, and suggest it might occur in four distinct circumstances where:

1 the meaning of play goes unrecognised
2 the adult's response is inappropriate
3 the containment breaks
4 the cycle becomes hybrid.

In the last case especially, they feel the child is likely to start forming neuroses. This is crucial to their thesis. Many well-established therapies involve the replaying of neuroses formed in childhood. Thus, Else and Sturrock are suggesting that playworkers are in a potentially important position because they are 'active at the precise point where potential neuroses are being formed' (1998, p. 5). They therefore ask whether playwork might be seen as either curative or at least cathartic, and suggest that playworkers might be seen as *freely associating in the free associations of* children.

Thus, for Else and Sturrock play is a drive active in a *frame* of a particular nature. The frame is the setting for the child's driven material – his/her cues and themes. The play drive requires accommodation and/ or return. Some elements of the playwork setting will inevitably be compensatory for, and contribute to, the child's emotional equilibrium. At the deeper levels of functioning, children express, in symbolic form, unconscious material crucial to their psychic development. This requires containment, reflection, return, and thoughtful engagement by the playworker; all of which means that playworkers must develop a consistent interpretative or analytic perspective out of which to issue their responses.

The BRAWGS continuum and the Edge of Recalcitrance

Frost and Woods (2006, p. 338) describe playworkers as 'adults who support and help children play through providing resources, and an atmosphere of safety and security in environments dedicated to children's play'. In

Playwork: Theory and Practice (Brown, 2003b, p. 4) I suggested that one of the essential concerns of playwork is 'enabling children to pursue their own play agenda'. Thus, playwork is about empowering children in their play, yet at the same time ensuring they come to no harm. The potential contradiction here is all too apparent, and has been taxing playworkers for the last 50 years. How is it possible for an adult to provide safe and secure provision that still offers children the complete freedom to explore their own ideas, feelings, skills and

Ideas in action

Author's observational notes

I once watched a playworker playing with a 10-year-old boy called Nicolae, in a hospital ward. The pair were engaged in a game of chase. Nicolae was chasing the playworker, but seemed to want her to chase him. As they were running round the cots, Nicolae stopped at a table and banged it noisily twice with his hand. The playworker kept on running, having missed the play cue she had just been given. Nicolae resumed his chase. Next, he knocked over a mattress, and clasped his hands to his face in mock horror. He even said, 'Oh dear!' This was a much more obvious play cue, and yet the playworker missed it altogether and continued to run away from him. That left Nicolae with no option but to take his cue from the playworker, and so he started to chase her again. Almost immediately he ran past the playworker's coat, which was hanging from a door handle. He stopped and put his hand into the coat pocket, pretending to steal something. At last the playworker got the message, and started to chase him. Nicolae yelled excitedly. He allowed himself to be caught quite quickly, and the pair ended up rolling around on the floor with Nicolae giggling triumphantly.

Comment

The unstated meaning of the play cues in this example is fairly clear – 'Stop running away, and start chasing me.' When the playworker eventually responded, Nicolae's reaction was not simply to start running away. His excited yell showed a real sense of accomplishment, and the fact that he allowed himself to be caught seemed to reflect a desire to confirm his achievement.

Else and Sturrock (1998) emphasise the importance of the playworker's ability to interpret children's play cues. They suggest that a consistent failure to do so may have damaging effects for the children concerned.

Play cues are often quite subtle, which means playworkers have to be highly sophisticated in their ability to interpret the meaning of each child's behaviour. However, it is fortunate that one of the functions of play is to provide us with the opportunity to engage with the non-verbal messages of other human beings. Through play we develop those interpretative skills (Brown, 2008). Therefore, so long as the playworker has had a reasonably well-balanced childhood, there should be no problem interpreting children's play cues.

It is also significant that Nicolae had been born ten weeks premature, and weighing less than 2 pounds. He was abandoned at birth, and subsequently spent most of his life tied in a cot. He had considerable brain damage, although it was not clear whether this was the result of his genetic make-up or his life experience – probably a combination of the two. At the time of my observation, Nicolae had only been free of his abuse for about nine months. In that time he had learned to walk, developed some rudimentary language, and was now engaged in social play. His use of quite sophisticated play cues was a further indication of his development through play.

Stop and reflect

How successful are you at interpreting children's play cues? Can you identify examples from your own experience where you have misread the non-verbal messages of your children? What was your reaction? And theirs? What did you learn from this situation?

Can you draw parallels with the arguments provided in Chapter 7 and 11?

> **Didactic**
> Intending to instruct, an activity undertaken for the specific purpose of teaching.

Russell (2008) suggests that play provision has often been characterised as following one of two models: the **didactic** approach or the **ludocentric** approach. The didactic approach focuses on child development, and sees the adult's role as one of structuring and directing children in order to help them become successful adults. The ludocentric approach sees play as having value for its own sake, and views the adult's role as one of supporting, enabling and empowering children in order to help them become successful children. However, Russell says this is an oversimplification of the two positions that fails to take account of the complexity of play settings and the need for playworkers to develop a range of responses to children's playing.

Russell credits Arthur Battram (2002) with helping her come to an understanding that this dualistic perspective is erroneous.

> **Continuum**
> A chain, sequence or progression of events/areas where one thing leads logically to another.

Instead, Battram suggested the ludocentric principle should be about working towards a middle zone, somewhere between the edge of order and the edge of chaos. As a result Russell developed a model of a **continuum** from the didactic (directing and teaching) at one end, to the chaotic (negligent and egocentric) at the other end. A typical didactic setting would be characterised by an adult-designed, highly structured programme of activities, with a rigid set of rules, and so on. The chaotic approach might be typified by unreliable staff, unpredictable opening hours and resources that are dangerous or falling apart. In between these two extremes we find the ludocentric approach, which is about children's play, rather than any other adult agenda.

The model has been further developed, after discussions with Gordon Sturrock, who pointed out the need

abilities? Wendy Russell's BRAWGS[1] Continuum is an attempt to address that apparent contradiction.

to take account of emotions and feelings, rather than focusing simply on behaviour. This is an attempt to address problems of adulterating intervention such as adults joining children's playful competitions with the sole intention of winning; or dominating discussions with children about sensitive matters, as a result of a failure to come to terms with their own 'unplayed-out material' (Else and Sturrock, 1998). The important thing here is for playworkers to match their feelings to their behaviours. By seeking to become more aware of where our practice lies on the continuum, it should become easier to adopt a position that is consciously ludocentric.

Play deprivation and therapeutic playwork

The ideas of Bob Hughes regarding recapitulation and the evolutionary benefits of play and playwork have been explored in the first chapter. This subsection concentrates instead on Hughes's study of the effects of play deprivation and play bias, and especially the lessons to be drawn from his award-winning[2] study of children's play in urban Belfast during the period of 'The Troubles'.

Hughes (2002) has identified 16 distinct play types, which he says all children need to experience. His thesis is based on the idea that a lack of balance, or a deficit of one or more of these play types, during childhood will do lasting damage to the developing child. He suggests this might take two distinct forms, either play deprivation or play bias. Hughes (2003, p. 68) says *play deprivation* is the result of either 'a chronic lack of sensory interaction with the world', or 'a neurotic, erratic interaction'. *Play bias* refers to 'a loading of play in one area of experience or another, having the effect of excluding the child from some parts of the total play experience'. Hughes suggests that chronic deprivation and bias in children's play may be far more widespread than society acknowledges. This may be the result of a number of factors, including fear of traffic, perceived stranger danger, parental fears of children engaging in risky activity, and so on.

---

[1]BRAWGS is an anagram of the initials of the three people involved in the development of this idea: Wendy Russell, Arthur Battram and Gordon Sturrock.

[2]Bob Hughes was awarded the Mike Taylor Memorial Prize for Originality and Innovation in Professional Scholarship.

Ideas in action

Practitioner observations

Two examples illustrate these points. The first I have used elsewhere (Brown, 2003, pp. 61–2), but it bears repeating, as it offers an excellent example of the shortcomings of a didactic approach to playwork. It concerns an incident I once witnessed where a 'playworker' had organised a game of football for about 20 children. During the game, a dog chased a second ball on to the pitch. Quite spontaneously the children incorporated that ball into their play, and a very complex, almost three-dimensional game resulted. The adult blew his whistle forcefully, and stopped the game. The children moaned loudly, whilst he carried the spare ball to the touchline. Their body language should have sent a message to the whistle-blower, but he seemed completely unaware of their very obvious 'play cues' (Else and Sturrock, 1998). Not surprisingly, during the next ten minutes the players became more aggressive, even to the extent of a fight breaking out. After a while, four of the children simply walked away, and the game broke up in disarray.

The second example was provided by a work colleague, who told me of an especially chaotic situation at one of the local adventure playgrounds. Almost overnight, through no fault of their own, the management committee lost its funding. In the short term this meant the playworkers were made redundant, and the site closed. Over the next few months the playground committee made sterling efforts to raise the funds to reopen the site. On a number of occasions hopes were raised, only to be dashed, but in the mean time false impressions had been given to the children. Eventually small amounts of money were allocated to the project, with the result that it became possible to open for two or three nights per week. However, it was never predictable on which nights the playground would be open, because it was difficult to get reliable staff. Not surprisingly throughout this whole long saga the behaviour of the children deteriorated badly, and eventually violence became the norm.

Comment

In the first example the sports coach's didactic approach was ill-suited to the playscheme environment. Having tasted the thrill of creative play, the inflexibility of organised sport was too much for the children to bear. A simple understanding of the compound flexibility process, and the importance of working to the child's agenda, could have saved that playworker a great deal of stress, and made the experience that much more enjoyable for everyone.

In the second example, a stable group of children who were used to playworkers who adopted a predictably ludocentric approach were thrown into chaos by a chronic adulteration of their play environment. The fact that this was outside the control of a well-meaning committee is largely irrelevant. The children did not want their playground to close, and when it reopened they wanted it to be open at reliable times, with playworkers who showed commitment to their work. Since none of this happened it is hardly surprising that there was a build-up of resentment, and a general lack of trust.

Stop and reflect

In what ways might you ensure the children's wishes are given primacy in your setting? How could you be sure that a playwork ethos is adopted at all times?

On the basis of interviews conducted with subjects who grew up during the period of 'The Troubles', Hughes concluded that play had been 'adulterated'. Adulteration is the term Hughes (2000, p. 13) uses to describe the 'negative impact of adults on children's play'. He found four main effects on play:

1 deprivation and substitution of play types
2 saturation by adulterating images and events
3 range, choice and mastery deprivation
4 traumatic violation of the play process.

Ideas in action

Observations from a Romanian paediatric hospital

Studies of abandoned children in Romania by Sophie Webb and myself (2005) have provided some confirmation of the conclusions of Harlow, and thus offer support for the recommendations of Hughes. Our work investigated the impact of a therapeutic playwork project on a group of children in a Romanian paediatric hospital. The children, who were between 18 months and 12 years old, had been abandoned at birth, and subsequently received little positive input into their lives. They spent most of their time tied in the same cot, in the same hospital ward. They were fed no more than once a day, and their nappies were rarely changed. Some of the children were HIV positive, and yet when sick, they were treated with shared needles.

In 1999 White Rose Initiative (WRI), a Leeds-based charity, employed the first Romanian playworker (Edit Bus) to work with the children. This was a direct result of the new director's awareness of Harlow's research into the effects of play deprivation in monkeys reared in isolation. WRI brought Edit Bus to Leeds Metropolitan University, where we designed a specially focused training course for her, consisting of work at the Leeds General Infirmary and Ebor Gardens Nursery, coupled with daily reflective tutorials. Edit returned to Romania in October 1999, and began working exclusively with the children in a rudimentary playroom provided by the hospital.

At the start of every day Edit had to untie the children, feed them, bathe them and change their nappies, before taking them to the playroom, where she (play)worked with them during the day before returning them to their cots in the evening. As soon as she left the hospital, the nurses would enter the ward and tie the children up again. Apart from the therapeutic playwork project, during the first year little else changed in the children's lives. They still spent the rest of their day, and most weekends, tied in the same cots, experiencing hardly any interaction with anyone else.

Comment

During the first year of the project two researchers from Leeds Metropolitan University spent more than 500 hours working at the hospital. We used a combination of research methods to identify developmental changes in the children, such as research diaries, participant and non-participant observation, and our own play development assessment tool. In some cases the changes were dramatic, providing strong evidence of the power of play as a therapeutic and developmental agent. The children showed a speed of 'recovery' that was quite unexpected, and which casts doubt on the 'ages and stages' view of play development, as seen in the work of Piaget, Parten, Sheridan and others (Webb and Brown, 2003).

These extracts from Sophie Webb's research diary illustrate the change from October 1999:

8th March 2000: Virgil plays well with other children and is usually the instigator in made-up games; although when he plays on his own he is more serious. He's always busy collecting objects and putting them in the yellow box; he'll move the box around and then empty whatever is inside. This is repeated so many times and he never gets tired of it. He likes to be in control, but is learning to share his 'work' with the others and is definitely gaining in confidence. It struck me how much enjoyment he got from the building blocks and it was so lovely to watch him laughing and laughing to himself when he knocked them over.

29th March 2000: Olympia was dancing to the music on the radio this morning with Virgil. They were holding hands and moving around the room. When I joined in, Carol came over and wanted to be involved and this progressed into running up and down the room with them still holding hands and wanting to stay linked together. This might appear to be something very normal, but considering how unsteady these children were only six weeks ago, it's a major achievement.

Hughes suggests four damaging outcomes from all this: the adulteration of social play fostered the continued propagation of sectarianism; the militaristic nature of the child's environmental experience encouraged the adoption of an extremely limited range of play narratives; restrictions on children's range behaviour created mental mapping deficits; and the stress, trauma and play deprivation of everyday life resulted in neurochemical and neurophysiological mutation of the brain.

Hughes (2000, p. 58) refers to work by Harlow and Suomi (1972) and Einon *et al.* (1978) in suggesting that 'symptoms from play deprivation in other species can be significantly reduced when the subjects are given the opportunity to play again'. He therefore proposes a role for playworkers in alleviating the ill effects of play deprivation, but suggests they would need specialist training in the effects of conflict on play.

Summary and review

Children's play is a complex phenomenon with implications far beyond childhood. This chapter set out to explore the following questions:

- What do more recent theories of playwork and the ideas of Brian Sutton-Smith tell us about the nature and purpose of playwork?
- What are the implications for playwork practice?

As we have seen, Sutton-Smith (2008) offers the proposition that play may well represent the mutant gene that enabled us to develop along a different path from the reptiles in the course of evolution. Burghardt (2005) suggests that reptile behaviour patterns are essentially reflexive. Most other sentient beings are reflective to a greater or lesser extent. Human beings appear to be the most reflective of all, and Sutton-Smith feels that ability is developed through play. Thus, he is placing play right at the heart of the evolutionary process. The paradoxical nature of human play, and its inherent complexity, set us apart from all other species.

We are also the species that takes most risks with our personal future. Again Sutton-Smith suggests that characteristic has helped cement our place in the evolutionary process. Risk takers are not always popular, but they move the species forward. Playworkers generally view risk as an essential part of play, and have a belief that children are broadly capable of making their own risk assessments. Thus, playwork settings tend to be risky settings: not just in the physical sense, but also in the social and emotional sense. This means that playworkers are often working at the edge of what others in society would find acceptable. They are likely to be more tolerant of the extremes of behaviour than most adults. That is why Battram talks about playwork being 'on the edge of recalcitrance', as opposed to merely steering a gentle path between the didactic and the chaotic.

But, what is playwork really about? From my own theorising about compound flexibility (see Chapter 1), through Else and Sturrock (1998) exploring the play cycle, and on to Hughes's work on play deprivation, we can see that playwork is essentially compensatory. Playworkers assess what is lacking in the child's play environment, and attempt to address those play deficits.

Unfortunately this work has been generally undervalued by governments, although in the United Kingdom the recent Children's Plan (DCSF, 2007c) gives cause for optimism.

Transforming thinking and practice: over to you!

The playwork profession has never really managed to develop a cohesive and sustained lobby, with the result that most playwork provision is poorly funded. That funding is often short term in nature. As a result provision is patchy and the political base is weak. Like most infant professions playwork has sadly been plagued by inter- and intra-professional conflicts. That has affected the profession's ability to develop effective networks. All this leads to insecurity among playworkers, and results in them adopting a somewhat defensive approach to other professions.

Questions for consideration

Playwork is still a fledgling profession, and as such there are many unresolved issues facing the profession today:

- To what extent, and for what reasons is supervision acceptable?
- Is it ever acceptable to structure children's play for them?
- Which is the best funding regime: public or independent?
- Should children and their families expect to pay an entry fee?
- Does payment always remove the potential for free play opportunities?
- What are the pros and cons of open access provision when compared to care provision?

- Where do we draw the line between safety/danger on the one hand, and risk/challenge on the other?
- To what extent is it possible for this work to be done by volunteers?

Ideas for research

The greatest need for the playwork profession is some form of longitudinal impact research. At present playworkers are fond of swapping stories of their long-term success with children who other institutions have found troublesome. However this is generally anecdotal, unverifiable, evidence. One of the very few pieces of research that focused on the impact of playwork was my own study with Sophie Webb of the impact of a therapeutic playwork project on a group of abandoned children in a Romanian paediatric hospital. However, this focused on a very extreme situation. What is needed is similar longitudinal studies, but focusing on 'normal' children, so that playworkers will at last be able to point to meaningful research to back up their funding applications.

Further reading

Brown, F. (ed.) (2003) *Playwork: Theory and Practice.* Buckingham: Open University Press.

Brown, F. and Taylor, C. (eds) (2008) *Foundations of Playwork.* Maidenhead: Open University Press.

Gill, T. (2007) *No Fear: Growing Up in a Risk Averse Society.* London: Calouste Gulbenkian Foundation.

Hughes, B. (2001) *Evolutionary Playwork and Reflective Analytic Practice.* London: Routledge.

Sutton-Smith, B. (1997) *The Ambiguity of Play.* London: Harvard University Press.

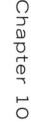

Opening Play: Research into Play and Dramatherapy

PHIL JONES

Editors' Note: *This chapter is presented in a slightly different format to the other chapters in the book. It describes a highly specialist area in which play is used in therapeutic interactions and, as such, the practice described is that of counsellors in the therapeutic arena, rather than that of mainstream practitioners in care and education settings. It is hoped that students will be able to benefit from the contents of this chapter as a source for reflection on the wider benefits of play, and that the chapter will serve as a source of information for qualified practitioners currently considering postgraduate training in this area.*

Colette was referred to Family Futures for an assessment because of absconding and school refusal. The referral had been triggered by an incident when the police picked up Colette late one night in a local park with a large group of older boys who were taking drugs. She spent the first 45 minutes of the individual therapy session eyeing me and picking at her fingers. After a long silence she suddenly said, 'I never feel happy you know, never. Why is that?' . . . I asked her what was the main feeling she has most of the time: angry, sad or scared? Colette explained that most of the time she felt scared . . . I asked Colette what she thought she did when she was scared. Colette sat bolt upright and widened her eyes, she said, 'Well I run as fast as I can and I just keep running.'

Up until this point the conversation had largely been one-sided with me doing most of the talking. I suggested that perhaps using a sandtray might help Colette think about her need to run and keep running . . . I brought the sandtray closer to Colette, who said it was silly, but with a sort of question in her voice. Colette's hand drifted to the sand and she stroked it lovingly. I put my own hand in the sand and joined with Colette in touching the sand . . . Colette ran the sand through her fingers enjoying the sensation and sprinkled the sand over my hand very gently.

(Vaughan, interview in Jones, 2007, p. 89)

Introduction

Play, as this book testifies, is flexible and varied in its forms. Children reach to it in a number of ways, and for a number of reasons. There is not one way of playing, nor one meaning of play. This chapter deals with some specific qualities that some forms of playing have. These concern the way play has within it what has been described as *therapeutic potential* or *curative possibilities*.

> **Therapy**
> A form of intervention where a client and therapist meet with an intention to assist development, reduce identified symptoms or resolve conflicts (Oatley, 1984).

The spontaneous play that children create is allied to, but different from, the play created for intentional **therapy**. The following questions relate to this difference:

- How do therapists see the potentials and benefits for children of playing within therapy?

- How is access to play's therapeutic possibilities created within therapy?

This chapter will report on research that explores how play can be allied to the ways in which adults can offer opportunities to children who need a therapeutic space. It explores the ways in which the potentials and possibilities of play are opened up by therapists and children working together in dramatherapy. The chapter will give a background to the connections between play, therapy and the **arts therapies**, followed by a description of the research approach taken, along with some **dramatherapy** research vignettes from *Drama As Therapy* (Jones, 2007). The two questions above will be used to help look at the research, to explore how therapists see the process of play in therapy.

> **Arts therapies**
> Forms of individual or group therapy using the arts.
>
> **Dramatherapy**
> The use of drama in therapy, involving processes such as role enactment, mask work or play.

Play, therapy and the arts therapies

The focus of this chapter is on play which occurs within a specific context, that of the arts therapies. Play therapy has been established as a distinct modality with clear professional boundaries (Gil and Drewes, 2004; Schaefer and Kaduson, 2006). Yet, for children who come to therapy, it is not the only arena where play can be offered therapeutically. Increasingly, children are able to access a variety of forms of therapy, depending on their needs and the availability of different therapies within their local provision (Malchiodi, 1999; Evans and Dubowski, 2001). The arts therapies are offered to children in a number of countries and in a number of different settings: for example in schools, hospitals and family contexts (Weber and Haen, 2004; Jones, 2005; Karkou and Sanderson, 2005). The specific research that will be drawn upon examines the ways in which play features within dramatherapy (Jones, 2007). My research looked at the ways in which 30 therapists saw the nature of processes such as play within their work with clients. This chapter presents some of that research – looking at how therapists see the effectiveness of play-related processes within their work with children. The contexts of the work drawn on in this chapter vary widely, from children in the United Kingdom to children and young people living with HIV in South Africa and child survivors of the tsunami in Sri Lanka.

The following gives a background to play within the arts therapies. In previous publications I have discussed the ways in which play and playing is central to the efficacy of the arts therapies and to dramatherapy (Jones, 1996, 2005, 2007). Play is a close relative to drama and is a source for both content and process within dramatherapy. Evreinov speaks of this close relationship between play and drama in his discussion of the Soviet Malachie-Mirovich's work on the educational value of toys: 'All children have the ability to create a new reality out of the facts of life' (1927, p. 36). The child plays naturally, without instruction, creating their 'own theatre', proving that 'nature herself has planted in the human being a sort of "will to theatre"' (1927, p. 36). I have noted how many key figures within the development of dramatherapy and the arts therapies began their initial thinking and work in the areas of play and dramatic playing with children (Jones, 1996, 2005, 2007). From Moreno's work with children in Viennese parks in 1908 (Blatner and Blatner, 1988) to Slade's work with child drama (1954) and his initial use of the term 'dramatherapy', the inspiration for the use of drama as therapy has been found in play. Play has a great deal of relevance to the therapeutic use of drama. Blatner and Blatner (1988, p. 51) have spoken of the 'common basis of drama, **psychodrama** and the play of children'.

> **Psychodrama**
> A specific form of drama as therapy developed by Moreno focusing on exploring the roles people play in their lives.

For the dramatherapist and for a child coming to dramatherapy, play is a part of the expressive range that can be drawn on in creating meaning, exploring difficulties and achieving therapeutic change. Literature indicates that crucial to this relationship is the way in which a child in therapy finds meaning in play processes (Klein, 1961; Erikson, 1963; Winnicott, 1974; Johnson *et al.*, 1987). The reasons for children coming to therapy can vary enormously. A recent national survey in the United Kingdom (Meltzer, 2000) offered some of the reasons in its analysis of mental health of children and adolescents:

- Amongst children aged 5–10 years 10 per cent of boys and 6 per cent of girls had a 'mental health problem' defined as a clinically recognisable set of symptoms or behaviour associated with considerable distress and substantial interference with personal functions.

- One in five children has officially recognised special educational needs – those with a mental health issue are about three times more likely than other children to have special needs (49 per cent compared with 15 per cent).

- Those with a mental health problem are about four times more likely than other children to have played truant (33 per cent compared with 9 per cent).

As the vignettes from practice analysed in this chapter will show, the emotional and mental health of children is connected to their life situation and the events they experience. Examples of these include living with illness; the attitudes of the society they live within; traumatic events; their family life and issues such as social exclusion including poverty, or prejudice. Aynsley-Green (2003, p. 35) illustrates the ways these factors are often seen to be connected when he says, 'while it is true that the vast majority of children lead rich and fulfilled lives, nonetheless, there are widening inequalities of health, wealth and education, with many children, young people and families not benefiting from society'. In engaging with children's lives through therapy drawing on play, the emphasis can be placed on play's capacity to reflect and work with these complex, interconnecting areas. The therapeutic space creates opportunities for the child and therapist to use these qualities of play. Stevens (2000, p. 177) summarises this: 'it is through play that children learn about the world, develop abilities and explore their needs and anxieties: in other words, help to develop and transform themselves'.

In her research conversation, therapist Van Den Bosch refers to this idea of a 'play space' in talking about a client, Brenda:

> Van Den Bosch: Yes, and for Brenda (the therapy) gave her space to acknowledge the presence of her sons. As up to this point she had never really spoken about family. I think this was like the idea of a play space, which apart from trying things out without consequences gives distance between the client and the material and enables both therapist and client to explore the material (Jones, 2007, p. 83).

Authors have identified a number of different ways in which play features within dramatherapy (Jennings, 1992; Langley, 2006; Jones, 2007). A state of playfulness is created whereby the client can enter into a playing *state*. A key aspect of this state concerns the ways in which the dramatherapy space can be said to create a playful relationship with reality. This 'playfulness' concerns the ways a child in dramatherapy can enter a state that has a special relationship to time, space and everyday rules and boundaries. This relationship is characterised by a more creative, flexible attitude towards events, consequences and held ideas (Jones, 1996, 2007). As Van Den Bosch mentioned in the excerpt from her research interview above, this space enables the client to adopt a playful, experimenting attitude towards themselves and their life experiences.

Playfulness also refers to the ways in which playing can often involve the representation of events or feelings which a child, for example, is trying to assimilate, come to terms with or master. This sometimes can involve the playing out of an event or situation, and at other times the play taking on the theme or issue that reflects the material the child is concerned with, or troubled by.

Within dramatherapy, play is also seen as part of an expressive continuum – as a part of drama. As such, it is a specific language (for example object play, toys, games) that can be a part of the way a client explores or expresses material in dramatherapy. Play content in dramatherapy usually includes play with objects and **symbolic toys**, **projective work** with objects in the creation of small worlds, rough and tumble play or make-believe or dramatic play involving taking on characters and games (Weber and Haen, 2004; Karkou and Sanderson, 2005).

Playing can be seen within a developmental continuum of different stages such as **sensorimotor play** or **symbolic play** (Johnson *et al.*, 1987; Jennings, 1992; Jones, 2007). This continuum is often connected to cognitive, emotional or interpersonal development. For some clients in dramatherapy, the therapy will consist of moving to a new **developmental level** through play. For a client with severe learning difficulties,

---

Symbolic toys
Small representative objects, e.g. a toy tree or animal.

Projective work
A way of playing that enables children to express feelings or concerns from their lives by using objects or pretend scenarios.

Sensorimotor play
Play that emphasises movement or physical expression.

Symbolic play
Play that emphasises imagining and transforming.

Developmental level
The idea that most children progress through different stages in play, each one offering new potentials and opportunities.

---

for example, the therapeutic work might involve engaging in a shift from one level to another. This might be a change from playing in a solitary fashion to cooperative play with other children. This change would entail a therapeutic shift in the way the client can interact with people and with their environment. They begin to be aware of others through playing, for example, and to use objects in interactions with others rather than staying involved in solitary play activity.

A developmental perspective can also involve interpreting a client's problem as concerning a blockage or problem at some stage in their life. Cattanach describes this as 'a stage in our journey where we got stopped and got stuck' (1994, p. 29). Dramatherapy's use of play can involve the re-creation of a state where such a block occurs, and the reworking of that stage in a more satisfactory way. The playing process within the dramatherapy session would aim to revisit that aspect of the client and their life and to assist them in renegotiating the developmental stage.

All of these ways show how a child can engage with, and make full use of, the therapeutic possibilities of play. The next section will explore research into how this is seen to happen in specific examples.

Narratives and meanings: the approach to research

The research I will draw on (Jones, 2007) concerned the impact of the core therapeutic processes described within *Drama as Therapy* (Jones, 1996, pp. 99–129) on thinking and practice in the field. The research question was: 'How are dramatherapists making use of the therapeutic core processes in analysing the processes at work within their practice?' One of these core processes was defined as playing:

Drama and play are part of a developmental continuum. As a part of this continuum, play is included in the expressive language which the client uses to create meaning and explore material in Dramatherapy. For clients in Dramatherapy, playing is a way of discovering or creating access to their own spontaneity. For some clients this process forms the main therapeutic benefit within Dramatherapy. Dramatherapy creates a playful relationship with reality. The Dramatherapy space enables clients to play with elements of their life – to rework issues, to try out new configurations or possibilities. This can be described as a 'play shift'. This playful exploration can produce changes, which can be integrated into the client's life outside the Dramatherapy . . . Cognitive, emotional and social development can be worked with using a developmental understanding of the play–drama continuum. Changes in the dramatic developmental level that a client is able to use in Dramatherapy, for example, can be accompanied by cognitive or social changes for clients.

(Jones, 1996, pp. 194–5)

A request was made for vignettes in written form from practising therapists who were making use of the therapeutic core processes, such as the one defined above, in analysing their practice. The short vignette from practice could either be a part of a session, or a broader description of a process through a session. The remit was that the participants considered it practice that drew on their understanding of, and use of, the core therapeutic processes as defined in *Drama As Therapy* (Jones, 1996). This would be followed by a reflective conversation with respondents based on the vignette and rooted in approaches drawing on narrative research. The conversation was normally undertaken by **MSN messenger** and each participant saw the final version to agree it. The research became not purely about the gathering of the vignette as data to be analysed by the researcher, but about researcher and respondent reflecting on the vignettes together: trying to understand how processes such as play helped the clients. The research offered a framework as a starting point, the 'Research conversations' try to identify how the therapy works: allowing the meaning and significance of what happens in the vignettes to be developed between the researcher and therapist.

> **MSN messenger**
> A live, typed online conversation.

Both vignette and conversation were conducted with care for ethical issues.[1]

Examples from the research

The excerpts in 'Ideas in Action' on p. 236 are from the full research findings (Jones, 2007). They are selected to indicate the ways in which the therapists see play as a core therapeutic process in their work with children. The extracts from the vignettes and the research conversations (Jones, 2007) show something of the variety of different contexts and situations that children experience. They also illustrate the flexibility and potency of play as a therapeutic language and process in being used by the children. They illustrate examples of the ways therapists see play at work, and the way they see it as bringing benefits to children and dealing with the issues that they bring to therapy.

Key reflections in dramatherapy

How is access to play's therapeutic possibilities created within therapy?

I will now return to the questions asked at the start of this chapter as a way of gathering together some of the material offered within the research vignettes and questions. This section will look at the implications of the research into dramatherapists' accounts for understanding play in working with children therapeutically. These are: 'How do therapists see the potentials and benefits for children of playing within therapy?' and 'How is access to play's therapeutic possibilities created within therapy?'

---

[1]Respondents were referred to the Health Professions Council Standards of Conduct, Performance and Ethics, Duties of Registrant (http://www.hpc-uk.org) and the British Association of Dramatherapists Code of Practice (www.badt.isoin.co) as well as Leeds Metropolitan University's Code of Ethics. This included clear guidelines that reflected and met all ethical requirements concerning areas such as permission to include examples of someone's therapy and confidentiality: for example, that the research participant and myself would anonymise the client work so that they would not be identifiable.

Ideas in action

Play, therapy and children after a tsunami

Debra Colkett is a dramatherapist working with children who had recently survived the tsunami in 2005. The vignette was part of a number of initiatives in Sri Lanka offering ongoing support for children. The dramatherapy was part of the 'Psycho-Social Program' headed by Unicef for the whole of Sri Lanka, and was within an initiative funded by the Ministry of Education 'arts in schools' and Funforlife, which supports work with children in countries experiencing war and natural disasters. The practice also connected with the local organisation The Foundation of Goodness, which provided resources such as resident psychologists and translators. Colkett as a dramatherapist worked with the children on an ongoing basis with additional support and aftercare being provided by the Foundation:

> **Post-traumatic stress disorder**
> A psychological reaction occurring after experiencing a highly stressful event often reflected in depression, anxiety, flashbacks and recurrent nightmares.

The circumstances we were going into were unclear. Only that we would be working in villages and camps with children, many of whom had been orphaned by the tsunami . . . The group ran everyday for one month initially. It was an open group, so children of all ages could attend . . . The group settled down to around 12–24 children per day. Not all came everyday.

(Jones, 2007, p. 150)

Colkett describes the aims of the work as being:

- to provide a safe space
- to provide some relief from **post-traumatic stress disorder** (PTSD)
- to offer containment
- to offer support.

The following is from one of the first groups.

Research vignette excerpt

We began by holding hands in a circle; me, a co-worker and a translator and some thirty children who had come to join us.

I had placed a blue cloth in the centre and waited to see what would emerge. The children began to move their arms up and down and we all began to sway spontaneously. The energy began to build and a section of the circle lunged into the centre and then another section. There was a lot of laughter, the lunging became more intense and I requested that the translator ask 'What is the sound to this movement?' Then it came, 'Whoosh!' others joined in. We were running in and out of the circle, hands linked 'Whoosh'. The energy and the noise built further bouncing off the temple walls, a sort of contained chaos. 'What's happening?' I shouted above the din. They told my translator 'It's tsunami!' 'Tsunami coming!'

'What can you see?' I yelled. The children were laughing, playing with the movement and replying 'House!' 'My house!' 'My grandfather!' 'My grandmother!' 'My sister!' 'Mango tree!' 'Gone tsunami!' The noise became more intense. We were in the thick of it. Then the howling, ear-piercing, soul-wrenching howling. I tried to ask 'What is the howling sound?' No one heard. It was almost unbearable.

B caught my eye. The other children were still in the 'play' of the enactment. B's face had changed. He had broken off from the circle, everywhere else it remained intact. The movement and sound built to a crescendo and died down and we were back to stillness, panting and smiling with the effort. B sat just outside the circle. His eyes were downcast and his face sad. I checked the rest of the children. They seemed to be having fun.

▶

My attention was drawn back to B. I asked the children to sit. He was now sitting with his head bowed and he had isolated himself slightly. I felt that he was back there with the full horror of the tsunami. How could I bring B back into the present? I desperately searched my intuition to somehow reach out to him. The right intervention was important. I asked my translator to ask him, 'What was he feeling?' He looked up, fear and sadness in his eyes. He said nothing. It was unspeakable.

After a long moment I shuffled a little closer to B still unsure of what to do, and the other children followed. In an inspired moment they picked up the blue cloth, gathered around him so that he was encased in the circle, and sensitively placed the cloth over him like a shroud. Aware that we were all watching him, I spoke to the children; I knew they had the answer. 'How can we make B feel better? I can see that playing at tsunami has upset him.' 'We can sing to him' they replied. 'Would you like that?' I asked B. He nodded. My connection with him and the loss he was feeling were palpable. We carefully edged closer, the distance seemed important. Not too close as to overwhelm him and not too distant to isolate him. After a count of three, 'Iren Handen' (a popular Sri Lankan song meaning Sun and Moon. It's the theme tune to a popular film in Sri Lanka, about two boys who go through many struggles together but their friendship, faith and spiritual bond keeps them strong) echoed around the temple and everyone was focused on B.

'Iren Handen' (Sun and Moon)

Iren Handen elija aran
Gahen velen suwanda aran
Elen dolen sisila aran
Apata sebuna ape lokaye
Sathuta wenna enne galuwe

Translation

Getting light from the Sun and Moon
Getting cool from the rivers and waterfalls

Fresh smells from the trees and bushes
This world is for us.

He looked into all our faces and eyes. We were clapping smiling and singing to him. Soon he began to smile and Tsunami no longer had him in its cruel grip. B was back with us.

Research conversation excerpt

Jones: I was very moved by the work you and the children created with the tsunami in the temple – looking back how did you make that space for them? How did you prepare, for example?

Colkett: Safe buildings were at a premium after the tsunami. It was very difficult to find a safe enclosed space. After a week or so it was suggested we use the temple. I got children of all ages involved in the task of finding a place for us. We stood in a circle. We said our name and made a movement to match it. The name was the music and the movement the dance. Then we all mirrored the movement and the name of the person creating their personalised 'dance'. My translator Rajhita spoke in Singhalese to the children. Their English was limited as was my Singhalese, so the universal language of movement and mime was very useful.

Jones: From the vignette it sounded like you managed to hold the processes that the children naturally reached out to in their play – almost like you were taking cues and holding the way they were going – the reaching for the cloth, the shrouding. Is that how it felt or was it different?

Colkett: Yes, I completely followed their lead. I had preconceptions about PTSD and how this might manifest itself. During the therapeutic process they didn't get angry . . . they experienced emotions and got on with it. It was a lesson to be learnt from them. I was in a very feeling, intuitive state. I had to trust my solid training and my instincts.

(Jones, 2007, pp. 192–5)

▶

Play, therapy and children living with HIV

In the following vignette dramatherapist Kirsten Meyer describes practice with a group of adolescents. The work took place in a project in South Africa. Recent statistics show that if one is under the age of 20 years there is a 50 per cent chance of contracting HIV. Meyer notes that, 'Statistics South Africa produced a report on death registration data showing that deaths among people 15 years of age and older increased by 62 per cent from 1997–2003 due to Aids-related conditions. Craig Higson-Smith in his evaluation report on work done by my NGO says that

> the potential impacts of HIV/AIDS on childhood are enormous and complex. To begin to explore this question it is essential to move beyond thinking about children as a homogenous group but to think about the impact of HIV/Aids on children at different developmental stages in different social, economic and cultural contexts.
>
> (Higson-Smith et al., 2006, p. 6)

Meyer also places her work in the context of the ways that the stigmatisation of HIV does 'not allow expression amongst the "normal" peer group (at school or at home), so a psychosocial support group of adolescents living with HIV provides a space for the "unspeakable" (HIV).'

The group formed part of a project that was set up between Zakheni Arts Therapy Foundation, which Meyer founded with an art therapist, a UK-based funder, Hope HIV and a Perinatal HIV Research Unit at a hospital in South Africa. The doctors are mainly paediatricians who see the children on the clinical trials once every three months or so. The project was initially set up to run groups with positive children (ages 7–11), for psychosocial support, and to see if adherence to medication improved. Meyer says,

> my Non Government Organisation, funded by Hope HIV, set up four groups. Two art therapy groups with children were run for a year. I ran one dramatherapy children's group for 6 months and, after that, one adolescent group for 12 sessions.
>
> (Jones, 2007, p. 152)

The specific goals of the group were:

- to develop **self-esteem**
- to develop a containing environment in which to explore feelings around living with a chronic illness
- to encourage different ways of expressing feelings.

The short-term therapy was for 12 weeks, sessions lasting one and a half hours, and referral was from medical doctors within the unit. Meyer described the group as being composed of five adolescents (one male and four females) ranging from 12 to 15 years of age. They had all been disclosed to (advertently or inadvertently) about their HIV status. Two had contracted HIV through sexual abuse and three had contracted it at birth through mother-to-child transmission. She notes that,

> **Self-esteem**
> The way an individual sees aspects of themselves relating to areas such as self-confidence and self-worth.

> some of the group members had also suffered earlier bereavements and traumas such as the loss of parents, rape, physical and sexual abuse. None of them had disclosed their status to anyone but their families, and they were living with the 'weight' of their secret and the 'unspeakable', also the fear of rejection if they disclosed.
>
> Group members were aware of their status but had not disclosed to anyone outside of their families. During the pre-group assessment and interviews, all participants were informed that the group was for adolescents like themselves, living with HIV. They all expressed both to their referring doctors and me how much they would appreciate a group like this, in which they could explore and talk about their feelings around living with HIV. Until this point no one had mentioned the word 'HIV' in the group; it was still the 'unspeakable'.
>
> (Meyer, in Jones, 2007, p. 96)

In the session prior to the vignette below, a very confident and open group member Zandile disclosed to the

▶

group that she had been raped. The group was supportive and expressed their concern for her. When asked what it felt like to tell the group, she answered that she was scared to tell us in case we laughed at her. The discussion then led into feelings around disclosing very personal information to others. Zandile then said she wanted us to know this fact as it is the reason she comes to the clinic (*the reason she contracted HIV*).

I was reminded that in our society having HIV is perceived as very shameful, as if having the virus were confirmation of having done something really bad or sinful. Zandile had never had the space to explore her feelings around being raped, and appeared to be emotionally 'stuck'. Her relief in telling the group was not about working through her feelings of being raped but having an opportunity to explain her HIV status. I understood her and the group to be saying it is okay to be raped but not to have HIV.

Zandile was not able to attend the following session when Nomsa and Busisiwe disclosed their status to the group.

Research vignette excerpt

At the beginning of session four one of the girls, Nomsa, was speaking about how her teacher had told her she has got 'adolescence': 'I've got adolescence,' she said, as if it was some kind of affliction or disease. (I was struck by how much easier this was to talk about.) The group then went on to explore what it meant to have 'adolescence'. They spoke of romance, bodily changes and mood swings. Nomsa said the thing she missed most about being 10 years old was that you could 'play and get dirty'; now, she said, things were different.

I was struck by the poignancy of her comment and wondered about interpretations of play and dirt, that is, contamination; and who is contaminated; and what it must feel like to live with HIV in a society that views it as dirty. Also, at a time in her life when it is vital for her to 'play' with her identity, what it meant to be living with HIV. I was struck too by the fact that at the time when she should have just been playing (8 years old), her father had begun to continuously sexually abuse her.

I responded by saying that I wondered what felt different for them now.

The group went quiet for a long time, then I said, 'Well maybe some things are difficult to speak about.' They nodded. I invited them to think about secrets and we threw a ball around the group, free-associating around secrets. After this, there was a brief discussion of different types of secrets, feelings around trust and what it meant to keep others' secrets. This led into a role-play around secrets. In the previous sessions the group had engaged well with role-play and seemed to enjoy the process.

Nomsa suggested they do a role-play and the rest of the group said they would like this very much, and then the session moved very quickly.

Nomsa wanted to 'act' first and asked Miriam to join her. Miriam accepted. After a warm-up, I invited the audience group members to say what the two girls' relationship could be. Busi suggested they were 'best friends'. I then asked for suggestions as to where they might be. Busi also suggested they were in the playground during break. With this in mind I suggested that one of them had something to tell the other that is important. Nomsa said she would like to be that person and commenced the role-play. (They chose to keep their names.)

It was a very brief role-play. Both were sitting on chairs. Nomsa turned to Miriam and said:

Nomsa:	Can I trust you?
Miriam:	Yes.
Nomsa:	I am HIV positive.
Miriam:	[Giggles with hand over her mouth.]
Nomsa:	Did you hear me?
Miriam:	Yes.
Nomsa:	Well?
Miriam:	Just don't tell anybody else.

After this we de-roled, during which Nomsa said she felt 'relieved' and that that was the first time she had ever told anyone she was HIV. I felt relief too, holding this 'secret' had been difficult and intense.

We regrouped on our cushions in a circle and I invited the group to reflect on what had happened. This led into a very intense silence. Nomsa then said it felt so

▶

good to say it out loud. We spoke about the difficulties of disclosure and other people's perceptions. Nomsa also said she would like to set up a support group at her school at some stage. There were long periods of silence and I reflected on how difficult it was to talk about HIV. Then very quietly Busi said: 'I have something to say. I am HIV.'

The group fell quiet again.

In reflecting on the group afterwards, I wondered about the significance of saying out loud (naming), 'I am HIV.' They all knew their status and they were aware that the others were positive as well. It felt as though a process had been necessary in which they could begin to name it for themselves. Through embodiment and distance (lack thereof), they were able to summon the courage needed.

Here the two group members seemed to need to create a degree of distance from themselves by creating roles in which they are talking as 'friends', yet they keep their own identities in that they choose not to play other people or invented characters. Here the dramatising creates a combination of **distancing** and **empathy** within the group. For Nomsa the distance of dramatising herself provides a way of expressing the secret. For Busi, witnessing the dramatised roles creates empathy with the scenario and with Nomsa's disclosure, and she is able to talk for the first time also. This shows how the processes of distancing and empathy can work in a number of ways within the therapeutic process.

Distancing

A way of relating to others and to the self that stresses thought, reflection and critical distance.

Empathy

A way of relating to others that emphasises understanding, sensitivity and awareness of their feelings, thoughts and perspective.

Research conversation excerpt

Meyer: I think the process of empathy was core. The witnessing of each other's processes and words was very moving and powerful from my perspective as therapist; and I think for them too, the very many quiet moments as they looked at each other and the tone of their voices. I think that having a space made for this group of teenagers was very meaningful to them. In my view it somehow represented the possibility of the idea that space could be made internally to contemplate the illness. Creating the safety of the space was very important for them and I think they only really began to trust it towards the end. So in the vignette, as in the session before, it felt as if they were 'testing the waters'.

Jones: I'm just wondering about your thoughts/ways of looking at that space: the space of the group/the individual's internal space. In the next sentences you use the word 'play' twice: something being 'played out' and 'play out telling'. In a profound way do you think the space was linked to ideas about a play space? Am just wondering about your thoughts about your use of the term there – be interested to hear your reflections about why you used it/what it might mean?

Meyer: Something was being played out in the sessions around 'telling' and 'trusting' between and within them. I had a sense that if they could play out 'telling' in dramatherapy, an internal shift may occur around acknowledgement and the very beginnings of the process of integrating the 'unwanted' aspects/'sick' parts of themselves. In my view, this is what needed to happen long before they could even contemplate speaking about it outside the therapy space.

Jones: I was very interested in the way the young women acted as 'best friends' so in role not just playing themselves and yet chose to keep their names – what did you make of that when you were in the session?

Meyer: For them it made no sense to change their names (as they told me). I think it relates to the 'me and not me' process in role-play. They needed to say 'I've got HIV' as 'themselves' but needed a context to say it in, and the context of best friends allowed this. (Jones, 2007, pp. 152–7)

▶

Play, therapy and a child refusing school

The following vignette concerns a 13 year old, and shows her developing a relationship with the therapeutic space and the dramatherapist, Jay Vaughan. Within the vignette it is possible to see the therapeutic potentials of play language, the revisiting of a developmental stage and time along with the notion of the play space giving permission for Colette to try different ways of expressing, communicating and assimilating her experiences. Vaughan contextualises a part of the work with Colette by noting that: 'Colette was 5 when she and her siblings were removed from their birth family for physical and sexual abuse and placed in foster care.'

Colette was 13 years old when she was referred to Family Futures for an assessment because of absconding and school refusal. The referral had been triggered by an incident when the police picked up Colette late one night in a local park with a large group of older boys who were taking drugs. Colette was already known to social services and to the education welfare officer as a difficult and troubled young person who often refused to talk when they interviewed her. Vaughan says that, 'Everyone agreed that Colette needed help; the only problem to date had been getting Colette to engage with anyone to think about the choices she was making and why.'

In this initial assessment session, which was part of a whole assessment day involving the rest of her family, an individual arts therapist specialising in working with adolescents sees Colette. The aim of the session was 'to see whether or not Colette could be helped to engage with the therapist and begin to consider the reasons for her troubled behaviour'.

Research vignette excerpt

Colette was very wary. She spent the first 45 minutes of the individual session eyeing me and picking at her fingers. After a long silence she suddenly said, 'I never feel happy you know, never. Why is that?' I said that lots of young people find it hard to enjoy life when they have had difficult things happen to them when they are little. Colette breathed out, relaxing her shoulders, and looked curiously at me. I asked her what was the main feeling she has most of the time: angry, sad or scared?

Colette explained that most of the time she felt scared. I explained that when scary things happen all human beings have a sort of animal response to try to save themselves from whatever is scary. This animal response is either to fight or take flight or freeze. I asked Colette what she thought she did when she was scared. Colette sat bolt upright and widened her eyes; she said, 'Well I run as fast as I can and I just keep running.'

Up until this point the conversation had largely been one-sided with me doing most of the talking. I suggested that perhaps using a sandtray might help Colette think about her need to run and keep running . . . Colette looked at the sandtray in the corner of the room, allowing her eyes to linger. Colette said that she did not want to use the sandtray but after talking for some time about Colette's problems I saw her look once more to the sandtray. I said gently, 'Why don't you give it a go, it might help.' I brought the sandtray closer to Colette, who said it was silly, but with a sort of question in her voice. Colette's hand drifted to the sand and she stroked it lovingly. I put my own hand in the sand and joined with Colette in touching the sand. I said how many young people find it helpful to express themselves using such things as sandtrays, not just little children. Colette ran the sand through her fingers enjoying the sensation and sprinkled the sand over my hand very gently. I then asked Colette to choose ten objects from three boxes of toys and arrange them in the sand.

She slowly gathered all the babies together from boxes of toys and put them in one corner of the sandtray. She worked intently, stroking the babies as she gently placed them in the sand. At one point she brought a baby up to her lips and kissed it. She then built a wall of wooden blocks with no door cornering the babies in one end of the sandtray. On the other side of the wall Colette put two large monsters that towered over it and the babies on the other side. Colette then rearranged the monsters so that they were nose to nose and facing one another and, to all intents and purposes, seemed to be fighting. Colette sat back and looked at the scene. She sighed and began to run her hands up and down her legs in an agitated way. I asked her to describe what was happening in her body. Colette said

►

she felt cold and could feel tingling all up and down her legs. She went on to say that looking at the sandtray with its picture of the trapped babies made her feel like running away.

Colette then began to talk as if she would never stop, tears slowly trickling down her face, which she kept brushing angrily away. Colette said she had tried to run away from her birth family but always felt bad about leaving the babies. Every time she ran away somehow she ended up back there and eventually she gave up running away and tried to barricade herself and her baby sisters in the bedroom. It did not work. They still got in. Sometimes she took the beatings and hoped that they wouldn't hurt her baby sisters. But sometimes she let them take the babies and hurt them, and she didn't try to protect them. She said, through convulsed sobs, that she had covered her ears trying not to listen when her sisters cried. She said she felt so bad that she had let that happen and often thought about it. Colette looked up at me and whispered, 'I still want to run away but all the pictures in my head of what happened to me come as well.'

Research conversation excerpt

Jones: I was thinking about how it seems that so many things were happening at the same time! Colette seemed to be building an appetite, or an interest, or an ease to allow herself permission to project into the dramatic materials, she seemed to be building a relationship with you through them, as well as testing herself, the capacity of the materials to 'hold' her and your new relationship. Do you see it that way or do you see the process working differently?

Vaughan: I would absolutely agree that whilst at one level a simple unfolding of the story of running away is told there are many levels of different things happening at the same time. Colette is absolutely learning in this small way to trust the therapist as well as to trust the process of working with the art.

As the sandtray facilitates Colette to tell part of her story the feelings come with the story. It feels like it is a first time for Colette. Whilst lots of children are able to tell their story, and Colette may well have told hers before, what is significant is that she allows the feelings to emerge and the therapist to witness them.

I am also very aware that for many of these young people and children they have not had the opportunity to work in this way ever before, and it is a tremendous relief to work with a therapist who knows about the sort of things they may well have experienced, who uses the arts to help them express what is inexpressible in words, and who is able to pick up their non-verbal cues that they are actually still a scared small child. It is often unhelpful to listen just to what is said because so much is held within the non-verbal communications that often contradicts the verbal communication. I believe that if a therapist can attune to the child's non-verbal messages as well as respecting their verbal messages then the whole story that they need to tell can be heard.

Jones: What difference do you see your playing as making (compared to if you'd just watched)?

Vaughan: Whilst there is a time and a place for watching the process, there are also times when it is helpful to play alongside (parallel play) with children and young people in order to work with them. One crucial part of an assessment of a child is to assess what developmental stage they are at, whether or not it is possible to get close to them in some way and join with them in play. I suppose our work is ultimately about the relationship between the child/young person and the adults around them. In order to think about how the child makes, or does not make, relationships and attachments the therapist has to think about how to form a relationship with the child. (Jones, 2007, pp. 172–5)

In all the vignettes the creation of a play space in dramatherapy involves the development of an area set apart from, but connected to, the everyday world, and which has specific rules and ways of being. All three accounts see the space as enabling the child in dramatherapy to create, within the sessions, a playful relationship with reality. Dramatherapist Vaughan, in her research conversation analysis of the vignette, describes the work of

Family Futures and play in a way that summarises how playing is a core process in dramatherapy:

> 'The play space offers . . . an opportunity to step out of the daily life and try something different with enough distance to allow them to feel safe. In the play they can explore all the possibilities of what can happen and a range of different endings, the beauty of it being that it is safely contained within the play space.   (Jones, 2007, p. 152)

In Colkett's account of the use of core processes we can see a picture of play emerging that emphasises the ways in which the therapist tries to stay sensitive to the child discovering their own way through the forms and directions of play. In her account Colkett talks about this in a number of ways. She describes 'waiting' to see 'what emerges': the group suggest singing, for example; she talks about the ways in which in response to B's feelings the group 'in an inspired moment . . . picked up the blue cloth'. When introducing ideas she suggests cues for the group to develop, for example by asking, 'What sound emerges'? The emphasis is also on forms that the children make their own, rather than external structures given by the therapist which they have to use. This is shown by Colkett's description of a 'person-alised dance', for example, which the children create. Her own description of her state echoes this position: a 'feeling intuitive state'. She has to confront rather than follow her own preconceptions of what needs to be done, and refers to the children providing *her* with a 'lesson to be learnt'. She, in this way, sees the play processes and directions as flexible vehicles for the children in their expression, exploration and shifting relationship to the things they bring.

Similarly, Meyer's account bears testimony to the ways in which the therapist retains a deep awareness of the potential meanings and significances of play, but does not impose activity or interpretation. She shows in her account the different levels the playing therapist holds. She notes the way the client talks about missing playing, the experiences of the playground, and both acknowledges the overt, as well as the potential for other meanings given the client's experiences – her HIV status, her youth, about playing and getting dirty, and the lost opportunities to 'play' with her identity.

In reflecting on a vignette not included in this chapter, dramatherapist Jo Rogers summarises a key aspect of the way the therapist creates as open a space as possible for the child's own play to emerge. This can be seen in all three accounts included within this chapter. She emphasises the importance of being aware that their role might be to facilitate access and development of play as a child may have previously experienced barriers to playing,

> Rogers: I feel my main role as first and foremost to accept whatever they bring, and whoever they are, without judgement. I feel that there has been a real obstacle against playing for many of them: that experiences in society can lead to people with a severe disability looking to see what they have got wrong. So, yes, first and foremost I model that every sound, movement, gesture, feeling is 'right'.
>   (Jones, 2007, p. 52)

Vaughan reflects this awareness as she offers a potential structured to Colette, for example, indicating the sandtray and a wide variety of objects to the client. Within this the attention is on 'suggestion': she sees this in the following way,

> I think that she needed to feel joined in the sand, as if the therapist was prepared to play too. I followed her lead and joined in the invitation from Colette to play. In my view my willingness to join with her and play enabled her to engage with the sandtray.

The emphasis is on the ways she can give permission to the client to enable free play. Vaughan's touching the sand deliberately parallels the client's movement, and seeks to communicate contact and empathy. Her words, 'followed her lead' parallels Colkett's approach, whereby the therapist works to hold, witness and foster the emerging play directions and ideas of the client.

Vaughan makes the interesting distinction between watching the play emerge and engaging in parallel play – both are seen by her as important and needed at different times. The emphasis is upon the therapist's role in enabling the play to emerge and to be with the child as meaning forms and is worked with.

How do therapists see the potentials and benefits for children of playing within therapy?

The play space within the dramatherapy becomes an arena for material to emerge. Once the material is present, it can be given access to play processes, and to the relationship with the therapist as presence, as witness to what is emerging and as sympathetic player. The relationship that is created with the therapist is seen by Vaughan to be an important part of the work of the therapy. She says, part of the significance of the play in the therapy is, 'In order to think about how the child makes, or does not make, relationships and attachments the therapist has to think about how to form a relationship with the child.' In this way the relationship formed can offer a different experience to ones the child may have experienced outside the therapy. In all three excerpts the concept of the presence of the therapist and the space offering safety and trust is key. The importance of this is central to a child allowing material that cannot be expressed elsewhere to emerge.

Meyer, for example, speaks of 'the safety of the space' and of material that can be allowed to be given expression and access to others and to the processes at work in play and therapy. In her account she links this to trust. Within Colkett's account ideas of the play space as protected by boundaries are also present; she calls it a 'safe enclosed space' and the idea of 'contained chaos'. The play develops a relationship with the events the children have experienced – this is described by her as 'full horror' and as a 'cruel grip' – the play, though, is described as assimilating, developing a relationship with what cannot be easily expressed outside the space. The combination of group expression, playful expression and exploration allows material to emerge and to be touched together. The implications of her analysis are that the play space within therapeutic boundaries creates a safety and permission.

The idea in all the accounts is that play permits expression of material that a verbal account alone could not create – that play creates a particular kind of access for the child to express and encounter their life experience. This is seen in part as assimilation, the creative work touches the material and starts to personalise it: the overwhelming tsunami and its effects – embodied by the group – for example. Colkett says of the children's experience, 'it was unspeakable': that the experiences could not find words. At times in her account the presence of the re-created tsunami is described by her in a way that indicates the testing of the boundaries of what can be held and expressed, for example in her words, 'No one heard. It was almost unbearable.' This can be contrasted with her account of the children's access to play and the arts when she speaks of the 'universal language of movement and mime'. The play is also typified as very physical and deeply involving – with personalised dances, moving in the circle. This deep involvement is seen to be key to the potency of play as being able to powerfully evoke and contain previously silenced experiences. Meyer also uses the word 'unspeakable' – and for me this is no coincidence. As in the comparison I pointed to in Colkett's account between unspeakable experience that cannot have words, or is not ready for words, and the expressions of movement and mime, so in Meyer's account, the play space and play language, the relationship between the play space and reality outside creates opportunities and permissions; a real difference for her clients. She says 'long before they could even contemplate speaking about it outside the therapy space' playing creates an opportunity to tell, and to receive support. Vaughan also speaks of these qualities. She sees part of the value of play and the arts as being 'to help . . . express what is inexpressible in words' and that a part of the value of the therapist for the client is their awareness of communication beyond words, and 'who is able to pick up their non-verbal cues'. She also talks of the safety of the space contrasting with the 'horror' experienced elsewhere and about a key element of the play space in the therapy being to do with a sense of the child reclaiming power or 'control' over experiences in their lives. As with Colkett's account she focuses on the contrast between the client's silence about the issue outside the playing and the level of involvement and eloquence of Colette's play: 'she worked intently', the images of the babies, the monsters and the sand become a powerful evocation of her life experience and become visible to her and the therapist, and access is followed by being able to assimilate, to express and begin to resolve or reach a new relationship to the previously silenced issues.

A part of the benefit for children in all three vignettes is seen to be the way in which play within the therapeutic space and relationship involves an unburdening, of something the child has been holding on to, something that play language allows to be shared. Vaughan touches on this when she talks about the 'tremendous relief' of sharing something that has been silenced. Meyer observes about the teenagers in her group, 'they were hungry to say it and the roles gave them the space to say it and say it and say it again'. Meyer also refers to the complexity that can accompany the sharing of material which has been silenced when she says, 'Nomsa then said it felt so good to say it out loud. We spoke about the difficulties of disclosure and other people's perceptions.'

In part this permission is seen to be due to the way in which the content of play language allows the forming of images that permit something to be shared in a way that verbal language is seen not to permit. This is seen in different ways. An aspect of this is the way in which images communicate in a manner that allows distance, or a lack of direct reference that is different from a direct verbal description of the experience. This is seen to give the child permission, to be safer than a direct reference. In another way, the images create a form that allows the child to communicate in play language – this is seen to be owned by them as something which they feel familiar with – as if play is their own terrain.

Another aspect is that by which play is seen to be an 'as if' state. In the world outside the play space sharing the difficult material is seen to be problematic, even dangerous. Meyer talks about the forces that silence the sharing of the adolescents' HIV status, for example. She sees this in different ways. In part the space becomes one to create opportunities for the children to begin to touch and assimilate their situation within themselves: 'it somehow represented the possibility of the idea that space could be made internally to contemplate the illness'.

The play space is also seen by her as becoming a safer arena for the children to test something before accessing it in the world outside the therapy, 'I had a sense that if they could play out "telling" in dramatherapy, an internal shift may occur around acknowledgement and the very beginnings of the process of integrating the "unwanted" aspects/"sick" parts of themselves.'

In the dramatherapy, the safe boundaries of the therapy space and therapeutic relationship and the playful state created combine to form a 'playful safety' by which such material can be allowed into the 'play space'. Meyer talks of the processes of distancing, whereby play allows the child to touch material in a way that is given a connected yet separate quality from the experiences outside the play space it represents: 'I think it relates to the "me and not me" process in role-play. They needed to say "I've got HIV" as themselves but needed a context to say it in, and the context of best friends allowed this.'

The three accounts and research conversations have been explored using the two questions concerning how access to play within the arts therapies is created, and how therapists see play as a core process with their dramatherapy practice. The analysis has shown the ways in which therapists see the creation of a safe, contained space as essential to the child being able to bring material to therapy. The development of a relationship with the therapist was also seen as crucial, and the accounts spoke of the importance of trust, witnessing and permission within this. The therapist's role was both to be aware of issues that might hinder the child's access to play, whilst following cues and offering potential directions to help the space and relationship to be used by the child to create and discover their own play's potential. Play is seen by the therapists as a way to help a child deal with the complex issues they face in their lives. The analysis of the vignettes and conversations illustrated perceptions of play as a rich and varied source of assimilation, exploration, empowerment and creativity. The therapists all had these perceptions in common as they described and reflected on the core processes they made available to children who need the therapy space.

How does society silence children?

This chapter has shown how children can benefit from play within the therapeutic context of dramatherapy. It has illustrated the ways in which therapists see play as forming a natural vehicle for children to express, test, explore, assimilate and recover from difficult life experiences. It has shown how play language and play process can reflect issues from children's lives in both indirect and direct ways. This way of looking at play can be valuable for all those who live and work with children, both in being aware of the value of play, but also being sensitive to the possible issues and meanings that might be expressed in a child's spontaneous play. Within the vignettes and the analysis a key theme was the ways in which children can become silenced. This issue bears reflecting on in a number of ways for those living and working with children. The following offers some points for reflection on this theme.

In the accounts contained in the vignettes, children bring encounters with complex and violent experiences: from physical disaster to abuse within families and within their communities, from social stigma to disease. In different ways, the situations they are in are connected to their being silenced. The analysis referred to the ways in which such silencing takes place, and it is important to consider the different factors that result in such silencing. This reflection can be usefully linked both to how we, as adults, may participate in such factors, as well as the ways in which

adults can work towards combating the factors that produce silencing.

Children as active agents in their own lives

Within the vignettes and the research conversations a key theme was the idea of active involvement and play as a way of children assimilating and gaining a sense of power over experiences. Within this is a tension that is important to consider in all work with children. One way of seeing this concerns the extent to which children are seen as passive vessels to which things happen, compared to them being seen as active agents who are able to have insight, opinions and rights in determining what happens to them. It can be useful to ask questions relating to this issue in all aspects of relating to children.

Ideas in action

Stop and reflect

Explore the material contained in the research vignettes within this chapter.

- What factors combine to produce the silencing of children in the experiences they bring to the therapy?
- What are the benefits and limitations of play within the therapy described in addressing children's experiences of being silenced?

Ideas in action

Stop and reflect

Based on the accounts of the children's lives contained in the vignettes, what issues do you think might be present relating to children being seen as passive vessels or as active agents by the communities they live in?

What are the potentials and limitations of play within the therapy described in encouraging children to see themselves as active agents in their own lives?

Improving practice
Referral

The use of play as a therapy, or within therapy, has both parallels and clear differences with other playwork. Parallels include the language of play, and the facilitating nature of the relationship between adult

▶

and child. Differences include the fact that play within therapy occurs within a therapeutic space with clear, specific boundaries concerning areas such as confidentiality, personal exploration and disclosure. Another key difference is that the relationship between child and adult is not only one of facilitating play, but of doing so within a defined therapeutic relationship that abides by codes of conduct, ethics and professional guidelines.[2] This difference of space and relationship needs to be clear to child, parents or guardians and organisations. Otherwise, as has been argued elsewhere, the space and relationship is unethical and potentially harmful.

In terms of improving practice, it is, naturally, important for those involved in contact with children, whether in play, care or education, to know when a child might be indicating that there are issues in their life that may need referral.

Stop and reflect

As this chapter has argued, children naturally reflect and assimilate many life experiences within their playing. However, in certain circumstances those working with play may encounter expressions or issues that they feel might be indicators of a child's need for specialist attention. What might these look like?

A referral might be to specialist work with therapists, or professionals with a remit and training to deal with specific aspects of a child's life. What might these be?

Comment

Examples of these include a child who practitioners may suspect is being abused, and/or who has emotional and behavioural needs that may require particular support and space, complementary to activities such as play.

---

[2]Examples of such guidelines can be found on the following websites: www.bapt.info/ethicalbasis.htm for the British Association for Play Therapists Ethical Guidelines and www.badth.org.uk/downloads/information for the British Association of Dramatherapists Code of Practice.

The knowledge of how to appropriately raise concerns with other workers, or to refer a child, can be a key element in maintaining or improving good practice. General and specific information about what to do if you have concerns about a child are available (see below). All individuals who work with children need to be clear about relevant policies and procedures.

Who to talk to?

The following gives some illustrations of the kinds of information you will find or need to find. It is important to stress that these may differ depending on the context of your practice. Issues within referral include who to take your concerns to, for example,

> Discuss your concerns with your manager, named designated health professional or designated member of staff, depending on your organization setting. If you still have concerns you or your manager could also, without necessarily identifying the child in question, discuss your concerns with senior colleagues in another agency in order to develop an understanding of the child's needs and circumstances.
>
> What to Do if You're Worried a Child is being Abused
> http://www.everychildmatters

We must also remember that suspected abuse within the family is not the *only* reason you might want to refer a child. Becoming a victim of abusive behaviour outside the family, including bullying by peers, might also be a reason, or difficult events within the child's family, such as death or severe illness of a parent or sibling, or parents divorcing may also result in deep unhappiness that may be alleviated by therapeutic intervention.

Referral systems

Some settings may have particular systems in place for referral to particular services for children. Here is a sample of advice to practitioners about arts therapies access in schools.

> How the referral process works in schools can differ depending on the staff team and the art therapist. However, art therapy referrals in schools

▶

generally come from class teachers, SENCos (special education needs coordinators) and head teachers. Other outside agencies might include social workers or educational psychologists. The art therapist may be given a list of pupils, whom staff would like to be considered. From this, the art therapist and other professionals, such as the SENCo or head teacher, can begin the process of selection. This can also include a therapist's observation of a pupil in class . . . Parental consent is another important part of the referral process. This is generally done via a letter being sent home, which is accompanied by an information leaflet for parents. Parents are given the opportunity to meet with the therapist prior to therapy to discuss any queries or concerns.   Art Therapy in Schools Service
www.atiss.co.uk

The child's involvement

All material on referral to support services stresses the importance of vigilance, of care to protect children, and the need to be clear about lines of communication and responsibility. In addition the way a child is consulted is a key part of any such process, taking into account factors such as age, whether the child's language of preference is English, and how best to communicate with a child if disability is a factor in their understanding or expressing themselves. It is crucial that children's rights and needs are respected. Ethical guidelines and codes of practice, as referred to earlier, are one key facet of looking after this area. One aspect concerns the ways children can be involved in, and informed about, any process of referral. The following is a sample of material given to children about referral made by a UK play therapy organisation.

Why am I going to see a Play Therapist?

The Play Therapist has been asked to see you because you feel sad or angry or scared about some-

thing or perhaps because something horrible has happened. Maybe you can't help fighting or crying or you feel bad about yourself. Sometimes, it is hard to talk about your feelings so your Play Therapist will try to help you feel better without you having to explain things. That's because children play their feelings better than they talk about them.

Children's Information, British Association
of Play Therapists www.bapt.info

The following are websites that provide information about what do to if a worker has concerns, how to communicate and proceed with any concerns, and what referral can entail. They are included as examples, some are specific to play and the arts, others are general. As mentioned above, any worker needs to be clear what applies to their specific context.

- On sharing information about children:

Information Sharing; Practitioners Guide HM Government 2006 Section 4 guidance on confidentiality and information sharing.

www.ecm.uk/deliveriungservices/informationsharing

- On structures around care and referral:

Framework for the Assessment of Children in Need and their Families.

http://www.dh.gov.uk/PublicationsPolicyAndGuidance/
PublicationsPolicyAndGuidanceArticle/fs/en

- On inter-agency collaboration and communication:

Working Together to Safeguard Children: A guide to inter-agency working to safeguard and promote the welfare of children.

http://www.everychildmatters.gov.uk/
resources-and-practice/IG00060

- On referral if you think a child may be being abused:

What to Do if You're Worried a Child is being Abused.

http://www.everychildmatters.gov.uk

Summary and review

This chapter has shown how play is seen as a core process in the way a child can be offered an arts therapy. The accounts all concerned the ways in which the potentials and possibilities of play are opened up by therapist and children working together in dramatherapy.

Play is part of the expressive language a child can use to create meaning and explore material in dramatherapy. The research vignettes, conversations and analysis have shown how therapists see playing as a way of children discovering or creating access to their own spontaneity and power.

The chapter has illustrated how the therapists see dramatherapy as creating a playful relationship with reality. The dramatherapy space enables children to play with elements of their life – to express and assimilate experiences, to rework issues, to try out new configurations or possibilities. The research into dramatherapists' views of how their work is effective has shown that they see play as a valuable core process in their therapeutic practice. The analysis has illustrated the ways in which the therapists view how they create access to the therapeutic potentials of play for children. It also looked at the ways in which different factors such as the creation of a safe space, the therapeutic relationship and the child's creativity can be brought together. The accounts and the conversations have shown that they see playful exploration as an opportunity for children to use in a number of different ways to produce changes, which can be integrated into the child's life outside the dramatherapy.

Further reading

The following texts concern the arts therapies

Bunt, L. and Hoskyns, S. (2002) *The Handbook of Music Therapy*. London: Routledge.

Case, C. and Dalley, T. (2006) 2nd edn, *The Handbook of Art Therapy*. London: Routledge.

Jones, P. (2005) *The Arts Therapies*. London: Routledge.

Jones, P. (2007) *Drama as Therapy*, 2nd edn. London: Routledge.

Karkou, V. and Sanderson, P. (2005) *Arts Therapies: A Research Based Map of the Field*. Elsevier Health Science.

Langley, D. (2006) An Introduction to Dramatherapy. London: Sage.

Payne, H. (1992) *Dance Movement Therapy: Theory and Practice*. London: Routledge.

The following texts concern play therapy

Gil, E. and Drewes, A.A. (eds) (2004) *Cultural Issues in Play Therapy*. London: Routledge.

Schaefer, C.E. and Kaduson, H.G. (eds) (2006) *Contemporary Play Therapy*. London: Routledge.

The following texts are on the arts therapies and children:

Evans, K. and Dubowski, J. (2001) *Art Therapy with Children on the Autistic Spectrum*. London: Jessica Kingsley Publishers.

Malchiodi, C. A. (ed.) (1999) *Medical Art Therapy with Children*. London: Jessica Kingsley Publishers.

Weber, A.M. and Haen, C. (eds) (2004) *Clinical Applications of Drama Therapy in Child and Adolescent Treatment*. London: Routledge.

Websites and professional development opportunities

Play therapy and the arts therapies are professions requiring specialist training and registration. Short courses introducing approaches and understanding of these therapies can be attended. Graduate and postgraduate programmes exist.

British Association of Art Therapists http://www.baat.org

UK Association for Dance Movement Therapy http://admt.org.uk

British Association of Dramatherapists http://badth.ision.co.uk

British Society for Music Therapy http://www.bsmt.org

Association of Professional Music therapists UK http://www.apmt.org

British Association of Play Therapists www.bapt.info

Play Therapy http://www.playtherapy.org.uk

Health Professions Council Standards of Conduct, Performance and Ethics, Duties of Registrant (2003) http://www.hpc-uk.org

Concluding Perspectives

Play, Learning for Life: The Vital Role of Play in Human Development

PAM JARVIS AND JANE GEORGE

Looking back through my school years, the experiences that have best managed to shape me as an individual have taken place during social interaction with my peers. Therefore, I feel the most educational grade to students is kindergarten . . . it was in kindergarten that I learned to share . . . and basically get along with people in general. When I entered the first grade . . . I was all of a sudden expected to sit in a desk, in an assigned row, and feel some sort of 'connection' with a teacher at the front of the room, lecturing to thirty-plus students at once . . . Recess [break] was the biggest relief to me! Ever since kindergarten I have become increasingly disappointed with the lessons taught within the classroom. Of course, a certain amount of math, English, history and science is necessary for later in life, but so is a certain amount of interaction with other people. My classroom education has fallen short of giving me the most vital skills needed to survive in the world today.

Amy Peterson, US high school honours student, in Schultz and Cook-Sather (2001, p. 98)

Introduction

Now you have nearly arrived at the end of this book, and (we hope!) feel that you know a lot more about the complex concept of play than you did at the beginning, this chapter will attempt to explore some current, often theoretically complex and controversial debates relating to the place of play in children's lives in the early

Sibling
A brother or a sister.

twenty-first century. It will initially consider research relating to **sibling** relationships, peer interaction and friendships, then move on to consider 'spaces' both in time and location where children played together in earlier generations, and why recent generations may have had problems in finding sufficient spaces for such play. It will close by making some tentative suggestions relating to how adults, hopefully including readers of this book, may create new opportunities for children to access such spaces in contemporary western post-industrial societies. Peer and sibling interaction is a key area for research in the early twenty-first century, focusing on children's development in a complex, holistic fashion, building on the Vygotskian socio-cultural tradition outlined in detail by Olusoga in Chapter 2.

Olusoga in Chapter 2 ⇨

This chapter will consider the following questions:

- How does peer and sibling interaction research suggest that such interactions are vital for healthy human development?

- What 'spaces' in time and location did playing children inhabit in the past, how did these become less 'open' over the last quarter of the twentieth century, and what might be the emergent effects?

- How might adults attempt to reopen some 'spaces' in time and location that will be successfully utilised by children in the cultural environment of our current society?

Play in sibling interaction

In the early days of child development theory there was little research interest in children's peer relationships; the principle focus was upon the role of the parent (particularly the mother) and child. For example, eminent developmentalist John Bowlby proposed that the key pivot upon which the success of a child's social and emotional development hung was the existence of 'a warm, intimate and continuous relationship with his mother (or permanent mother-substitute – one person who steadily "mothers" him) in which both find satisfaction and enjoyment' (1953, p. 13). Intellectual development was also seen very much by mid-twentieth-century western theorists as quite an isolated affair; however Lindon (2005) proposed that Piaget's views on **egocentricity** in children between the ages of 2 and 6 were increasingly succumbing to more modern research findings, indicating that far more complex, socially interactive processes must underlie children's holistic

Egocentricity
To be focused on the self, but not in the same sense as being *selfish* – small children do not yet understand that other people are individuals like themselves, with a complex internal mental world that is hidden from others – they have to learn this through social interaction.

development. Our current view of children from the first months of life depicts highly social beings, interacting in many different environments, and with many different people, both adults and other children.

Researchers have increasingly widened their focus to take in a broader panorama of children's early relationships, with research considering not only the roles of a multitude of adults within a child's developmental processes, but that of other children, commonly referred to as 'peers'. The sibling studies of Judy Dunn, carried out over a period of 25 years, from the early 1980s to the present, comprise a key body of research in this area. What all peer interaction has in common is the central activity that young children carry out together; that of play. A range of sibling and friendship research will be considered below; the chapter will then move on to consider research relating to problems that may arise when children lack experience of peer interaction in early childhood.

Rutherford (2005, p. 90) states that, in an individual's developmental period, siblings have five functions:

1 the provision of affection and security;

2 the provision of companionship and intimacy;

3 the provision of support and help;

4 the provision of models for imitation for learning skills and language;

5 through conflict and cooperation siblings develop their own internal working model of relationships and feelings of others.

It could be argued that the first three functions have the potential to continue throughout the lifespan. Dunn (1983) carried out a comprehensive review of the then current knowledge of sibling relationships, noting that previous findings had indicated that the relationships between siblings were significant, distinct, reciprocal and continuous over time. She found from her review of the literature that findings relating to sibling play and associated perspective-taking development indicated that there was the potential for much developmental learning to occur through sibling interactions. Furthermore, she proposed that the sibling relationship was also structured through a complex set of interactions between the sibling relationship and the parent–child relationship. Subsequently, in her own longitudinal study of families before and after the birth of a new child, she found that where siblings played together, especially in pretend play, by the age of 2 years the younger child was likely to show a more sophisticated understanding of 'other minds' than the older child had done at the same age. She theorised that this difference was due to the variable of exposure to the influence of a slightly older playmate. This idea has been supported more recently by Flynn (2004), who suggested that the pretend play, deception, teasing and talking about feelings which occur in sibling interaction support the development of **theory of mind** in the younger sibling.

> **Theory of mind**
> A skill that is shared by only a few species on Earth – the ability to understand what another creature might be thinking, and to change one's own behaviour to account for this – sometimes in order to deceive.

Lamb (1978) carried out a study that involved observing siblings at play in a laboratory playroom, subsequently describing a set of findings which indicated that younger siblings would typically (although not exclusively) follow an older sibling's lead in play. This can clearly be seen to address the younger child's 'zone of proximal development', allowing her/him to become 'a head taller than himself' (Vygotsky, 1978, p. 102) in the collaborative activity than s/he could become alone. Schaffer (1996, p. 265) suggested that siblings have a huge, mainly positive influence on each other, which includes much imitation. He proposed that, in fantasy play, siblings are 'full partners in a pretend shared world' and through this play children learn social rules such as possession, fairness, sharing and turn taking. He noted that the shared play develops over time and that it varies depending on the age, gender and temperament of the siblings involved.

These ideas are supported by Barr and Hayne (2003), who studied acquisition of new behaviours in younger siblings and only children. Whilst both groups of children acquired at least one new behaviour a day through imitation, those with siblings imitated more new behaviours with no instructions than only children. They accomplished such learning principally through collaborative 'pretend' and rough and tumble play interactions.

Research indicates that the relationship between siblings develops over time. Pike and Coldwell (2005), researching sibling relationships in mid-childhood (between 4 and 8 years), suggested that positive sibling relationships are strongly linked to adjustment rather than conflict. They proposed that the quality of the relationship which develops between siblings is closely associated with the older sibling's adjustment to the new family member; a factor that will no doubt also be closely connected to the pattern of relationships between the adults and children in the family. Kim et al.'s (2007) studies of sibling relationships through middle childhood and adolescence concur with this view. These researchers also proposed that good adjustment to the sibling relationship, and high levels of sibling intimacy, are linked to high levels of peer competence in adolescence.

Researchers therefore overwhelmingly agree that there are many potential benefits to be gained through sibling relationships. Curtis and O'Hagan (2003) considered the situation of children with no siblings. They noted that whilst such children have full parental attention, they may lack the opportunity to develop skills in turn taking and sharing unless they are encouraged to interact with other children from a young age. Such a finding is an indication that parent and toddler groups, pre-school play groups and children's centres may have a vital role to play in the early lives of children from single-child family structures.

It must be noted that much of the current body of research on sibling relationships has been carried out in western, working- or middle-class, two-parent families with two or three children. There is much still to do in widening the research focus to take in sibling relationships in larger families and in non-western societies, particularly in areas of the world where many families live in poverty and need. Such a lack of access to vital resources is highly likely to create many difficult choices for parents and subsequent tensions (and possibly even collaborations) between siblings that will not be experienced by siblings in the western world. Additionally, whilst there is a small body of research relating to siblings in twin and other 'multiple' relationships (for example Lowe *et al.*, 1988) this is also an area in need of

> **In vitro fertilisation (IVF)**
> A modern fertility treatment, where the egg is fertilised in a laboratory test-tube, i.e. outside the mother's body.

expansion, particularly in modern times, where the advent of **in vitro fertilisation (IVF)** has raised the numbers of multiple births in western society.

Ideas in action

Sibling play, learning and development (Author's observational notes)

Siblings Claire (just 5), and twins Sian and Andrew (2½) are spending a sunny afternoon playing in their back garden. Sian is bouncing on a small trampoline, whilst Claire and Andrew are playing on the swings/climbing frame apparatus. Claire is twisting around on the single seat swing, whilst Andrew sits quietly on one seat of the boat swing, looking around. Claire leans over to the boat swing and swings Andrew gently back and forth. He smiles. Claire then asks Sian if she can have a go on the trampoline. Sian agrees. Sian moves over to the single swing, and Claire bounces up and down singing and clapping, whilst both twins watch. After a minute or two, Claire asks Sian if they can swap places again. Sian agrees, and as she

bounces up and down on the trampoline she claps and sings an extremely jumbled version of the song that Claire previously sang. When Claire arrives back on the single swing, Andrew, who is sitting on the nearby boat swing, says, 'Push me.' Sian leaves the trampoline and goes to sit on the other seat of the boat swing. Claire stands in the middle of the boat swing and swings it back and forth, whilst the twins giggle . . .

As afternoon becomes early evening, Andrew sits down in the doorway. He looks tired, and his expression is very serious. Claire moves over towards him. She bends down so they are face to face, and touches him gently on the head saying 'Androoooooo.' As she moves away, his face breaks into a wide smile.

Figure 11.1 Learning together (children)

Comment: Learning together

This observation is taken from a video of one of the authors' children, which was filmed on a summer afternoon in the late 1980s. This observation describes some very common everyday events experienced by many children in a western environment, but if we analyse it carefully we can see that this interaction supports previous research findings, by indicating that there is a wealth of learning occurring throughout this interaction for all three siblings. They all learn about communicating and sharing; the younger children learn language from the older child, and this is clearly demonstrated by Sian singing a version of Claire's song, in contrast to her earlier silent play. The older child also takes a purposive leading role in the play by taking responsibility for swinging her younger siblings, who are too young to use the large play equipment to its fullest extent unaided. Later on in the interaction, she provides gentle entertainment for Andrew when he tires towards the end of the afternoon. Of course, not all sibling interactions are always this positive, either for these two sisters and their brother, or within other families. But children also learn valuable lessons from their disagreements, which relates to the 'social hardiness' that Jarvis outlines in Chapter 7. These children are now in their early 20s, and maintain a close sibling relationship, although the activities in which they interact are, of course very different!

Figure 11.2 Learning together (children grown up)

Play in peer interaction

Peers do not have to be siblings; they may be from the extended family, or unrelated children. Olusoga raises this wider perspective on peer relationships in Chapter 2. In particular, she outlines vital collaborative and social learning occurring between groups of peers from different cultural backgrounds. She goes on to make the key point that children from single-child families may continue to lack the interaction with different-aged peers described in the sibling studies above, if this opportunity is never provided in the education and care settings that children inhabit outside the family. Maguire and Dunn (1997) suggested that both sibling relationships and early friendships play a key role in the development of emotional understanding in the young

Olusoga raises this wider perspective on peer relationships in Chapter 2.

child, evidenced by the greater success of children in understanding the emotional states of others when their everyday routines involved interaction in peer and/or sibling relationships. These authors concluded:

> It appears that the experience of sharing a pretend world, or establishing connected, co-ordinated play with another child (sibling or friend) are linked to developments in social understanding. Common sense, as well as our data, suggest that there is a two-way process of influence between relationships and understanding.   (Maguire and Dunn, 1997, p. 683)

Peters (2003) found that children who made strong friendships in the nursery years were more emotionally robust over the transition to primary school, and settled down more comfortably to the academic requirements of formal schooling. Those who did not carry strong peer relationships over from the nursery correspondingly experienced a more difficult transition. Sebanc (2003) studied nursery children's (ages 3–4) friendship patterns alongside their teachers' reports of their in-school behaviours, and found clear positive correlations between children who had strong friendships and **pro-social** behaviour, and children who experienced problems with friendships and aggressive behaviour. Lindsey's (2002) longitudinal research with 3–6-year-old children indicated that

---

Pro-social

Behaviour or thought that is aimed at building relationships.

---

children who had at least one mutual friend at the beginning of the study were better liked by peers one year later than children who did not have any mutual friends at the beginning of the study; and that this finding was not correlated with each child's place on the liked/disliked continuum created at the beginning of the study. Lindsey concluded that, as early as 3 years of age, mutual friendships are vital in children's social developmental processes.

Many researchers (for example Coie and Kupersmidt, 1983; Ladd *et al.*, 1988; Pellegrini, 1989a; Dodge *et al.*, 1990; Boulton, 1993) found that primary school children who are popular amongst their peers deal skilfully with the society of the playground, competently recognising overtures from other children seeking rough and tumble as invitations to play. In contrast,

In Chapter 7 Jarvis ⇨ identifies situations in the outdoor environment where learning is evident in play activities.

children who are rejected by their peers are more likely to mistake such overtures as aggression, and respond in kind. Empirical evidence suggests that this is an enduring effect, particularly amongst groups of boys. Boulton (1993a) proposed that an important aspect of problematic social cognition in 4–10-year-old boys could be seen in an inability to differentiate between playful and aggressive interactions, leading to a 'vicious circle' effect, as the child responds with 'acts of interpersonal aggression, which in turn may lead to poor interpersonal acceptance' (Boulton, 1993a, p. 262). All of the studies listed above make some reference to this kind of 'feedback loop'; for example, Dodge *et al.* (1990, p. 1307) reflected that much evidence suggested that early disliking by peer groups was typically correlated with long-term behavioural problems, proposing: 'rejected boys seem to have failed to master the task of benign rough play'. Pellegrini and Blatchford (2000) concluded that, for 5½-year-old boys, the amount of time spent in active social play with other boys directly predicts their level of success in social problem solving one year later.

In an observational study of children's playground-based behaviour, Braza *et al.* (2007, p. 209) concluded that engaging in R&T and pretend play allows children to create complex social hierarchies that 'seem to reduce aggressive behaviour and help children develop sociocognitive skills not required in other types of play (for instance, social intelligence, theory of mind)'. In a biological study which studied the R&T play of rats, Pellis and Pellis (2007, p. 95) concluded that such experience led to neuronal reorganisation and development of connections 'especially [in] those areas [of the brain] involved in social behaviour'. With regard to the expression of such learning within a child's external environment, Pellegrini (1989a, p. 51) proposed: 'It may be that the ability of popular children to discriminate social information enables them to treat R&T and aggression as distinct categories.' MacDonald and Parke (1984, p. 1273) proposed that such skills are initially learned in infanthood in gentle R&T with parents, particularly fathers and other close male relatives: 'children may be learning the social and communicative value of their own affective displays as well as how to use these emotional signals to regulate the social behaviour of others'.

In support for the suggestion that children who misunderstand the 'language' of playground interaction have subsequent problems with aggression response, Orobio de Castro *et al.* (2002) found that there was a highly significant positive correlation between children's tendency to attribute hostile intent to others and their own expressed aggressive behaviour, particularly amongst 8–12 year olds. This investigation was carried out by combining data from several previous studies, creating a mainly male combined sample. From the statistical analyses, there appeared to be a greater tendency to attribute aggression and response in kind amongst males, but no firm overarching conclusions relating to gender difference could be drawn, due to the highly unbalanced gender sample.

Unfortunately much of the research relating to active free play in the twentieth century was **androcentric**, based on the fact that developmental researchers in the past have tended to view boys' play as potentially more 'dangerous' and hence more worthy of their attention than girls' play. With regard to developmental research, this inequality of gender focus has had mixed effects for girls, on the one hand perpetuating the stereotype of the androcentric model of humanity, with female differences viewed as 'non-standard', but on the other allowing more negative female play activities to unfold to some extent 'under the [adult] radar', as described by Olusoga in Chapter 2 with her discussion of girls' play involving quite aggressive fantasies around the power of 'magic wands'.

> **Androcentric**
> Centred on males/a masculine view of the world.

Ideas in action

Problems with play? (Author's observational notes)

Five and a half year old Michael is in his school playground at lunchtime, playing with a group of six or seven other boys. They have decided to play at 'races' and they are taking it in turns to be the starter. The starter stands to one side of the runners with his hand up, the runners line up and then the starter says 'Go', bringing his hand down at the same time. Michael has already had two turns at being the starter, and the group have decided that it is now Huw's turn. Michael however refuses to line up with the other runners, and stands to one side with his hand up. Aiden says to him, 'Put your hand down.' Huw stands on the other side of the group with his hand up. Michael runs over to Huw and gets hold of his coat, saying, 'You go.' Huw gets hold of Michael's coat and pushes him back against the wall. They shake one another for a moment, and then break apart. Huw returns to the original group of boys, who are still waiting for him to start their race. Michael does not join the runners, but walks off and joins a group of slightly younger boys that includes Jason and David. Michael joins the group in a 'tig'-style running game for a few minutes. When the younger boys take a break from their game, Jason and David come to a halt standing side by side. Michael puts an arm around each boy's shoulders, and then purposely bangs their heads together. Both start to cry and Jason has a growing bump and bruise on his forehead. Later I ask Michael's teacher, Jackie, if this is an unusual occurrence with Michael. She says, no, not really, Michael has a fair history of problems when he engages in social play with the other children. She adds that he is effectively an only child; the only offspring from a reconstituted family where there is a much older half-brother and sister who live in a different house with their mother and attend secondary school.

Comment: Supporting socialisation

There is no suggestion that Michael behaved in this way because he lacked near-age siblings, but possibly that at an earlier stage in his development he may have lacked interaction with similar-aged peers. The teacher

▶

went on to say that she thought that both the parents and older children in the family tended to 'spoil' Michael by 'letting him have his own way, so this is always what he expects'.

Whilst teachers' reflections of this nature are often useful, we do need to treat them cautiously as they are what is known as '**hearsay**' information, in that they are not the product of direct, focused observation (as was the behaviour in the playground), or a matter of concrete fact (as is a child's basic family structure and day-to-day living arrangements). A key focus should be how to move on from the immediate situation, in the first instance by helping the child to recognise the inappro-

---

Hearsay
Repeating information that has been communicated by another person, describing something that is not the result of one's own direct experience.

---

priateness of his or her behaviour. In this case, Jackie approached this outcome by asking Michael if he would like it if someone banged *his* head. When he answered that he wouldn't, Jackie asked him why not. 'Because it would hurt', he replied.

Stop and reflect

Decentre
To move away from one's own point of view and consider the point of view of another creature.

Have you ever dealt with a situation such as that described above? Did you attempt to encourage the child to '**decentre**' into the 'shoes' of the child that s/he upset or injured? This helps the child to consider how unpleasant it would have felt to be on the other side of such an interaction.

Comment

The research outlined so far in this chapter indicates that the more peer interaction young children experience (both with siblings and unrelated peers), the more competent they become in this type of decentring. Hence it is very important that children do not get into a 'vicious circle' where their behaviour in peer interaction is poor because they lack experience of peer interaction, leading other children to reject them, which in turn leads the child in question to lag further and further behind in his/her development of key social interaction skills. Jackie was attempting to avoid this situation for Michael by scaffolding his development of theory of mind, which underpins the ability to decentre.

Improving practice

Carry out some observations of peer interactions in your setting. As you analyse them, consider what the children may have been learning from the interactions in which they engaged, remembering that children may sometimes learn as much from disagreement as they learn from more obviously positive interactions. You could also consider how much peer interaction the children in your setting are able to acquire, and whether they get sufficient chances to engage in play with older/younger children and children from a wide range of cultural backgrounds.

A place to play: free play in the past

British researchers Opie and Opie carried out an extensive study of children's free play in streets and playgrounds during the 1950s and 1960s, either interviewing or directly observing the play of some 10,000 children across England, Scotland and Wales. In

1969, they reported 'there is no town or city known to us where street games do not flourish' (p. vi), and further suggested that successive generations of playing children might be the sole guardians of many ancient oral traditions, proposing that: To understand the "wanton sports" of the Elizabethan day, and the horseplay of even earlier times is to watch the contemporary child engrossed in his traditional pursuits on the metalled floor of a twentieth-century city (Opie and Opie, 1969, p. ix).

It is clear, however, that these researchers would find something distinctly different on British streets today, due to the fears of parents who do not allow their children out unaccompanied until they are in early adolescence. The Children's Society (2007a) interviewed 1148 British adults on this topic, of whom 43 per cent proposed that children should not be allowed to go out unaccompanied by an adult until they were 14.

Chapters 6 and 9 ⇨ explore further findings from this research.

The gradual narrowing of opportunities for children to engage in outdoor play in spaces around their local neighbourhoods over the final quarter of the twentieth century is described in more detail by O'Brien et al. (2000, p. 273) who proposed: 'letting children play out is becoming a marker of neglectful or irresponsible parenting'. In A Child's-eye View of Social Difference, research sponsored by the Joseph Rowntree Foundation, Sutton et al. (2007) interviewed inner city and suburban children in Britain about their out-of-school activities. One of the inner city participants explained:

> There's only one park and no one goes on anything because the 18 year olds go on and vandalise everything. There's a playground near the shops and if the police catch you they take you back to your house. You're not allowed to go in.
>
> (Sutton et al., 2007, p. 29)

The suburban children, by contrast, described spending their free time in adult-organised activities, for example riding, tennis, swimming, dancing and gymnastics lessons, and after-school clubs for activities such as chess and learning to play various musical instruments.

Such a lifestyle ⇨ reflects the day in the life of 'Aimee' described by Jarvis in Chapter 1.

The authors reflected: 'This left [the children] very little time when they got home from school to play or do anything else' (Sutton et al., 2007, p. 26).

Opie and Opie reported that some of the terms their 1950s and 1960s child participants used in their outdoor free play could be directly related back to much earlier forms of spoken English. They discovered a range of terms that children used to call 'truce' on play fighting or chasing which were specific to their regional location, for example 'fainites' in southern England, and 'kings', 'crosses', 'keys' or 'barley' across northern England, Wales and Scotland. Children in the area around Cornwall used 'bars', which would seem more closely related to the northern than the southern terms, suggesting an aspect of Celtic similarity between these areas that is also found through the Gaelic languages of Cornwall, Wales and Scotland. Opie and Opie recorded that J.R.R. Tolkien (of Lord of the Rings fame, who was an English scholar in his professional life) described how, in the fourteenth-century collection of published moral stories, The Canterbury Tales, Chaucer tells us that 'lordes mowe nat been yfeyned'; in modern English translation: 'lords' orders must not be declined'. This indicates that 'fainites' has descended from 'fains I', in both cases meaning 'I decline'. 'Barley' is also found in fourteenth-century literature, in the poem 'Gawayne and the Grene Knight': 'to dele him an other barley . . . and yet gif him respite' (Opie and Opie, 1959, p. 148). This appears to be used in a similar frame to the term 'parley', (from the French parlez, to speak) which was used mainly in the English vernacular to mean a halt in a battle for peace talks. This would seem to have a clear similarity to pleading for a halt in a game or to miss a turn to take a rest, or to catch one's breath before engaging once more with the (pretend) 'enemy'.

It is sobering to think that generations of playing children dating back at least to Chaucer's time, probably much longer, have transmitted scraps of dialect directly to one another that are the only echoes of linguistic forms which are otherwise dead. It is even more thought provoking to consider that this has been halted during the contemporary lifetimes of adults aged 35 and over at the turn of the twentieth century by the intrusion of motorised vehicles designed to reach ever-increasing speeds into children's traditional play areas, and by the relentless output of a global mass media engaged in a modern witch-hunt for predatory stranger 'paedophiles'. Such societal factors come together to convince parents that children are not safe outside the company of familiar adults until they are far too old to play such games. These fears are likely to be exacerbated by the socio-cultural environment of city life where neighbours may be strangers to one another, spending their working lives many miles away from their home environments. This reduces the likelihood that an underpinning society of 'known' adults might provide an unseen, almost casual network of underpinning vigilance to oversee the neighbourhood children's seemingly independent activities around a local area. The Children's Society (2007b) also pointed out that flexible 'wraparound' child care arrangements for the children of working parents means that they may be transported by adults between a range of areas on a daily basis, meaning that these children may find it very hard to cement ongoing independent friendships with peers.

Ideas in action

Two very different mid-twentieth-century childhoods: (Author's interview data)

In writing the required reflexive analysis for her PhD thesis Pam Jarvis, one of the writers of this chapter, commented

[during] my own inner-city upbringing in a district of Inner London, [I was] surrounded by buildings and traffic. My primary school playground was wholly laid to tarmac and faced a busy main road. There was a tiny walled garden off to one side which we were told belonged to the school caretaker. This garden was beautifully kept, with a tiny lawn and flower beds full of roses, but it was not, by any stretch of the imagination, a child's play area. On warm summer days we were sometimes taken to read or draw in the garden, as long as we 'sat nicely' and did not run around (which spoilt the lawn) or touch the flowers. I am sure that my captive experience within this beautiful outdoor prison, besides creating a lifelong irritation with 'Keep off the Grass' and 'No Ball Games' notices, has led me through the years to focus my research efforts upon children's school-based outdoor free play'. (Jarvis, 2005, p. 123)

I have a male friend, almost exactly my age (born in 1959) with whom I have previously sometimes discussed completely different childhood experiences of outdoor environments, but I did not formally interview him about this until I was constructing the chapter for this book. Here are some of his memories of his much less restricted play space:

I must have been about 6 when I first played in the woods – I don't remember a summer holiday when I wasn't out in the woods; every day I would be out with my schoolmates. The church was the beginning of the woods. You went down through the church-yard and then into the woods. We spent whole days out there; we walked all the way down to the golf course. It took a long time for a kid to walk that far, so you'd spend all day in the woods and walk for what seemed like miles and miles. We took packed lunches and bottles of water because we were out for so long.

I don't remember getting instructions from adults about strangers – there weren't any, we generally knew everybody. There were TV ads telling you not to talk to strangers, and on the odd occasion we saw someone we didn't know we ignored them . . . I wouldn't have liked to have been in a town. Once you were in the woods you could do whatever you liked.

Games he remembered playing included:

- Play battles, 'mostly World War II stuff, sometimes cowboys and Indians. "Truce" in war games was called by saying "fainites". We used to try and avoid being seen, like Indian scouts. Then we wouldn't use the path at all. It was fun to avoid the older boys. You used to pretend that they were the bad guys and hide; they were the enemy. You'd try to avoid being seen just for the fun of it. We used to try tracking each other, which generally didn't work. You ended up getting separated and going home on your own. It was never scary, but it could be a bit annoying.'

▶

- Digging places up to make hides, and making fires ('We'd try two sticks for about a minute then we would use matches'), and making pretend traps.
- Damming little streams 'very unsuccessfully'.

Compare these examples of play with those of the 'tweenies' cited by Dodds in Chapter 6. ⇨

The end of the summer was marked by playing with the bales of hay in the farmer's field:

I think the farmer saw this as useful because we used to pile up the bales of hay to make castles, and the machine he used dropped the bales at regular intervals across the field, so we made some piles for him that were useful when he loaded the hay on to his wagon. He never got cross with us as long as we didn't break the bales apart. Playing with the hay meant that it was nearly the end of the summer holidays.

Improving practice
A research point

These very different memories illustrate an important point for novice researchers. Whilst much recent research suggests that children are less free to 'roam' than the children of previous generations, this does not mean that there will not be wide variations between children of the same generation. In this case the difference was clearly underpinned by location and, possibly, to some extent by gender, as the male participant did not remember playing with or even seeing any girls in the woods before he was of secondary school age, even though he remembered seeing girls playing in the streets around his home.

My own children, born in the mid-1980s, grew up in a suburb of a large northern English city, in a house with a fairly generous garden, located in a quiet cul-de-sac. The area was encircled by an area of footpaths, set within wide grass banks upon which (from approximately 7 years old) neighbouring children congregated to play. Location rather than generation decreed that they had far more freedom to roam than their mother. In a possible reflection of a more equal orientation to gender issues in the later years of the twentieth century, no gender differences were applied in the 'roaming' rules set for them.

Remember that large-scale pieces of research such as those undertaken by the Children's Society (2007a, 2007b) mentioned earlier in this chapter, can only give a very general picture. As such, it is very valuable to undertake small-scale research, in order to capture rich, descriptive narratives from individuals.

Stop and reflect

If you work with, or have access to children aged between 7 and 13, it would be very interesting to carry out some short interviews with them (no longer than 15 minutes) to study how they spend their time when they are not in the setting environment, and how far they are allowed to 'roam'. Do make sure that you have their parents' explicit permission for your interviews. It would also be useful to interview these parents to try to understand the rationales that they use when setting 'roaming' boundaries for their children.

Decreasing opportunities to play in school

English schools have consistently reduced break time during the school day, due to concerns about behaviour management, and in order to have more time in the classroom to address the demands of the adult-directed, highly outcome-driven English National Curriculum (Pellegrini and Blatchford, 2002). The National Curriculum also emerged as a key problematic issue from Santer *et al*.'s (2007) review of the literature relating to children's free play, in that the time consumed by curriculum delivery left little time, either outside *or* inside the classroom, for children to develop original, independent and peer **co-constructed cognitions**. This classroom practice

Co-constructed cognition

A thought or idea that has been arrived at by the collaboration of two or more people.

concern was echoed by Reay and Williams (1999), who proposed that the emphasis on testing individual performance against narrowly defined targets at 7, 11 and 14 years of age had the cumulative result that many creative and collaborative activities which had previously been part of day-to-day classroom practice in English schools were quashed in favour of 'spoon feeding' an individually learned, outcome-focused curriculum, in order for children to perform at the maximum possible level in the Key Stage tests.

A particular concern, also raised by Brock in Chapter 5 and Dodds in Chapter 6, is the curtailment of the pedagogical technique of discovery learning, which is 'an approach to instruction through which students interact with their environment – by exploring and manipulating objects, wrestling with questions and controversies, or performing experiments' (Ormrod, 1995, p. 442). The National Curriculum tightly specifies precisely what pupils from Year 1 ('**rising 6s**') are to learn, including the provision of exacting instructions relating to what constitutes an 'acceptable' answer for markers of Key Stage tests, GCSEs and A-levels, and schools are

Rising 6

A reference to the age of children in an English Year 1 classroom, all of whom will have had their fifth birthday before 1st September, and will have their sixth birthday between 1st September and 31st August during the relevant school year.

ranked and funded based on their overall results. Education managers have inevitably been subsequently pressurised to encourage teachers to engage in a 'transmission' style of teaching, which communicates the bare information required to answer predictable test questions correctly, rather than facilitating play-based 'discovery' learning, which takes more time and resources, and generates a deep, flexible understanding, and a 'what if . . .' approach to further investigation.

To add to this problematic culture in state education, the advent of 'performance management' in schools is the culmination of a 'payment by results' policy currently favoured by the English state education system. This dictates that pupils taught by a particular teacher must collectively reach a specific statistical level of progression before the teacher can receive his/her yearly pay increment. The last time payment by results was declared a national failure in the education system, however, was in the mid-nineteenth century! This was elegantly satirised by Charles Dickens in *Hard Times* (1863), in the character of 'Mr Gradgrind', who constantly insists that 'all children must be taught is facts'. It is of great concern that the current Government-imposed practice in education conspires to restrict children's experience of the 'open-ended' problems associated with discovery learning activities. Pollard *et al.* (2000) suggested that those who set the agenda need to consider such issues more deeply, recognising the difference between 'curriculum as intended' and 'curriculum as experienced'.

An overriding result of engagement in free play, particularly in activities undertaken in peer groups, is that children exercise their natural ability to use ideas and objects flexibly in the creation of co-constructed cognitions. The narratives that unfold between the participants are open ended, as are the uses of objects within them. Such interactions can be harnessed by teachers to underpin guided activities in discovery learning. Logically, if children do not have sufficient experience of being confronted with open-ended problems, they will not effectively learn how to find open-ended solutions; all problems will be perceived as having one fixed solution, to which a teacher will provide a standard answer. Guy Claxton (1997) proposed in his book *Hare Brain, Tortoise Mind* that adults also produce more original and insightful solutions to work-based problems when they are encouraged to 'play' creatively with ideas, particularly in groups. Claxton reflected: 'The slow ways of knowing will not deliver their delicate produce when the mind is in a hurry . . . people need to know how to make use of slow knowing . . . This . . . must surely be the true function of education' (pp. 214–15).

Ideas in action

What English children say about school in the early twenty-first century (Author interview data)

The continual testing of children at school, and the huge emphasis on individual achievement, rather than a balance between individual and collective activity, leaves those children who are judged to be at the bottom of the pile feeling '"thick", "stupid", not wanted in the school' (Riley and Docking, 2004, p. 166). One of the writers of this chapter carried out a series of 'student voice' interviews in several schools during the summer of 2006, with children of both genders aged between 11 and 15, who had experienced teaching and learning under the direction of the National Curriculum for at least seven years, including six years of primary education. These participants were from a wide range of ethnic groups and socio-economic backgrounds, and their placement in assessed ability groups reflected a broad spread of ability across the mainstream range. The overwhelming content of their combined 'voice' was a general perception that school-based activities were essentially artificial and alienating. One working-class white boy who had been placed in the bottom ability group in his cohort contributed a vivid metaphor for how he and his friendship group felt in school: 'It's like saying if a black person came in, like take your skin off, you're the wrong colour. That's how we feel.' Children in higher ability groups were also not insensitive to the ways in which pupils' individual value was perceived by the school, with one from a mid-range ability group commenting: 'some people are known, but some people are just numbers to the school, it's like they don't care'.

Others more straightforwardly complained that a lot of the work teachers set them in preparation for tests was 'pointless and repetitive'. A pupil from the highest ability group in his cohort made the point that countless revision sheets 'just get stuck in your book – a bit pointless'. Even when pupils were set collective tasks in group work, the culture of the contemporary classroom appeared to dictate that the entire goal was perceived by the pupils concerned as to individually reach a particular target or standard rather than to collectively discover and reflect. The consequent result was outlined by a pupil in a mid-range ability group, that the 'not so clever [relied] on the brainy person to do it for them'. Another pupil from the highest ability group in her cohort commented: 'when teachers try and mix it . . . so . . . the clever people are with people who are not as clever . . . it tends to happen that those people don't really want to work so you just get kind of left [to do all the work]'.

The researcher was led to a key reflection point by finding that homework or tests set on topics where 'the answers' had not been previously directly communicated by the teacher in the classroom was unanimously perceived as extremely unfair by a focus group of 11 year olds representing a mixed range of abilities. One member of this group doggedly insisted: 'If the teacher hasn't taught it, it shouldn't be on the test.' The main purpose of writing was seen across the board by 11- and 12-year-old participants as 'to revise for your tests', and several participants went on to reflect that 'writing' and 'fun' were polar opposites in their estimation. Many of the children interviewed also proposed that the reading they were required to do at school was dull, difficult and boring, but they also reported prolific engagement with multi-media activities requiring competency in communication skills, particularly MSN conferencing and texting. Many of the sample were also keen readers of magazines, comics and horror novels. One girl from a low–mid-range ability group in her cohort smiled at the researcher's question about how 'school' reading could be made more interesting and softly commented, 'But really, it's just education in the end, isn't it?'

Comment: Bridging the gap

One criticism that could be made of this research is that from mid-childhood onwards children traditionally

▶

show some amount of resistance to 'schoolwork'. However, the researcher did not find just *some* resistance, but a deep cynicism and disinterest, even in children who had been placed in the higher ability groups, who gave the impression that school for them was to a great extent 'going through the motions'. This is surely not how we would like our children to experience their education, and we do need to consider how the relentless regime of testing and its associated dominant 'transmission' styles of teaching and learning are impacting upon their views of their world during the most formative years of their lives.

Stop and reflect

Pick an activity that you have undertaken in the past with children in your setting, and consider how this would be approached from the perspective of 'transmission' learning, and then from the perspective of 'discovery' learning. Ask yourself the following questions:

- Which method would be likely to have the quickest result?
- Which method would be likely to result in the deepest learning?
- Which method would be likely to create the most interesting experience for the children?

Improving practice

If you get into the habit of this sort of reflective practice at the start of your career, you will be well on the way to providing what several of these 'student voice' participants referred to as 'funner' things to do.

So what are the core problems?

All primate species have evolved to undergo a substantial developmental period during which active social free play forms much of their necessary developmental experience. There is growing evidence to indicate that, over the past 25 years, various sociological factors have unwittingly banded together to deprive our children of play spaces, both in time and in location, with the result that many children in contemporary British society are unable to undertake sufficient independent collaborative activities to promote their healthy psychosocial development. A recent piece of research carried out for the Children's Society (2007b, p.) reports that:

> Since 1986, the number of teenagers with no best friends has increased from around one in eight to almost one in five. Over the same period 16 year olds who were assaulted by a peer increased by almost 50% while those threatened with violence more than doubled. More girls report that they are not popular today than they did 20 years ago.

Broadhead (2007) reports that child mental health problems are steadily rising, and that in the past few years there have been increasing reports of children as young as 4 suffering from clinical depression. The UNICEF report *An Overview of Child Well-being in Rich Countries* (2007) indicates that British children report having by far the poorest peer relationships amongst all the countries surveyed, and this is reflected in the research undertaken by the Children's Society (2007b) outlined above.

The more complex the adult society, the longer animals spend in their developmental period, and the more complex the play activities in which they engage. 'Play . . . is what children are "intended" to do. Remembering this may cause us to think twice before modifying children's environments to achieve . . . more focused learning opportunities in schools at the expense of play' (Bjorklund and Pellegrini, 2002, p. 331). To parody the common Thatcher misquote, there clearly *is* such a thing as society, and the society of the playground forms the basis of the social skills that the children of each generation carry forward to underpin their adult interactions.

The curtailment of children's risk taking in contemporary western society forms a related debate. Perceptions amongst adults that children will not be safe to stray unaccompanied outside the home and school environment until they are adolescent (the Children's Society, 2007b) creates physically risk-aversive behaviour amongst children that may also be further inculcated by the culture of psychological and intellectual dependence which underlies the 'transmission' style of teaching and learning. Some theorised results of such 'hot housing' are reflected in comments taken from a survey undertaken by a body of private employers, which creates a picture of socially awkward and emotionally fragile young people:

> There should be a greater emphasis placed on teaching [school leavers] 'social skills', such as encouraging pupils to communicate clearly, instilling a modicum of respect for others, and promoting in them enthusiasm for a useful working life . . . [so they don't] fall apart emotionally if they don't get what they want. (Management Issues, 2005)

It is impossible to directly 'teach' social skills; such learning comes from complex social interaction with peers, something that the demands of the National Curriculum and the construction of the UK physical environment currently seem to mitigate against. In conclusion, if a significant proportion of children are not allowed out to play unaccompanied by adults until they are in early adolescence (the Children's Society, 2007a), and spend their time in school being crammed with teacher-transmitted 'facts' towards maximum individual test performance, rather than engaging in collaborative 'discovery' learning activities, a large part of their necessary developmental learning may never be addressed; such children are not being afforded sufficient physical or intellectual 'space' to fully engage in the social development activities that are necessary for highly social human primates. Previous chapters in this book by Brock and Dodds have dealt at length with what measures might be taken to address this requirement in the classroom environment. Therefore, the question that will be addressed in the remainder of this chapter is: how might we work forwards from our existing physical environment to allow children more pleasant arenas for out-of-school free play than they can currently access?

Ideas in action

An urban play project (Author's interview data)

Andrea works on a play project in a large northern city. When she started in 2006 the project consisted of three people going out to facilitate play sessions for after-school clubs, but this has now grown to a team of a dozen people who manage an inner city adventure playground, and originate other projects that involve taking play experiences out to children in various settings around the city. The ethos of their practice is to encourage practitioners to let children take the leading role in their play activities.

The core funding for the project is from **SureStart** and **The Children's Fund**, but 'little pots of money from all over the place' often pay for one-off initiatives. These have included creating 'play pods', which are shipping containers full of art and craft materials, sports equipment and other play resources, which are taken to an area and opened up for two hours for children to come along and play. A current objective (October 2007) is to get other agencies involved so that these play pods can find more permanent homes, in areas where children can access them when they want, without the play project staff being present. Another such initiative is 'play rangers' where the play workers take a van full of equipment to a local park, open it up for the children there to play with for two hours, and then pack up and move on to another area.

Andrea describes the children's reaction:

> most of them have never seen anything like it . . . they don't usually understand that we don't want anything from them . . . It takes a while for them to understand that we are not there to teach them anything. But when they 'get it', we have fantastic relationships with the children.

SureStart
A government initiative created in 1998, aimed at improving services for children under 5 and their families.

The Children's Fund
A government initiative launched in 2000 to improve the lives of disadvantaged children and young people.

▶

Teachers were inclined to view the project with some suspicion:

> one teacher sat me down and said, OK, can you tell me exactly what they are learning from this? I said well, in terms of wood play, you can look at what tools they use and what conversations they are having when they are doing it . . . look at the self-directed things that are going on, like there's a lot of investigation going on. For example, they might try to make a cart and put different size wheels on one side, and then they figure out it will only go round in a circle, it won't go forwards, all those investigative things.

One teacher got enthusiastically involved, but 'ended up squashing [the children's] play; he said like, ten minutes to make a den, and then he tore one den down saying that it wouldn't withstand any kind of strong weather'. Even the settings that were more in tune with the ethos of the play project seemed nervous about using the equipment and wanted a lot of training, so the playworkers then had to explain that they were not 'expert' in wood play or in any specified uses of any of the other play equipment and resources. When the children fill in evaluation forms 'we did what we wanted to do' always comes top of the 'good points' list.

The future of play

How can we 'mainstream' or 'normalise' the work in which Andrea is engaged, so that the good practice she is promoting is not seen by other practitioners as just something connected with a (possibly rather 'fringe') project, but as something that happens everyday in playgrounds throughout the country, both during school break times, and when children are out of school? UN Article 31 within the United Nations Convention on the Rights of the Child, to which the United Kingdom is a signatory, 'sets out the right of the child to rest and leisure, to engage in play and recreational activities appropriate to the age of the child' (New Policy Institute, 2001, p. 7). Given the combination of factors outlined above that appear to have unwittingly conspired to remove such rights from the current generation of British children, it is suggested that policy makers urgently consider making space, both in time and location, for children's social free play, both within the school environment and beyond. To encourage parents to allow their children to use such areas during out-of-school hours in the heavily vehicle populated, mass media saturated, hence highly safety conscious twenty-first century, attention should be paid to providing permanent safe, suitable spaces for all-weather active play, ensuring that these contain suitable surfaces and resources, and the provision of a range of discrete areas designed to address the developmental needs of specific age groups. These play spaces should be overseen by adult playworkers, trained in the promotion of free play and child-led activities. It is recommended that resulting initiatives should be underpinned by a clear recognition of human beings' origins as social primates and the multicultural nature of contemporary British society, and all that this entails in the consideration of the necessary breadth of socialisation experiences.

There is currently (late 2007) some indication that UK social policy is moving towards this outcome. A new ministry for Children, Families and Schools was created in mid-2007, and the British Government has recently set aside some funding streams (including the 'transformation' fund) aimed at improving the breadth and quality of the children's workforce. Additionally, the Children's Workforce Development Council was set up in 2006 to oversee the management of such initiatives, and a five-year project called Play England (www. playengland.org.uk) was created in March 2007 with funds from the National Lottery to 'promote strategies for free play and create a lasting support structure for play providers in England . . . [and to] provide information and a range of resources for the strategic development of play provision and play space' (Play England, 2006). Amongst many other play promotion activities, Play England is currently engaged in producing a practical 'how-to' guide to risk management in play space provision. The Children's Plan, published in

December 2007, has promised support and funding for 'play space' ventures.

We are therefore currently living in a time and in a location where, despite some continuing challenges, such as the narrow focus of the National Curriculum on outcome-based learning for children aged 'rising 6', and over, and the traffic-clogged streets of our towns and cities, opportunities are opening up that may yet allow current and future generations of children to reclaim physical play spaces that have been redesigned to be a better 'fit' with the cultural background of a postmodern twenty-first-century society. It is hoped that our readers will become some of the adults who will lead us into an exciting new phase of play for enjoyment, and play for learning.

Ideas in action

An early twentieth-century childhood

Where am I going? I don't quite know.
Down to the stream where the king-cups grow –
Up on the hill where the pine-trees blow –
Anywhere, anywhere. I don't know.
Where am I going? The clouds sail by,
Little ones, baby ones, over the sky.
Where am I going? The shadows pass,
Little ones, baby ones, over the grass.
If you were a cloud, and sailed up there,
You'd sail on water as blue as air,
And you'd see me here in the fields and say:
'Doesn't the sky look green today?'
Where am I going? The high rooks call:
'It's awful fun to be born at all.'
Where am I going? The ring-doves coo:
'We do have beautiful things to do.'
If you were a bird, and lived on high,
You'd lean on the wind when the wind came by,
You'd say to the wind when it took you away:
'*That's* where I wanted to go today!'
Where am I going? I don't quite know.
What does it matter where people go?
Down to the wood where the blue-bells grow –
Anywhere, anywhere. I don't know.

'Spring Morning' by A.A. Milne, from
When We Were Very Young, 1921

Comment: Back to the Future?

There are probably very few adults currently living in Britain who were allowed the 'roaming' scope described above during their own childhoods. This poem describes an English childhood in a period before the last great push of **urbanisation**, and in which 'motorway' was not yet a word in the English language. We are unlikely ever to get this world back again; but we may yet be able to reclaim some spaces, both in time and location, for children to engage in some of the same sorts of play and flexible thinking described in this poem. A clear goal would be to give every child in Britain enough free time and a suitable place to lie on the grass on a sunny day and engage in the type of flexible thinking that underpins ideas about how, for example, s/he might see the world if the sky was the ground and the ground was the sky.

One of the most poignant lines in this poem is 'It's awful fun to be born at all.' How many children actually think this today? The evidence suggests that this was not the viewpoint of the children interviewed in 'What English children say about school' above; although we must remember that individuals vary (see 'A research point' above), and that, of course, not all children would have had such a free and happy childhood during the 1920s as A.A. Milne depicts in his poem.

> **Urbanisation**
> A process that occurs when a society is industrialized – as factories and large businesses are set up, people start to live in 'urban' areas (towns) rather than 'rural' areas (farms and countryside).

▶

Improving practice

In this penultimate 'Improving practice' box we are not going to make any specific suggestions about how you might attempt to promote the facilitation of play for contemporary children that is as rich as the experience described in the poem above, although we do strongly suggest that you consider the huge body of research findings, theory and practical suggestions you will find in the chapters in this book to help you towards this goal.

Now you have considered some of *our* ideas, you could make a start on *your own* 'perspectives on play' by sketching out some ideas relating to an ideal outdoor play area for the children in your setting. Once you have done this, ask colleagues, parents and most importantly the children for their suggestions. Once you have collated these, you will be well on your way to a working proposal. The next step is for you and your colleagues to seek funding for such a venture – you may find that this is not as difficult as you may have initially thought!

Summary and review

As we draw to the end of this chapter, we can begin to suggest some tentative answers to the questions we posed at the beginning:

- How does peer and sibling interaction research suggest that such interactions are vital for healthy human development?

We can see from the examples provided in this chapter that such relationships underpin experiences that children simply could not have if they were unable to engage in play with a wide range of peers. Research carried out with children who experience problems in social interaction additionally suggests that there may be negative consequences for human primates who do not receive enough 'space' either in time or in location to carry out such activities during the developmental period.

- What 'spaces' in time and location did playing children inhabit in the past, how did these become less 'open' over the last quarter of the twentieth century, and what might be the emergent effects?

The school curriculum was not nationally imposed before 1988, and although there was little discovery or play-based learning undertaken in mainstream British primary schools before the late 1960s, children used their out-of-school time, including longer break periods within the school day, to engage in independent collaborative free play. In the past, children were able to play in streets that did not contain the hazard of a constant stream of fast-moving motor vehicles, and parents were not constantly bombarded by the sensational output of myriad global multi-media sources on the activities of predatory stranger 'paedophiles'. Until the last quarter of the twentieth century, therefore, children tended to do most of their collaborative free play in the streets, woods and fields that are now commonly designated by adults as dangerous environments. There is recent evidence to suggest that many children and young people in Britain are not seeing their lives in a very positive light. A range of such evidence has been cited in this book, including the 'friendlessness' contained in the UNICEF (2007) and Children's Society (2007a, 2007b) reports and the dissatisfaction with education reported in the smaller-scale 'student voice' studies that have been highlighted in this chapter.

- How might adults attempt to reopen some 'spaces' in time and location that will be successfully utilised by children in the cultural environment of our current society?

It is not only this chapter, but this book as a whole that has led us to a point where we can usefully pose a question of this nature, considering the provision of 'safe' play areas which will fit into the highly complex outdoor environments in modern towns and cities. The good news is that government funding for such initiatives is coming on stream, and there are also plans to create a network of extended schools and children's centres that are accessible to children in every area in Britain. As we move towards the 2010s, these centres could form ideal 'hubs' around which outdoor *and* indoor play space initiatives could be piloted, and this potential has been explicitly recognised by the Children's Plan (DCSF, 2007c). In terms of *'Over to you' for transforming practice and ideas for research*, all the chapters in this book should have given you a wealth of ideas about 'where we go from here'. This area of transformation is a key issue for children's services within contemporary Britain, to enable children to experience their childhoods as a holistic, enjoyable phase of their whole life experience, rather than experiencing them as a rushed period of 'cramming' adult-transmitted learning on a sprint towards adulthood.

Further reading

Claxton, G. (1997) *Hare Brain, Tortoise Mind*. London: Fourth Estate.

Dunn, J. (2004) *Children's Friendships: The Beginning of Intimacy*. Oxford: Blackwell.

Opie, I. and Opie, P. (1969) *Children's Games in Street and Playground*. London: Oxford University Press.

Santer, J., Griffiths, C. and Goodsall, D. (2007) *Free Play in Early Childhood*. London: National Children's Bureau.

UNICEF (2007) *An Overview of Child Well-being in Rich Countries*, available at: http://www.unicef-icdc.org/presscentre/presskit/reportcard7/rc7_eng.pdf

Chapter 12

Afterword: What Now for Play?

PAM JARVIS, SYLVIA DODDS AND AVRIL BROCK

'The Teaching with Games project was a one-year study designed to offer a broad overview of teachers' and students' use of and attitudes towards commercial off-the-shelf computer games in school. It aimed to identify the factors that would impact the use of these entertainment games in school.' (Sandford *et al.*, 2006) These researchers found that whilst the predictable generation gap emerged, with students exhibiting more confidence in game playing than teachers, effective use of such games in the context of teaching and learning depended far more on the individual teacher's curriculum knowledge and teaching skills than it did on the content of the game or the players' IT skills. The game therefore did not 'take over' the classroom in any way; teachers continued to play the key role in scaffolding the learning of their students.

Introduction

We have now reached the end of this book and we believe that, at the time of writing in Britain, there is an exciting new **zeitgeist** that has inspired the authors. National and global discussions relating to finding new ways to support children's play in twenty-first-century urban environments have only just started. Hopefully, 'the [new]

> **Zeitgeist**
> The spirit of the time; general trend of thought or feeling characteristic of a particular period of time (Dictionary.com).

journey is just beginning', as Doherty suggests in Chapter 8.

The panorama of play that has unfurled for the reader within the pages of this book touches upon many areas of professional and academic investigation. These will be ripe for research activities (particularly practitioner-led action research) well beyond the career lifetimes of our first generation of readers. For example, in an increasingly multi-cultural global society, the socio-cultural approach to children's play activities described by Olusoga in Chapter 2 will become standard practice in all democratic societies, necessitating a body of knowledgeable, reflective practitioners in this area.

Ongoing discoveries relating to human genetics will inform the bio-cultural approach to human development (outlined by Jarvis in Chapter 7) for many years to come. Effective practitioners will need to update their understanding of the complex interactions of nature and nurture in human development on an ongoing basis. Discoveries relating to the living, functioning human brain are beginning to show us a considerable sophistication in human cognition even from the earliest months of life, hence there is a developmental need for human beings to have access to suitable play experiences from the very beginning. Some excellent suggestions for such activities are made by Doherty, Brock and Jarvis in Chapter 4.

The occupational area of playwork introduced by Brown in Chapters 1 and 9 is on a sharply upward trajectory in the United Kingdom, as the new Children's Workforce Development Council expands the career arena for those working with children. Such new roles will largely encompass supporting play-based out-of-school activities for children, located within the new extended schools and children's centres referred to by Jarvis and George in Chapter 11. It is to be hoped that all future provision for children, whether in school or out-of-school environments, will increasingly start with the needs of the child, as espoused by Doherty in Chapter 8, rather than crushing the holistic development of individual children under a monolithic one-size-fits-all curriculum, which labels many aspects of a child's individuality as stigmatising 'special needs'. Moreover, such curricula at best can only achieve the superficial transmission of contemporary skills and knowledge that will quickly become outdated as the child becomes a young adult. To consider the huge possibilities for deep, flexible discovery play-based learning in the classrooms of the future, we can find a wealth of information in the concepts outlined by Brock in Chapters 3 and 5 and Dodds in Chapter 6.

In summary, then, the advent of various government initiatives, some of which are outlined by Jarvis and George in Chapter 11, indicate that the future for play in Britain seems much brighter than it has done for many years, providing we can avoid the temptation to turn this new adult gaze upon free play into adult direction, as Jarvis warns in Chapter 7. However, such

advances have only been won through a debate that has continued across two play-arid decades over the closing years of the twentieth century. As the experience of childhood in Britain changed rapidly via its immersion in an equally rapidly changing society, concerns were steadily raised by many adults working with children in many different capacities. This sadly culminated in a UNICEF report (2007) branding the United Kingdom the worst place in the developed world to be a child (see Jarvis and George, Chapter 11). As a myriad of experts increasingly raised issue after issue that can be seen to simultaneously negatively impact upon children and childhood, lack of time and space for free play consistently featured highly on this list. Jones provides a background to some such issues in Chapter 10, visiting the devastating effects of natural disaster, HIV and child abuse upon individual children, and the healing capacity of play to help them begin to reconcile what may initially seem to be overwhelming circumstances.

Living (and playing) in the twenty-first century

Children today engage in types of play that did not exist even 20 years ago. The development of technology has not only impacted on traditional toys but has also created the existence of a whole new world of virtual adventures and play. Take for example the game battleships – if you were a child 50-plus years ago, you would have played this simply with a pencil and paper. Partners would draw grids, decide on how many squares an aircraft carrier, submarine and so on would cover and then they would commence the game to 'seek and wipe out'. In the mid-twentieth century, this game was further developed (and commercialised) by manufacturers who, taking the same basic idea, created plastic pegboards that would not only receive miniature vessels but also different coloured pegs to represent hits and misses. More recently there have been electronic versions that not only simulate the sounds of firing missiles and air strikes but also have a 'mission command' and a whole range of inbuilt, pre-programmed battle plans.

Ideas in action

Defining the problem(s)

On 12 September 2006 a letter was published in the *Daily Telegraph* signed by 100 professionals, academics and authors, all of whom had successful career backgrounds either directly working with and/or writing for or about children and childhood. This letter raised a summary of contemporary issues regarding the effects of ever more rapid technological and cultural change on children's lives. It is reproduced below.

We are deeply concerned at the escalating incidence of childhood depression and children's behavioural and developmental conditions. We believe this is largely due to a lack of understanding, on the part of both politicians and the general public, of the realities and subtleties of child development.

Since children's brains are still developing, they cannot adjust – as full-grown adults can – to the effects of ever more rapid technological and cultural change. They still need what developing human beings have always needed, including real food (as opposed to processed 'junk'), real play (as opposed to sedentary, screen-based entertainment), first-hand experience of the world they live in and regular interaction with the real-life significant adults in their lives.

They also need time. In a fast-moving hyper-competitive culture, today's children are expected to cope with an ever-earlier start to formal schoolwork and an overly academic test-driven primary curriculum. They are pushed by market forces to act and dress like mini-adults and exposed via the electronic media to material which would have been considered unsuitable for children even in the very recent past.

Our society rightly takes great pains to protect children from physical harm, but seems to have lost sight of their emotional and social needs. However, it's now clear that the mental health of an unacceptable number of children is being unnecessarily compromised, and that this is almost certainly a key factor in the rise of substance abuse, violence and self-harm amongst our young people.

This is a complex socio-cultural problem to which there is no simple solution, but a sensible first step would be to encourage parents and policymakers to start talking about ways of improving children's well-being. We therefore propose as a matter of urgency that public debate be initiated on child-rearing in the 21st century; this issue should be central to public policy-making in coming decades.

The *Daily Telegraph*, 2006

Improving practice
Dealing with complex issues

Although the text of this letter is not very long, it raises multiple issues. Go through the text highlighting the main points made, and then list them as bullet points. On which points do you agree with the authors of the letter? Go back to each bullet point and consider how you might start to deal with the issues raised. In so doing, take heed of the authors' point that what they are describing 'is a complex socio-cultural problem'. You will meet some very intricate issues as you carry out this activity. It would help to discuss such issues with your colleagues and tutors.

The ongoing development of the internet, and the potential for online game playing with strangers located across the globe, is increasingly changing the nature of play and leisure for human beings as a species, both for children and adults. Individuals of all ages can explore virtual, animated worlds, for example taking on the role of a medieval knight or science-fiction character, looking after a virtual pet, playing a godlike role to a whole cyber family or even 'driving' virtual cars and 'flying' virtual planes, helicopters or even spacecraft. As technology advances and computer graphics become more and more realistic, the possibilities seem endless.

Figure 12.1 Children playing computer games

Ideas in action

The future for play is online? (Author's reflection)

The first time I became fascinated by possible futures for computer-based play was watching various episodes of the US science-fiction programme *Star Trek: The Next Generation* in the late 1980s. The characters had what they termed a 'holo-suite' on their ocean liner sized spacecraft. This 'holo-suite' was one of the principal places they went to relax when off duty, and it was able to create any type of virtual, 3D, completely interactive world they pleased. For example, the ship's dignified senior executive captain assumed the leading role of a seedy private detective in a series of murder mysteries, whilst several other members of the crew simply created pleasant surroundings and 'holo-people' for relatively mundane interactions (for example a sultry jazz nightclub in New Orleans). There was no problem in dealing with arguments or even full-blown physical fights with 'holo-characters', as the program could be paused or ended by a single command from a 'real' player. There were of course some episodes where the 'pause button' malfunctioned; one I remember well entailed a holo-character asking a 'real' character, 'Where do I go when you turn me off?' Clearly, this hints at a whole new set of (hypothetical) questions about moral and ethical issues that might arise if technological advance ever leads us to the creation of a real leisure device that resembles a holo-suite. A subsequent *Star Trek* series, *Voyager*, contained an episode that told the story of a little girl who could interact with characters in

▶

a children's fantasy novel in her holo-suite, which led me to muse that if I could have entered the world of *Alice in Wonderland*, *Little Women*, *The Famous Five* or any of Robert Heinlein's science-fiction novels in such a way during my own childhood, I would never have wanted any real friends!

I didn't consider this topic as anything more than an interesting hypothetical situation until some 10–12 years later, when I made the acquaintance of a person who was a dedicated online game player. In the game he played he inhabited a *Star Trek*-type universe where he was a spacecraft pilot running a freight business, outrunning galactic pirates and engaging in some of his own shady dealings when he had the chance. He had online, fellow game player partners in his 'business' who he did not know outside the game, and kept 'accounts' of his 'earnings' which he could 'spend' on a multitude of 'planets' within the game. I remember being fascinated that he had to 'secure his spacecraft' after being online, as the game continued when he was not there, and an 'unsecured vehicle' could be 'stolen' by other players when one was offline! It concerned me that the game seemed more interesting to him in many ways than his real life (small, neat suburban home and

a 9–5 office job). I did wonder about the eventual long-term effects on mental health from such activities, for both children and adults. (PJ)

Reflection

As generations who are more and more computer literate progress into their 60s and 70s, and begin to suffer from mobility-limiting infirmities, will they be tempted to live a greater proportion of their lives online, not necessarily in extreme fantasy games, but on websites such as 'second life' where neither age nor infirmity needs to be incorporated into the online identity? If so, will this be a benefit or a detriment to society as a whole? On the one hand, the problem of isolated elderly people may abate to some extent, but will children begin to lack contact from a grandparent generation who are more attracted by continually available online adult interaction, than a rather more restricted real-world conversation with a small child? I already shudder when I see young parents pushing their children along in front-facing pushchairs, staring blankly ahead, their ears plugged into the music on their ipods, or talking over the child's head into a mobile phone or bluetooth.

Playing in Cyberspace: a blessing or a curse?

Senario 1: Jeff's new lease of life in cyberspace

Jeff is 64 years old, and only a few months away from retirement. He works shifts for a local security company, which means his hours are not always sociable. In his spare time he loves to play golf and when he has leisure time available he is frequently on the fairways. However the British climate is not always conducive to a round of golf and now Jeff is getting older he is finding long walks around golf courses more difficult due to ageing joints and general fatigue. Three years ago he acquired

his first computer. Whilst hesitant at first, with a little help from family and friends he is now able to send and receive emails from his golfing buddies, surf the internet to find the latest deals on green fees and book his golfing holidays, but most importantly have a round of 'virtual' golf with Tiger Woods, his hero. He has participated in many 'virtual' US golf tournaments and 'won' over $1 million – if only real life could be so rich! As Jeff says, 'It keeps my mind busy, it has helped my game on the ground and it gives me something to do when it is wet outside – I think it's marvellous!'

▶

Senario 2: Cyber-tracking Santa

When Santa Claus leaves the North Pole to begin his epic delivery tomorrow, he will be tracked closely by radar and satellite, and by jet fighters following the sleigh. And this Christmas Eve there will be more men and women and boys and girls watching than ever, as the website showing his progress around the world in real time expects a billion hits.

'Norad Tracks Santa' – run by the deadly serious North American Aerospace Defense Command – has become a massive festive phenomenon. For one night only each year, the organisation set up to defend the US from incoming missiles sets its sights on Santa.

Originally an American craze, tracking Santa is rapidly picking up fans in this country and many others. Last year Jonathan Ross gave an excited commentary as the sleigh swooped over Big Ben, and broadcasters from other nations were also hired to describe Rudolph blazing across their night skies. This time the images from Santa Cams will be in 3D and the audience the largest yet, thanks to a link-up with the search engine Google.

The *Independent on Sunday* online, 23 December 2007

Senario 3: Game over for internet addicts: a Chinese perspective

Combining sympathy with discipline, a military-style boot camp near Beijing is at the front line of China's battle against Internet addiction, a disorder afflicting millions of the nation's youth. The Internet Addiction Treatment Center (IATC) in Daxing County uses a blend of therapy and military drills to treat the children of China's nouveau riche addicted to online games . . .

Concerned by a number of high-profile Internet-related deaths and juvenile crime, the government is now taking steps to stem Internet addictions by banning new Internet cafés and mulling restrictions on violent computer games . . .

'Many of the Internet addicts here have rarely considered other people's feelings. The military training allows them to feel what it's like to be a part of a team,' said Xu Leiting, a psychologist at the hospital. 'It also helps their bodies recover and makes them stronger.'

The IATC has treated 1,500 patients in this way since opening in 2004, and boasts a 70 per cent success rate at breaking addictions . . . Internet addiction rates posted in western studies vary wildly, with little consensus as to what constitutes addiction and whether the concept exists . . .

'The main cause of Internet addiction is that parents' expectations for their children are too high,' Mr Xu said. With education perceived by many parents as the only means of advancement in an ultra-competitive society of 1.3 billion people, some lock their children up to study and ask teachers to assign them extra homework. 'The pressure can be too much for some children,' said Mr Xu, especially if they fail. 'Then they escape to the virtual world to seek achievements, importance, and satisfaction, or a sense of belonging,' he added.

Red Herring online, 11 March 2007

Reflection

While the internet appears to have invigorated Jeff's life, and created a huge amount of fun for 'Santa-watching' children and adults around the world at Christmas time, the final scenario above outlines possible problems that may arise for children and young people from over-reliance on the internet for leisure activities, particularly when this is paired with problems in real-world relationships. It could be suggested that eventual progression lies in educating individuals to use their online leisure environments safely, although we will need to develop new skills to protect our psychological rather than our physical safety in this new recreation environment. Perhaps educating children in such an increasingly core life skill will eventually underpin at least one of the new child education/care occupations referred to above.

What now for play?

The authors wholeheartedly support the points made by the writers of the letter to the *Daily Telegraph* with regard to their initiation of a debate relating to the best ways to fulfil children's core needs:

- to develop in environments where they both are, and *comprehend* that they are protected, safe and loved;

- to receive sufficient time and space for free play;

- to be both sensitively supported and given enough freedom to engage in independent social interaction, developing positive relationships with a wide range of peers;

- to receive the correct amount and level of structured teaching from engaged and well-trained adults, appropriate to the child's own highly individual stage of development and ongoing needs.

However, from the socio-cultural viewpoint, we would urge practitioners to be wary of glib references to '*real*' play. Cyber interaction is indeed very real in today's world, and it is a medium that children must become accustomed to in their developmental period if they are to fully and effectively engage in their cultural worlds when they become adult. Of course, such cyber experience needs to be carefully balanced with interaction in the concrete, physical environment, and perhaps it is this element of balance that we need to look more carefully towards in our endeavours to create a more nurturing environment for our children; balanced both in terms of cyber and concrete interaction opportunities, and in terms of the provision of structured and unstructured activities.

One aspect it is important to remember is that we cannot accurately predict the world in which our children are going to live as adults; it is therefore vitally important to support every generation of children in their development of transferable skills. This must essentially include the development of the skills and attitudes that underpin the ability to self-regulate one's own educational experiences as an independent learner (for which play provides such valuable experiences), not the transmission of chunks of disjointed knowledge in the pursuit of good 'performance' on a highly artificial paper and pencil test.

The chapters in this book are designed to take you a few steps along the road in your professional journey, and within them we have attempted to communicate some (inevitably time-bound) ideas to help you in your pursuit of educating and nurturing a generation of playful, developing children. We have had great pleasure in inviting you to join us as lifelong learners in this fascinating endeavour, and to take this process forward into as yet unknown cultures of the future.

Ideas in action

'On children'

Your children are not your children.

They are the sons and daughters of Life's longing for itself.

They come through you but not from you,

And though they are with you, yet they belong not to you.

You may give them your love but not your thoughts.

For they have their own thoughts.

You may house their bodies but not their souls,

For their souls dwell in the house of tomorrow, which you cannot visit, not even in your dreams.

You may strive to be like them, but seek not to make them like you.

For life goes not backward nor tarries with yesterday.

You are the bows from which your children as living arrows are sent forth.

▶

The archer sees the mark upon the path of the infinite,

and He bends you with His might that His arrows may go swift and far.

Let your bending in the archer's hand be for gladness;

For even as He loves the arrow that flies, so He loves also the bow that is stable.   Gibran, 1923

These words were written by Khalil Gibran (1883–1931) shortly after World War I. Gibran was thus a member of one of the earlier generations who experienced the **psychosocial dissonance** that rapidly changing technology can evoke. Perhaps if we as adults can learn this one lesson that he phrases so beautifully – that every successive generation of children will 'dwell in the house of tomorrow, which [adults] cannot visit, not even in your dreams . . . For life goes not backward nor tarries with yesterday' – every successive generation of adults will subsequently be motivated to fiercely guard the independent, flexible free play activities in which their children develop the vital foundations of independent learning abilities. Such a culture could also helpfully underpin the central quest for each successive generation of teachers: to hone and further develop existing pedagogical systems that inculcate the transferable skills and knowledge that each new generation will need to meet new and unforeseen challenges in an unknown future.

> **Psychosocial dissonance**
> Psychosocial: relating to both the psychological and the social; dissonance: inharmonious or harsh sound; discord or incongruity (Dictionary.com). Psychosocial dissonance is therefore a description of a feeling that one's society and one's place within it is somehow unbalanced, in particular that some societal factors do not properly synchronise with others, or with one's own ideas of how interactions with others ought to proceed.

Glossary

Accommodation   From Piagetian theory, to build a new schema in response to a new experience.

Adapted   A species that has undergone evolutionary changes that have enabled it to fit neatly into the environment which it naturally inhabits.

Agency   The capacity, condition, or state of acting or of exerting power (Merriam Webster).

Agentive   Active participation in the social creation of meaning (within a constructivist learning model).

Androcentric   Centred on males/a masculine view of the world.

Anglo-American   Relating to the nations inhabited by British-derived, English-speaking populations.

Anthropologist   One who studies human beings and their ancestors through time and space and in relation to physical character, environmental and social relations, and culture (Merriam Webster).

Apprenticeship   The period of Legitimate Peripheral Participation where learners are engaged in the active process of acquiring the knowledge and skills of a community of practice until they are deemed sufficiently knowledgeable to practice on their own, e.g. apprentice bricklayer, community nurse, dentist, etc.

Arousal modulation   To independently regulate one's arousal.

Arts therapies   Forms of individual or group therapy using the arts.

Assimilation   From Piagetian theory, to use an existing schema to deal with a new experience; in teaching the term can be used to mean to absorb, take in, fully understand a particular element of learning.

Attachment theory   A psychological and ethological theory that describes how an infant can become attached to an individual with whom they spend prolonged periods of time, e.g. mother.

Behavioural knowledge   Enactive (physical) knowledge that is represented in the senses and is developed 'by doing'.

Bioculturalism   A theory that suggests that people are constructed equally by their biology and their cultural surroundings.

Bio-psychology   In full, biological psychology, a branch of psychology that is based on the physical properties of the brain.

Bookstart   Bookstart is the world's first national books-for-babies programmme, delivering free packs of books to babies and toddlers in the UK.

Catharsis   Elimination of a complex by bringing it to consciousness and affording it expression (Merriam Webster).

Cerebellum   The part of the brain that coordinates sensory perception and motor control. It integrates the pathways which cause the muscles to move.

Child-centred approach   Education that tailors the learning style to the particular interests of the child, e.g. allowing a child who has an interest in trains to read about trains, write a story about trains, etc.

Child initiated   Allowing children the opportunity to develop their knowledge and skills through play without adult direction.

Co-constructed cognition   A thought or idea that has been arrived at by the collaboration of two or more people.

Co-construction   When more than one individual is actively involved in the learning process.

Cognition   The processing of information; how one understands the world.

Communities of practice   Describes how differences may exist between different cultures in that they may have different ways of accomplishing everyday tasks, e.g. educating children or preparing food.

Computational view of mind   An individualised view of mind that involves the simple transmission of knowledge without interaction with one's surroundings, either biological, psychological or sociological.

Constructivists   Researchers who adhere to the notion that meaning is individually constructed from one's own perceptions and experiences, through interaction with the environment in which one exists.

Continuum   A chain, sequence or progression of events/areas where one thing leads logically to another.

Cortisol   One of several steroid hormones produced by the adrenal cortex, it is produced by mammals in situations of stress to increase metabolism of fats and carbohydrates in order to fuel the animal to run or fight.

Critical pedagogy   An approach that attempts to help teachers or students question and challenge ideologies and practices that exist in education.

Cultural evolution   The unfolding of cultural practices to fit the environment in which a population live, e.g. the cultural norm of very swift disposal of the newly dead in hot countries.

Cultural–historical theory   Describes the role of the 'collective mind' (or 'distributed cognition') that exists in a community's culture in underpinning the future of that society.

Culture   The customary beliefs, social forms and material traits of a racial, religious or social group, also the characteristic features of everyday existence (as diversions or a way of life) shared by people in a place or time (Merriam Webster).

Curriculum   A body of knowledge/skills to be transmitted to the learner; the coursework and content taught at a school; a programme of learning.

Darwin's theory of evolution   A theory which proposes that features that give a particular creature an advantage in the environment it inhabits are more likely to survive in that species, due to the fact that more successful animals are more likely to survive to mate and pass on their genes to the next generation.

Decentre   To move away from one's own point of view and consider the point of view of another creature.

Department for Children, Schools and Families   A new government department, replacing the Department for Education and Skills.

Desirable learning outcomes   A curriculum for pre-school children in England from 1996 to 1999.

Developmental level   The idea that most children progress through different stages in play, each one offering new potentials and opportunities.

Developmental movement play   The Jabadao National Centre term for movement, learning and health.

Developmental psychologist   A psychologist who specialises in the psychology of infants and children, particularly how this changes as the child matures.

Developmentally appropriate   Practice based on what is known about how children develop taking account of age, social situation and emotional well-being.

Dichotomy   Division into two mutually exclusive, opposed, or contradictory parts.

Didactic   Intending to instruct, an activity undertaken for the specific purpose of teaching.

Didactic teaching   Teacher-led, direct instruction, where children are passive learners/simply take in information.

Discourse   Literally a conversation, but frequently used by social scientists to describe an ongoing theoretical debate.

Discovery learning   Inquiry-based learning/instruction.

Distancing   A way of relating to others and to the self that stresses thought, reflection and critical distance.

Diversity   Recognises the uniqueness of individuals in terms of needs, aspirations, abilities, weaknesses and strengths.

Dizygotic   Twins who begin life as two separate eggs fertilised by two separate sperm and therefore having differing DNA.

Dramatherapy   The use of drama in therapy, involving processes such as role enactment, mask work or play.

Dynamic relationships   A relationship where one part complements (but is not the same) as the other(s), and when one part changes, the others also change to continue the complementary relationship.

Dynamic systems   A system that works in interaction with other systems within the same organism or mechanism, each system regulating the other. For example the human body is a such an organism, and a car engine is such a mechanism.

Early learning goals   The six main areas of development and learning, which define what children are expected to achieve from age 3 to the end of Reception.

Early Years Foundation Stage   Statutory guidelines for the education and care of children aged 0–6 in England, to be introduced September 2008.

Education Action Zone   Schools that receive special assistance from the Department for Education and Employment to run projects designed to raise pupils' achievement levels.

Egocentricity   To be focused on the self, but not in the same sense as being *selfish* – small children do not yet understand that other people are individuals like themselves, with a complex internal mental world that is hidden from others – they have to learn this through social interaction.

Emotional intelligence   Level of awareness of one's own emotions and those of others, and using this to inform one's own behaviour and interaction patterns.

Empathy   A way of relating to others that emphasises understanding, sensitivity and awareness of their feelings, thoughts and perspective.

Empirical   Based on observation or experience.

Enactive representation   How a child stores memories from their past experience according to appropriate motor response, i.e. riding a bike – the actions are imprinted on our muscles.

Endomorph   A heavy person with a soft and rounded body (dictionary.com)

English as an additional language   Where English is not the child's first language.

Equilibration   To bring into balance. In Piagetian theory, this specifically refers to bringing one's ideas into balance with reality.

Ethological   The scientific and objective study of animal behaviour, especially under natural conditions (Merriam Webster).

Ethologist   A person who studies animals in their natural environment.

Every Child Matters   The English government's new approach to ensuring the well-being of children from birth to age 19, encompassing five main areas.

Evolutionary developmental psychology   A theory that proposes that children are born with a basic set of evolved features, which need to be further developed in interaction with the environment.

Evolutionary forces   Forces that shape creatures, creating a situation where creatures with a specific set of features are more likely to survive to mate and have offspring than those who do not possess such features; e.g., if birds with hooked beaks are better at catching worms, then birds with hooked beaks will survive and reproduce, whilst those with straight beaks will not.

Evolutionary theory   A theory proposing that features which give a particular creature an advantage in the environment it inhabits are more likely to survive in that species, due to the fact that more successful animals are more likely to survive to mate and pass on their genes to the next generation.

Exclusion   When a pupil is prohibited from attending school on the grounds of a serious offence.

Feely bag   A bag in which items can be placed so that pupils can guess the contents through touch or by asking questions.

Fine motor skills   Involve the movement of the muscles in smaller actions such as holding a pen or wriggling the toes in sand.

Focal area observation   An observation carried out by focusing on one area, recording everything that occurs within this area for a stated amount of time.

Focal child observation   An observation carried out by focusing on one child, recording everything that the child does and says for a stated amount of time.

Formal and informal curriculum   The formal curriculum is the planned programme of objectives, content, learning experiences, resources and assessment offered by a school. It is sometimes called the 'official curriculum'. Informal curriculum is another term for hidden curriculum.

Foundation Stage   Prior to September 2008, this was the first part of the National Curriculum, aimed at children between the ages of 3 and 5.

Free time   When a learner is given the opportunity to make their own choice about the nature of their activity.

Gendered   Reflecting or involving gender differences or stereotypical gender roles (Merriam Webster).

Genes   The functional unit of inheritance controlling the transmission and expression of one or more traits (Merriam Webster).

Golden time   A short period, often in the afternoon or at the end of the week, where children and their teachers either sit down together and celebrate achievement or children are offered a range of activities in which to engage. It is often used as a method for modification of inappropriate behaviours and rewarding children who behave well. Governed by 'golden rules' it is an opportunity, at its best, for self- and peer reflection.

Gross motor skills   Involve the movement of the muscles in larger actions such as running, jumping or riding a bike.

Guided participation   Describes how children are led to participate in the community into which they were born by being supported by adults to engage in mundane/everyday activities, many of which will vary from culture to culture.

Habitus   A set of thoughts, values, tastes and behaviours that have been culturally acquired in childhood which the individual nevertheless frequently presumes are universally 'normal' and/or 'what everyone does'.

Hand–eye coordination   Is the ability of the vision system to control and guide the hand to perform tasks such as catching a ball or writing a letter.

Hard wiring   The fixed inborn aspects of a creature's brain physiology.

Hearsay   Repeating information that has been communicated by another person, describing something that is not the result of one's own direct experience.

Heuristic play   Play in a controlled environment without adult intervention with various types of object.

Hidden curriculum   Areas of the curriculum that are not necessarily directly taught but which are learned, such as codes of behaviour, unwritten social rules, or all the lessons that are indirectly taught by the school not necessarily in formal lessons; e.g. rules about time keeping, dress-code, etc.

Holistic   Relating to or concerned with wholes or with complete systems rather than with the analysis of, treatment of, or dissection into parts (my definition – educating the whole person, i.e. not just the intellect but emotions and mind and body).

Homo sapiens   Latin name for the version of the human species currently living on Earth.

Human instincts   A natural or inherent aptitude, impulse, or capacity, specific to the human species (Merriam Webster).

Hunter–gatherer   The way that early human beings organised their societies prior to the advent of farming, hunting animals for meat and gathering edible vegetation.

Iconic knowledge   How the brain uses sensory images or icons to store knowledge.

Iconoclast   One who destroys culturally important symbols and monuments; in the sense the chapter uses this term, it is suggesting that play might enable a player to experiment with ideas that are unconventional in his/her culture.

Impactive movement   Movement play between adult and baby in which movement starts away from the child and as the adult gets close the movement gathers speed and force, often culminating in the child being picked up by the adult.

Impairment   To be damaged or diminished in strength or ability.

Impulsive movement   Movement play between adult and baby in which movement starts strongly and gradually fades in speed and force to nothing, such as being lifted into the air and finishing being lowered to the adult's arms.

Inclusion   Allowing all children to be able to fully participate in mainstream institutions whatever their individual needs or abilities.

Inclusive education   Ensuring that all children have access to appropriate and effective education irrespective of physical disabilities.

Inclusive play   Providing equipment and apparatus in school and in out-of-school activities that allow disabled children to participate.

Individual development and species 'evolution'   Play creates situations which do not simply help the individual to develop skills, but help whole groups of players to develop skills that they can then teach other people, which in turn helps the whole human race to progress.

Individualistic consumer subjectivity   The excessive amount of choice created by a modern consumer society means that people constantly have to choose between which items to buy, such as clothes, food, furnishings, in a subjective fashion on the basis of trivial factors; hence consumption becomes highly subjective and individualistic.

Infant direct speech or parentese   The adaptation of simplified language by adults when communicating with very young children, which includes changing the tone of voice; altering words; using sounds; simple repetition and frequent questions.

Integrated topic approach Interconnecting several subjects within a curriculum into one topic to make cohesive 'human' sense to the learner.

Integration The inclusion of disabled children in the mainstream education system.

Internalisation To make something that is initially external to the self part of one's mind – e.g. in learning a language.

Intersubjectivity Describes shared meanings between people; the ability to be 'intersubjective' suggests that they are 'reading' symbols in the same way.

Intrinsic motivation The stimulus for learning inherent in children that is not dependent on external factors such as money or grades.

In vitro fertilisation (IVF) A modern fertility treatment, where the egg is fertilised in a laboratory test-tube, i.e. outside the mother's body.

Jabadao A national charity that works in partnership with the education, health, arts and social care on developing natural movement for young children.

Kin groups Groups of people who are genetically related.

Lactation Literally, to secrete milk, refers to the period that a mother is breast feeding an infant.

Learning communities A group of persons who share a set of relations, expectations and opportunities to ensure full participation and a positive learning environment.

Legitimate Peripheral Participation The actions of a newcomer into a community of practice that lead him or her to full participation of that community; e.g. a trainee doctor enters the community of doctors (e.g. hospital). They will spend some of their time shadowing experienced colleagues; increasingly they will take a more active role in that community, participating in activities that involve other professionals, patients and their families. Eventually the knowledge-ability of the individual will be indicated by the success of interactions, extent of participation and accuracy of judgement.

Leuven Involvement Scale Ferre Laevers' Involvement Scale for Young Children is a process-oriented monitoring system – a tool for quality assessment of educational settings that looks at how 'involved' the children are in their work and their 'emotional well-being'.

Linguistic Relating to language.

Ludic paradox Ludic refers to play, and a paradox is a strange contradiction that might not be expected, but nevertheless exists, so 'ludic paradox' refers to a complex contradiction relating to play behaviour.

Ludic play Play activities that are either engaged in, or have the outcome of, pleasure.

Mammal A group of warm-blooded, hairy animals that secrete milk to feed their young.

Mediation To bring about an understanding; a mediator is someone who liaises between two or more others to help them to understand one another.

Messy play Allows children to explore play involving different textures and resources without being labelled 'naughty', e.g. moulding clay and finger painting.

Metacognition Reflection or analysis of one's own process of learning and thinking.

Meta-cognition The awareness of one's cognitive processes and the efficient use of this self-awareness to self-regulate thinking and understanding.

Metacommunicative play Metacommunication is communicating about communicating, used to describe conversations where people are talking about aspects relating to communication; children frequently do this in their play interactions.

Meta-play Thinking about, communicating or reflecting on play experiences.

Monozygotic Identical twins who share the same fertilised ovum and sperm, and therefore the same DNA.

MSN messenger A live, typed online conversation.

Multiple intelligences A theory developed in 1983 by Dr Howard Gardner that challenges the traditional IQ test-based notion of intelligence. Gardner suggests there is a broad range of different intelligences (such as Linguistic, Intrapersonal, Bodily-kinaesthetic) to describe adult and child potential and that these exist in different combinations within an individual. Thus a teacher must use a range of different teaching methods or pathways to reach a learner effectively.

Multi-sensory Relating to or involving several physiological senses, e.g. sight, sound, etc.

Narrative Literally something that is spoken (narrated), the term is often used by social scientists to refer to the way people explain things by explaining a background 'story'.

National Curriculum The National Curriculum introduced in 1989 into state schools sets out the compulsory curriculum through the subjects and stages for children throughout primary and secondary schooling.

National Literacy and Numeracy Strategies Prescribed/ structured teaching and learning activities aimed at instructing learning activities in literacy and numeracy skills and knowledge.

Natural environment   The environment that a creature evolved within; for people this is a world of animals to hunt and plants to gather, not a world of farms and cities, which have been made by people.

Nature   The inherited aspects of a creature's appearance, personality and intelligence. Theorists have continually debated the proportions of each of these qualities that are due to 'nature' and which proportions are due to 'nurture', with as yet no definitive agreement.

Neural pathways   The connection between one part of the nervous system to another.

Neuronal pathways   The pathways along which thought occurs in human and animal minds, involving an electro-chemical reaction between cells in the brain called 'neurons'.

Non-participant [research]   A piece of research (most frequently observation) where the researcher does not interact with the participants, but collects data relating to their behaviour/interactions.

Nurture   The environmentally created aspects of a creature's appearance, personality and intelligence. Theorists have continually debated the proportions of each of these qualities that are due to 'nature' and which proportions are due to 'nurture', with as yet no definitive agreement.

OECD (Organisation for Economic Co-operation and Development)   An international organisation helping governments tackle the economic, social and governance challenges of a globalised economy (OECD website).

Offspring   The product of reproduction, the young produced by an organism.

Paradigm   A philosophical or theoretical framework of any kind (Merriam Webster).

Peak experiences   A peak experience is one where the individual feels intense joy and sense of purpose.

Pedagogic setting   The practice that a teacher, together with the particular group of learners, creates, enacts and experiences.

Pedagogy   The art, science, or profession of teaching.

Peers   Those belonging to the same societal group, especially based on age, grade, or status (Merriam Webster).

Perturbations   A term coined by Jerome Bruner to describe the moments in learning, where one might feel unsettled, uneasy or anxious, that should be an expected and accepted part of cognition.

Philosopher   A person who seeks wisdom or enlightenment (Merriam Webster).

Physical activity play   Play that incorporates physical vigour such as rhythmic play in infants, exercise play and rough and tumble.

Physiology   The organic processes and phenomena of an organism (Merriam Webster).

Plasticity/neuroplasticity   The lifelong ability of the brain to change as we learn or experience new things.

Play   A dynamic, active and constructive behaviour. An essential and integral part of all children's healthy growth, development and learning across all ages, domains and cultures.

Play 'gene'   A concept proposing that the desire to play is encoded in human beings' biology. The reference to 'a gene' is a figure of speech, as what we know of genetics indicates that the need for play would be the result of complex interactions between many genes.

Play plans   The planning of a range of activities for parents to support their children at home.

Play text   An imaginary story a child or group of children creates to underpin and explain their play actions (can also be called a 'play narrative').

Playful learning   Having fun and enjoyment whilst learning.

Portage   A home-visiting service for those children who have special needs.

Post-traumatic stress disorder   A psychological reaction occurring after experiencing a highly stressful event often reflected in depression, anxiety, flashbacks and recurrent nightmares.

Potentiation of adaptive variability   A potential for a player to carry out/practise varied behaviours that will help him/her adapt to life beyond the play situation.

Practice wisdom   A feature of a professional culture, similarly to habitus, 'practice wisdom' is a set of thoughts, values and behaviours, but in this instance it is shared between members of a profession (e.g., teachers, doctors) and is acquired through training and subsequent frequent association between professional colleagues.

Pretend fantasy play   Where children either enact or create imaginary situations within their own play. This type of play emerges when an environment sparks or allows the freedom for imagination and creativity.

Primate   A member of a group of mammals that developed particularly large brains and an ability to grasp objects. It encompasses both apes and monkeys.

Profanity   Using abusive or vulgar language – in modern English-speaking societies such language is usually connected to Anglo-Saxon words for bodily functions; in the past and in some other cultures such words are more likely to be connected to religious concepts, particularly relating to hell and damnation.

Projective work   A way of playing that enables children to express feelings or concerns from their lives by using objects or pretend scenarios.

Proprioception   The ability to recognise movements in the joints that helps to assess where in the world the body is and how agile it moves.

Pro-social   Behaviour or thought that is aimed at building relationships.

Psychodrama   A specific form of drama as therapy developed by Moreno focusing on exploring the roles people play in their lives.

Psychological tools   Describes the ways in which human beings support the building of knowledge, e.g. story telling, writing, possibly even the internet!

Psycholudics   Psyche – of the mind; ludic – relating to play; psycholudics is therefore the study of the mind at play.

Psychosocial dissonance   Psychosocial: relating to both the psychological and the social; dissonance: inharmonious or harsh sound; discord or incongruity (Dictionary.com). Psychosocial dissonance is therefore a description of a feeling that one's society and one's place within it is somehow unbalanced, in particular that some societal factors do not properly synchronise with others, or with one's own ideas of how interactions with others ought to proceed.

Pupil voice   Research undertaken to collect interview data from pupils who have been asked to give honest opinions about their experiences in education, and possibly make suggestions for positive change.

Radical Constructivism   A view of learning whereby individual meaning is constructed from individual experiences within reality.

Rating scales   Used to numerically quantify levels of attainment and/or environments, frequently in the form of 'scores'. In child assessment processes, this can mean comparing a child's actual level of attainment to a notional 'average level of attainment'.

Received curriculum   What children actually learn; what they actually take with them from the classroom and is remembered.

Reciprocal   A return in kind, mutually corresponding (Merriam Webster).

Reconceptualised   To reframe a concept and subsequently attempt to communicate this effectively, usually done within teaching and learning to extend/improve a learner's grasp of the to-be-learned material.

Reflective practitioners   Are teachers who actively evaluate their professional competence and look for ways in which to improve their knowledge and expertise.

Reflexive schemas   How a baby assimilates stimuli in the environment.

Relative   A thing having a relationship to or necessary dependence upon another thing (Merriam Webster).

Representational knowledge   How knowledge is stored and processed in the mind.

Rhythmic play   Patterns of language or movement that are carried out in rhythmic fashion.

Rising 6   A reference to the age of children in an English Year 1 classroom, all of whom will have had their fifth birthday before 1st September, and will have their sixth birthday between 1st September and 31st August during the relevant school year.

Scaffolders   Supporting learning by knowledgeable others, often through adult–child dialogue that is structured by the adult.

Scaffolding   Assistance provided by an adult in context to aid a child's learning.

Schema   A term from Piagetian theory, referring to a collection of concepts or ideas that are highly organised within the brain.

Self-efficacy   Confidence to behave in a certain way – the belief that one has the ability to achieve.

Self-esteem   The way an individual sees aspects of themselves relating to areas such as self-confidence and self-worth.

Self-regulation   Involves the individual child deliberately attending to, thinking about and reflecting on his or her actions.

SEN statement   A statement of special educational needs sets out the help required by a child with learning difficulties that falls outside of the regular provision of the education system.

Sensorimotor play   Play that emphasises movement or physical expression.

Separation   Placing children of particular difficulties and similar needs together, but separated from other children of their age.

Sexual selection   A theory which proposes that the genders evolved slightly different attributes, due to the different roles that they play in parenting.

Sibling   A brother or a sister.

Social constructivists   Researchers who adhere to the notion that meaning is socially constructed from joint perceptions and experiences, through interactions with the wider environment and everything within it.

Social inclusion   Is concerned with reducing the inequality that exists between disadvantaged groups of society and the rest of society.

Social interaction   A dynamic sequence of social actions between individuals or groups who modify their own actions in response to the interaction with others.

Social model of disability   Seeks to reduce the barriers that hinder a disabled person from being an equal participant in society.

Socially constructed   An attribute, behaviour or belief developed through social interaction with others.

Socio-cultural   Of, relating to, or involving a combination of social and cultural factors (Merriam Webster).

Socio-culturalism   Describes the role of the community and culture in underpinning the psychological development of the human being. The theory suggests that psychological development is rooted in the collective ideas and conventions of a specific culture.

Special educational needs   Refers to children with learning difficulties or disabilities that can hinder their ability to learn or to have access to education.

Special needs   Those with a particular need different or extra to those children in the same social situation.

Special needs coordinator (SENCO)   The teacher with overall responsibility for ensuring that the requirements of children with special needs are met and for monitoring childrens' progress.

Special schools   Provide education for children whose needs cannot be catered for in mainstream institutes of education.

Stability   Relationship of the body with the force of gravity to achieve upright posture.

Stakeholders   Those who have an interest in children's education such as parents, teachers and school governors.

SureStart   A government initiative created in 1998, aimed at improving services for children under 5 and their families.

Sustained thinking   The ability of an adult to intuit a child's interest and level of understanding.

Symbolic knowledge   Representing knowledge by ideas and concepts, symbolic knowledge provides an understanding of the interconnectedness of life experiences.

Symbolic play   Play that emphasises imagining and transforming.

Symbolic toys   Small representative objects, e.g. a toy tree or animal.

Synapses   The junction between two neurons over which information is transmitted.

Synaptogenesis   The formation of synapses that occurs throughout a person's life; it is greatest in early brain development.

Taxonomy   An orderly classification of a group of related concepts.

Technical rationalisation   Reducing teaching and learning to specific skills and practices, so it becomes a technical process that teachers can be instructed to use on a national basis.

Testosterone   A hormone produced by the testes that creates male sex characteristics.

The Children's Fund   A government initiative launched in 2000 to improve the lives of disadvantaged children and young people.

Theory of mind   A skill that is shared by only a few species on Earth – the ability to understand what another creature might be thinking, and to change one's own behaviour to account for this – sometimes in order to deceive.

Therapy   A form of intervention where a client and therapist meet with an intention to assist development, reduce identified symptoms or resolve conflicts (Oatley, 1984).

Transferable skills   Marketable job skills can be broken down into five basic categories, or skills sets, that job seekers can use in showing applicable skills from one job/career to the next. These encompass communication (the skilful expression, transmission and interpretation of knowledge and ideas); research and planning (the search for specific knowledge and the ability to conceptualise future needs and solutions for meeting those needs); interpersonal skills; organisation, management and leadership.

Transformation of practice   Describes how things may change in a society when new discoveries are made; e.g., the invention of the microwave created a difference in the way food is prepared in western households; such changes may permeate into the culture and create wider effects, such as a curtailment of 'home cooking'.

Transitional object   A transitional object is created in a child's belief that one object can 'stand for' something else in the sense of a fantasy experience.

Transmission-acquisition model   A model of education that argues that the teacher needs to input knowledge in order for children to acquire knowledge.

Transmission learning   Where the learning experience is inactive and consists of didactic teaching, where information is conveyed to the student and the student is simply expected to remember it.

Treasure baskets   A collection of everyday articles that can be used to stimulate a child or baby's senses.

Tweenies   A phrase used to describe children between the toddler and teenage phase of development.

UN Rights of the Child   An international agreement providing a comprehensive set of rights for all children.

Urbanisation   A process that occurs when a society is industrialised – as factories and large businesses are set up, people start to live in 'urban' areas (towns) rather than 'rural' areas (farms and countryside).

Western people   People from Europe, Australia or North America.

Whatever you want it to be place   An area where children are provided with materials that encourage them to use their imagination and engage in free play.

Zeitgeist   The spirit of the time; general trend of thought or feeling characteristic of a particular period of time (Dictionary.com).

Zone of Proximal Development (ZPD)   From Vygotskian theory, the gap between the learner's current level of development as compared to his/her immediate potential level of development when s/he is aided by an adult or more competent peer.

References

Aasen, W. and Waters, J. (2006) The new curriculum in Wales: a new idea of the child? *Education 3 – 13*. Vol. 34, No. 2, 123–9.

Abbot, L. and Hevey, (2001) Training to work in the early years: developing the climbing frame in G. Pugh (ed.) *Contemporary Issues in the Early Years: Working Collaboratively with Children*. London: Sage.

Abbot, L. and Nutbrown, C. (2001) *Experiencing Reggio Emilia: Implications for Pre-school Provision*. Buckingham: Open University Press.

Abbott, L. and Langston, A. (eds) (2005) *Birth to Three Matters: Supporting the Framework of Effective Practice*. Maidenhead: Open University Press.

Abernethy, D.W. (1968) *Playleadership*. London: National Playing Fields Association.

Acheson, D. (1998) *Independent Inquiry into Inequalities in Health Reports*. London: The Stationery Office.

Ainscow, M. (1995) Education for all: making it happen. *Support for Learning*. Vol. 10, No. 4, 147–54.

Alexander, R. (1995) *Versions of Primary Education*. Buckingham: Open University Press/Routledge.

Alexander, R. (2007) Where there is no vision . . . *FORUM*, Vol. 49, Nos. 1 & 2, 187–200.

Alexander, R. and Hargreaves, L. (2007) *Community Soundings – The Primary Review Regional Witness Sessions*. Cambridge: University of Cambridge Faculty of Education.

Allen of Hurtwood, Lady (1968) *Planning for Play*. London: Thames & Hudson.

Anderson, M. (1998) The meaning of play as a human experience in D. Fromberg and D. Pronin (eds), *Play from Birth to 12 and Beyond: Contexts, Perspectives and Meanings*. New York: Garland, 103–7.

Anning, A. (1991) *The First Years at School*. Buckingham: Open University Press.

Anning, A. (1998) Appropriateness or effectiveness in the early childhood curriculum in the UK: some research evidence. *International Journal of Early Years education*. Vol. 6, No. 3.

Anning, A. (2005) in Moyles, J. (2005) *The Excellence of Play*. Buckingham: Open University Press.

Anning, A., Cullen, J. and Fleer, M. (2004) *Early Childhood Education: Sociology and Culture*. London: Sage.

Anning, A. and Edwards, A. (1999) *Promoting Children's Learning from Birth to Five*. Buckingham: Open University Press.

Anning, A. and Ring, K. (2004) *Making Sense of Young Children's Drawing*s. Maidenhead: Open University Press.

Anzul, M., Ely, Downing, M. and Vinz, R. (1997) *On Writing Qualitative Research*. London: Falmer.

Appiah, K.A. (1994) Identity, authenticity, survival: multicultural societies and social reproduction in A. Gutmann (ed.), *Multiculturalism*. Princeton: Princeton University Press.

Apple, M.W. (2004) *Ideology and Curriculum*, 3rd edn. New York and London: Routledge.

Arnold, C. (2000) *Endangered: Your Child in a Hostile World*. Roberts bridge Plough Publishing.

Arnold, C. (2003) *Observing Harry: Child Development and Training 0–5*. Maidenhead: Open University Press.

Art Therapy in Schools Service www.atiss.co.uk [accessed 19 October 2007].

Athey, C. (1990) *Extending Thought in Young Children: A Parent–Teacher Partnership*. London: Paul Chapman.

Atkins, J. and Bastani, J. (1988) *Listening to Parents: An Approach to the Improvement of Home–school Relations*. London: Croom Helm.

Aubrey, C. (2004) Implementing the foundation stage in reception classes. *British Educational Research Journal*. Vol. 30, No. 5, 633–56.

Aynsley-Green, A. (2003) Children's health: an overview', in C. Horton (ed.) *Working with Children 2004–05*, London: Society Guardian and NCH (formerly known as National Children's Home).

Bailey, R.P. (1999) Play, health and physical development in T. David (ed.), *Young Children Learning*. London: Paul Chapman Publishing.

Ball, C. (1994) *Start Right: The Importance of Early Learning*. London: Royal Society for the Encouragement of the Arts, Manufacture and Commerce.

Ball, D. (2002) *Playgrounds: Risks, Benefits and Choices*. (HSE contract research report 426/2002). Middlesex University. Sudbury, HSE Books.

Ball, S.J. (1999) Labour, learning and the economy: a 'policy sociology' perspective. *Cambridge Journal of Education*. Vol. 23, No. 3, 257–74.

Banich, M.T. (2003) *Neuropsychology: The Neural Bases of Mental Function*. New York: Houghton Mifflin.

Barr, R. and Hayne, H. (2003) It's not what you know, it's who you know: older siblings facilitate imitation during infancy, *International Journal of Early Years Education*. Vol. 11, No. 1, 7–21.

Barton, L. (1998) *The Politics of Special Educational Needs*. Lewes: Falmer.

Bateson, G. (1955) A theory of play and fantasy, *Psychiatric Research Reports*. Vol. 2, 39–51.

Battram, A. (2008) The edge of recalcitrance: playwork in the zone of complexity in F. Brown and C. Taylor (eds), *Foundations of Playwork*. Maidenhead: Open University Press.

Battram, A. and Russell, W. (2002) The edge of recalcitrance: playwork, order and chaos. Paper presented at the *Spirit of Adventure Play is Alive and Kicking*, Play Wales conference, Cardiff: June.

BBC (2007a) Tests 'stopping children playing', available at: <http://news.bbc.co.uk/1/hi/education/6530827. stm> [accessed 25 June 2007].

Beardsley, G. and Harnett, P. (1998) *Exploring Play in the Primary Classrooms*. London: David Fulton Publishers.

Bengtsson, A. (1974) *The Child's Right to Play*. Sheffield: International Playground Association.

Benjamin, J. (1974) *Grounds for Play: An Extension of In Search of Adventure*. London: Bedford Square Press of the National Council for Social Service.

Bennett, N., Desforges, C., Cockburn, A. and Wilkinson, B. (1984) *The Quality of Pupil Learning Experiences*. London: Erlbaum.

Bennett, N. and Kell, J. (1989) *A Good Start? Four year olds in Infant Classrooms*. Oxford: Blackwell.

Bennett, N., Wood, L. and Rogers, S. (1997) *Teaching Through Play: Teachers' Thinking and Classroom Practice*. Buckingham: Open University Press.

Bera (2003) *Good Practice in Educational Research Writing*. Notts: British Educational Research Association.

Berenbaum, S. and Snyder, E. (1995) Early hormonal influences on childhood sex-typed activity and playmate preferences. *Developmental Psychology*, 31, 31–42.

Berk, L. and Winsler, A. (1995) *Scaffolding Children's Learning: Vygotsky and Early Childhood Education*. Washington, DC: National Association for the Education of Young Children.

Berlyne, D. (1960) *Conflict, Arousal and Curiosity*. New York: McGraw-Hill.

Berry, P. (1993) Young children's use of fixed playground equipment. *International Play Journal*. Vol. 1, No. 2, 115–31. London: E. & F.N. Spon.

Bertrand, M. (1976) Rough and tumble play in stumptails in J. Bruner, A. Jolly and K. Sylva (eds), *Play and its Role in Development and Evolution*. New York: Basic Books, 320–27.

Bilton, H. (1998) *Outdoor Play in the Early Years*. London: David Fulton.

Bilton, H. (2002) *Outdoor Play in the Early Years: Management and Innovation*. London: David Fulton.

Bishop, J. and Curtis, M. (2001) *Play Today in the Primary School Playground*. Buckingham: Open University Press.

Bjorklund, D. and Pellegrini, A. (2002) *The Origins of Human Nature*. Washington DC: American Psychological Association.

Bjorkvold, J.-R. (1989) *The Muse Within: Creativity and Communication, Song and Play from Childhood through to Maturity*. New York: HarperCollins.

Black, P. (1999) Assessment, learning theories and testing systems in P. Murphy (ed.), *Learners, Learning and Assessment*. London: OUP.

Blakely, K.S. and Hart, R. (1987) The playground for all children: some lessons in supporting creative play in a public recreation setting for disabled and non-disabled children in *Report from the IPA 10th World Conference, Creativity Through Play*, Stockholm: June.

Blakemore, C. (1998) *The Mind Machine*. London: BBC Books.

Blakemore, C. (2001) What makes a Developmentally Appropriate Early Childhood Curriculum? Lecture at the Royal Society of Arts, 14 February.

Blakemore, C. (2003) Movement is essential to learning. *Journal of Physical Education, Recreation and Dance*. Vol. 74, No. 9, 22–8.

Blatner, A. and Blatner, A. (1988) *The Art of Play*. New York: Springer.

Blenkin, G. and Kelly, A. (1994) *The National Curriculum and Early Learning*. London: Paul Chapman.

Blenkin, G. and Kelly, A.V. (1997) *Principles into Practice in Early Childhood Education*. London: Paul Chapman.

Blurton Jones, N. (1967) An ethological study of some aspects of social behaviour of children in nursery school in D. R. Morris (ed.), *Primate Ethology*. London, Weidenfeld & Nicolson, 347–68.

Booth, T. (2000) Reflection: Tony Booth in P. Clough and J. Corbett, *Theories of Inclusive Education*. London: PCP/Sage.

Boulton, M. (1988) A multi-methodological investigation of rough and tumble play, aggression and social relationships in middle school children. Unpublished PhD thesis, University of Sheffield/6742.

Boulton, M. (1993a) Children's ability to distinguish between playful and aggressive fighting: a developmental perspective. *British Journal of Developmental Psychology*. Vol. 11, 249–63.

Boulton, M. (1993b) A ComChrison of adults and children's abilities to distinguish between aggressive and playful fighting in middle school pupils, *Educational Studies*. Vol. 19, No. 3, 193–204.

Boulton, M. and Smith, P. K. (1989) Issues in the study of children's rough and tumble play in M. Bloch and A. Pellegrini (eds), *The Ecological Context of Children's Play*, Trenton, NJ: Ablex, 57–81.

Bourdieu, P. (1977) *Outline of a Theory of Practice*. Cambridge: Cambridge University Press.

Bourdieu, P. (2001) (translated by Richard Nice) *Masculine Domination*. Cambridge: Polity.

Bower, T., Broughton, J. and Moore, M. (1971) Development of the object concept as manifested in the tracking behaviour of infants between 7 and 20 weeks of age. *Journal of Experimental Child Psychology*. Vol. 23, 182–93.

Bowlby, J. (1953) *Child Care and the Growth of Love*. London: Penguin.

Bowlby, J. (1969) *Attachment and Loss, Vol. 1: Attachment*. London: Hogarth.

Braggio, J.T., Nadler, R. D., Lance, J. and Miseyko, D. (1978) Sex differences in apes and children. *Recent Advances in Primatology*, Vol. 1, 529–32.

Braza, F., Braza, P., Carreras, M., Munoz, J., Sanchez-Martin, J., Azurmendi, A., Sorozaba, A., García, A. and Cardas, J. (2007) Behavioral profiles of different types of social status in preschool children: an observational approach. *Social Behavior and Personality*. Vol. 35, No. 2, 195–212.

Bredo, E. (1994) Reconstructing educational psychology: situated cognition and Deweyan pragmatism. *Educational Psychologist*. Vol. 29, No. 1, 23–35.

British Association of Play Therapists www.bapt.info [accessed 19 October 2007].

Broadhead, P. (2001) Investigating sociability and cooperation in four and five year olds in Reception class settings. *International Journal of Early Years Education*. Vol. 9, No. 1, 24–35.

Broadhead, P. (2003) When children play, what are they thinking? Critical reflection on my own thinking, understanding and learning. Paper presented at the BERA Conference, Heriot Watt: September.

Broadhead, P. (2004) *Early Years Play and Learning: Developing Social Skills and Cooperation*. London: RoutledgeFalmer.

Broadhead, P. (2006a) Inaugural lecture at LeedsMet University, November.

Broadhead, P. (2006b) Developing an understanding of young children's learning through play: the place of observation, interaction and reflection. *British Educational Research Journal*. Vol. 32, No. 2. 123–9.

Broadhead, P. (2007a) Playful learning: time to come out of the shadows, Keynote address at Play Symposium conference, Birmingham: April.

Broadhead, P. (2007b) Working together to support playful learning and transition in J. Moyles (ed.), *Early Years Foundations: Meeting the Challenge*. Maidenhead: Open University Press.

Brock, A. (1999) Into the Enchanted Forest: Language, Drama and Science in the Primary School. Stoke-on-Trent: Trentham Books.

Brock, A. (2004) Eliciting early years educators voices: rhetoric or reality? *TACTYC International Journal of Early Years Education*. Online discussion page: www.tactyc.org.uk.

Brock, A. and Power, M. (2006) Promoting learning in the early years in J. Contch (ed.), *Promoting Learning for Bilingual Pupils 3–11: Opening Doors to Success*. London: Paul Chapman/Sage.

Brock, A. and Rankin, C. (2008) *Communication, Language and Literacy from Birth to Five*. London: Sage.

Bronfenbrenner, U. (1979) *The Ecology of Human Development*. Cambridge, MA: Harvard University Press.

Bronfenbrenner, U. (1989) Ecological systems theory in R. Vasta (ed.), *Annals of Child Development, 6*. Greenwich, CT: JAI, 187–251.

Brooker, L. (2005) Learning to be a child: cultural diversity and early years ideology in Yelland, N. (ed.), *Critical Issues in Early Childhood Education*. Maidenhead: Open University Press.

Brown, F. (2003a) Compound flexibility: the role of playwork in child development in F. Brown (ed.), *Playwork: Theory and Practice*. Buckingham: Open University Press.

Brown, F. (ed.) (2003b) *Playwork: Theory and Practice*. Buckingham: Open University Press.

Brown, F. (ed.) (2003c) Introduction: childhood and play in *Playwork: Theory and Practice*. Buckingham: Open University Press.

Brown, F. (2007) *The Venture: A Case Study of an Adventure Playground*. Cardiff: Play Wales.

Brown, F. (2008) Playwork theory in F. Brown and C. Taylor (eds), *Foundations of Playwork*. Buckingham: Open University Press.

Brown, F. (2008) The fundamentals of playwork in F. Brown and C. Taylor (eds), *Foundations of Playwork*. Maidenhead: Open University Press.

Brown, F. and Webb, S. (2002) Playwork: an attempt at definition. *Play Action*. Spring. Bognor Regis: Fair Play for Children.

Brown, F. and Webb, S. (2005) Children without play, *Journal of Education*. No. 35, March, special issue: Early childhood research in developing contexts.

Bruce, T. (1991) *Time to Play in Early Childhood Education*. London: Hodder & Stoughton.

Bruce, T. (2002) *What to Look for in the Play of Children Birth To Three*. London: Hodder & Stoughton.

Bruce, T. (2004) *Developing Learning in Early Childhood 0–8 Series*. London: Paul Chapman.

Bruce, T. (2005) *Early Childhood Education*, 3rd edn. Abingdon: Hodder Arnold.

Bruce, T. (2006) *Early Childhood Education: A Guide for Students*. London: Sage.

Bruer, J.T. (1991) The brain and child development: time for some critical thinking. *Public Health Reports*. Vol. 113, No. 5, 388–97.

Brundrett, M. (2006) Educational research and its implications for educational practice. *Education 3–13*, Vol. 34, No. 3, 99–101.

Bruner, J. (1966) *Towards a Theory of Instruction*. Cambridge, MA: Harvard University Press.

Bruner, J. (1976) Nature and uses of immaturity in J.S. Bruner, A. Jolly and K. Sylva (eds), *Play: Its Role in Development and Evolution*. New York: Basic Books, 28–64.

Bruner, J. (1983) *Child's Talk: Learning to Use Language*. New York: Norton.

Bruner, J. (1986) *Actual Minds, Possible Worlds*. Cambridge, MA: Harvard University Press.

Bruner, J. (1996a) Culture, mind, and education in B. Moon and P. Murphy *Curriculum in Context*. London: Paul Chapman.

Bruner, J. (1996b) *The Culture of Education*. New York: Harvard University Press.

Bruner, J.S. (1962) *On Knowing: Essays for the Left Hand*. Cambridge, MA: Harvard University Press.

Bruner J.S. (1999) Culture, mind and education in B. Moon and P. Murphy, *Curriculum in Context*. London Paul Chapman.

Bruner, J. S., Jolly, A. and Sylva, K. (eds) (1976) *Play: Its Role in Development and Evolution*. Harmondsworth: Penguin.

Bruner, J. S., Jolly, A. and Sylva, K. (eds) (1976) *Play: Its Role in Development and Evolution*. New York: Basic Books.

Budilovsky, J. and Adamson, E. (2006) *The Complete Idiot's Guide to Yoga*: New York: Alpha.

Burgess, H. (2004) The primary strategy: a chance for a 'whole' curriculum. *Education 3–13*. Vol. 32, No. 2, 10–17.

Burgess, H. and Miller, L. (2004) Editorial curriculum issues in the primary and early years. *Education 3–13*,

Burghardt, G.M. (2005) *The Genesis of Animal Play: Testing the Limits*. London: MIT Press.

Calaprice, A. (1966) *The Expandable Quotable Einstein*. Princeton, NJ: Princeton University Press.

Candland, D.K. (1993) *Feral Children and Clever Animals: Reflections on Human Nature*. Oxford: Oxford University Press.

Carnegie Task Force Report (1994) *Starting Points: Meeting the Needs of Our Youngest Children*. New York: Carnegie Corporation.

Carpenter, B. (ed.) (1997) *Families in Context: Emerging Trends in Family Support and Early Intervention*. London: David Fulton.

Carr, M. (1999) Learning and Teaching Stories: New Approaches to assessment and Evaluation, available at http://www.aare.edu.au/99pap/pod99298.htm [accessed 5 July 2005].

Carr, M. (2001) A sociocultural approach to learning orientation in an early childhood setting. *International Journal of Qualitative Studies in Education*. Vol. 14, Issue 4 , 525–42.

Carroll, J. (2004) *Literary Darwinism*. London: Routledge.

Casey, T. (2004) *The Play Inclusive Research Report.* Edinburgh: The Yard.

Casey, T. (2005) *Inclusive Play: Practical Strategies for Working with Children aged 3 to 8.* London: Paul Chapman.

Cattanach, A. (1994) The developmental model in dramatherapy in S. Jennings, A. Cattanach, S. Mitchell, A. Chesner, and B. Meldrum (eds), *The Handbook of Dramatherapy.* London: Routledge.

Chafel, J.A. (2003) Socially constructing concepts of self and other through Play. [1] *International Journal of Early Years Education.* Vol. 11, No. 3, 213–22.

Charlesworth, W. and Dzur, C. (1987) Gender Com-Chrisons of pre-schoolers' behavior and resource utilization in group problem solving. *Child Development.* Vol. 58, 191–200.

Chaucer, G. (c.1388) *The Canterbury Tales,* available at: http://www.bibliomania.com/0/2/14/24/frameset. html [accessed on 10 April 2008].

Chiang, L. (1985) *Developmental Differences in Children's Use of Play Materials.* Austin, TX: University of Texas Press.

Children's Society (2007a) Reflections on childhood, available at: <http://www.childrenssociety.org.uk/ NR/rdonlyres/DA92712B-5C3F-47C2-87E6-51B8F0C11FFE/0/ReflectionsonChildhoodFriendship. pdf> [accessed 10 September 2007].

Children's Society (2007b) Reflections on childhood: The Good Childhood: Evidence Summary one: Friends, available at: <http://www.childrenssociety. org.uk> [accessed 10 September 2007].

Chilton, T. (2003) Adventure playgrounds in the twenty-first century in F. Brown (ed.), *Playwork: Theory and Practice.* Buckingham: Open University Press.

Christie, J. F. and Wardle, F. (1992) How much time is needed for play? *Young Children.* Vol. 47, No. 3, 28–32.

City & Guilds (2004) The transient 21st century workforce (25 February), available at http://www. cityandguilds.com/cps/rde/xchg/SID-204447A6-17BA8A7F/cgonline/hs.xsl/1395.html.

Clancy, M.E. (2006) *Active Bodies, Active Brains: Building Thinking Skills through Physical Activity.* Champaign, IL: Human Kinetics.

Claxton, G. (1997) *Hare Brain, Tortoise Mind.* London: Fourth Estate.

Clough, P. and Corbett, J. (2000) *Theories of Inclusive Education.* London: Paul Chapman.

Cohen, D. and Stern, V. (1983) *Observing and Recording the Behavior of Young Children.* New York: Teachers College Press.

Cohen, L., Manion, L. and Morrison, K. (2004) *A Guide to Teaching Practice,* 5th edn. London: Routledge-Falmer.

Coie, J., Dodge, K. and Coppotelli, H. (1982) Dimensions and types of social status: a cross age perspective. *Developmental Psychology.* Vol. 8, No. 4, 557–70.

Coie, J. and Kupersmidt, J. (1983) A behavioural analysis of emerging social status in boys' groups. *Child Development.* Vol. 54, 1400–16.

Collishaw, S., Maughan, B., Goodman, R. and Pickles, A. (2004) Time trends in adolescent mental health. *Journal of Child Psychology and Psychiatry.* Vol. 45, No. 8, 1350–62.

Conteh, J. (2006) *Promoting Learning for Bilingual Pupils 3–11.* London: Paul Chapman.

Conway, M. and Farley, T. (2001) *Quality in Play: Quality Assurance for Children's Play Providers.* London: London Play.

Cook, R.E., Tessier, A. and Klein, M.D. (2000) *Adapting Early Childhood Curricula for Children in Inclusive Settings.* Englewood Cliffs, NJ: Merrill.

Cooper, H. (2004) *Exploring Time and Place Through Play: Foundation Stage – Key Stage 1.* London: David Fulton.

Corbett, J. (1998) *Special Educational Needs in the Twentieth Century: A Cultural Analysis.* London: Cassell.

Corbett, J. (2001) Teaching approaches which support inclusive education: a connective pedagogy. *British Journal of Special Education.* Vol. 28, No. 2, 55–60.

Corker, M. (2002) Profile: Mairian Corker in P. Clough and J. Corbett, *Theories of Inclusive Education.* London: PCP/Sage.

Corsaro, W. (1997) *The Sociology of Childhood.* Thousand Oaks, CA: Pine Forge Press.

Costabile, A. (1983) Five expressive motor patterns of rough and tumble behaviour in pre-school children. *Monitore Zoologico Italiano:* 17, 187.

Costabile, A., Matheson, P. and Aston, J. (1991) A cross national ComChrison of how children distinguish between serious and play fighting. *Developmental Psychology.* Vol. 7, 881–7.

Cowie, B. and Carr, M. (2004) The consequences of socio-cultural assessment in A. Anning, J. Cullen and M. Fleer (eds), *Early Childhood Education: Society and Culture.* London: Sage.

Craft, A. (2000) *Creativity Across the Primary Curriculum: Framing and Developing Practice.* London: Routledge.

Craft, A. (2002) *Creativity and Early Years Education.* London: Continuum.

Cranwell, K. (2003) Towards playwork: an historical introduction to children's out-of-school play organisations in London (1860–1940) in F. Brown (ed.), *Playwork: Theory and Practice.* Buckingham: Open University Press.

Creasey, G.L., Jarvis, P. A. and Berk, L. E. (1998) Play and social competence in O.N. Saracho and B. Spodek (eds), *Multiple Perspectives on Play in Early Childhood Education*. Albany, NY: SUNY Press.

Cresswell, H. (1995) *The Gift from Winklesea*. London: Young Puffin Books.

Crick, N. (1996) The role of overt aggression, relational aggression and pro-social behaviour in the prediction of children's future social adjustment. *Child Development*. Vol. 67, 2317–27.

Crystal, D. (1988) *Listen to Your Child: A Parent's Guide to Children's Language Development*. Harmondsworth: Penguin.

Curtis, A. and O'Hagan, M. (2003) *Care and Education in Early Childhood: A Student's Guide to Theory and Practice*. London: Routledge.

Dadds, M. (2001) The politics of pedagogy. *Teachers and Teaching: Theory and Practice*, Vol. 7, No. 1, 44–58.

Damasio, A.R. (1994) *Descartes' Error: Emotion, Reason and the Human Brain*. New York: Grosset-Putnam.

Daniels, H. (2001) *Vygotsky and Pedagogy*. London: RoutledgeFalmer.

Daniels, H. and Garner, P. (eds) (1999) *Inclusive Education: World Yearbook of Education*. London: Kogan Page.

Darwin, C. (1859, reprinted 1979) *Origin of Species*. London: Random House.

David, T. (1999) *Teaching Young Children*. London: Paul Chapman.

Davies, M. (2003) *Movement and Dance in Early Childhood*. London: Paul Chapman.

Davy, A. (2008) Exploring rhythm in playwork in F. Brown and Taylor, C. (eds) (2008), *Foundations of Playwork*. Buckingham: Open University Press.

DCSF (2007a) *Early Years Foundation Stage Statutory Framework and Guidance*. London: HMSO.

DCSF (2007b) *Early Years Foundation Stage Statutory Framework and Guidance*. Nottingham: DfES.

DCSF (2007c) *Every Child Matters and Standards for Daycare*. Nottingham: DfES.

DCSF (2007d) The Children's Plan, available at: <http://www.dfes.gov.uk/publications/childrensplan/?cid=childrens_plan&type=sponsoredsearch&gclid=COOa0LzKsJACFQvkXgodIkcGqQ> Accessed on 11th December 2007.

DCSF (2007e) Special Educational Needs in England: Statistical First Releases, January 2007. Available at www.dfes.gov.uk/rsgateway/DBSFR/500732/index.shltml.

De Bono, E. (1973) *Lateral Thinking: Creativity Step by Step*. New York: Harper & Row.

DeCasper A. and Fifer W. (1980) Of human bonding: new borns prefer their mothers' voices, *Science* 208, pp.1174–1176.

DES (1978) *Special Educational needs: Report of the Committee of Enquiry into the Handicapped Children and Young People* (The Warnock Report). London: HMSO.

DES (1981) *Education Act*. London: HMSO.

DES (1982) *Mathematics Counts Report of the Committee of Inquiry into the Teaching of Mathematics in Schools* (The Cockroft Report). London: HMSO.

DES (1990) *Starting with Quality: The Report of the Committee of Inquiry into the Quality of Educational Experience Offered to 3 and 4 year olds*. Norwich: The Stationary Office.

DfEE (1988) *Education Reform Act*. London: HMSO.

DfEE (1989) *The National Curriculum*. London: HMSO.

DfEE (1994) *Code of Practice on the Identification and Assessment of Special Educational Needs*. London: HMSO.

DfEE (1997) *Excellence for All Children: Meeting Special Educational Needs*. London: DfEE.

DfEE (1999) *The National Numeracy Strategy: A Framework for Teaching Mathematics from reception to year 6*. London: DfEE.

DfEE (1999) *The National Curriculum: Handbook for Primary Teachers in England*. London: DfEE.

DfES (1996) *The Standards Site: Early Years Foundation Stage*, available from: <http://www.standards.dfes.gov.uk/primary/faqs/foundation_stage/eyfs/?subject=S_953489> [accessed on 25th October 2006].

DfES (1999) *All Our Futures: Creativity, Culture and Education*. The National Advisory Committee on Creative and Cultural Education (NAECCE) Report. London: HMSO.

DfES (2000) *The National Curriculum: A Handbook for Primary Teachers in England*. London: DfEE.

DfES (2001a) *National Standards for Under Eights Day Care and Childminding*. London: DfES.

DfES (2001b) *Special Educational Needs Code of Practice*. Nottingham: DFES.

DfES (2002a) *Birth To Three Matters* framework. London: DfES Publications.

DfES (2002b) *Inclusive Schooling: Children with Special Educational Needs*. London: HMSO.

DfES (2002c) Siraj-Blatchford, I., Sylva, K., Muttock, S., Gilden, R., Bell, D. *Researching effective pedagogy in the early years*. Research Report No RR356. Institute of Education.

DfES (2003a) *Birth to Three Matters*. Nottingham: DfES.

DfES (2003b) *Excellence and Enjoyment: A strategy for primary schools*. Nottingham: DfES Publications.

DfES (2003c) *Every Child Matters*. London: HMSO.

DfES (2003d) *The Primary National Strategy*. Nottingham: DfES.

DfES (2004a) *Every Child Matters. Change for Children.* London: HMSO.

DfES (2004b) *The Five Year Strategy for Children and Learners.* London: HMSO.

DfES (2004c) *The Ten Year Strategy for Children and Learners.* London: HMSO.

DfES (2005) *Key Elements of Effective Practice.* London: DfES.

DfES (2006a) *The Primary National Strategy: Primary Framework for Literacy and Numeracy.* Nottingham: DfES.

DfES (2006b) *2020 Vision: Report of the Teaching and Learning in 2020 Review Group.* Nottingham: DfES.

DfES (2007a) *Special Educational Needs in England: 2007. A Summary of the DFES Statistical First Release.* June. Ref. SFR 20/2007.

DfES (2007b) *The Early Years Foundation Stage. Setting the Standards for Learning, Development and Care for children from birth to five.* Nottingham: DfES.

DfES (2007c) *The Report of the Teaching and Learning in 2020 Review.* Nottingham: DfES.

DfES and Department for Health (2002) *Together from the Start: Practical Guidance for Professionals Working with Disabled Children (Birth to 2) and their Families.* London: DfES.

DfES Standards, Early Years Foundation Stage website: http://www.standards.dfes.gov.uk/primary/faqs/foundation_stage/eyfs/?subject=S_953489.

DfES/SureStart Unit (2002) *Birth to Three Matters: A Framework to Support Children in their Earliest Years.* London: DfES.

Department of Health (1989) The Children Act 1987: Guidance and Regulations. London HMSO.

Department of Health (1991) *The Children Act Guidance and Regulations. Vol 2: Family Support, Daycare and Educational Provision for Young Children.* London: HMSO.

Department of Health and Social Security (2001) Disability Discrimination Act. London: HMSO.

Department of Heritage (2001) *Children's National Service Framework.* London: DoH.

Dickens, C (1863) *Hard Times.* New York: Sheldon & Co.

Dishman, R.K. (1986) Mental health in V. Seefeldt (ed.), *Physical Activity and Well-being.* Retson, VA: AAHPERD.

Dixon, J. and Day, S. (2004) Secret places: 'You're too big to come in here!' in H. Cooper, *Exploring Time and Place Through Play: Foundation Stage – Key Stage 1.* London: Cassell.

Dockett, S. and Perry, B. (2005) Starting school in Australia is 'a bit safer, a lot easier and more relaxing': issues for families and children from culturally and linguistically diverse backgrounds. *Early Years: An International Journal of Research and Development.* Vol. 25, No. 3, 271– 281.

Dodge, K., Coie, J., Pettit, G. and Price, J. (1990) Peer status and aggression in boys' groups: developmental and contextual analyses. *Child Development.* Vol. 61, 1289–1309.

Doherty, J. and Bailey, R.P. (2003) *Supporting Physical Development and Physical Education in the Early Years.* Buckingham: Open University Press.

Doherty, J. (2008) *Right from the Start: An Introduction to Child Development.* Harlow: Pearson Education.

Donaldson, M. (1978) *Children's Minds.* London: Flamingo/Fontana Paperbacks.

Dowling, M. (2000) *Young Children's Personal, Social and Emotional Development.* London: Paul Chapman.

Drake, J. (2001) *Planning Children's Play and Learning in the Foundation Stage.* London: David Fulton.

Drifte, C. (2005) *A Manual for the Early Years SENCO.* London: Paul Chapman.

Duffy, B. (1998) *Supporting Creativity and Imagination in the Early Years.* Buckingham: Open University Press.

Dunn, J. (1983) Sibling relationships in early childhood. *Child Development.* 54, 787–811.

Dunn, J. (2004) *Children's Friendships: The Beginning of Intimacy.* Oxford: Blackwell.

Dunn, J. and Kendrick, C. (1982) *Siblings: Love, Envy and Understanding.* Cambridge, MA: Harvard University Press.

Early Childhood Forum (2003) *Policy Statement: Definition of Inclusion.* London: HMSO.

Edgington, M. (2004) *The Foundation Stage Teacher in Action.* London: Paul Chapman.

Edwards, C. (2002) Three approaches from Europe: Waldorf, Montessori, and Reggio Emilia. *Contemporary Issues in Early Childhood.* Vol. 4, No. 1.

Edwards, C., Ghandini, L. and Foreman, G. (eds) (1993) *The Hundred Languages of Children: The Reggio Emilia Approach to Early Childhood Education.* Norwood, NJ: Ablex.

Einon, D.F., Morgan, M.J. and Kibbler, C.C. (1978) Brief period of socialisation and later behaviour in the rat. *Developmental Psychobiology.* Vol. 11, No. 3.

Eliot, L. (1999) *Early Intelligence: How the Brain and Mind Develop in the First Five Years of Life.* London: Penguin.

Elliott, J. (2005) *Using Narrative in Social Research, Qualitative and Quantitative Approaches.* London: Sage.

Ellis, M. (1973) *Why People Play.* Englewood Cliffs NJ: Prentice Hall.

Else, P. and Sturrock, G. (1998) The playground as therapeutic space: playwork as healing. *Proceedings of the IPA/USA Triennial National Conference, Play in a Changing Society: Research, Design, Application,* Colorado.

Ely, M. (1991) *Doing Qualitative Research: Circles within Circles.* London: Falmer.

Erikson, E. (1963) *Childhood and Society.* Harmondsworth: Penguin.

Evans, J. (2000) From Warnock to the market place: the development of Special Education Policy in England and Wales: 1978–1998, in C. Brock and R. Griffin (eds), *International Perspectives on Special Educational Needs.* Suffolk: John Catt Educational Limited.

Evans, K. and Dubowski, J. (2001) *Art Therapy with Children on the Autistic Spectrum.* London: Jessica Kingsley.

Evreinov, N. (1927) The Theatre in Life. New York: Harrap.

Every Disabled Child Matters. National Children's Bureau. London. www.edcm.org.uh

Farrell, M. (2005) *Key Issues in Special Education: Raising Standards of Pupil's Attainment and Achievement.* Abingdon: Routledge.

Fisher, J. (1996) *Starting from the Child.* Buckingham: Open University Press.

Fisher, J. (2005) *The Foundations of Learning.* Buckingham: Open University Press.

Fisher, R. (2004) What is creativity? In R. Fisher and M. Williams, *Unlocking Literacy: A Guide for Teachers.* London: Routledge.

Fisher, R. (2005) *Teaching Children to Think,* 2nd edn. Cheltenham: Nelson Thornes.

Fisher, K. (2008) Playwork in the early years: working in a parallel profession in F. Brown and C. Taylor (eds), *Foundations of Playwork.* Buckingham: Open University Press.

Fisher, R. and Williams, M. (2004) *Unlocking Literacy: A Guide for Teachers.* London: Routledge.

Fleer, M. (2003) Early childhood education as an evolving 'community of practice' or as lived 'social reproduction': researching the 'taken-for-granted'. *Contemporary Issues in Early Childhood.* Vol. 4, No. 1, 64–79.

Fleer, M., Anning, A. and Cullen, J. (2004) A framework for conceptualising early childhood education in A. Anning, J. Cullen and M. Fleer (eds), *Early childhood education: Society and Culture.* London: Sage.

Flewitt, R. (2006) Using video to investigate preschool interaction: educational research assumptions and methodological practices. *Visual Communication.* Vol. 5, No. 1, 25–50.

Flynn, E. (2004) Understanding minds in J. Oates and A. Grayson (eds), *Cognitive and Language Development in Children.* Oxford: Blackwell, 231–58.

Foot, H., Howe, C., Cheyne, B., Terras, M. and Rattray, C. (2002) Parental participation in pre-school provision. *International Journal of Early Years Education.* Vol. 10, No. 15–19.

Forbes, R. (2004) *Beginning to Play: Young Children from Birth to Three.* Maidenhead: Open University Press.

Frean, A. (2007) Stealth curriculum 'is threat to all toddlers' available at <http://www.timesonline.co.uk/tol/life_and_style/education/article2971600.ece>.

Frederickson, N. and Cline, T. (2002) *Special Education Needs: Inclusion and Diversity. A Textbook.* Buckingham: Open University Press.

Freud, S. (1974) *The Standard Edition of the Complete Psychological Works of Sigmund Freud,* 24 volumes, translated from the German under the general editorship of James Strachey, in collaboration with Anna Freud; assisted by Alix Strachey and Alan Tyson. London: Hogarth Press, Institute of Psychoanalysis.

Fromberg, D.P. (2002) *Play and Meaning in Early Childhood Education.* Boston, MA: Allyn & Bacon.

Frost, J. and Woods, I.C. (2006) Perspectives on play and playgrounds in D.P. Fromberg and D. Bergen, *Play From Birth to Twelve: Contexts, Perspectives and Meanings,* 2nd edn. Abingdon: Routledge.

Fry, D. (1987) Differences between play fighting and serious fighting among Zapotec children. *Ethology and Sociobiology.* Vol. 8, 285–306.

Fumoto, H., Hargreaves, D. and Maxwell, S. (2004) The concept of teaching: a reappraisal. *Early Years: An International Journal of Research and Development.* Vol. 24, No. 2, 179–91.

Gallahue, D.L. and Ozmun, J. (1982) *Understanding Motor Development: Infants, Children, Adolescents, Adults.* Boston, MA: WCB/McGraw-Hill.

Gallahue, D.L. and Ozmun, J.C. (1998) *Understanding Motor Development: Infants, Children, Adolescents, Adults.* Boston, MA: WCB/McGraw-Hill.

Gammage, P. (2006) Early childhood education and care: politics, policies and possibilities. *Early Years: An International Journal of Research and Development.* Vol. 26, No. 3, 235–48.

Gardner, H. (1993) *Multiple Intelligences: The Theory in Practice.* New York: Basic Books.

Gardner, H. (1999) *Intelligence Reframed: Multiple Intelligences for the 21st century.* New York: Basic Books.

Garrick, R. and Chilvers, D. (2003) Foundation stage units: a response to the foundation stage. Paper presented at the British Educational Research Association Conference, Edinburgh. 11–13 September.

Garvey, C. (1977) *Play*. London: Fontana/Open.

Garvey, C. (1990) *Play*, 2nd edn. Cambridge, MA: Harvard University Press.

Garvey, C. (1991) *Play*. London: Fontana.

Geary, D., Vigil, J. and Byrd-Craven, J. (2004) Evolution of human mate choice. *Journal of Sex Research*. Vol. 41, No. 1, 27–43.

Gerhardt, L. (1973) *Moving and Knowing: The Young Child Orients Himself in Space*. Englewood Cliffs, NJ: Prentice-Hall.

Gibran, K. (1923) *The Prophet*, available at: http://leb.net/~mira/works/prophet/prophet4.html. [accessed 23 December 2007].

Gil, E. and Drewes, A.A. (eds) (2004) *Cultural Issues in Play Therapy*. London: Routledge.

Gill, T. (2007) *No Fear: Growing Up in a Risk Averse Society*. London: Calouste Gulbenkian Foundation.

Gilligan, C. (1993) *In a Different Voice*, 2nd edn. Cambridge, MA: Harvard University Press.

Gitlin-Weiner, K. (1998) Clinical perspectives on play in D. Fromberg and D. Bergin, *Play from Birth to Twelve and Beyond*. New York: Garland, 77–92.

Gladwin, M. (2005) Participants' perceptions of risk in play in middle childhood. Unpublished MA dissertation, Leeds Metropolitan University.

Glaser, R. (1999) Expert knowledge and processes of thinking in R. McCormick and C. Paechter, *Learning and Knowledge*. London: Paul Chapman.

Goddard, S. (2002) *Reflexes, Learning and Behaviour: A Window into the Child's Mind*. Eugene, OR: Fern Ridge Press.

Golding, W. (1954) *Lord of the Flies*. New York: Capricorn Books.

Goldschmied, E. (1987) *Infants at Work* (training video). London: National Children's Bureau.

Goldschmied, E. and Hughes, A. (1992) *Heuristic Play with Objects: Children of 12–20 Months Exploring Everyday Objects* (VHS video). London: National Children's Bureau.

Goldschmied, E. and Jackson, S. (1994; 2nd edn 2004). *People Under Three: Young Children in Day Care*. London: Routledge.

Goncu, A. (1993) Development of intersubjectivity in social pretend play in M. Woodhead, D. Faulkner and K. Littleton (eds) (1998), *Cultural Worlds of Early Childhood*. London: Routledge.

Goodman, N. (1984) *Of Mind and Other Matters*. Cambridge, MA: Harvard University Press.

Gopnik, A., Meltzoff, A. and Kuhl, P. (1999) *How Babies Think: The Science of Childhood*. London: Weidenfeld & Nicolson.

Gottlieb, G. (1996) Commentary: a systems view of psychobiological development in D. Magnusson (ed.), *The Lifespan Development of Individuals: Behavioural, Neurobiological, and Psychosocial Perspectives. A synthesis*. Cambridge: Cambridge University Press.

Greenland, P. (2006) Physical development in T. Bruce (ed.), *Early Childhood: A Guide for Students*. London: Sage.

Greeno, J.G., Pearson, P.D. and Schoenfeld, A.H. (1999) Achievement and theories of knowing and learning in R. McCormick and C. Paechter, *Learning and Knowledge*. London: Paul Chapman.

Grenfell, M. and James, D. (1998) *Bourdieu and Education: Acts of Practical Theory*. London: Falmer.

Groos, K. (1896) *The Play of Animals*. New York: D. Appleton and Co.

Groos, K. (1901) *The Play of Man*. London: Heinemann.

Gruber, J.J. (1986) Physical activity and self-esteem development in children: a meta-analysis in G.A. Stull and H.M. Eckert (eds), *Effects of Physical Activity on Children*. Champaign, IL: Human Kinetics.

Gubrium, J. and Holstein, J. (eds) (2002) *Handbook of Interview Research: Context and Method*. Thousand Oaks, CA: Sage Publications Ltd.

Guha, M. (1987) Play in school in G. Blenkin and A.V. Kelly (1997) *Principles into Practice in Early Childhood Education*. London: Paul Chapman.

Haeckel, E. (1901) *The Riddle of the Universe at the Close of the Nineteenth Century*, translated by Joseph McCabe. London: Watts & Co.

Hall, G.S. (1920) *Youth*. New York: D. Appleton.

Hall, G.S. (1904) *Adolescence: Its Psychology and its relations to Physiology, Anthropology, Sociology, Sex, Crime, Religion and Education. Vol. 1*. New York: Appleton.

Hall, N. and Abbott, L. (1991) *Play in the Primary Curriculum*. London: Hodder & Stoughton.

Halldén, G. (1991) The child as project and the child as being: parents' ideas as a frame of reference. *Children and Society*. Vol. 5, No. 4, 334–46.

Hanline, M.F. and Fox, L. (1993) Learning within the context of play: providing typical early childhood experiences for children with severe disabilities. *Journal of the Association for Persons with Severe Handicaps*. Vol. 20, No. 1, 23–31.

Hannaford, C. (1995) *Smart Moves: Why Learning is Not all in Your Head*. Arlington, NJ: Great Ocean Publishers.

Harlow, H.K. and Harlow, M.K. (1965) The affectional systems in A.M. Schrier, H.F. Harlow and F. Stollnitz (eds), *Behaviour of Non Human Primates Vol. 2*. London: Academic Press, 319–42.

Harlow, H.F. and Suomi, S.J. (1971) Social recovery by isolation-reared monkeys in *Proceedings National Academy of Sciences USA*. Vol. 68, No.7, 1534–8.

Harms, T., Clifford, R.M. and Cryer, D. (1998) *Early Childhood Environment Rating Scale-Revised.* New York: Teachers College Press.

Harris, M. and Butterworth, G. (2002) *Developmental Psychology.* London: Psychology Press.

Hart, R. (1995) The right to play and children's participation in H. Shier (ed.), *Article 31 Action Pack: Children's Rights and Children's Play.* Birmingham: Play Train.

Heathcote, D. and Bolton, G. (1995) *Drama for Learning: Dorothy Heathcote's Mantle of the Expert Approach to Learning.* Oxford: Heinemann.

Hendy, L. and Toon, L. (2001) *Supporting Drama and Imaginative Play in the Early Years.* Buckingham: Open University Press.

Hendy, L. and Whitebread, D. (2000) Interpretations of independent learning in the early years. *International Journal of Early Years Education.* Vol. 8, No. 3, 243–52.

Herbert, E. (1998) Included from the start? Managing early years settings for all in P. Clough (ed.), *Managing Inclusive Education: From Policy to Experience.* London: PCP/Sage.

Hestenes, L.L. and Carroll, D.E. (2000) The play interactions of young children with and without difficulties: individual and environmental influences. *Early Childhood Education Journal.* Vol. 29, No. 2, 95–100.

High/Scope (2007) *All About High/Scope,* available at: <http://www.highscope.org/About/allabout.htm> [accessed on 11 February 2007].

Higson-Smith, C., Mulder, B. and Zondi, N. (2006) *Report on the Firemaker Project: A Formative and Summative Evaluation.* Johannesburg: South African Institute for Traumatic Stress.

Hines, M., Golombok, S., Rust, J., Johnston, K. and Golding, J. (2002) Testosterone during pregnancy and gender role behaviour of pre-school children: a longitudinal population study. *Child Development.* Vol. 73, No. 6, 1678–87.

HM Treasury (2003) *Every Child Matters* (the Green Paper). London: The Stationery Office.

HM Treasury (2004) *Choice for Parents, the Best Start for Children: A Ten Year Strategy for Childcare.* London: HMSO.

Hodgson, J. (2001) *Mastering Movement.* London: Methuen.

Hohmann, M., Banet, B. and Weikart, D. (1979) *Young Children in Action.* London: High Scope/Scope Press.

Holland, P. (2003) *We Don't Play with Guns Here.* Maidenhead: Open University Press.

Holland, R. (1997) What's it all about? How introducing heuristic play has affected provision for the under-threes in one day nursery in L. Abbott and H. Moyles (eds), *Working with the Under-3s: Responding to Children's Needs.* London: Routledge.

Horton, C. (2003) *Working With Children 2004-05.* London: Society Guardian and NCH (formerly known as National Children's Home).

House of Commons (2000) *Select Committee for Education and Employment: Minutes of Evidence.* www.publications.parliament.uk. January 2001.

Hrdy, S.B. (1999) *Mother Nature: Natural Selection and the Female of the Species.* London: Chatto and Windus.

Hughes, A.M. (2006) *Developing Play for the Under 3s: The Treasure Basket and Heuristic Play.* London: David Fulton.

Hughes, B. (1975) *Notes for Adventure Playworkers.* London: Children and Youth Action Group.

Hughes, B. (1990) Why is play a fundamental right of the child? *On Research and Study of Play.* Report of the IPA 11th World Conference, Tokyo: June.

Hughes, B. (1996) *Play Environments: A Question of Quality.* London: Playlink.

Hughes, B. (2000) A dark and evil cul-de-sac: has children's play in urban Belfast been adulterated by the Troubles? Unpublished MA dissertation, Cambridge: Anglia Polytechnic University.

Hughes, B. (2001) *Evolutionary Playwork and Reflective Analytic Practice.* London: Routledge.

Hughes, B. (2002) *A Playworker's Taxonomy of Play Types,* 2nd edn. London: Playlink.

Hughes, B. (2003) Play deprivation, play bias and playwork practice in F. Brown (ed.), *Playwork: Theory and Practice.* Buckingham: Open University Press.

Hughes, B. (2006) *Play Types Speculations and Possibilities.* London: The London Centre for Playwork Education and Training.

Hull, K., Goldhaber, J. and Capone, A. (2002) *Opening Doors: An Introduction to Inclusive Early Childhood Education.* Boston: Houghton Mifflin Company.

Humphreys, A. and Smith, P.K. (1987) Rough and tumble, friendship and dominance in schoolchildren: evidence for continuity and change with age. *Child Development.* Vol. 58, 201–12.

Hutchin, V. (1996) *Right from the Start: Effective Planning and Assessment in the Early Years.* London: Hodder and Stoughton.

Hutt, C. (1979) Play in the under-fives: form development and function in J. G. Howells (ed.), *Modern Perspectives in the Psychiatry of Infancy.* New York: Brunner/Marcel.

Hutt, S. J., Tyler, C., Hutt, C. and Christopherson, H. (1989) *Play, Exploration and Learning.* London: Routledge.

Jackson, D. and Tasker, R. (2004) *Professional Learning Communities.* Networked Learning Communities. National Schools Centre for Learning.

James, O. (2003) Children before cash, The *Guardian*, 17 May, available at: <www.guardian.co.uk> [accessed on 29 December 2003].

Jarvis, P. (2005) The role of rough and tumble play in children's social and gender role development in the early years of primary school. Unpublished PhD thesis, Leeds Metropolitan University.

Jarvis, P. (2006) Rough and tumble play: lessons in life. *Evolutionary Psychology*. Vol. 4, 268–86; 330–46.

Jarvis, P. (2007) Monsters, magic and Mr Psycho: a biocultural approach to rough and tumble play in the early years of primary school. *Early Years: An International Journal of Research and Development*. Vol. 27, No. 2, 171–88.

Jennings, S. (1992) *Dramatherapy: Theory and Practice for Teachers and Clinicians*. London: Routledge.

Jensen, E. (2000) *Learning with the Body in Mind*. San Diego, CA: The Brain Store, Inc.

JNCTP (2002) *The New JNCTP Charter for Playwork Education, Training and Qualifications,* adopted at the Annual General Meeting held on 26 November 2002, Derby.

Johnson, C. (2004) Creative drama: thinking from within in R. Fisher and M. Williams, *Unlocking Literacy: A Guide for Teachers*. London: Routledge.

Johnson, J., Christie, J. and Yawkey, T. (1987) *Play and Early Childhood Development*. Illinois: Scott Foresman and Co.

Jones, P. (1996) *Drama as Therapy*, 1st edn. London: Routledge.

Jones, P. (2005) *The Arts Therapies*. London: Routledge.

Jones, P. (2007) *Drama as Therapy*, 2nd edn. London: Routledge.

Jones, L., Holmes, R. and Powell, J. (eds) (2006) *Early Childhood Studies: A Multiprofessional Perspective*. Maidenhead: Open University Press.

Jordan, B. (2004) Scaffolding learning and co-constructing understandings in A. Anning, J. Cullen and M. Fleer (eds), *Early Childhood Education: Society and Culture*. London: Sage.

Jordan, E. (1995) Fighting boys and fantasy play: the construction of masculinity in the early years of school. *Gender and Education*. Vol. 7, No. 1, 69–87.

Jupp, V. (ed.) *The Sage Dictionary of Social Research Methods*. London: Sage.

Karkou, V. and Sanderson, P. (2005) *Arts Therapies: A Research Based Map of the Field*. Elsevier Health Science.

Karrby, G. (1989) Children's concepts of their own play. *International Journal of Early Childhood*. Vol. 21, No. 2, 49–54.

Katz, L. (1988) What should young children be doing? *American Educator*. Summer, 28–33; 44–5.

Keating, I., Basford, J., Hodson, E. and Harnett, A. (2002) Reception teacher responses to the Foundation Stage. *International Journal of Early Years Education*. Vol. 10, No. 3, 193–203.

Kelly, A. V. (2004) *The Curriculum: Theory and Practice*, 5th edn. London: Sage.

Kieff, J. and Wellhousen, K. (2000) Planning family involvement in early childhood programs. *Young Children,* 18–25.

Kilderry, A. (2004) Critical pedagogy: a useful framework for thinking about early childhood curriculum. *Australian Journal of Early Childhood*, available at: http://goliath.ecnext.com/coms2/ [accessed 11 January 2007].

Kim, J.-Y., McHale, S. M., Crouter, A. C. and Osgood, D. W. (2007) Longitudinal linkages between sibling relationships and adjustment from middle childhood through adolescence. *Developmental Psychology*. Vol. 43, No. 4, 960–73.

Klein, M. (1961) *Narrative of a Child Analysis*. London: Hogarth.

Kolb, D. (1984) *Experiential Learning*. London: Prentice Hall.

Konner, M. J. (1972) Aspects of the developmental ethology of a foraging people in N. Blurton Jones (ed.), *Ethological Studies of Child Behaviour*. Cambridge: Cambridge University Press, 285–304.

Kress, G. (1997) *Before Writing: Rethinking the Paths to Literacy*. London: Routledge.

Kyratzis, A. (2000) Tactical uses of narratives in nursery school in same sex groups. *Discourse Processes*. Vol. 29, No. 3, 269–99.

Kyratzis, A. (2001) Children's gender indexing in language: from the separate worlds hypothesis to considerations of culture context and power. *Research on Language and Social Interaction*. Vol. 34, No. 1, 1–14.

Ladd, G., Price, J. and Hart, C. (1988) Predicting pre-schoolers' peer status from their playground behaviours. *Child Development*. Vol. 59, 986–92.

Laland, K. and Brown, G. (2002) *Sense and Nonsense: Evolutionary Perspectives on Human Behaviour*. Oxford: Oxford University Press.

Lamb, M. (1978) The development of sibling relationships in infancy: a short-term longitudinal study. *Child Development*. Vol. 49, No. 4, 189–96.

Langley, D. (2006) An Introduction to Dramatherapy. London: Sage.

Langsted, O. (1994) Looking at quality from the child's perspective in P. Moss and A. Pence (eds), *Valuing Quality in Early Childhood Services*. London: Paul Chapman.

Lansdown, G. and Lancaster, P. (2001) Promoting children's welfare by respecting their rights in G. Pugh (ed.), *Contemporary Issues in the Early Years: Working Collaboratively for Children*. London: Paul Chapman.

Laszlo, J. I. and Bairstow, P. J. (1985) *Perceptual-Motor Behaviour, Assessment and Therapy*. London: Holt, Reinhart & Winston.

Lave, J. and Wenger, E. (1991) *Situated Learning: Legitimate Peripheral Participation*. Cambridge: Cambridge University Press.

Lave, J. and Wenger, E. (1999) Legitimate Peripheral Participation in Communities of Practice in R. McCormick and C. F. Paechter (eds), *Learning and Knowledge*. London: Paul Chapman/The Open University.

Lee, C. (1984) *The Growth and Development of Children*. London: Longman.

Let our children play (2007) *The Daily Telegraph* Letters page 10 September.

Levinson, M. (2005) The role of play in the formation and maintenance of cultural identity: Gypsy children in home and school contexts. *Journal of Contemporary Ethnography*. Vol. 34, No. 5. October, 499–532, available at: http://jce.sagepub.com/cgi/content/abstract/34/5/499. [accessed: 14 June 2007].

Lewis, M. (2002) The Foundation Stage in England. *Early Education*. Vol. 38, Autumn, 6.

Libraries Linking Idaho (LiLi) (2003) Facts about brain development and how children learn. Idaho State Library, available at: http://www.lili-org.read/readtome/braindevelopment.htm.

Liebermann, A.F. (1995) *The Emotional Life of a Toddler*. New York: Free Press.

Lindon, J. (2005) *Understanding Child Development: Linking Theory and Practice*. Abingdon: Hodder Arnold.

Lindsey, E. (2002) Pre-school children's friendships and peer acceptance: links to social competence. *Child Study Journal*. Vol. 32, No. 3, 145–56.

Lingard, B. (2000) Profile: Bob Lingard in P. Clough and J. Corbett, *Theories of Inclusive Education*. London: PCP/Sage.

Linklater, H. (2006) Listening to learn: children playing and talking about the reception year of early years education in the UK. *Early Years: An International Journal of Research and Development*. Vol. 26, No. 1, 63–78.

Loizos, C. (1976) An ethological study of chimpanzee play in J.S. Bruner, A. Jolly and K. Sylva (eds), *Play: Its Role in Development and Evolution*. New York: Basic Books, 345–51.

Lowe Vandell, D., Tresch, M., Owen, K., Shores Wilson, V. and Henderson, K. (1988) Social Development in Infant Twins: Peer and Mother–Child Relationships. *Child Development*. Vol. 59, No. 1, 168–77.

Lyle, S. (2000) Narrative understanding: developing a theoretical context for understanding how children make meaning in classroom settings. *Journal of Curriculum Studies*. Vol. 32, No. 1, 45–63.

MacDonald, K. and Parke, R. (1984) Bridging the gap: parent–child play interaction and peer interactive competence. *Child Development*. 55, 1265–1277.

MacIntyre, C. (2001) *Enhancing Learning through Play*. London: David Fulton.

MacIntyre, C. and McVitty, K. (2004) *Movement and Learning in the Early Years: Supporting Dyspraxia (DCD) and Other Difficulties*. London: Paul Chapman.

MacNaughton, G. (2003) *Shaping Early Childhood: Learners, Curriculum and Contexts*. Maidenhead: Open University Press.

MacNaughton, G. and Williams, G. (2004) *Teaching Young Children: Choices in Theory and Practice*. Maidenhead: London.

Magill, R.A. (1988) *Motor Learning: Concepts and Applications*. Oxford: WCB/McGraw-Hill.

Maguire, M. and Dunn, J. (1997) Friendships in early childhood, and social understanding. *International Journal of Behavioural Development*. Vol. 21, No. 4, 669–86.

Mahoney, G., Robinson, C. and Powell, A. (1992) Focusing on parent–child interaction: the bridge to developmentally appropriate practice. *Topics in Early Childhood Special Education*. Vol. 12, No. 1, 105–20.

Malaguzzi, L. (1995) History, ideas and basic philosophy: an interview with Lella Gandini in C. Edwards, L. Gandini and G. Forman (eds), *The Hundred Languages of Children: The Reggio Emilia Approach to Early Childhood Education*. Greenwich, CT: Ablex, 41–89.

Malchiodi, C.A. (ed.) (1999) *Medical Art Therapy with Children*. London: Jessica Kingsley.

Mallon, R. and Stitch, S. (2000) The odd couple: the compatibility of social constructionism and evolutionary psychology. *Philosophy of Science*. Vol. 67, 133–54.

Management Issues (2005) Employers slam 'unemployable' school leavers, available at: <http://www.management-issues.com/2006/8/24/research/employers-slam-unemployable-school-leavers.asp> [accessed 9 September 2007].

Manning-Morton, J. and Thorp, M. (2003) *Key Times for Play: The First Three Years*. Maidenhead: Open University Press.

Marder, N. (1987) Gender dynamics and jury deliberations. *Yale Law Journal*. Vol. 96, No. 3, 593–612.

Marsh, J. (2000) But I want to fly too: girls and superhero play in the infant classroom. *Gender and Education*. Vol. 12, No. 2, 209–20.

Maude, P. (2001) *Physical Children, Active Teaching: Investigating Physical Literacy*. Buckingham: Open University Press.

Maxim, G. (1997) *The Very Young: Guiding Young Children from Infancy through the Early Years*. Upper Saddle River, NJ: Merrill/Prentice-Hall.

Maynard, T. (2007) Forest Schools in Great Britain: an initial exploration. *Contemporary Issues in Early Childhood*. Vol. 8, No. 4, 320–31.

McCormick, R. and Paechter, C. (eds) (1999) *Learning and Knowledge*. London: Paul Chapman.

McCrae, R.R. *et al.* (2000) Nature over nurture: temperament, personality, and life span development. *Journal of Personality and Social Psychology*. Vol. 78, No. 1, 173–86.

McCrum, M. and Sturgis, M. (1999) *The 1900 House*. London: Macmillan.

McLaughlin, M.J. (1995) Defining special education: a response to Zigmond and Baker. *Journal of Special Education*. Vol. 29, No. 2, 200–8.

McNess, E., Broadfoot, P. and Osborn, M. (2003) Is the effective compromising the affective? *British Education Research Journal*. Vol. 29, No. 2, 243–57.

McQuail, S. and Pugh, G. (1995) *Effective Organisation of Early Childhood Services*. London: National Children's Bureau.

Meadows, S. (1993) *The Child as Thinker: The Development and Acquisition of Cognition in Childhood*. London: Routledge.

Meadows, S. (2006) *The Child as Thinker: The Development and Acquisition of Cognition in Childhood*, 2nd edn. London: Routledge.

Meaney, M.J. and Stewart, J. (1985) Sex differences in social play: the socialisation of sex roles. *Advances in the Study of Behaviour*. Vol. 15, 2–58.

Melillo, R. and Leisman, G. (2004) *Neurobehavioral Disorders of Childhood: An Evolutionary Approach*. New York: Kluwer, 2004.

Mellou, E. (1994) Play theories: a contemporary review. *Early Child Development and Care*. Vol. 102, 91–100.

Meltzer, H. (2000) *Mental Health of Children and Adolescents in Great Britain*. London: The Stationery Office.

Mental Health Foundation (1999) *Bright Futures: Promoting Children and Young People's Mental Health*. London: Mental Health Foundation.

Miller, L., Cable, C. and Devereux, J. (2005) *Developing Early Years Practice*. London: Open University Press/David Fulton.

Miller, L., Drury, R. and Campbell, R. (eds) (2002) *Exploring Early Years Education and Care*. London: David Fulton.

Milne, A. A. (1921) *When We Were Very Young*. London: Methuen.

Ministry of Education (1996) *Te Whäriki*. Wellington: Learning Media Limited.

Moon, B. and Murphy, P. (1999) *Curriculum in Context*. London: Paul Chapman.

Moore, R.C. (1974) Patterns of activity in time and space: the ecology of a neighbourhood playground in D. Cantor and T. Lee (eds), *Psychology and the Built Environment*. London: Architectural Press.

Morgan, N. and Saxton, J. (1987) *Teaching Drama: A Mind of Many Wonders*. Oxford: Heinemann.

Mortimer, H. (2001) *Special Needs and Early Years Provision*. London: Continuum.

Moss, P. and Petrie, P. (2002) *From Children's Services to Children's Spaces: Public Policy, Children and Childhood*. London: RoutledgeFalmer.

Moss, P. (2006) Bringing politics into the nursery: early childhood education as a democratic practice. Keynote speech, European Early Childhood Research Association Conference. Reykjavik: September.

Moyles, J. (1989) *Just Playing*. Buckingham: Open University Press.

Moyles, J. (1990) *Just Playing*. Buckingham: Open University Press.

Moyles, J. (1994) *The Excellence of Play*. Buckingham: Open University Press.

Moyles, J. (2002) *The Excellence of Play*. Buckingham: Open University Press.

Moyles, J. (2005) *The Excellence of Play*. Buckingham: Open University Press.

Moyles, J. (2006) *The Excellence of Play*. Buckingham: Open University Press.

Moyles, J. and Adams, S. (2001) *Steps: Statements of Entitlement to Play: A Framework for Playful Teaching*. Buckingham: Open University Press.

Moyles, J., Adams, S. and Musgrove, A. (2002) *SPEEL: Study of Pedagogical Effectiveness in Early Learning*. DfES Research Brief and Report 363. London: DfES.

Murphy, B. (2004) Practice in Irish infant classrooms in the context of the Irish primary school curriculum.

Murphy, P. (1999) *Learners, Learning and Assessment*. London: Paul Chapman.

Murray, L. and Andrews, E. (2000) *The Social Baby: Understanding Babies' Communication from Birth*. London: Richmond Press.

Murray, L and Trevarthen, C. (1985) Emotional regulation of interactions between two-month-olds and their mothers in T.M. Field and N.SA. Fox (eds), *Social Perception in Infants*. Norwood: NJ: Ablex.

National Assembly for Wales (2003) *The Learning Country: The Foundation Phase – 3 to 7 years.* Cardiff: National Assembly for Wales.

NAEYC (National Association for the Education of Young Children) (1997) Developmentally appropriate practice in early childhood programs serving children from birth through age 8. A position statement of NAEYC, available at: www.naeyc.org [accessed 15 January 2007].

National Children's Society (2007) The Good Childhood Inquiry, available at: www.childrenssociety. org.uk [accessed 14 December 2007].

Nelson Sofres, T., Quick, S., Lambley, C., Newcombe, E., in conjunction with Aubrey, C. in C. Aubrey (2002) *Implementing the Foundation Stage in Reception Classes.* DfEE Brief 350. London: HMSO.

Neuman, M. (2005) Governance of early childhood education and care: recent developments in OECD countries. *Early Years: An International Journal of Research and Development.* Vol. 25, No. 2, 129–41.

New Policy Institute (2001) *The Value of Children's Play and Play Provision: A Systematic Review of the Literature,* available at: <www.npi.org.uk/reports/ play%20-%20literature.pdf> [accessed 27 January 2003].

Newton, M. (2002) *Savage Girls and Wild Boys: A History of Feral Children.* London: Faber & Faber.

Nicholls, M. (2004) Cultural perspectives from Aotearoa/New Zealand: Te Whäriki as an Intergenerational Curriculum. *Journal of Intergenerational Relationships.* Vol. 1, No. 4, 8 January, 25–34.

Nicholson, S. (1971) The theory of loose parts in *Landscape Architecture Quarterly.* Vol. 62, No. 1, October 30–4; also in *Bulletin for Environmental Education.* No. 12, April 1972, London: Town & Country Planning Association.

Nicholson, S. and Schreiner, B.K. (1973) *Community Participation in Decision Making.* Social Sciences: a second level course, Urban development Unit 22. Milton Keynes: Open University Press.

Norén-Björn, E. (1982) Survey undertaken of play activities on 27 playgrounds in Sweden in E. Norén-Björn, *The Impossible Playground.* West Point, NY: Leisure Press.

Norman, (1978) in J. Moyles (1989) *Just Playing.* Buckingham: Open University Press.

Nutbrown, C. (1996) *REAL Project Early Literacy Education with Parents: A framework for Practice.* Sheffield University.

Nutbrown, C. (1999) *Threads of Learning,* 2nd edn. London: Paul Chapman.

Nutbrown, C. (2006) *Key Concepts in Early Childhood Education and Care.* London: Sage.

O'Brien, M., Jones, D., Sloan, D. and Rustin, M. (2000) Children's independent spatial mobility in the urban public realm. *Childhood.* Vol. 7, No. 3, 257–77.

Oberhaumer, P. and Colberg-Schrader, H. (1999) in L. Abbott and D. Hevey, (2001) Training to work in the early years: developing the climbing frame. In G. Pugh (ed.), *Contemporary Issues in the Early Years: Working Collaboratively for Children,* 3rd edn, London: Paul Chapman.

Ofsted (2004) Registered childcare providers and places in England, available at: www.ofsted.gov.uk [accessed 29 April 2004].

Opie, I. and Opie P. (1959) *The Lore and Language of Schoolchildren.* London: Oxford University Press.

Opie, I. and Opie P. (1969) *Children's Games in Street and Playground.* London: Oxford University Press.

Ormrod, J. (1995) *Educational Psychology: Principles and Applications.* Englewood Cliffs, NJ: Prentice-Hall.

Orobio de Castro, B., Veerman, J.W., Koops, W., Bosch, J. and Manhowwer, H. (2002) Hostile attribution of intent and aggressive behavior: a meta-analysis. *Child Development.* Vol. 73, No. 3, 916–34.

Pahl, K. (1999) *Transformations: Meaning Making in Nursery Education.* Stoke-on-Trent: Trentham Books.

Parker Rees, R. (2000) Time to relax a little: making time for the interplay of minds in education. *Education 3–13.* Vol. 28, No. 1, 29–35.

Parker-Rees, R. (2004) Moving, playing and learning: children's active exploration of their world in J. Willan, R. Parker-Rees and J. Savage (eds), *Early Childhood Studies.* Exeter: Learning Matters.

Parkinson, C. (1987) *Children's range behaviour.* Birmingham: Play Board.

Parten, M. (1932) Social participation among pre-school children. *Journal of Abnormal and Social Psychology.* 27, 243–69.

Parten, M. (1933) Social play among pre-school children. *Journal of Abnormal and Social Psychology,* 28, 136–47.

Paul, R. (1993) *Critical Thinking.* Rohnert Park, CA: Center for Critical Thinking, Sonoma State University.

Pellegrini, A. (1989a) Categorising children's rough and tumble play. *Play and Culture.* 2, 48–51.

Pellegrini, A. (1989b) What is a category? The case of rough and tumble play. *Ethology and Sociobiology.* 10, 331–42.

Pellegrini, A. (1993a) Boys' rough and tumble play, social competence and group composition. *British Journal of Developmental Psychology.* 11, 237–48.

Pellegrini, A. (1993b) Boys' rough and tumble play and social competence, contemporaneous and longitudinal relations in A. Pellegrini (ed.), *The Future of Play Theory.* New York: State University of New York, 107–26.

Pellegrini, A. (1996) *Observing Children in their Natural Worlds: A Methodological Primer.* Mahwah, NJ: Lawrence Erlbaum.

Pellegrini, A. (1998) Rough and tumble play from childhood through adolescence in D. Fromberg and D. Pronin (eds), *Play from Birth to 12 and Beyond: Contexts, Perspectives and Meanings.* New York: Garland, 401–8.

Pellegrini, A. (2005) *Recess: Its Role in Education and Development.* Mahwah, NJ: Lawrence Erlbaum.

Pellegrini, A. and Blatchford, P. (2000) *The Child at School.* London: Arnold.

Pellegrini, A. and Blatchford, P. (2002) Time for a break. *The Psychologist.* Vol. 15, No. 2, 60–2.

Pellegrini, A. and Galda, L. (1993) Ten years after: a re-examination of symbolic play and literacy re-search. *Reading Research Quarterly.* June, 163–73.

Pellegrini, A. and Smith, P.K. (1998) Physical activity play: the nature and function of a neglected aspect of play. *Child Development.* 69, 557–98.

Pellis, S. and Pellis, V. (2007) Rough and tumble play and the development of the social brain. *Current Directions in Psychological Science.* Vol. 16, No. 2, 95–8.

Pepler, D.J. (1982) Play and divergent thinking in D.J. Pepler and K.H. Rubin (eds), *The Play of Children: Current Theory and Research.* Basel: S. Karger.

Peters, S. (2003) I didn't expect that I would get tons of friends . . . more each day . . . children's experiences of friendship in the transition to school. *Early Years.* Vol. 23, No. 1, 45–53.

Petrill, S.A. *et al.* (2004) Chaos in the home and socio-economic status are associated with cognitive development in early childhood: Environmental mediators identified in genetic design. *Intelligence.* Volume 32, Issue 5, 445–460.

Piaget, J. (1951) *Play, Dreams and Imitation in Child-hood.* London: Routledge & Kegan Paul.

Piaget, J. (1955) *The Child's Construction of Reality*, translated by M. Cook. London: Routledge & Kegan Paul.

Piaget, J. (1968) *Six Psychological Studies.* London: University of London Press.

Piaget, J. (1962) Play, dreams and imitation in child-hood. New York: Nation.

Piaget, J. and Inhelder, B. (1969) *The Psychology of the Child.* London: Routledge & Kegan Paul.

Pike, A. and Coldwell, J. (2005) Sibling relationships in middle/early: links with individual adjustment, *Journal of Family Psychology.* Vol. 19, No. 4, 523–32.

Pitcher, E. and Schultz, L. (1983) *Boys and Girls at Play: The Development of Sex Roles:* Brighton Harvester.

Play England (2007) Guide to managing risk in play provision, available at: http://www.playengland. org.uk/ [accessed 20 September 2007].

Plomin, R. (ed.) (2002) *Behavioural Genetics in the Postgenomic Era.* Washington, DC: American Psychological Association.

Plowden Report (1967) Central Advisory Council for Education (CACE) England. *Children and their primary schools.* London: HMSO.

Pollard, A. (ed.) (2002) *Readings for Reflective Teaching.* London: Continuum.

Pollard, A., Trigg, P., Broadfoot, P., McNess, E. and Osborn, M. (2000) *What Pupils Say: Changing Policy and Practice in Primary Education.* London: Continuum.

Portchmouth, J. (1969) *Creative Crafts for Today.* London: Studio Vista.

Porter, L. (2002) *Educating Young Children with Special Needs.* London: Paul Chapman.

Post (The Parliamentary Office for Science and Tech-nology) (2000) Early Years Learning. June Report, available at: www.parliament.uk/commons/selcom/ edehome.htm.

Powell, D.R. (1994) Parents, pluralism, and the NAEYC statement on developmentally appropriate practice in B.L. Mallory and R.S. New (eds), *Diversity and Developmentally Appropriate Practices: Challenges for Early Childhood Education.* New York: Teachers College Press.

Power, T. (1999) Play and Exploration in Children and Animals. Mahwah, NJ: Lawrence Erlbaum.

PPSG (2005) Playwork Principles, held in trust as honest brokers for the profession by the Playwork Principles Scrutiny Group, available from: <http://www.playwales.org.uk/page.asp?id=50> [accessed 5 August 2007].

Promislow, S. (1999) *Making the Brain–body Connec-tion: A Playful Guide to Releasing Mental, Physical and Emotional Blocks to Success.* Vancouver: Kinetic.

Pugh, G. (ed.) (1996) *Training for Work in the Early Years.* Report of the Early Years Training Group. London: Paul Chapman.

Pugh, G. (ed.) (2001) *Contemporary Issues in the Early Years.* London: Paul Chapman.

QCA/DfES (2000) *Curriculum Guidance for the Founda-tion Stage.* London: DfEE.

Ramsey, P. (1998) Diversity and play in D. Fromberg and D. Pronin (eds), *Play from Birth to 12 and Beyond, Contexts, Perspectives and Meanings.* New York: Garland, 23–33.

Reaney, M.J. (1916) *The Psychology of the Organized Game.* Cambridge: Cambridge University Press.

Reay, D. and Williams, D. (1999) I'll be a nothing: structure, agency and the construction of identity through construction. *British Education Research Journal.* Vol. 25, No. 3, 343–54.

Red Herring (2007) Game over for internet addicts, available at: http://www.redherring.com/Home/21604 [accessed 24 December 2007].

Reed, T. and Brown, M. (2000) The expression of care in the rough and tumble play of boys. *Journal of Research in Child Education.* Vol. 15, No. 1, 104–16.

Reiser, R. and Mason, M. (1992) *Disability Equality in the Classroom: A Human Rights Issue.* London: Disability Equality in Education.

Rennie, J. (1996) Working with parents in G. Pugh (ed.), *Contemporary Issues in the Early Years: Working Collaboratively for Children.* London: Paul Chapman.

Riley, J. (ed.) (2003) *Learning in the Early Years.* London: Paul Chapman.

Riley, K. and Docking, J. (2004) Voices of disaffected pupils: implications for policy and practice. *British Journal of Educational Studies.* Vol. 52, No. 2, 166–79.

Roberts, R. (1996) In the schema of things in *Times Educational Supplement,* November.

Robinson, K. (2006), available on http://www.ted.com/index.php/talks/view/id/66

Robsen, S. (2006) *Developing Thinking and Understanding in Young Children.* London: Routledge.

Robson, A. (1989) Special needs and special educational needs. Unpublished paper, Inner London Education Authority.

Robson, S. and Smedley, S. (1999) *Education in Early Childhood.* London: David Fulton.

Rogoff, B. (1998) Cognition as a collaborative process in D. Kuhn and R.S. Siegler (eds), *Handbook of Child Psychology Vol. 2,* 5th edn. New York: Wiley, 679–744.

Rogoff, B. (1990) *Cognitive Development in Social Context.* New York: Oxford University Press.

Rogoff, B. (2003) *The Cultural Nature of Human Development.* New York: Oxford University Press.

Rose, R. Fletcher, W. and Goodwin, G. (1999) Pupils with severe learning difficulties as personal target setters. *British Journal of Special Education.* Vol. 26, No. 4, 206–12.

Roth, W.M (1999) *Authentic School Science: Intellectual Traditions* in R. McCormick and C.F. Paechter (eds), *Learning and Knowledge.* London: Paul Chapman/The Open University.

Rouse, D. and Griffin, S. (1992) Quality for the under threes in G. Pugh (ed.), *Contemporary Issues in the Early Years.* London: Paul Chapman/National Children's Bureau.

Rowlett, W. (2000) To what degree does mobility enrich the personal, social and emotional development, within the outside play curriculum for children under three? BA (Hons) degree project, University of North London.

Roy, R. and Benenson, J. (2002) Sex and contextual effects on children's use of interference competition. *Developmental Psychology.* Vol. 38, No. 2, 306–12.

Russell, W. (2008) Modelling playwork: Brawgs Continuum, dialogue and collaborative reflection in F. Brown and C. Taylor (eds), *Foundations of Playwork.* Maidenhead: Open University Press.

Rutherford, D. (2005) Children's relationships, in J. Taylor and H. Woods, (eds), *Early Childhood Studies: An Holistic Introduction.* London: Hodder Arnold, 89–92.

Sammons, P., Eliot, K., Sylva, K., Melhuish, E., Siraj-Blatchford, I. and Taggert, P. (2004) The impact of pre-school on young children's cognitive attainments at entry to reception. *British Educational Research Journal.* Vol. 30, No. 5, 692–707.

Sandford, R., Ulicsak, M., Facer, K. and Rudd, T. (2006) Teaching with games: using commercial off-the-shelf computer games in formal education, available at: http://www.futurelab.org.uk/resources/documents/project_reports/teaching_with_games/TWG_report.pdf [accessed 23 December 2007].

Santer, J., Griffiths, C. and Goodsall, D. (2007) *Free Play in Early Childhood.* London: National Children's Bureau.

Saracho, O. and Spodek, B. (2003) *Studying Teachers in Early Childhood Settings.* Connecticut: Information Age Publishing.

Sax, L. (2005) Why Gender Matters. New York: Doubleday.

Sayeed, Z. and Guerin, E. (2000) *Early Years Play.* London: David Fulton.

Sayeed, Z. and Guerin, E. (2001) *Early Years Play: A Happy Medium for Assessment and Intervention.* London: David Fulton.

Schachter, R. (2005) The end of recess. *The District Administrator,* August, available at: http://www.districtadministration.com

Schaefer, C.E. and Kaduson, H.G. (eds) (2006) *Contemporary Play Therapy.* London: Routledge.

Schaffer, H.R. (1996) *Social Development.* Oxford: Blackwell.

Scheffler, I. (1999) Epistemology and education in R. McCormick and C. Paechter (eds), *Learning and Knowledge.* London: Paul Chapman.

Schore, A.N. (2001) Effects of a secure attachment relationship on right brain development, affect regulation and infant mental health. *Infant Mental Health Journal.* Vol. 22, Nos. 1–2, 7–66.

Schultz, J. and Cook-Sather, A. (2001) *In Your Own Word: Students' Perspectives on School.* Oxford: Rowman and Littlefield.

Schwartzman, H. (1978) *Transformations: The Anthropology of Children's Play*. New York: Plenum.

Schweinhart, L.J. and Weikart, D.P. (1993) *A Summary of Significant Benefits: The High/Scope Perry Pre-school Study Through Age 27*. Ypsilanti, MI: High/Scope Press.

Scott, J. (2000) Children as respondents in A. James and P. Christensen (eds), *Research with Children: Perspectives and Practices*. Sussex: Falmer, 98–119.

Scruggs, T.E. and Mastropieri, M.A. (1994) Successful mainstreaming in elementary science classes: a qualitative study of three reputational cases. *American Education Research Journal*. Vol. 31, No. 4, 785–811.

Sebanc, A. (2003) The friendship features of pre-school children: links with pro-social behaviour and aggression. *Social Development*. Vol. 12, No. 2, 249–68.

Sebba, R. (1991) The landscapes of childhood: the reflection of childhood's environment in adult memories and in children's attitudes. *Environment and Behaviour*. Vol. 23, No. 4, 395–422.

Shaffer, H.R. (2006) *Key Concepts in Developmental Psychology*. Oxford: Blackwell.

Sharp, C. (1998) Age of starting school and the early years curriculum. Paper prepared for *National Foundation Educational Research Annual Conference*, London: 6 October.

Sharp, C. (1998) What parents want from a preschool. *Education Journal*. Issue 20, Item 4, 20–1.

Sheldon, A. (1990) Pickle fights: gendered talk in pre-school disputes. *Discourse Processes*. 13, 5–31.

Shephard, R.J., Volle, M., Lavallee, H., La Barre, R., Jequier, J.C. and Rajic, M. (1984) Required physical activity and academic grades: a controlled study, in J. Ilmarinen and I. Valimaki (eds), *Children and Sport*. Berlin: Springer Verlag.

Shonkoff, J.P. and Phillips, D.A. (2000) *From Neurons to Neighborhoods: The Science of Early Childhood Development*. USA: National Academy Press.

Shore, R. (1997) *Rethinking the Brain: New Insights into Early Development*. New York: Families and Work Institute.

Shulman, L.S. (1987) *Knowledge and Teaching: Foundations of the New Reform*. Cambridge, MA: Harvard University Press.

Sims, M., Guilfoyle, A. and Parry, T. (2006) Child care for infants and toddlers: where in the world are we going? The first years – Nga Tau Tuatahi. *New Zealand Journal of Infant and Toddler Education*. Vol. 8, No. 1, 12–19.

Singer, D.G. and Singer, J.L. (1990) *The House of Make Believe*. London: Harvard University Press.

Singer, J. (1973) *The Child's World of Make-believe: Experimental Studies of Imaginative Play*. New York: Academic.

Siraj-Blatchford, I., Sammons, P., Taggert, B., Sylva K. and Melhuish, E. (2006) Educational research and evidence-based policy: the mixed method approach of the EPPE Project. *Evaluation and Research in Education*. Vol. 19, No. 2, 62–82.

Siraj-Blatchford, I. and Sylva, K. (2004) Researching pedagogy in English pre-schools. *British Educational Research Journal*. Vol. 30, No. 5, 713–30.

Siraj-Blatchford, I. and Sylva, K. (2005) *Monitoring and Evaluation of the Effective Implementation of the Foundation Phase Report*. Cardiff: Welsh Assembly.

Siraj-Blatchford, I., Sylva, K., Muttock, S., Gilden, R. and Bell, D. (2002) Researching Effective Pedagogy in the Early Years. Research Report No. 356, DfES. London: HMSO.

SkillsActive (2002) *Assumptions and Values of Playwork*. London: SkillsActive.

Slade, P. (1954) *Child Drama*. London: University Press.

Sluckin, A. (1981) *Growing up in The School Playground*. London: Routledge & Kegan Paul.

Smidt, S. (2007) *A Guide to Early Years Practice*. London: Routledge.

Smilansky, S. (1968) *The Effects of Socio-dramatic Play on Disadvantaged Preschool Children*. New York: Wiley.

Smith, P. and Connolly, K. (1980) *The Ecology of Preschool Behaviour*. Cambridge: Cambridge University Press.

Soler, J. and Miller, L. (2003) The struggle for early childhood curricula: a comparison of the English Foundation Stage curriculum, *Te Whäriki* and Reggio Emilia. *International Journal of Early Years Education*. Vol. 11, No. 1, 57–67.

Sorenson, E.R. (1979) Early tactile communication and the patterning of human organisation: a New Guinea case study in M. Bullowa (ed.), *Before Speech: The Beginning of Interpersonal Communication*. Cambridge: Cambridge University Press, 289–305.

SPRITO (1992) *National Occupational Standards in Playwork*. London: Sport and Recreation Industry Lead Body.

Star Trek series: *The Next Generation* and *Voyager* © Paramount Pictures 2004.

Stephenson, A. (2003) Physical risk taking: dangerous or endangered? *Early Years*. Vol. 23, No. 1, 35–43.

Stern, D.N. (1985) *The Interpersonal World of the Infant: A View from Psychoanalysis and Developmental Psychology*. New York: Basic Books.

Stevens, R. (2000) *Understanding the Self*. Milton Keynes: Open University Press.

Stonehouse, A. (ed.) (1988) *Trusting Toddlers: Programming for 1–3 Year Olds in Child Care Centres*. Maidenhead: Australian Early Childhood Association.

SureStart Unit (2002) *Birth To Three Matters: A Framework to Support Children in Their Earliest Years.* London: DfES.

Survey of Laws Relating to SEN. UNESCO.

Sutton, E., Smith, N., Deardon, C. and Middleton, S. (2007) *A Child's Eye View of Social Difference,* available at: <http://www.jrf.org.uk/bookshop/eBooks/2007-children-inequality-opinion.pdf> [accessed on 7 October 2007].

Sutton-Smith, B. (1977) Towards an anthropology of play in S. Phillips (ed.), *Studies in the Anthropology of Play: Papers in Memory of B. Allan Tindall.* New York: Leisure Press, 222–32.

Sutton-Smith, B. (1992) In Channel 4 documentary: *Toying with the Future.* London: Channel 4 TV.

Sutton-Smith, B. (1997) *The Ambiguity of Play.* Cambridge, MA: Harvard University Press.

Sutton-Smith, B. (1999) Evolving a consilience of play definitions: playfully. *Play and Culture Studies.* 2, 239–56.

Sutton-Smith, B. (2008) Beyond ambiguity in F. Brown and C. Taylor (eds), *Foundations of Playwork.* Maidenhead: Open University Press.

Sutton-Smith, B. and Kelly-Byrne, D. (1984) The idealization of play in P.K. Smith (ed.), *Play in Animals and Humans.* Oxford: Blackwell.

Sylva, K. (1994) School influences on children's development. *Journal of Child Psychology and Psychiatry.* Vol. 35, 135–70.

Sylva, K., Bruner, J.S. and Genova, P. (1976) The role of play in the problem-solving of children in J.S. Bruner, A. Jolly and K. Sylva (eds), *Play: Its Role in Development and Evolution.* New York: Basic Books.

Sylva, K. and Czerniewska, P. (1985) Play (Open University E206, Unit 6, *Personality Development and Learning*). Milton Keynes: The Open University.

Sylva, K., Roy, C. and Painter, M. (1980) *Childwatching at Playgroup and Nursery School.* London: Grant McIntyre.

Sylva, K., Roy, C. and Painter, M. (1994) *Observation and Record Keeping.* London: Pre-school Playgroups Association.

Sylva, K., Siraj-Blatchford, I., Taggart, B., Sammons, P., Elliot, K. and Melhuish, E. (1997–2002) *The Effective Provision of Preschool Education* [*EPPE*] *Project* Summary of Findings, DfES Research Brief. London: DfES and Institute of Education, University of London.

Sylva, K., Siraj-Blatchford, I., Taggart, B., Sammons, P., Elliot, K. and Melhuish, E. (2004) *The Effective Provision of Preschool Education*[*EPPE*] *Project* Technical Paper 12 – The Final Report: Effective Preschool Education. London: DfES and Institute of Education, University of London.

Sylva, K., Siraj-Blatchford, I., Taggart, B., Sammons, P., Melhuish, E., Elliot, K. and Totsika, V. (2006) Capturing quality in early childhood through environmental rating scales. *Early Childhood Research Quarterly.* Vol. 21, 76–92.

Sylva, K., Taggart, B., Siraj-Blatchford, I., Totsika, V., Ereky-Stevens, K., Gilden, R. and Bell, D. (2007) Curricular quality and day-to-day learning activities in pre-school. *International Journal of Early Years Education.* Vol. 15, No. 1, 49–65.

Talay-Ongen, A. (1998) *Typical and Atypical Development in Early Childhood: The Fundamentals.* England: BPS Books.

Taggart, B. (2004) Editorial. Early years education and care: three agendas. *British Educational Research Association Journal.* Vol. 30, No. 5, 619–22.

Taylor, C. (1994) The politics of recognition in A. Gutmann (ed.), *Multiculturalism.* Princeton, NJ: Princeton University Press.

Taylor, C. (2008) Playwork and the theory of loose parts in F. Brown and C. Taylor (eds), *Foundations of Playwork.* Maidenhead: Open University Press.

Teacher Training Agency (2003) *Qualifying to Teach: Professional Standards for Qualified Teacher Status and Requirements for Initial Teacher Training.* London: TTA.

Teacher Training Agency (2005a) *Meeting the Professional Standards for the Award of Higher Level Teaching Assistant Status. Guidance to the Standards.* London: TTA.

Teacher Training Agency (2005b) *Teacher Training Agency Handbook of Guidance. Accompanies Qualifying to Teach: Professional Standards for Qualified Teacher Status and Requirements for Initial Teacher Training.* London: TTA.

The Children's Society, The Good Childhood Inquiry, available at http://www.childrenssociety.org.uk/all_about_us/how_we_dp_it/the_good_childhood_inquiy/1818.html or www.goodchildhood.or.uk, [accessed 17 April 2008].

The *Daily Telegraph* (2006) Modern life leads to more depression among children, available at: http://www.telegraph.co.uk/news/main.jhtml;jsessionid=2UB5R5X1L22Y5QFIQMGCFF4AVCBQUIV0?xml=/news/2006/09/12njunk112.xml&page=1 [accessed 23 December 2007].

The *Independent on Sunday* (2007) On the trail of Santa Claus, available at: http://news.independent.co.uk/world/americas/article3278491.ece> [accessed 23 December 2007].

The Plowden Report (1967) *Children and their Primary Schools A Report of the Central Advisory Council for Education (England).* London: HMSO.

The Primary Review (2007) available at: <http://www.primaryreview.org.uk/index.html>

Thelen, E. and Smith, L.B. (1994) *A Dynamic Systems Approach to the Development of Cognition and Action.* Cambridge, MA: MIT Press.

Thompson, I. (1999) *Issues in Teaching Primary Numeracy.* London: Paul Chapman.

Thurman, S. (1997) The congruence of behavioural ecologies: a model for special education programming. *Journal of Special Education.* Vol. 11, 329–33.

Tinbergen, N. (1975) The importance of being playful. *Times Education Supplement,* January.

Tizard, B. and Hughes, M. (1984) *Young Children Learning.* London: Fontana.

Tizard, B., Blatchford, P., Burke, J., Farquhar, C. and Plewis, I. (1988) *Young children at school in the inner city.* Hove: Lawrence Erlbaum.

Tomasello, M. (1999) The Cultural Origins of Human Cognition. Cambridge, MA: Harvard University Press.

Tovey, H. (2007) *Playing Outdoors: Spaces and Places, Risk and Challenge.* Maidenhead: McGraw-Hill.

Training and Development Agency (2007) *The Revised Standards for the Recommendation for Qualified Teacher Status (QTS).* London: TDA.

Trevarthen, C. (1992) An infant's motives for speaking and thinking in the culture in A.H. Wold (ed.), *The Dialogue Alternative.* Oxford: Oxford University Press.

Trevarthen, C. (1995) The child's need to learn a culture in M. Woodhead, D. Faulkner and K. Littleton (eds) (1998), *Cultural Worlds of Early Childhood.* London: Routledge.

Trevarthen, C. (1996) How a young child investigates people and things: why play helps development. Keynote speech to TACTYC Conference: A Celebration of Play, London: November.

Trevarthen, C. (1998) The child's need to learn a culture in M. Woodhead, D. Faulkner and K. Littleton (eds), *Cultural Worlds of Early Childhood.* London: Routledge/Open University Press.

Trivers, R. (1972) Parental investment and sexual selection in B. Campbell (ed.), *Sexual Selection and the Descent of Man.* Chicago IL: Aldine de Gruyter, 136–79.

Turner-Bisset, R. (2001) *Expert Teaching: Knowledge and Pedagogy to Lead the Profession.* London: David Fulton.

Tymms, P. and Merrell, C. (2007) Research Survey 4/1: Standards and quality in English primary schools over time: the national evidence, available at www.dfes.gov.uk [accessed 10 November 2007].

United Nations (1989) *Convention on the Rights of the Child.* Brussels: United Nations Assembly.

UNICEF (1989) *Convention on the Rights of the Child.* New York: United Nations.

UNICEF (1991) *United Nations Convention on the Rights of the Child.* Svenska: UNICEF Kommitten.

UNICEF (2007) An overview of child well-being in rich countries, available at: http://www.unicef-icdc.org/presscentre/presskit/reportcard7/rc7_eng.pdf [accessed 14 February 2007].

UNESCO (1994) *Salamanca Statement on Principles, Policy and Practice in Special Needs Education.* Paris: UNESCO.

UNESCO (1996) *Legislation Pertaining to Special Needs Education.* Paris: UNESCO.

Van Dyk, A. (2006) Hyperactivity and four-year-old-children, available from: <http://www.sandplay.net/hyper4year.htm> [accessed on 6 January 2007].

Van Hoorn, J., Nourot, T., Scales, B. and Alward, K. (1993) *Play as the Center of the Curriculum.* New York: Macmillan.

Villalón, M., Suzuki, E., Herrera, M. O. and Mathieson, M.E. (2002) Quality of Chilean early childhood education from an international perspective. *International Journal of Early Years Education.* Vol. 10, No. 1, 49–59.

Vygotsky, L.S. (1967) Play and its role in the mental development of the child. *Soviet Psychology.* Vol. 5, 6–18.

Vygotsky, L.S. (1976) Play and its role in the mental development of the child in J.S. Bruner, A. Jolly and K. Sylva (eds), *Play: Its Role in Development and Evolution.* New York: Basic Books (original work published 1933, *Soviet Psychology,* 5, 6–18).

Vygotsky, L.S. (1978) *Mind in society: The Development of Higher Psychological Processes.* Cambridge, MA and London: Harvard University Press.

Wade, B. and Moore, M. (1998) *A Gift for Life. Bookstart: The First Five Years.* London: Booktrust.

Wall, K. (2006) *Special Needs and Early Years: A Practitioner's Guide.* London: Paul Chapman.

Wallace, M. (1996) When is experiential learning not experiential learning? in G. Claxton, T. Atkinson, M. Osborn and T. Wallace (eds), *Liberating the Learner: Lessons for Professional Development in Education.* London: Routledge.

Wallace, M. (1999) When is experiential learning not experiential learning in P. Murphy, *Learners, Learning and Assessment.* London: Paul Chapman.

Ward, C. (1978) The Child in the City. London: Architectural Press.

Warnock M. (1986) Children with special needs in ordinary schools: integration revisited in A. Cohen and L. Cohen (eds), *Special Needs in the Ordinary School.* San Francisco, CA: Harper & Row.

Webb, J., Schirato, T. and Danaher, G. (2002) *Understanding Bourdieu.* London: Sage.

Weber, A.M. and Haen, C. (eds) (2004) *Clinical Applications of Drama Therapy in Child and Adolescent Treatment*. London: Routledge.

Wells, G. (1986) *The Meaning Makers: Children Learning Language and Using Language to Learn*. Portsmouth: Heinemann.

Wells, G. (1987) *The Meaning Makers*. Sevenoaks: Hodder & Stoughton.

Wenger, E. (1998) *Communities of Practice: Learning, Meaning and Identity*. Cambridge: Cambridge University Press.

Whardle, F. (2007) Play as curriculum, available at: http://www.gymboreeplay.ch/pdf/articles/play_as_curriculum.pdf What to do if you're worried a child is being abused, available at: http://www.everychildmatters [accessed 19 October 2007].

Whitebread, D. (2005) C.IND.LE Project: *Supporting Young Children in Becoming Self-regulated Learners*. Cambridge: CUMIS.

Whitebread, D. (2007) Self-regulation in children's play, Workshop at the TACTYC Play, Diversity and Heritage in the Early Years Conference, Brighton, 16–17 November.

Whiting, B. and Edwards, C. (1973) A cross cultural analysis of sex differences in behavior of children 3 through 11. *Journal of Social Psychology*. Vol. 41, 171–88.

Whiting, B.B. and Whiting, J.W.M. (1975) *Children of Six Cultures: A Psycho-cultural Analysis*. Cambridge, MA: Harvard University Press.

Willan, J., Parker-Rees, R. and Savage (eds) (2004) *Early Child Studies*. Exeter: Learning Matters.

Williams, M. (2004) Creative literacy: learning in the early years in Fisher and Williams, *Unlocking Literacy: A Guide for Teachers*. London: Routledge.

Wilson, R.A. (1998) *Special Education in the Early Years*. London: Routledge.

Wilson, R.A. (2002) The wonders of nature: honouring children's ways of knowing. *Earlychildhood*.

Excelligence Learning Corporation. Available from: > http://www.earlychildhoodnews.com/earlychildhood/article_view.aspx?ArticleId=70 [accessed 4 February 2007].

Winnicott, D.W. (1951) Transitional objects and transitional phenomena in D.W. Winnicott, *Collected Papers*. New York: Basic Books, 29–242.

Winnicott, D.W. (1974) *Playing and Reality*. London: Pelican.

Wolfe, P. (2001) *Brain Matters: Translating Research into Classroom Practice*. Alexandria, VA: Association for Supervision and Curriculum Development.

Wolfendale, S. (2000) Special needs in early years: prospects for policy and practice. *Support for Learning*. Vol. 15, No. 4.

Wood, D. (1998) *How Children Think and Learn*. Oxford: Blackwell.

Wood, E. and Attfield, J. (1996) *Play, Learning and the Early Childhood Curriculum*. London: Paul Chapman.

Wood, E. (2004) A new paradigm war? The impact of national curriculum policies on early childhood teachers' thinking and classroom practice. *Teaching and Teacher Education*. Vol. 20, Issue 4, 361–74.

Wood, E. and Attfield, J. (2005) Play, Learning and the Early Childhood Curriculum, 2nd edn. London: Paul Chapman.

Wrigley, T. (2003) *Schools of Hope: A New Agenda for School Improvement*. Stoke-on-Trent: Trentham Books.

Wylie, C. and Thompson, J. (2003) The long-term contribution of early childhood education to children's performance: evidence from New Zealand. *International Journal of Early Years Education*. Vol. 11, No. 1, 69–78.

Young, M. (1999) *The Curriculum as Socially Organised Knowledge* in R. McCormick and C. Paechter (eds), *Learning and Knowledge*. London: Paul Chapman.

Websites

www.aaac.org.uk National Assembly for Wales (2003) The Learning Country: Foundation Phase 3-7 years.

www.badt.isoin.co British Association of Dramatherapists Code of Practice

www.bapt.info British Association of Play Therapists

www.bapt.info/ethicalbasis.htm British Association for Play Therapists Ethical Guidelines

www.cmslive.curriculum.edu.au Curriculum Corporation, Australia

www.dfes.org.uk Department for Children, Schools and Families

www.dictionary.reference.com

www.everychildmatters.gov.uk/ Every Child Matters

www.foresteducation.org/ Forest Schools Initiative

www.highscope.org – High/Scope Educational Research Foundation

www.hpc-uk.org Health Professions Council Standards of Conduct, Performance and Ethics, Duties of Registrant

www.inclusion.org.uk Centre for Studies on Inclusive Education

www.learning.wales.gov.uk/foundationphase

www.ltscotland.org.uk/earlyyears/resources/publications/ltscotland/reggioemilia

www.merriam-webster.com Merriam Webster

www.minedu.govt.nz/index. Te Whāriki

www.montessori.org.uk/Montessori St Nicholas Charity.

www.ncaction.org.uk National Curriculum

www.oecd.org Organization for Economic Cooperation and Development

www.ofsted.gov.uk/ The official body for school inspection

www.playengland.org.uk Play England

www.qca.org.uk Qualifications and Curriculum Authority

www.reggioinspired.com/ Reggio Emilia

www.standards.dfes.gov.uk The Nationals Standards Site including Primary National Strategy

www.standards.dcsf.gov.uk/eyfs/The Early Years Foundation Stage

www.standards.dfes.gov.uk/primaryframeworks/

www.steinerwaldorf.org.uk Steiner/Waldorf

Index

Terms in **bold** indicate glossary entries.